Contents

BARRON'S

AP*

ENGLISH LANGUAGE
AND COMPOSITION

7TH EDITION

George Ehrenhaft, Ed.D.
Former Chairman, English Department
Mamaroneck High School
Mamaroneck, New York

BARRON'S

*AP and Advanced Placement Program are registered trademarks of the College Board, which was not involved in the production of, and does not endorse, this product.

All inquiries should be addressed to:
Barron's Educational Series, Inc.
250 Wireless Boulevard
Hauppauge, New York 11788
www.barronseduc.com

ISBN: 978-1-4380-0864-6 (book only)

ISBN: 978-1-4380-7690-4 (book with CD-ROM)

ISSN: 2164-0939 (Print)

ISSN: 2156-5775 (Print with CD-ROM)

PRINTED IN THE UNITED STATES OF AMERICA

9 8 7 6 5 4 3 2 1

10%
**POST-CONSUMER
WASTE**
Paper contains a minimum
of 10% post-consumer
waste (PCW). Paper used
in this book was derived
from certified, sustainable
forestlands.

If you're aiming for a score of **5** on the AP English Language and Composition exam, this book can help. But to reach your goal, here are five things that you **MUST** do:

Barron's Essential

1   **Familiarize yourself with the language of rhetoric.** Both the short-answer and essay questions require that you know how authors employ rhetorical strategies to create effects and convey meaning. Become conversant with the functions of tone, syntax, imagery, irony, point of view, and the other rhetorical techniques.

2   **Become an annotation addict.** Nothing will build your skill in prose analysis better than a steady diet of annotation. Begin by reading nonfiction prose passages in this book and elsewhere. Resolve to figure out exactly what each author did to compose the passage. Identify rhetorical techniques, but more important, try to explain why the author chose each rhetorical component.

3   **Review documentation basics.** By learning the anatomy of footnotes you'll be ready to answer multiple-choice questions that ask you to interpret documentation. Also, to earn a top score on the "synthesis" essay, know how to weave source material into your text and correctly document where it came from.

4   **Brush up on basic grammar skills.** Don't bother memorizing terminology. Few, if any, multiple-choice questions require it. Concentrate on writing error-free essays because essay scores suffer when grammar rules are broken. Proofread all your practice essays. Look particularly for

- sentences errors
- lack of agreement between subjects and verbs
- incorrect pronoun usage
- errors in verb choice

5   **Plan and practice an essay-writing process.** Develop a process for writing an essay in no more than forty minutes. Build in time to read the question, pick a main idea and decide how to support it. Before you start writing, list your ideas and arrange them in sensible order. While composing your essay, be mindful of the need to:

- introduce your topic
- develop coherent paragraphs
- vary sentences
- choose the best words to express ideas
- provide a brief conclusion

Set aside time for editing and proofreading.

Acknowledgments

Grateful acknowledgment is made to the following sources.

Page 12, Byron Williams, "Revolution Was Only the Start of the American Experiment," *Contra Costa Times*, December 17, 2015, p. A19.

Page 25, Alfie Kohn, "Homework: An Unnecessary Evil?" *www.psychologytoday.com*, November 24, 2012.

Page 26, Brian P. Gill and Steven L. Schlossman, "My Dog Ate My Argument," *Los Angeles Times*, December 11, 2003.

Page 27, Tom Loveless, "Do Students Have Too Much Homework?" Brown Center on Education Policy, Brookings Institution, October 1, 2003.

Page 28, "Average NAEP Reading Scale Scores of Students by Age and Amount of Assigned Daily Reading Homework," *Digest of Education Statistics*, National Center for Educational Statistics, 2012.

Page 29, Brian Haley, "What Is the Value of Homework?" July 6, 2006. *SearchWarp.com*.

Page 30, Gloria Chaika, "Help! Homework Is Wrecking My Home Life," *Education World*, August 8, 2000. © *EducationWorld.com*.

Page 33, F. M. Esfandiary, "The Mystical West Puzzles the Practical East," *New York Times Magazine*, February 6, 1967. © F. M. Esfandiary.

Page 35, Clyde Kluckhorn, "An Anthropologist Looks at the United States," *Mirror for Man*, McGraw-Hill Book Co., NY, 1949.

Page 45, Richard Maxwell Brown, "Historical Patterns of Violence in America," *The History of Violence in America*, eds. Hugh Davis Graham and Ted Robert Gurr. National Commission on the Causes and Prevention of Violence. Task Force on Historical and Comparative Perspectives, U.S. Government Printing Office, Washington, D.C.

Page 52, N. Scott Momaday, *The Way to Rainy Mountain*, University of New Mexico Press, 1976.

Page 55, Richard Wright, *White Man, Listen!*, John Hawkins & Associates, New York, 1957.

Page 58, Daniel Goleman, "The Man Without Feelings," *Emotional Intelligence*. Copyright © 1995. Reprinted with permission of Bantam Books, a division of Random House, Inc.

Page 63, Katherine Hansen, "What Good Is a College Education Anyway?" © Quintessential Careers, *www.quintcareers.com*.

Page 64, Lori Kurtzman, "Remedial Classes Teach Freshmen What They Should Already Know," *The Cincinnati Enquirer,* posted online July 30, 2006.

Page 67, Gregg Toppo and Anthony DeBarros, "Reality Weighs Down Dreams of College," *USA Today,* posted online February 2, 2005.

Page 68, Online blog, "Rob," "Declining College Standards," *Say Anything,* posted January 3, 2006.

Page 104, Joe B. Frantz, "The Frontier Tradition: An Invitation to Violence," *The History of Violence in America,* eds. Hugh Davis Graham and Ted Robert Gurr. National Commission on the Causes and Prevention of Violence. Task Force on Historical and Comparative Perspectives, U.S. Government Printing Office, Washington, D.C.

Page 120, J. H. Pryor, K. Eagan, L. Palucki Blake, S. Hurtado, J. Berdan, and M. H. Case, "Trends of Reasons in Deciding to Go to College," *The American Freshman: National Norms Fall 2012,* Los Angeles, CA: Higher Education Research Institute, UCLA, 2012.

Page 134, Julie Hilden, "Does Celebrity Destroy Privacy?" *FindLaw* website, accessed 6/28/06.

Page 135, "*jenblacksheep,*" "Do Public Figures Have Privacy Rights?" *Hubpages.com,* 2010.

Page 136, Vincent M. deGrandpré, "Understanding the Market for Celebrity, An Economic Analysis of the Right of Publicity," Simpson Thacher and Bartlett, LLP, posted September 15, 2001, *www.stb.com.*

Page 137, "Entertainment to Environment Headlines of Prominent News Sources (Ratio of 5 to 1 or Greater)," Pew Research Center's Project for Excellence in Journalism, 2013.

Page 138, GNL, "For Today's Public Figures, Private Lives Really Matter," *www.Buzzle.com.,* Buzzle.Com, Inc., Costa Mesa, CA, November 30, 2004.

Page 139, Jamie Nordhaus, "Celebrities' Rights to Privacy: How Far Should the Paparazzi Be Allowed to Go?" University of Texas School of Law, *Review of Litigation,* Volume 18, 1999.

Page 147, Laura Eirmann, DVM, "The Facts About Euthanasia," Cornell University Pet Loss Hotline, *vet.cornell.edu,* November 2004.

Page 151, Carl Binger, "Emotional Disturbances Among College Women," *Emotional Problems of the Student* by G. B. Blaine, Jr. and C. C. McCarthur, Appleton-Century-Croft, 1961.

Page 227, Excerpt from *West with the Night* by Beryl Markam, © 1942, 1983 by Beryl Markham. Northpoint Press, a division of Farrar, Straus, and Giroux, LLC.

Page 231, Henry Allen, "The Corps," *The Washington Post,* March 5, 1972. © *The Washington Post.*

Page 238, Deanna Paoli Gumina, *The Italians of San Francisco, 1850–1930,* Center for Migration Studies, 1978.

Page 246, "What Benefits Have Come from Medical Research Using Animals?" American Association for Laboratory Animal Science (AALAS), *www.foundation.aalas.org.*

Page 248, "Numbers of Animals Used in Research in the United Kingdom," Home Office (2004), *Statistics of Scientific Procedures on Living Animals,* Great Britain, 2003.

Page 249, Stuart Derbyshire, Ph.D., "Animal Experimentation," speech at Edinburgh Book Festival, August 19, 2002.

Page 250, "The Ethics of Research Involving Animals: A Guide to the Report," Nuffield Council on Bioethics, May 25, 2005. Reprinted by permission.

Page 251, Clare Haggarty, "Animals in Scientific Research: The Ethical Argument," National Anti-Vivisection Society, *www.navs.org.*

Page 252, Albert Einstein, *Out of My Later Years*, The Philosophical Library, Inc., 1950.

Page 264, Arnold Toynbee, *Civilization on Trial*, © 1958 by Oxford University Press, Inc.

Page 273, Aldous Huxley, *Music at Night and Other Essays*, Harper and Row, © 1931, renewed 1958 by Aldous Huxley.

Page 277, George Bernard Shaw, *Shaw on Music: A Selection from the Music Criticism of George Bernard Shaw*, 1927, ed. Eric Bentley, Anchor Books, Doubleday. © The Society of Authors, London.

Page 280, Barbara W. Tuchman, *The Proud Tower*, MacMillan Company, New York, 1962, pp. 117–118.

Page 285, "Stop Cyberbullying," *www.stopcyberbullying.com, Wired Kids*, accessed, July 31, 2010.

Page 286, "The Legality of School Responses to Cyberbullying," Constitutional Rights Foundation, Chicago. Posted by *www.deliberating.org*, 2007.

Page 287, Victoria Kim, "Suit Blends Internet, Free Speech, School," *Los Angeles Times*, August 3, 2008.

Page 289, Nancy Willard, "School Response to Cyberbullying and Sexting," Center for Safe, Responsible Internet Use, August 2, 2010.

Page 290, Cindy Hsu, " N.J. School District Set to Battle Cyber Bullies," *HD2, wcbs.com*, August 1, 2008.

Page 291, Edward P. Gyokeres, "Camp Muckamungus," © by Edward P. Gyokeres, from *Operation Homecoming*, ed. Andrew Carroll.

Page 311, T. S. Eliot, "On Teaching the Appreciation of Poetry," *The Critic* XVIII, 1960, © the estate of T. S. Eliot, Harcourt, Brace, Jovanovich, and Faber and Faber, Ltd.

Page 319, *From the Island at the Center of the World: The Epic Story of Dutch Manhattan and the Forgotten Colony That Shaped America*, Russell Shorto, © 2004 by Russell Shorto.

Page 325, "Q & A About Military Recruitment at High Schools," ACLU of Washington, *www.aclu-wa.org*, September 14, 2007.

Page 328, "EP," "Military Recruitment Day," SouthWest Organizing Project, *swop.net*, Albuquerque, NM, July 2010.

Page 329, Ruby Hawk, "Military Recruitment in High Schools," *Socyberty.com.*, February 15, 2010.

Page 330, Mike Hardcastle, "What Should You Do After High School?: A Look at Your Postgraduate Choices," *about.com.*

Page 358, Excerpt from pp. 180–182 from *Stiffed: The Betrayal of the American Man*, Susan Faludi, © 1999 by Susan Faludi.

Page 363, Enda Tuomey, "Should Dangerous Sports Be Banned? Yes!" posted on *Writefix.com*, 2005.

Page 364, Associated Press, "Big Hits, Macho Players and Dangers of NFL" published in *Abilene Reporter-News* online, January 2009.

Page 365, Lola Jones, "Banging on About High Diving and Extreme Sports Rules and Regulations," *www.extremesport4u.com*, April 24, 2009.

Page 367, British Broadcasting Company, "Are Sports Becoming Too Dangerous?" "Talking Points," BBC Online Network, 1999.

Page 368, "Is Boxing the Most Dangerous Sport?" *The Irish Independent*, December 7, 2007, posted on *www.independent.ie*.

Page 383, Jon Gertner, "Ice", *New York Times Magazine*, November 15, 2015, pp. 48–57.

CD-ROM ACKNOWLEDGMENTS

Test 1

Frank Lloyd Wright, "Modern Architecture," Kahn Lectures. Princeton University Press, 1930.

John Irving, "My Dinner at the White House," *Trying to Save Piggy Snead*, Arcade Books, 1996.

Bill Bryson, from *A Short History of Nearly Everything*, Broadway Books, a division of Random House, Inc., 2003.

"Year-Round School Has Educational Advantages," *HometownSource.com*, ECM Publishers, Inc., December 6, 2000.

Duke Helfand, "Year Round Discontent at Hollywood High," *Los Angeles Times*, November 20, 2000.

"Know the Facts," National Center for Summer Learning, 2006.

Graeme MacKay, MacKay Editorial Cartoons, *The Hamilton Spectator*, Hamilton, Ontario, Canada, August 16, 2001.

Ann McGlynn, "Districts That School Year Round, *The School Administrator*, American Association of School Administrators, March 2002.

Christopher Newland, "Academics, the Year-Round Calendar, and the Color of School Buses," *Offspring Magazine*, June 2000.

Test 2

Gloria Steinem, "Ruth's Song (Because She Could Not Sing It)," *Family Portraits*, ed. Carolyn Anthony, Doubleday, New York, 1989.

Robert V. Rimini, *Henry Clay: Statesman for the Union* by Robert Rimini. W.W. Norton & Company, Inc., 1991.

Kelly Walsh, "Pros and Cons of Digital Devices in the Hands of Young Students," *www.EmergingEdTech*, June 20, 2012.

Iris Adler, "How Our Digital Devices Are Affecting Our Personal Relationships," National Public Radio, WBUR, Boston, January 17, 2013.

Mike Kegle, Untitled cartoon, *Denver Post*, August 20, 2010.

Angela Barnes and Christine Laird, "The Effects of Social Media on Children," *Communications and Social Media*, 2012.

Pamela De Loatch, "The Four Negative Sides of Technology," *Endemic-Connecting Education and Technology*, May 2015.

Welcome

Welcome to the AP English Language and Composition exam. This book will take you on a virtual trip through every nook and cranny of the test. Its pages will acquaint you with the types of questions asked on the exam and show you how to write high-scoring essays. Along the way you'll find hundreds of sample questions and crucial test-taking tips. You'll also be introduced to principles of rhetoric and find a review of the grammar you need to know for the exam. The book contains five practice tests (plus two more on the optional CD-ROM and one more online)—all designed specifically to help you boost your AP score.

You probably know that the AP English Language and Composition exam tests your understanding of how writers use language to convey meaning. It does this by asking you to respond to roughly 55 **multiple-choice questions** about the text of four or five nonfiction prose passages written for different purposes and drawn from a range of historical periods.

The exam also contains three **essay questions**. The first essay, called a synthesis essay, requires you to state an opinion on a given issue and argue on behalf of your point of view. In constructing your argument, you must incorporate, or *synthesize*, material from at least three of several sources that accompany the question, or *prompt*, as it is called.

To answer the second essay question, you must identify and analyze the rhetorical techniques used in a passage of nonfiction prose. A third question asks you to write an essay that argues for or against a disputable idea expressed in a brief statement or passage.

The exam lasts three hours and 15 minutes and consists of two sections. The short-answer section takes one hour and counts for 45 percent of the total score. The essay section, lasting two-and-a-quarter hours, comprises 55 percent of your grade.

SECTION I	SECTION II
Up to 55 multiple-choice questions based on your reading of four or five nonfiction passages about history, science, art, language, and virtually any other topic (One hour)	**Question 1** • A synthesis essay that uses sources to support your position on a given issue **Question 2** • An essay that analyzes the style, rhetoric, and use of language in a selected prose passage **Question 3** • An essay in which you discuss the validity of an idea expressed in a given statement or brief prose passage (Two hours and 15 minutes)

Your score on the test is reported on a scale of 1–5. In general, scores are interpreted to mean that you are:

5 Extremely well qualified
4 Well qualifed
3 Qualified
2 Possibly qualified
1 Not recommended for AP credit

A high score on the exam demonstrates a proficiency in English at least on a par with students who've passed an introductory college-level course in composition or rhetoric. Some colleges award academic credit or offer more advanced English courses to high-scoring students. Because each college and university makes its own policies regarding AP scores, be sure to check with the admissions office of the institution you hope to attend.

Keep in mind that preparation for the exam isn't instantaneous. For most students it's a gradual and often painstaking process of study, review, and more study. In other words, give yourself time. Take it slowly. If the exam is months away, set aside, say, 30 minutes a day to work your way through the pages of this book. Yes, 30 minutes takes a big bite out of a high school student's day, but to get ready for the AP exam, there's no substitute for the steady accumulation of knowledge over a long period of time. If time is short between now and the exam, cramming may help you earn a good score, especially if you familiarize yourself with the test instructions and the format of the exam—but frankly, cramming is a less than perfect approach.

Regardless of how you go about preparing for the exam, I wish you luck. In May, when test day comes around, over 300,000 students will be taking the exam. I wish every one of them lots of luck, but because you have used this book to prepare, I'll be rooting especially for you.

George Ehrenhaft

A NOTE TO AP ENGLISH TEACHERS

Many AP teachers across the country find this book to be an invaluable resource. Questions and exercises throughout the book stimulate thinking and inspire students to write high-scoring essays. Some teachers use the book as an instant syllabus for their AP classes because it contains so much of what a high-level course in language and composition might offer, including:

✔ Reading passages that range from easy to hard
✔ Numerous exam questions, discussed and analyzed
✔ Essential rhetorical terms
✔ Sample student essays (with comments by AP readers)
✔ Annotated passages
✔ An analysis of the synthesis essay question
✔ A full-length self-assessment exam
✔ Four complete practice exams
✔ Two additional exams on CD-ROM (CD-ROM edition only) and one more online
✔ Full explanations of all answers

As a veteran AP teacher, I'm aware of both the rewards you enjoy and the hardships you encounter every day. If anything, I hope this book will lighten your load and help you provide the best possible instruction for your students.

Getting Acquainted with the Test

1

→ **A PREVIEW OF THE TEST**

→ **TYPES OF SHORT-ANSWER QUESTIONS**

→ **FOUR WAYS TO READ THE PASSAGES**

→ **WHEN TO GUESS**

→ **SYNTHESIS ESSAY AND ANALYTICAL ESSAY: HOW THEY DIFFER**

→ **USING AND CITING SOURCES**

→ **HOW ESSAYS ARE SCORED**

→ **WHAT YOU CAN LEARN FROM PAST EXAMS**

Putting it simply, the AP exam tests your reading and writing skills. Understanding the words in a bunch of passages doesn't guarantee success, however. Rather, top scores are awarded to anyone who can do two additional things:

1. Analyze how authors of nonfiction prose use various techniques to convey meaning and create effects, and
2. Write three well-organized and insightful essays, each with a different purpose.

To succeed in both these tasks, you need to know something about rhetoric, such as how an author's choice of details contributes to the meaning of the passage or in what ways the structure of a passage relates to its content.

You'll also need to be well acquainted with such concepts as *theme, tone, diction, syntax, allusion, imagery, paradox, irony, satire,* and a variety of other rhetorical devices that you've probably studied in English classes.

STRUCTURE OF THE EXAM

The exam lasts three hours and 15 minutes. For the first 60 minutes you'll read a handful of relatively short nonfiction passages and answer roughly 10 multiple-choice questions about each one. During the remaining time you'll write essays in response to three questions.

The prompt for the first essay question consists of a statement about an issue of concern in today's world. Accompanying the statement are several published documents—they are called **sources**—related to the issue, each less than a page long. One source will be an image—a photo, chart, map, cartoon, or other visual presentation also related to the issue. Fifteen minutes are allotted to read the sources. Then you are expected to write an essay that takes a position on the issue and incorporates, or *synthesizes,* at least three of the sources into your discussion. In AP terminology, this essay goes by the name **synthesis essay**.

A second question consists of a prose passage about a page long and an assignment to write an **analysis essay** that discusses the rhetorical strategies used by the author of the passage.

The third question calls for a **persuasive essay**. The prompt consists of a brief passage that expresses an opinion on a particular subject. Your essay must support, refute, or qualify the opinion stated by the author of the passage.

OUTLINE OF THE EXAM

Total time: Three hours and 15 minutes

Section I: One hour (45 percent of total score)
50–60 multiple-choice questions about several nonfiction prose passages

Section II: Two hours and 15 minutes
Three essays (55 percent of total score)

Essay 1: an argument for or against an idea presented in a short passage incorporating provided published sources
Essay 2: an analysis of a prose passage
Essay 3: an essay commenting on the validity of an opinion expressed in a statement or short passage

MULTIPLE-CHOICE QUESTIONS

TIP

Ordinarily, it pays to answer each question as it comes, but if a question gives you trouble, skip it for the time being and return to it later.

Multiple-choice questions can be about virtually anything that the author of a passage has done to convey meaning or create an effect. For instance, you may be asked about why the passage has been structured in a certain way, the purpose of a particular word or phrase, the function of a certain paragraph, or how a specific idea contributes to the development of the passage as a whole.

To answer some questions, you need a sense of sentences, including how sentences function in a passage; how sentences of different lengths, structure, and type (simple, compound, complex, compound complex) relate to tone and meaning. You must be aware of the uses of subordination, coordination, periodic and loose sentences, and parenthetical ideas. You may also be asked about word order, tone, diction (word choice), transitions, repetition, parallelism, and use of alliteration, allusion, antithesis, apostrophe, and figurative language, including metaphors, allusions, similes, hyperbole, paradox, and irony. At least one of the passages will include footnotes or a bibliography, and some of the questions will ask you about the meaning, purpose, or effect of these citations.

If your grasp of any of these topics is weak, be sure to look them up while preparing for the exam. They're all explained and discussed in this book.

One final hint: The order of multiple-choice questions usually coincides with the progress of each passage. Neither the passages nor the questions are presented in order of difficulty.

Typical Questions

RHETORIC

Most questions relate in some way to rhetoric. Such questions are typically worded as follows:

The primary rhetorical function of lines 15–19 is to

- (A) provide a transition between paragraphs 1 and 2.
- (B) reiterate the main idea of the passage.
- (C) introduce an idea that will be discussed later in the passage.
- (D) develop the controversial statement made in the first sentence of the passage.
- (E) prove the validity of the statistics cited in the previous sentence.

TIP

Rhetoric is a catch-all term loosely referring to the techniques and strategies an author uses to compose a passage.

TONE

A question on the tone of a passage may be worded like this:

The speaker's tone in the last sentence of the passage can best be described as which of the following?

- (A) Hateful
- (B) Satirical
- (C) Pretentious
- (D) Resentful
- (E) Arrogant

MOOD

A mood question may be worded like this:

The mood of the second paragraph of the passage is best described as

- (A) anxious.
- (B) sentimental.
- (C) humorous.
- (D) suspenseful.
- (E) sarcastic.

TIP

In literary criticism, the term *mood* refers to the feelings that a poem or prose piece arouses in the reader. Mood, therefore, is technically different from *tone*, which refers to the author's or speaker's feelings about the subject.

FOOTNOTES

A documentation question on footnoting is likely to be worded this way:

The function of footnotes 2 and 4 is to tell readers that the quotations in lines 13–14 and 26–28

- (A) come from the same source but are attributed to two different authors.
- (B) were both published in 2013.
- (C) are found in the same edition of the *Oxford Companion to American Literature*.
- (D) appear in books that are no longer in print.
- (E) reveal that the author quoted material from *The Modern Family* by Robert Winch.

This question won't stump anyone acquainted with the conventions of footnoting. Although systems of documentation differ in their details, they all cite titles, authors, dates, and publishers. A complete footnote tells you where to find the cited quotation or information. It may also tell you, among other things, where the material originated, whether it was translated, and a great deal more. If you've ever labored on a research paper or project during your school career, you've probably written footnotes and prepared bibliographies, or lists of works cited. The AP exam won't give you esoteric or highly specialized footnotes or citations to interpret. Rather, it will serve up ordinary samples—those that a college freshman would be expected to know.

LANGUAGE

A question about language may be worded as follows:

> The second paragraph of the passage contains all of the following EXCEPT
>
> (A) a simple sentence.
> (B) a compound sentence.
> (C) a complex sentence.
> (D) a declarative sentence.
> (E) an interrogative sentence.

To answer this question you need to know sentence terminology and be able to identify sentence types. The review of sentence types later in this book will help you do just that.

TIP

It pays to brush up on the terminology of grammar and usage.

GRAMMAR

Another type of grammar question is apt to be phrased like this:

> Lines 12–18 contain which of the following?
>
> (A) Subordinate clauses
> (B) Hyperbole
> (C) A single periodic sentence
> (D) An allusion
> (E) Parallelism

Strictly speaking, only choices (A), (C), and (E) relate to grammar. The others are more rhetorical in nature. The nature of each choice, however, matters less than your ability to identify various examples of grammatical usage and rhetoric when you see them.

Typically, no more than two or three multiple-choice questions on the exam pertain to grammar. Most questions—other than a few comprehension questions—relate in some way to rhetoric.

The foregoing questions represent only a few of the many types on the exam. The following list will give you an idea of other kinds that have appeared on recent exams.

1. **IDENTIFY** the relationship of a sentence in the first paragraph to the passage as a whole.

2. **SELECT** the rhetorical strategy or device used in a particular section of the passage.

3. **IDENTIFY** the function of a sentence within a paragraph, or a paragraph within the whole.

4. **CHOOSE** the best title or main topic of a passage.

5. **DISCERN** shifts in theme, tone, style, sentence structure, diction, syntax, effect, or rhetorical purpose between the two sections of the passage.

6. **DETERMINE** how unity (or point of view, emphasis, contrast, or other feature) is achieved in all or part of the passage.

7. **RECOGNIZE** the overall genre of the passage.

8. **NAME** the author's implied or stated purpose, or the purpose of particular images, diction, organization, sentence structure, or other stylistic choice.

Many of the questions direct you to particular lines of the passage. To answer most of those questions you need to read the specified lines and respond. Some questions, however, require more than that. Some raise broad issues that can't be addressed without a fuller understanding of the context in which the lines appear. In such cases, you must read at least the two or three lines that precede the lines designated by the question and the two or three lines that follow.

For multiple-choice questions, AP test writers ordinarily choose passages written between the 17th and 21st centuries, although they might occasionally toss in a passage from ancient Greece or Rome. In each exam, they attempt to balance genre, time period, and individual style. Passages are nonfiction and are composed by essayists, historians, journalists, diarists, autobiographers, political writers, philosophers, and critics. You won't find simple passages that leave little room for interpretation, nor will you find passages comprehensible only to those with sky-high IQs.

Authors and titles of the passages are not given, although the source of each passage is briefly identified: "*a nineteenth-century memoir,*" "*a twentieth-century book,*" "*a contemporary journalist's diary,*" and so on. By and large, if you've taken an AP English class, you'll probably understand the passages and correctly answer the majority of questions. A robust reading background, both in school and on your own, as well as practice in close textual analysis, will serve you well.

READING TECHNIQUES

By this time in your school career you've probably taken numerous tests like the SATs or ACTs for which you have read passages like those on the AP English exam and answered multiple-choice questions. No doubt you've developed certain techniques of test taking and have observed that there is no technique that serves everyone equally. What works for others may not work for you, and vice versa.

Nevertheless, it's helpful to know which techniques help you do your best. Prepare for the exam by trying the alternatives described below. Experiment with each one as you make your way through the exercises and practice tests in this book. Gradually, you'll discover which technique, or combination of techniques, you can count on. Lean on them and ignore the others.

Technique 1: Read the Passage in Its Entirety

Read everything, including footnotes, from start to finish with pencil in hand. As you read, keep in mind that on this test you will be asked questions primarily about the language and rhetoric of the passage. (You may also get a small number of comprehension questions.) While reading, underline any unusual turns of phrase. Make a note of particularly vivid images and of figures of speech. Try also to figure out the tone of the passage. Ask yourself, "What is the author's attitude or feeling about the subject?" Then mark any words, phrases, or ideas that clearly illustrate or contribute to the tone. Finally, observe how the passage is organized. Is there a progression of ideas? What does each paragraph contribute to the main point of the passage? Finally, turn to the questions, referring to the passage as necessary to find or check your answers.

Technique 2: Skim the Passage

To get the general idea of the passage, read faster than you normally would. Try only to identify the general topic and the approach used by the author: Is the passage formal or informal? Personal or objective? Is it mainly a narrative? A description? An argument for or against some issue? The answers to these questions will be fairly apparent during a quick read-through. Make a mental note of any unusual words and phrases. Read intently enough to get an impression of the content and writing style of the passage, but don't dawdle. Then, as you answer the questions, refer to the passage.

Technique 3: Read Twice

Skim the passage for a general impression; then go back and read it more thoroughly, using your pencil to mark the passage and take notes. Two readings, one fast and one slow, allow you to pick out features of language and rhetoric that you might overlook during a single reading. Why? Because from the first reading you'll know what the passage is about, and during the second you'll be able to focus on the features that contribute to the overall meaning and effect of the passage. After the second reading proceed to the questions, referring to the passage to check your answers.

Technique 4: Read Only the Questions

Do <u>not</u> look at the answer choices. Because it's virtually impossible to remember 10 or 12 questions about material you haven't read, go through the questions quickly—only to become acquainted with the kinds of information you are expected to draw out of the passage. Label each question with a notation: "MI" (main idea), "T" (tone), "POV" (point of view), "SS" (sentence structure), and so on. (Or you can devise your own system.) When you know the questions beforehand, you can read the passage more purposefully, taking into account the matters raised by the questions.

Some students methodically read one question, then scour the passage in search of the answer before moving on to the next question. Before they know it, time has run out, and they are far from finishing. Moreover, such a fragmented approach reduces the likelihood of grasping the overall point of the passage.

HOW TO INCREASE YOUR READING POWER

Strong readers often get that way by habitually analyzing what they read word by word, sentence by sentence, and paragraph by paragraph. They recognize that good authors carefully select every syllable they write, leaving nothing to chance—not the words, the sentences, the punctuation, the footnotes, the order and content of paragraphs, nor the overall structure of their work. Every bit of their prose has a point and purpose behind it.

Your job on the AP exam is to read the passages and analyze how they were written. The good news is that you can train yourself to make insightful analyses by dissecting whatever you read. Practice with a pencil in hand, and as you read almost any respectable piece of prose, jot down reasons why the author chose particular words and details. Examine sentence structure and the sequence of ideas. Identify how the author creates a tone and develops a main idea.

Like every other worthwhile skill, annotating a passage in this manner takes time, and to do it well takes even more time, especially at the beginning. It can be burdensome, frustrating, and even discouraging, but just a single reasonably astute insight can beget another and another after that. With regular practice, close reading can become almost addictive. Laying bare an author's creative process has whet the appetite of many students who now do it all the time. Even better, a heightened awareness of the reasons behind every choice that an author has made will lift your score on the AP exam. And perhaps even more important in the long run, it's likely to raise the level and maturity of your own writing. Considering all these potential rewards, how can you not try it?

How to get started as an annotator:

✔ Condense the main idea of whatever you read into a pithy sentence or two. (You might even jot down a brief summary.) If you can clearly and accurately identify the thesis, you've come a long way. Sometimes the thesis will be stated outright. In that case, underline or highlight it in some way. If the thesis is only implied by content, however, put it into your own words. Writing it down on paper or on a computer screen is a sure sign that you're serious about finding the essence of a passage.

✔ Look for clues to the author's attitude, purpose, and intent. Is the passage meant largely to entertain? To inform? To provoke controversy? To inspire or to enlighten the reader? Does the author have a bias, an ax to grind, an ulterior motive? It's hard to conceive of a piece of writing in which the author's attitude is totally hidden. Take the paragraph you've just read. Can you tell what the author—me!—hoped to accomplish with his words? Well, if you're the least bit tempted to dissect a passage, then I've achieved my purpose—to convince you to give annotation a try.

✔ Analyze structure. Which ideas come first? Second? Third? Is there a reason for the sequence of ideas? How are ideas linked to each other? Does the end contain echoes of earlier ideas?

✔ Examine how the author creates an effect on the reader. Study word choice, sentence structure and length, the order of ideas, figures of speech, the use of rhythm and sound. How does the author keep you interested? Is the writing formal or informal? Is the author friendly or stand-offish, enthusiastic or cool?

✔ Think about the author's qualifications to write on a topic. Details usually reveal the authority of the writer. Authors who don't know what they are talking about often hide behind prose top-heavy with generalities. Study the footnotes, if any. Do they refer to sources that are reliable and up-to-date?

✔ Become an annotator. Mark up passages profusely, writing in margins and underlining noteworthy ideas and features.

What follows are three annotated passages. Although the notes are not exhaustive, they suggest what an alert reader might observe during a close reading of each passage.

TIP

To become a first-rate annotator, get into the habit of dissecting passages line by line.

PASSAGE 1

This passage, written early in the twentieth century by Virginia Woolf, is an excerpt from an essay about the art of biographical writing. (Note: This passage is about one-quarter the length of passages typically used on the AP exam.)

[1] Thus the biographer must go ahead of the rest of us, [2] like the miner's canary, detecting falsity, unreality, and the presence of obsolete conventions. His [3] sense of truth must be alive and on tiptoe. Then again, since we live in an age when a thousand cameras are pointed, by newspapers, letters, and diaries, at every character from every angle, he must be prepared to admit contradictory versions of the same face. Biography will enlarge its scope by hanging up looking glasses at odd corners. And yet from all this diversity it will bring out, [4] not a riot of confusion, but a richer unity. And again since (so much is known that used to be unknown), the question now [5] inevitably asks itself whether the lives of great men only should be recorded. [6] Is not anyone who has lived a life and left a record of that life worthy of biography—the failures as well as the successes, the humble as well as the illustrious? And what is greatness? And what is smallness? [7] We must revise our standards of merit and set up new heroes for our admiration.

Line (5) ... *(10)* ... *(15)*

—From *The Death of the Moth and Other Essays* by Virginia Woolf

[1] "Thus" is a transitional word telling you that this paragraph is a continuation of a longer passage about writing biographies.

[2] "like the miner's canary" is a simile admonishing biographers to be wary of information that appears to be the "truth," but isn't.

[3] "sense of truth . . . alive and on tiptoe" is a personification. This figure of speech, along with the synecdoche "face" (line 8) and the metaphors, "a thousand cameras" (line 5) and "looking glasses" (line 9), indicates that figurative language is an important rhetorical feature of the passage.

[4] Author uses sentences containing contrasts: "not . . . but" (line 11) and "known . . . unknown" (line 12) for emphasis.

[5] The word "inevitably," along with the use of "must" as the main verb in several sentences (lines 1, 4, 7, and 18), adds assertiveness and confidence to the writer's tone.

[6] Three rhetorical questions (lines 14–18) draw the reader into the discussion.

[7] The concluding sentence articulates this passage's main idea and introduces the topic for the next paragraph—that biographers of the future may find a rich source of subjects (i.e., "heroes") not only among the rich and famous but also in the mass of ordinary people.

Annotation Summary

The passage consists entirely of Woolf's thoughts about the art of biographical writing. To strengthen her presentation, she adopts an earnest and self-confident tone. Almost half of the sentences in the passage use the verb "must," a sure sign that Woolf aims to instruct biographers in the requirements of their craft if they expect to tell the truth about their subjects.

Figurative language gives the passage its literary quality. The use of metaphor fits the topic because biography, after all, is not an objective, literal account of everything in a person's life. Rather, it is a figurative rendering of the subject, its details carefully chosen to create a certain image for the reader. Accordingly, since Woolf asserts that subjects for biography can be found among all types of people, her references to cameras and looking glasses—instruments that help us see things more clearly—are particularly apt.

A WORD FROM YOUR AUTHOR

If the Woolf passage has been your first brush with annotation, you may now find yourself muttering "Are you kidding me?" or "No way, man!" or some even less delicate expressions of self-doubt.

Well, that's not an uncommon initial reaction. But please, don't give up. Sure, annotating passages can be a challenge, especially at the start. It's not all that difficult if you work at it, however. It's guaranteed to get easier, but it does take practice. And that's one of the purposes of this book—to help you master this annotation stuff.

Remember, too, that annotation is merely a means to an end: writing a perceptive analytical AP essay. As you annotate a passage, you'll gradually learn what to look for and begin to see the author's rhetoric becoming more and more apparent. And as you grow accustomed to annotating passages, you'll begin to find more and more rhetorical elements—maybe more than you ever expected. Then, as you plan your AP essay, you'll have some decisions to make—namely, which elements to write about, which of them to emphasize, and which to discuss first, second, third, and so on.

PASSAGE 2

The following passage is by the renowned ornithologist John James Audubon. It is about half the length of passages typically used on the AP exam.

As soon as the pigeons discover a sufficiency of food to **[1]** entice them to alight, they fly around in circles, reviewing the countryside below. During these *Line* **[2]** evolutions the dense mass which they form presents (5) a **[3]** beautiful spectacle, as it changes direction; turning from a glistening sheet of azure, as the backs of the birds come simultaneously into view, to a suddenly presented rich, deep purple. After that they pass lower, over the woods, and for a moment are lost among the foliage. (10) Again they emerge and glide aloft. They may now alight, but the next moment take to wing **[4]** as if suddenly alarmed, the flapping of their wings producing a noise like the roar of distant thunder, as they sweep through the forests to see if danger is near.

[1] The verbs "discover" (line 1) and "reviewing" (line 3) attribute human qualities to a flock of pigeons, as though the author knows what goes on inside pigeons' heads. Likewise, "hunger" (line 15) brings the birds to the ground. In lines 23–24, the author ascribes frustration ("find his labor completely lost") to one of the birds. Note, too, the use of the personal pronoun "his" instead of "its."

[2] The word "evolutions" suggests progressive change. As the passage continues, the writer portrays the birds in different stages: alighting, turning en mass, getting lost in the foliage, etc.

[3] The "beautiful spectacle" of the birds in flight is captured by visual imagery and poetic language in lines 5–8. Sibilant sounds ("s," "sh," "z") suggest the swoosh of birds' wings. Sound imagery continues with a simile in lines 12–13 ("a noise like the roar of distant thunder . . .")

[4] Writer continues to ascribe human qualities to the birds: "as if suddenly alarmed" (lines 11–12), "to see if danger is near" (line 14).

(15) **[5]** However, hunger soon brings them to the ground. On alighting they industriously throw aside the withered leaves in quest of the fallen mast.[1] The rear ranks continually rise, passing over the main body and alighting in front, and in such rapid succession that the whole

(20) flock seems still on the wing. **[6]** The quantity of ground swept in this way is **[7]** astonishing. So completely has it been cleared that the gleaner who might who follow in the rear of the flock would find his labor completely lost. While their feeding **[8]** avidity is at times so great

(25) that in attempting to swallow a large acorn or nut, they may be seen to gasp for a long while as if in the agonies of suffocation.

—Excerpt from "Passenger Pigeon"
by John James Audubon (1813)

---

[1] *nuts, acorns*

[5] A turning point in the passage: The pigeons are in flight during the entire first paragraph, but on the ground in the second paragraph. The use of active verbs shows the birds in constant motion: e.g., "throw aside," "continually rise," "passing over," "alighting . . . in rapid succession" etc.

[6] Allusion to the notion of evolution, introduced earlier. See note [2].

[7] The writer reiterates astonishment over the birds' noteworthy behavior.

[8] The word "avidity" applies to the flock's feeding behavior but it also echoes the strength of the writer's own fondness for the birds.

Annotation Summary

Using a tone of admiration and wonder, Audubon describes a flock of passenger pigeons. His language and imagery emphasize the birds' beauty as well as their human-like qualities, a rhetorical strategy that encourages readers to view the pigeons not as just another species but almost as ingenious, alert, and intelligent creatures. In two paragraphs, one devoted to detailing the movement of the airborne flock, the other, the birds' behavior on the ground, the writer creates a multi-dimensional portrait of the passenger pigeon.

Footnote: Audubon's contemporaries might well have understood why he alludes to the flock's "evolution." The passenger pigeon, once among the most numerous of North American birds, in 1913 was on the verge of extinction. The last one died in a Cincinnati zoo on September 1, 1914. Audubon may well have written the passage as a tribute to the dying species.

PASSAGE 3

The passage below, a newspaper column, was published prior to the 2016 Presidential election, a time when candidates spoke often of "American exceptionalism," the proposition that the United States, because of its unique stature in the world, has both extraordinary responsibilities and extraordinary rights.

Its length (608 words) is about the same as passages typically used on the AP exam.

The notion **[1]** of American exceptionalism, first introduced by Alexis de Tocqueville[1] in his two-volume classic, *Democracy in America*, is incongruent with the contemporary use of the term. **[2]**

(5) Tocqueville wrote: "The position of the Americans is quite exceptional, and it may be believed that no democratic people will ever be placed in a similar one." **[3]**

Void of context this statement is vague and ambiguous enough for us to fill in whatever blanks we want, (10) even portraying America as the shining city of the hill where nirvana comfortably resides. But is this what de Tocqueville meant? **[4]**

In its full context the sentence reads: "The position of the Americans is therefore quite exceptional, and it may (15) be believed that no democratic people will ever be placed in a similar one. Their strictly Puritanical origin, their exclusively commercial habits, even the country they inhabit, have singularly concurred to fix the mind of the American upon purely practical objects. Their passions, (20) their wants, their education, and everything about them seem to draw the native of the United States earthward; although his religion bids him turn, from time to time, a transient and distracted glance to heaven."

[1] The word "notion" indicates that "American exceptionalism" is not a fact but rather a theoretical construct or idea that's open to interpretation.

[2] The opening sentence contains the thesis of the passage. All that follows is an argument meant to prove that de Tocqueville's notion has been misinterpreted.

[3] A direct quote showing precisely where the notion of American exceptionalism originated.

[4] This semi-rhetorical question implies that de Tocqueville's idea, when removed from its original context, invites faulty interpretations.

The question also helps to unify the passage by serving as a transition to a word-for-word rendering of de Tocqueville's text, included in the next paragraph (lines 13-23) as evidence meant to convince readers that de Tocqueville's idea has been distorted.

_____

[1] *A French political thinker and historian who toured the the U.S. in 1831 and had his observations published in an acclaimed book,* Democracy in America.

What de Tocqueville wrote bears little resemblance to
(25) the manner that American exceptionalism is touted in
contemporary discourse. **[5]** In fact, an honest assessment of de Tocqueville's definition calls into question if
he even meant the term as a compliment. **[6]**

In some circles, American exceptionalism has become
(30) the sophomoric **[7]** litmus test to ascertain one's allegiance to the nation. The contemporary definition is
nothing more than an anti-intellectual endeavor to rob
the nation of one of its key elements, which is dissent. **[8]** Dissent is the oxygen of any democratic soci-
(35) ety, and without it we risk choking on the fumes of our
self-induced megalomania.[2] The lack of dissent prohibits
a nation from self-reflection, which stagnates growth. It
is to infuse the society with the toxins of arrogance and
insularity. Rather than a foreign enemy, are not these
(40) weapons that topple superpowers? **[9]**

America, in my view, **[10]** is a unique nation, here is
where its greatness is realized. It is unique because it was
formed on an idea—an idea that was beyond the comprehension of the individuals who conceived it.

[5] The author again reminds readers of the passage's main point. The idea of exceptionalism has a deeper, more profound meaning than "America is different from other countries," as explained in lines 24-28.

[6] The author questions de Tocqueville's intent, thereby prodding readers to reassess the meaning of the quotation.

[7] An allusion to "sophomoric" (i.e., ignorant, biased, closed-minded, etc.) politicians who use the idea as a means to measure people's patriotism.

[8] The author not only abhors using the idea of American exceptionalism as a measure of patriotism, he claims that it destroys the right to dissent, one of America's basic values.

[9] The author's choice of words with negative connotations ("megalomania," "stagnates," "toxins," "arrogance," "topple") adds emotional power to the argument.

[10] Note the phrase "in my view." This shows the author's effort to reach out to the reader and acknowledge that he has a personal stake in what otherwise might be an academic argument. He strongly espouses American exceptionalism, calling the country a "unique nation," but for reasons far more noble than those cited by politicians.

---

[2]*Delusions of one's own greatness or grandeur.*

(45)   "We hold these truths to be self-evident: that all men are created equal; that they are endowed by their Creator with certain unalienable rights; that among these are life, liberty, and the pursuit of happiness," **[11]** is not only the nation's mission statement but has been expanded

(50)   upon, not without conflict, so that those words shine as bright today as they did when they were enshrined in the nation's ethos on July 4, 1776.

At a time when the world was dominated by inequality, along comes a cabal of great men, pledging to one another

(55)   their lives, fortunes and sacred honor for the unprecedented notion of equality. America need not rely on myth to support itself. Rather, it would be better served by embracing the words of Founding Father Benjamin Rush, who famously wrote: "The American war is over but this is

(60)   far from being the case with the American Revolution. On the contrary, nothing but the first act of this great drama is closed." **[12]** While there is something about American exceptionalism that suggests our work is complete, Rush is offering a more arduous task. The revolution is the

(65)   ongoing narrative **[13]** for what is commonly referred to as the American experiment.

It was an experiment first articulated by Thomas Jefferson, put into practice by Washington, held together by Lincoln, sustained by Roosevelt, and pushed to higher

(70)   greatness by King. What other nation can lay claim to such a unique history? **[14]**

—Adapted from Byron Williams, "Revolution Was Only the Start of the American Experiment," *Contra Costa Times*, December 17, 2015, p. A19.

[11] Using profoundly evocative words from the Declaration of Independence and a reference to July 4, 1776, the author lifts the notion of America's exceptionalism above the fray of everyday politics. Inspiring figurative language ("words shine as bright today . . . enshrined in the nation's ethos") is meant to stir the reader's mind and heart.

[12] Allusions to the Founding Fathers and to other inspiring figures from over two centuries of American history add still more substance and clarity to the notion of America's exceptionalism.

[13] The term "ongoing narrative" reminds readers that the notion of American exceptionalism is both timeless and transcendent and must not be reduced to a simplistic political slogan.

[14] The author leaves the reader with a rhetorical question that has only one possible answer.

Annotation Summary

The passage is an argument meant to persuade readers that the notion of American exceptionalism, originally articulated by de Tocqueville, has been distorted by politicians to mean a belief in American superiority. To prove his point, the author relies on a logical sequence of thought that includes the very words that de Tocqueville used to discuss the idea of America's exceptionalism. In its context the phrase refers to de Tocqueville's view that Americans differed from others because they are concerned with and devoted to mostly practical, everyday, down-to-earth matters.

Having shown that American exceptionalism is unrelated to patriotism, the author of the passage argues that the politicians' interpretation of the phrase undermines the very credo on which America was founded, especially the people's right to dissent. Quoting and paraphrasing evocative excerpts from the Declaration of Independence, he lauds the men who broke America's ties to England, fought the Revolution, and laid the foundation on which our democracy was built. To prove that America's spirit of revolt still survives, the author cites the contributions made to America's standing among nations by such legendary, almost mythic, figures as Lincoln, Roosevelt, and Martin Luther King.

Other annotators may have made different, yet equally valid, comments about each of the previous passages. What matters most is not that the details of the analyses differ from each other but that all of them more or less describe the essential anatomy of each passage.

Now try your hand at annotating a passage on your own. Read the following passage at least twice—first to see what it's about, and then, during the second reading, to jot down whatever you notice about its structure and composition. When you are done, write a summary of the main idea and state your perception of the author's tone. Afterwards, compare your notes to those made by the author of this book. Chances are that you will record ideas that he has missed and vice versa.

Passage for Annotation

There are two deep-seated idiosyncrasies of human nature that bear on our acceptance or rejection of what is offered us. We have, in the first place, an innate bias for
Line the familiar. Whatever we're thoroughly unfamiliar with
(5) is apt to seem to us odd, or queer, or curious, or bizarre. For it is no mere trick of speech, but one of those appallingly veracious records of human nature and experience in which the history of words abounds, through which "outlandish" and "crude" attained their present mean-
(10) ing. For "outlandish" meant in the beginning only what doesn't belong to our own land, and "uncouth" was simply "unknown." The change in meaning registers a universal trait. Whatever is alien to our own ways—the costume, manners, modes of speech of another race or
(15) of other times—is strange; and "strange" itself, which started out by meaning merely "foreign," is only another record of the same idiosyncrasy. But there is still another trait that is no less broadly human. Whatever is too familiar wearies us. Incessant recurrence without variety
(20) breeds tedium; the overiterated becomes the monotonous, and the monotonous irks and bores. And there we are. Neither that which we do not know at all, nor that which we know too well, is to our taste. We are averse to shocks, and we go to sleep under narcotics.
(25) Both the shock and the narcotic have, I grant, at times their fascination. But they are apt to be forward, not permanent, sweet, not lasting. The source of more or less abiding satisfaction for most normal human beings lies in a happy merging of the two—in the twofold delight
(30) in an old friend recognized as new, or a new friend recognized as old. The experience and the pleasure are universal. All the lovers who have ever lived have made experiment of it; a face that you have passed a hundred times, nor cared to see, remains the face you've always
(35) known, but becomes all at once the most beautiful and thrilling object in the world; the person you've never known before, you find all at once you've known from all eternity. Now art, like love, sends its roots deep into what we are. And our most permanent aesthetic satisfac-
(40) tion arises as a rule from things familiar enough to give the pleasure of recognition, yet not so trite as to rob us of the other pleasure of surprise. We are keen for the new,

but we insist that it establish some connection with what is friendly and our own; we want the old, but we want (45) it to seem somehow new. Things may recur as often as they please, so long as they surprise us—like the Ghost in *Hamlet*—each time they appear.

—From John Livingstone Lowes,
Convention and Revolt in Poetry, 1919

Your Annotation Summary

_____

_____

_____

_____

_____

_____

Here is the same passage annotated by the author:

[1] There are two deep-seated idiosyncrasies of human nature that bear on our acceptance or rejection of what is offered us. We have, in the first place, [2] an
Line innate bias for the familiar. [3] Whatever we're thor-
(5) oughly unfamiliar with is apt to seem to us odd, or queer, or curious, or bizarre. For it is no mere trick of speech, but one of those appallingly veracious records of human nature and experience in which the history of words abounds, [4] through which "outlandish" and "crude"
(10) attained their present meaning. For "outlandish" meant in the beginning only what doesn't belong to our own land, and "uncouth" was simply "unknown." The change in meaning registers a universal trait. Whatever is alien to our own ways—the costume, manners, modes of
(15) speech of another race or of other times—is strange; and "strange" itself, which started out by meaning merely "foreign," is only another record of the same idiosyn-crasy. [5] But there is still another trait that is no less broadly human. Whatever is too familiar wearies us.
(20) Incessant recurrence without variety breeds tedium; the overiterated becomes the monotonous, and the monoto-nous irks and bores. [6] And there we are. Neither that

[1] The passage begins with its topic sentence. It promises a discussion of two idiosyncrasies of human nature.

[2] The first trait is stated in lines 3–4.

[3] For clarity, the author explains "bias for the familiar," not by defining the term but by citing examples of its opposite—i.e., our aversion to the unfamiliar. Four adjectives ("odd," "queer," etc.) show subtle gradations of meaning, suggesting both the richness and the complexity of the subject.

[4] This may seem like a digression into word origins, but language is such an elemental part of what it means to be human that the author uses the history of words to show how deeply in our nature the rejection of the unfamiliar is embedded.

A compilation of diverse examples (lines 8–18) helps the author to build a convincing case that we tend initially, at least, to be wary of the new.

[5] The second trait is introduced and defined. Starting on line 21, the author plays with words by restating "monotonous" and using other redundant words and phrases—as though to give readers a taste of the very phenomenon being discussed.

[6] A short four-word sentence interrupts the ow of ideas, giving the reader a chance to absorb the author's ideas. The recapitulation of the passage thus far also serves as a transition to the discussion that follows.

which we do not know at all, nor that which we know too well, is to our taste. **[7]** We are averse to shocks, and we
(25) go to sleep under narcotics.

Both the shock and the narcotic have, I grant, at times their fascination. **[8]** But they are apt to be forward, not permanent, sweet, not lasting. The source of more or less abiding satisfaction for most normal human beings lies
(30) in a happy merging of the two—in the twofold delight in an old friend recognized as new, or a new friend recognized as old. **[9]** The experience and the pleasure are universal. All the lovers who have ever lived have made experiment of it; a face that you have passed a hundred
(35) times, nor cared to see, remains the face you've always known, but becomes all at once the most beautiful and thrilling object in the world; the person you've never known before, you find all at once you've known from all eternity. Now art, like love, sends its roots deep into what
(40) we are. **[10]** And our most permanent aesthetic satisfaction arises as a rule from things familiar enough to give the pleasure of recognition, yet not so trite as to rob us of the other pleasure of surprise. **[11]** We are keen for the new, but we insist that it establish some connection with
(45) what is friendly and our own; we want the old, but we want it to seem somehow new. Things may recur as often as they please, so long as they surprise us—like the Ghost in *Hamlet*—**[12]** each time they appear.

—From John Livingstone Lowes,
Convention and Revolt in Poetry, 1919

[7] The author introduces another way to look at the issue.

[8] Stylistically, the author is fond of using antitheses—juxtaposing contrasting ideas, as in lines 22-24: "that which we do not know at all, nor that which we know too well." See also lines 27-28, 31-32, 37-39, et al. The technique not only provides a lilting rhythm to the prose but helps develop the author's point that satisfaction comes from "a happy merging of the two" (line 30).

[9] A short, pithy sentence between two lengthy sentences adds variety and leaves an impact on the reader. The adjective "universal" is particularly apt because the entire passage deals with a defining characteristic of humankind. The author alludes to two widely understood experiences, love and friendship, to heighten readers' understanding. In line 39, however, the author expands the discussion to include the abstract world of art.

[10] The author reiterates the basic point of the discussion in terms of our emotional reactions to art.

[11] The author once again rephrases and reiterates the main idea of the passage, perhaps to prepare readers for the literary reference at the end of the passage.

[12] The allusion casts a new light on the ghost of Hamlet's father. We know beforehand that the ghost will show up, but its appearance nevertheless gives us a start.

Annotation Summary

The opening sentence of the passage states the author's thesis—that there is a predictable pattern in humans' responses to stimuli that are familiar and to stimuli that are not. This idea is presented not as a hypothesis or a theory but as an indisputable fact.

With an authoritative, analytical voice, the author sets out to prove the validity of his thesis, first by citing a number of everyday words, all with unfavorable connotations and all pertaining to our suspicion or outright rejection of things that are new and unfamiliar. Unexpectedly, the author also claims that we humans don't necessarily adhere to the opposite—embracing the well-known and familiar. Rather, because we are apt to find overly-familiar matters equally undesirable, he draws the conclusion that "Neither that which we do not know at all, nor that which we know too well, is to our taste" (lines 22-24).

This juxtaposition of contrasting ideas is a stylistic motif evident throughout the passage. Several sentences contain antithetical constructs, as in: "But they are apt to be forward, not permanent, sweet, not lasting" (lines 27-28), and "the twofold delight in an old friend recognized as new, or a new friend recognized as old" (lines 30-32), and "we want the old, but we want it to seem somehow new" (lines 45-46).

Such a pattern of sentence structure not only echoes a crucial component of the passage, i.e., "two deep-seated idiosyncrasies." It also leads naturally to the allusion to Hamlet's father's ghost—an always expected but nevertheless surprising dramatic occurrence.

The clock won't permit lengthy annotations during the AP exam, but if you get into the habit of underlining salient ideas, words, and phrases, and generally scrawling your insights all over the things you read, it's likely that you'll be primed to sail through the passages on the exam. But proficiency in annotation, like a skill in any endeavor, diminishes with disuse. So, keep at it because it's easy to slip out of the groove if you stop for any length of time.

See Appendix (pages 383–388) for more practice in annotation.

ANSWERING THE QUESTIONS

Multiple-Choice Questions

Multiple-choice questions separate well-qualified students from those who are less qualified. To earn a "5" on the exam you must answer most of the questions correctly and write good essays. To earn a "3," you need to get about 50 or 60 percent of the short-answer questions right—provided that your essays are generally acceptable.

Each correct answer is worth one point. In scoring the test, each wrong answer and each answer left blank will be deducted from the total number of questions. If, for example, you were to leave two blanks and answer four questions incorrectly, a total of six points will deducted from 55—the usual number of questions on the exam—making your short-answer score 49.

This scoring procedure means that it always pays to guess, even when a question stumps you completely. By guessing at random, you still have a one-in-five chance of getting it right, and by eliminating one or more choices, you dramatically increase the odds of picking the correct answer. In short, DON'T LEAVE BLANKS. ANSWER EVERY QUESTION.

When a question gives you trouble, and you can't decide among three choices, conventional wisdom says you should go with your first impulse. You may be right. Testing experts and psychologists agree there's a better than average chance of success if you trust your intuition. There are no guarantees, however. Because the human mind works in so many ways, relying on your initial choice may not always work.

Essay Questions

After an hour of answering multiple-choice questions, you'll have two hours to write three essays:

- A **synthesis essay** in which you use sources to argue your point of view on a given issue.
- An **analytical essay** that examines, interprets, and explains the meaning and structure of prose passage.
- A **persuasive** or **argumentative essay** that supports, refutes, or qualifies an opinion expressed in a statement or brief passage.

Before you've given the signal to begin writing your essays, you'll have 15 minutes to read the questions and the sources for the synthesis essay. However, you don't have to spend the whole time reading. During those 15 minutes you can plan your essay, underline noteworthy ideas, formulate a tentative thesis, or prepare a brief outline. You might even glance at the other essay questions. Essentially, the time is yours to fill as you wish but with one exception: you may not start writing your essay. That begins only after the proctor gives you the green light.

Write the essays in any order. The choice is yours. The suggested writing time for each essay is 40 minutes.

ESSAY QUESTIONS FROM PREVIOUS AP EXAMS

To give you an idea of the essays you are expected to write on the exam, here are essay topics that students were given during each of the last five years.

2012

1. Founded more than two-hundred years ago, the United States Postal Service (USPS) developed into a vital and efficient communication delivery system throughout America. During the last decade, however, with expanding digital communications and the growth of package delivery companies, postal business has declined precipitously. The resulting loss of revenue has forced the USPS to weigh reducing services, as, for example, cutting the number of mail delivery days per week.

   After reading seven sources about the current status of the postal service, write an essay that discusses whether the USPS should undertake steps to adapt to the present needs of the country, and if so, how.

2. Read remarks that President John F. Kennedy made in response to a 1962 decision by American steel companies to raise their prices at a time when the country's economy was in great distress. Then, write an essay which discusses the rhetorical strategies that Kennedy used to convey his views on the actions of the steel companies.

3. Write an essay that takes a position on the relationship between certainty and doubt as expressed by two brief quotations, one advocating the need to develop certainty in order to accomplish one's goals, the other supporting the inclusion of a degree of doubt in statements of one's opinions.

2013

1. This question is about the building of monuments that pay homage to renowned people, to great achievements, and to historic moments of deep sacrifice. Those who undertake to create such memorials must make numerous decisions regarding size, location, and materials—among many other things.

   After reading seven sources related to monument building, write an essay that examines the criteria that a group or agency should take into account not only in choosing an event or person to memorialize but also in creating an appropriate monument.

2. Read a passage written in 2008 that laments the growing separation of people from the natural world. Then, write an essay that analyzes the rhetorical strategies used by the author Richard Louv to express and develop his main idea.

3. Consider the question, "What does it mean to own something?" To put it another way, what is the relationship between ownership and our identities? The same question can also be asked this way: To what extent do we define ourselves by what we possess? Write an essay that explains your position on the importance of ownership and the development of self. Support your argument with evidence from your reading, experience, or observations.

2014

1. In recent years college graduates in great numbers have failed to find jobs for which their education has prepared them. As a result, many people, including high school students and their parents, question whether a college degree is worth the expense required to attain one. Others, however, argue that a college education is not meant solely to prepare students for a job or career.

   After reading six sources related to this issue, write an essay that discusses whether a college education is worth the cost. Synthesize information from at least three of the sources into your essay.

2. In 1780, Abigail Adams wrote a letter of advice to her son John Quincy Adams, then traveling in Europe with his father, John Adams, the future second president of the United States. Read the letter carefully. Then, write an essay that analyzes the rhetorical strategies that Mrs. Adams uses to advise the young man.

3. Research by experts in education reveals that the creativity of children from kindergarten through sixth grade has suffered in recent years. A decline in creativity is alarming, especially when present and future world problems related to climate, economics, war and peace, and much more will require increasingly creative solutions.

   One proposal to reverse the decline in creativity is to actively teach creative thinking in school. Opinion is divided on whether this approach is worthwhile. State your view on this issue by writing to your school board. Explain what you mean by creativity and argue for or against starting a course in creativity.

2015

1. Many schools, colleges, and universities have instituted honor codes meant to discourage such practices as cheating, stealing, and plagiarizing. Students violating established codes are subject to a variety of punishments.

   After reading six sources related to the issue of honor codes, compose an essay that supports your position on whether your school should establish, maintain, revise, or eliminate an honor code or honor system. Your argument should incorporate ideas, quotations, paraphrases, or summaries found in at least three of the six sources that accompany this question.

2. To commemorate the tenth anniversary of Dr. Martin Luther King's assassination, labor union organizer and civil rights leader Cesar Chavez wrote an article that discusses nonviolent resistance as a means to achieve certain social goals. After reading Chavez's words, write an essay that analyzes the rhetorical choices he uses to develop his argument.

3. Friendly phrases such as "How's it going?" and "Nice to meet you" are known as polite speech and are usually not taken literally. In an essay, develop your position on the value or function of polite speech in a culture or community with which you are familiar. To support your argument, use evidence drawn from your reading, experience, or observation.

2016

1. With the spread of globalization in recent decades, English has become the primary language for communicating in international finance, science, and politics. As the use of English has spread, foreign language learning in English-speaking countries has declined, making the use of only one language—English—the norm.

   Carefully read the six sources accompanying this question and then write an essay that takes a position on the claim that people who speak only English and no other language are at a disadvantage in today's world. In your discussion, synthesize appropriate quotations, ideas, paraphrases, or summaries found in at least three of the sources.

2. In 2004, upon the death of former president Ronald Reagan, the ex-prime minister of Great Britain, Margaret Thatcher, who had worked closely with Reagan, delivered a eulogy to the American people honoring her former colleague and friend. Read the eulogy carefully, and then write an essay that analyzes the rhetoric Thatcher used to convey her thoughts and feelings.

3. Back in the nineteenth century, the Irish author Oscar Wilde noted that "Disobedience, in the eyes of anyone who has read history, is man's original virtue. It is through disobedience that progress has been made, through disobedience and through rebellion." In an essay, argue your position on Wilde's claim that disobedience and rebellion promote progress. Support your views with evidence drawn from your reading, studies, experience, or observation.

SAMPLE SYNTHESIS ESSAY QUESTION

SUGGESTED TIME:
15 MINUTES FOR READING THE QUESTION AND SOURCES
40 MINUTES FOR WRITING AN ESSAY

Homework has always been part of going to school. In recent years, efforts to improve education have included assigning more homework to students from kindergarten to twelfth grade. Many teachers, parents, and others applaud this increase. Critics, in contrast, claim that heavier loads of homework do more harm than good, not only to children but also to their families.

Carefully read the following six sources, including the material that introduces each source. Then, in an essay that synthesizes at least three of the sources, take a position on the claim that large amounts of homework have more negative consequences than positive ones.

Be sure to focus the essay on your point of view and use the sources to support and illustrate your position. Don't simply summarize the sources. You may paraphrase, summarize, and quote material directly and indirectly from the sources. In your essay be sure to indicate which sources you use. Refer to them as Source A, Source B, and so on, or by the key words in the parentheses below.

Source A (Kohn)
Source B (Gill and Schlossman)
Source C (Loveless)
Source D (Chart)
Source E (Haley)
Source F (Chaika)

Alfie Kohn, "Homework: An Unnecessary Evil?" *Psychology Today*, published online at *www.psychologytoday.com*, November 24, 2012.

The following passage is an excerpt from an article written by an author and specialist in behavior and education. His books include The Homework Myth *and* What Does It Mean to Be Well Educated?

At the high school level, the research supporting homework hasn't been particularly persuasive. There does seem to be a correlation between homework and standardized test scores, but (a) it isn't strong, meaning that homework doesn't explain much of the variance in scores, and (b) one prominent researcher, Timothy Keith, who did find a solid correlation, returned to the topic a decade later to enter more variables into the equation simultaneously, only to discover that the improved study showed that homework had no effect after all.

. . . When homework is related to test scores, the connection tends to be strongest—or, actually, least tenuous—with math. If homework turns out to be unnecessary for students to succeed in that subject, it's probably unnecessary everywhere.

Along comes a new study, then, that focuses on the neighborhood where you'd be most likely to find a positive effect if one was there to be found: the effect of math and science homework on grades in high school . . . .

This result clearly caught the researchers off-guard. Frankly, it surprised me, too. When you measure "achievement" in terms of grades, you expect to see a positive result—not because homework is academically beneficial but because the same teacher who gives the assignments evaluates the students who complete them, and the final grade is often based at least partly on whether, and to what extent, students did the homework.

It's important to remember that some people object to homework for reasons that aren't related to the dispute about whether research might show that homework provides academic benefits. They argue that (a) six hours a day of academics are enough, and kids should have the chance after school to explore other interests and develop in other ways—or be able simply to relax in the same way that most adults like to relax after work; and (b) the decision about what kids do during family time should be made by families, not schools.

Brian P. Gill and Steven L. Schlossman, "My Dog Ate My Argument," Op/Ed page of the *Los Angeles Times*, December 11, 2003.

The following passage is an excerpt from an opinion article written by a social scientist at the RAND Corporation and a history professor at Carnegie Mellon University.

In our view, homework is the prime window into the school for parents to see, understand and connect with the academic mission of the teachers. It is the primary arena in which children, parents and schools interact on a daily basis. Yet it gets less systematic thought and attention than any other key component of education. Other than the admonition that kids should do more of it, we pay almost no attention to how to improve its design and content. Nor do we do much to prepare teachers to use and evaluate homework, to hold administrators accountable for monitoring the homework load or to cultivate parents' collaboration. Homework remains an orphan child of the educational excellence movement.

. . . After half a century of failure to increase student buy-in, it's time to rethink how to make homework a more valued part of the pedagogic process. In addition to promoting academic achievement, homework can inculcate habits of self-discipline and independent study and can help inform parents about the educational agenda of their school. We must find ways to make homework an interesting and challenging educational experience for students, instead of the uniform, seat-bound, memorization-focused solo exercise it has been. Otherwise, all our talk about high standards and improving student achievement will run up against the same roadblock that has stymied the pursuit of educational excellence in the past.

Tom Loveless, "Do Students Have Too Much Homework?" A report for the Brown Center on Education Policy at the Brookings Institution, Washington, D.C., 2003.

The following passage is excerpted from a report on American education.

The most reliable data support the following conclusions: 1) the typical student, even in high school, does not spend more than an hour per day on homework, 2) the homework load has not changed much since the 1980s, 3) the students whose homework has increased in the past decade are those who previously had no homework and now have a small amount, 4) most parents feel the homework load is about right and, of those who would like to change it, more parents would rather see homework increased than decreased.

. . . Research shows that the relationship of homework with student achievement is positive for both middle and high school students and neutral for elementary school students. The research does not prove causality, an ever-present difficulty with research on many educational practices. High-achieving students in high school, for example, may do more homework because they enjoy studying. They take tough classes that require a lot of work. That does not necessarily mean that homework is boosting their achievement. Low-achieving students in elementary school, on the other hand, may do more homework because they are struggling to catch up. The homework is not causing their learning problems.

"Average NAEP Reading Scale Scores of Students by Age and Amount of Assigned Daily Reading Homework," *Digest of Education Statistics*, National Center for Educational Statistics, 2012.

The table below has been adapted from research conducted by the National Association of Educational Progress, the nation's largest testing agency responsible for assessing what America's K–12 students know and can do in various subjects.

Average NAEP Reading Scale Scores of Students by Age and Number of Pages of Assigned Daily Reading Homework, 2012

Age	5 or fewer	6–10	11–15	10–20	21 or more
17	274	283	289	297	301
13	251	261	266	268	271
9	207	219	225	226	227

Brian Haley, "What Is the Value of Homework?" July 6, 2006. *SearchWarp.com*. Accessed August 2, 2006, *http://www.searchwarp.com/*

The passage that follows is adapted from an article published by a web site that promotes the writing of authors in many disciplines, including education.

Assigning homework serves various educational needs. It serves as an intellectual discipline, establishes study habits, eases time constraints on the amount of curricular material that can be covered in class, and supplements and reinforces work done in school. In addition, it fosters student initiative, independence, and responsibility, and brings home and school closer together.

. . . Like mowing the lawn or taking out the garbage, homework seems to be a fact of life. . . . But the value of homework extends beyond school. We know that good assignments, completed successfully, can help children develop wholesome habits and attitudes. . . . It can teach children to work independently, encourage self-discipline and responsibility (assignments provide some youngsters with their first chance to manage time and meet deadlines), and encourage a love of learning. . . . Homework can help parents learn about their children's education and communicate both with their children and the schools.

Research in the last decade has begun to focus on the relationship between homework and student achievement and has greatly strengthened the case for homework. Although there are mixed findings about whether homework actually increases students' academic achievement, many teachers and parents agree that homework develops students' initiative and responsibility and fulfills the expectations of students, parents, and the public. Studies generally have found homework assignments to be most helpful if they are carefully planned by the teachers and have direct meaning to students.

Gloria Chaika, "Help! Homework Is Wrecking My Home Life," *Education World*, August 8, 2000.

The following passage is from an article for school administrators published in an online educational journal.

"Teachers should devote energy to creating homework that is stimulating and provocative rather than banal," says Howard Gardner of the Harvard Graduate School of Education. "And parents or mentors should go shoulder-to-shoulder with youngsters, helping to motivate them, thinking of ways in which to help them without giving the answer, and being aware of the child's special gifts and weaknesses."

It sounds great, "but you need parent input for kids to perform, and with the increase in single-parent families, there's no one at home to help," veteran fifth-grade teacher Loretta Highfield told *Education World.*

"It isn't that the kids don't want to do homework; the majority of my students don't have the skills to go home and do it independently," added Highfield, a teacher at Florida Avenue Elementary in Slidell, Louisiana. "Even young students are not getting the help at home that they used to."

The same seems to hold true for older children. "I have students who have been thrown out of the house or have a financial situation brought on by an ill parent," Northshore High School (Slidell, Louisiana) teacher Kathleen Modenbach told *Education World.* "There are others whose after-school jobs pay for car insurance and clothes or whose involvement in extra-curricular activities, private lessons, or sports leaves little time for homework."

"For some students, a lot of homework can seem irrelevant," Modenbach added. "High school students become expert at evaluating the validity of assignments and assigning priorities to them. Kids who wouldn't dream of cheating on a test or copying a research paper think nothing of copying homework. I find students will do homework when it must be done to pass the class. Anything else is a waste of time and feeds into the vicious circle of beating the homework system."

Therefore, as kids deal with assigned homework in their own ways—or grow increasingly frazzled—their too-busy parents are uncertain what to do. Some, wanting their children to be academically competitive, demand extra homework, while others wonder just how much is too much.

Answering the Synthesis Question

Homework. Now, there's a topic that you must know something about. Being a seasoned doer of homework, you're probably bursting with ideas on the pros and cons of the stuff and could probably argue brilliantly for or against homework, or come down somewhere between the two poles. Regardless of where you stand, you're not apt find yourself short of ideas on the issue. In fact, you may be overloaded and find yourself sifting out only the best arguments among many to include in an essay on the subject.

But beware. This essay assignment is not intended simply to give you a chance to vent about homework. Although your biases will no doubt shape your argument, you mustn't rely solely on your personal experience and observations. This, after all, is what the AP people call a "**synthesis essay**," a label that you've got to take seriously.

What it means is that your essay must be based not solely on your personal opinion but to some extent on your interpretation of **at least three** of the sources. You can use the sources as evidence to support your point of view, or you can comment on them in other ways. For example, you can criticize them for inaccuracies or reject them as dead-wrong observations of the homework scene. You can quote from them directly, use indirect quotations, paraphrase ideas, or put ideas into your own words. But remember this: However you incorporate the sources, you must say where the material came from. That is, you must give credit to each source you use, as though you are writing a term paper for a class.

TIP

Cite three sources; there's no extra credit for more.

Cite Sources

Stylistically, it may serve you well to use phrases like "*According to Source C, . . .*" or "*In Loveless' opinion . . .*", or "*A study of students' reading scores (Source D) shows that . . .*," etc. Or you can simply cite your sources with parenthetical references—(*Source A, Source B*)—in your text. Another approach is to name the author or even the title of the sources, but writing out lengthy titles uses up precious time. AP essay readers will look for citations and will penalize essays that contain fewer than three. At the same time, however, you won't earn extra credit for citing more than three.

Whether or not you agree with the premise that "large amounts of homework have more negative effects than positive ones," your task is to write an argument that defends your point of view. Because a researched argument is meant to sway readers whose views may be contrary to yours, you need to gather compelling evidence in support of your position.

Let's say that you think homework is generally good for you and the more you get, the better. Right off the bat, then, you have a main idea, or thesis, for your essay. But even if you know immediately where you stand on the issue, take the time to read all the sources carefully, underscoring or circling those ideas you might consider mentioning in your essay. It's good to read the material with which you don't agree, too, because in making your case, you can bolster your argument by refuting and revealing the weaknesses in what you'd expect your opponent to say.

TIP

Be sure to read all the sources carefully.

Support Your Position

In building a convincing case, it often pays to gather at least three compelling reasons to support your position. Although AP students ought not be constrained by the familiar "five-paragraph" essay, you won't go wrong following its structure: an introduction, three paragraphs of development, and a conclusion. Why *three* paragraphs of development? Mainly because *three* is a number that works. If you can come up with three different arguments, you appear to speak with the voice of authority. One paragraph is too simple. Two is better but still shallow. Three is thoughtful. It suggests depth and insight. Psychologically, three also creates a sense of wholeness for the reader, like the beginning, middle, and end of a story. (Incidentally, it's no accident that the number three recurs in all literature, from *Goldilocks and the Three Bears* to *The Bible*.)

Use the sources to bolster your arguments for or against large amounts of homework. But you needn't depend totally on the sources. In fact, AP readers are likely to look kindly on your own original ideas, provided they are relevant to the issue, clearly expressed, and well-developed. On the positive side, you might pick out such ideas as:

- Homework permits parents to participate with teachers in the education of their children. (Source B)
- "[T]he relationship between the amount of reading homework and performance on reading tests is especially positive for high school students." (Source D)
- Homework fosters the development of individual initiative and effective study habits. (Source B)
- Homework provides opportunities for low-achieving students to catch up. (Source C)
- Homework leads to a lifelong love of learning. (Source F)

Or, if you have an unfavorable view of homework, the following ideas can be used to support your argument:

- Years of educational research have found only a weak correlation between homework and student achievement. (Source A)
- Large amounts of homework can keep a student from pursuing worthwhile personal interests. (Source C)
- Homework assigned during vacations is counterproductive; it turns kids away from the joys of learning and deprives them of reading for pleasure. (Source E)
- More homework does not necessarily lead to better grades. (Source E)

The given sources either support or decry homework. A middle-of-the-road position may be difficult to defend unless you build a case by refuting arguments presented on both sides of the issue. Source F, which argues against homework, for example, quotes an apparently frustrated teacher: "It isn't that kids don't want to do homework; the majority of my students don't have the skills to go home and do it independently."

Because the word "majority" can mean *almost all or just over half*, the teacher appears to have overlooked the fact that some students can be counted on to work on their own. By generalizing about all students, the teacher in effect deprives some of her kids the opportunity to learn at home. An essay that argues neither for nor against homework might emphasize that universal policies regarding homework don't work. In other words, when it comes to education, one size cannot fit all.

Determine Order

Once you've collected your ideas for or against the issue, stop for a moment to figure out which idea to put first, which to put second, and so on. Order is important. The best order is the clearest order, the arrangement that readers can follow with the least effort. No plan is superior to another, provided you have a valid reason for using it. The plan least likely to succeed is the aimless one, the one in which you state and develop ideas in random order as they happened to come to mind. It's better by far to rank your ideas in order of importance by deciding which provides the strongest support for your thesis. Although your best argument may be listed first in your notes, save it for last on the essay. Giving it away at the start is self-defeating because everything that follows will be anticlimactic. An excellent way to arrange your ideas is to lead with your second best, save your best for the end, and sandwich the others in between. This structure recognizes that the end and the beginning of an essay are its most critical parts. A good opening draws the reader in and creates an all-important first impression, but a memorable ending, coming last, is what readers have fresh in their minds when they assign you a grade. But, as always, don't just follow these guidelines slavishly. If you can justify another organization, by all means use it.

AP exam readers won't judge your essay based on the opinion you express. Even if they disagree with you, they are obliged to ignore their own biases and grade you according to the criteria of good writing. They may think that your view is off the wall, but a cogent, forceful essay that smoothly integrates the sources and demonstrates mastery of argumentation, will merit a high score.

TIP

Work *toward* your best point, not away from it.

No matter how skillfully written, your essay will be penalized for faulty reasoning and misinformation

SAMPLE ANALYTICAL ESSAY QUESTION

SUGGESTED TIME: 40 MINUTES

> **Directions:** Read the following passage published back in 1967 by *The New York Times*. Then write an essay in which you analyze how the structure of the passage and the use of language help convey the writer's views.

Americans and Western Europeans, in their sensitivity to lingering problems around them, tend to make science and progress their scapegoats. There is a belief that progress has precipitated widespread unhappiness, anxieties, and other social and emotional problems. Science is viewed as a cold mechanical discipline having

Line
(5) nothing to do with human warmth and the human spirit.

But to many of us from the nonscientific East, science does not have such repugnant associations. We are not afraid of it, nor are we disappointed by it. We know all too painfully that our social and emotional problems festered long before the age of technology. To us, science is warm and reassuring. It promises hope. It is helping us

(10) at long last gain some control over our persecutory environments, alleviating age-old problems—not only physical but also, and especially, problems of the spirit.

Shiraz, for example, a city in southern Iran, has long been renowned for its rose gardens and nightingales; its poets, Sadi and Hafiz; and its mystical, ascetic philosophy, Sufism. Much poetry has been written in glorification of the spiritual attributes

(15) of this oasis city. And to be sure, Shiraz is a green, picturesque town, with a quaint bazaar and refreshing gardens. But in this "romantic" city thousands of emotionally

disturbed and mentally retarded men, women, and children were, until recently, kept in chains in stifling prison cells and lunatic asylums.

(20) Every now and again, some were dragged, screaming and pleading, to a courtyard and flogged for not behaving "normally." But for the most part, they were made to sit against damp walls, their hands and feet locked in chains, and thus immobilized, without even a modicum of affection from their helpless families and friends, they sat for weeks and months and years—often all their lives. Pictures of these wretched men, women, and children can still be seen in this "city of poetry," this "city with a
(25) spiritual way of life."

It was only recently that a wealthy young Shirazi who, against the admonitions of his family, had studied psychology at the University of Teheran and foreign universities, returned to Shiraz and after considerable struggle with city officials succeeded in opening a psychiatric clinic, the first in those regions. After still more struggle, he
(30) arranged to have the emotionally disturbed and the mentally retarded transferred from prison to their homes, to hospitals, and to his clinic, where he and his staff now attend them.

They are fortunate. All over Asia and other backward areas, emotionally disturbed men and women are still incarcerated in these medieval dungeons called lunatic
(35) asylums. The cruel rejection and punishment are intended to teach them a lesson or help exorcise evil spirits.

The West, still bogged down in its ridiculous romanticism, would like to believe that emotional disturbances, dope addiction, delinquency are all modern problems brought on by technological progress, and that backward societies are too spiritual
(40) and beautiful to need the ministrations of science. But while the West can perhaps afford to think this way, the people of backward lands cannot. . . .

. . .The obstacles are awesome, the inertia too entrenched, the people's suffering too anguished, their impatience too eruptive. Moreover, the total cultural reorganizations such as Asia and Africa are undergoing inevitably engender their own tem-
(45) porary dislocations and confusions. But their goals, the direction, remain constant. We are on the move, however awkwardly at first, to a saner, better world.

How to Answer This Question

Go back to the original question, which asks you to analyze two features of the passage: (1) its structure, or organization, and (2) its language. The first aspect is fairly specific. As you read the passage, you need to observe what the author discusses first, second, third, and so on. Your essay should explain not only the order of ideas but the reasons the author may have chosen that order.

The second part of the question is more general. It invites you to analyze the use of language, which may include the author's choice of words (diction), syntax (word order), figures of speech, use of evidence (such as statistics or logical reasoning), sentence structure, rhythm, sound, tone, or just about any other characteristics of style and rhetoric you choose.

Although the question directs you to write about two different aspects of the passage, the essay itself should be unified. That is, a good essay should not consist of, say, two disparate paragraphs, one exclusively devoted to structure and another to language. Rather, the essay should include material that shows the interrelationship of structure and language in the passage and how those elements contribute to the meaning and effect of the passage. This might be covered in a separate paragraph, or it could be woven into the overall fabric of the essay.

Before you begin to write, read the passage at least *twice:* once for an overview and once as you write your analysis. You may notice early on that the opening paragraph contains generalizations about Westerners' concepts of science and progress. Then the author contrasts the Western view of science and progress with the Eastern view. Immediately, you see that the author, by using the first-person pronoun (as in "many of us") is speaking from the perspective of an Easterner. Consequently, his discussion of Eastern views is apt to come across as more well-informed, more authoritative, perhaps more personal.

To support his position, the author gives an extended example—the city of Shiraz—to illustrate just how different the East is from the West. The description and vivid images of Shiraz memorably convey the idea that the "spiritual way of life" has a side to it that Westerners don't know about. This is the heart of the passage. The use of quotation marks around "romantic" and "city of poetry" is meant to point out the discrepancy between the idealized and real versions of Shiraz.

Nearing the end, the author reiterates his initial contrast between West and East, with emphasis on the East. The last paragraph offers a generalized statement about conditions in Asia and Africa, reminding the reader of the contrast made at the very beginning of the passage. Tying the end to the beginning of the passage creates a sense of unity—a desirable feature in any piece of writing.

TIP

Read the passage at least twice— once for an overview and again as you write your analysis.

SAMPLE PERSUASIVE ESSAY QUESTION

SUGGESTED TIME: 40 MINUTES

> **Directions:** The following paragraph is adapted from *Mirror for Man*, a book written by anthropologist Clyde Kluckhorn in the middle of the twentieth century. Read the passage carefully. Then, write an essay that examines the extent to which the author's characterization of the United States holds true today. Use appropriate evidence to support your argument.

Technology is valued as the very basis of the capitalistic system. Possession of gadgets is esteemed as a mark of success to the extent that persons are judged not by the integrity of their characters or by the originality of their minds but by what they seem to be—so far as can be measured by the salaries they earn or by the variety and material goods which they display. "Success" is measured by the automobiles they drive—not by their number of mistresses as in some cultures.

How to Answer This Question

Whether you agree, disagree, or have mixed views on the content of the passage, your job is to write a convincing argument that expresses your opinion. Initially, the word *argument* may suggest conflict or confrontation. But rest assured that your essay need not be combative. Rather, make it a calmly-reasoned explanation of your opinion on a debatable subject. Your goal is to persuade the reader that your opinion, supported by examples, facts, and other appropriate evidence, is correct.

If you have strong feelings about the topic, of course you should state them in your essay. But express them in calm, rational language. Be mindful that the essay should not be an emotional rant for or against the issue.

TIP

A persuasive
essay should
not be an
emotional rant
for or against an
issue.

Consider first whether you agree with Kluckhorn's definition of "success." Is it, as Kluckhorn asserts, measured by income and material possessions? Or do you think that a more accurate standard of success in today's America should be determined by less tangible criteria—things such as happiness or self-respect? Or do you stand somewhere in between those two extremes?

The actual position you take on the issue is less crucial than your ability to support it fully by drawing from your knowledge, background, experience, or observation. Regardless of your position, be sure to include more than one example. An argument that relies on a single example, however compelling, will fall flat.

In the prompt, Kluckhorn's notion of success seems to refer broadly to American society. Resist responding in kind. That is, a short essay shouldn't focus on the whole of society but only on an identifiable segment—perhaps college-educated professionals or urban, blue-collar Americans. The point is that a narrowly-focused essay on a limited topic will always turn out better than one that tries to cover too much ground in just a few paragraphs.

HOW ESSAYS ARE SCORED

When it comes time to make judgments about writing, the word *effectively* comes up repeatedly. It's a popular word because it's easy to use. But it's also hard to define. It means so much, and yet so little. You probably know effective writing when you see it, but what the AP folks have in mind is the thoughtful organization of ideas, appropriate word choice, proper syntax, varied sentence structure, a mature style of writing, sensible paragraphing, coherent development, and correct mechanics (grammar, spelling, and punctuation).

AP readers
don't expect
three polished
pieces of
immortal prose,
just three good
essays.

AP readers don't sit there with a checklist to see whether your essay meets all these criteria, however. Rather, they read it *holistically*, meaning that they read it quickly for an overall impression of your writing and then assign your essay a grade from 1 (low) to 9 (high). Readers are trained to look for clearly organized, well-developed, and forceful responses that reveal a depth of understanding and insight.

Frankly, the 40 minutes suggested for each essay is not a great deal of time to read the question, plan what you will say, write a few hundred words, edit and proofread your draft, and submit a finished piece of work. In effect, you must condense into a short time what would normally take far longer. A saving grace, however, is that the AP test readers don't expect three polished pieces of immortal prose, but just three competently written essays.

Each year in early June, thousands of college and high school teachers get together to read and evaluate the essays written by students like you from across the country and overseas. Readers are chosen for their ability to make sound judgments about student writing and are trained to use a common set of scoring standards.

A WORD ABOUT WORD COUNT

Are 250 words enough? Yes, but the number of words in your essays is up to you. To AP essay readers, length takes a back seat to answering the question and covering the subject. A single paragraph most likely won't allow you to fully develop ideas. Multiparagraph essays allow you to be expansive, to use a variety of details to support your main idea, and to show that you have what it takes to cover a complex subject clearly and logically. Keep in mind that the number of words is less crucial than what the words say.

HOW ESSAYS ARE READ AND GRADED

As part of their training, AP readers are given guidelines that have the ring of common sense and stress the need for fairness. They are told:

✔ To read each essay once.

✔ To read quickly and to assign a grade immediately.

✔ To read mainly for what has been done well.

✔ To take everything into account, including organization, word choice, the mechanics of writing, and so on.

✔ To ignore poor handwriting as much as possible.

✔ Not to penalize a well-developed but unfinished essay.

✔ Not to use length as a criterion of evaluation.

✔ To keep in mind that any essay that contains even a marginal response to the question should be judged according to the logic of the argument developed by the writer.

✔ To remember that each essay is a first draft written under pressure in about 40 minutes by a seventeen- or eighteen-year-old.

Each essay is scored on a scale of 0 (low) to 9 (high) and is read by two different readers. If the scores assigned by the two readers differ by more than one grade, a third reader evaluates the essay.

What the Scores Say About Your Writing

By and large, the criteria used for evaluating the quality of both the synthesis essay and the analytical essays are identical—but with one important exception: While reading the synthesis essay, evaluators are required to judge how effectively you cite sources to support your position on the given issue.

Readers work hard to be both objective and fair while scoring essays. In general, scores on borderline essays—for example, one that's not quite 9 but is better than an ordinary 8—are raised to the higher number.

A 9 ESSAY

Essays deserving a score of 9 demonstrate the writer's exceptional control of effective writing techniques. They are clear, interesting, and correct. They analyze rhetorical strategies with insight and precision. They refer frequently to the text, directly or indirectly, and succinctly describe how such matters as tone, irony, diction, and use of examples contribute to the structure and meaning of a passage.

Synthesis essays present a persuasive argument cogently and convincingly, synthesizing material from at least three sources into the discussion of the issue.

If the essay contains an occasional flaw in analysis, prose style, or mechanics, the errors are inconsequential.

AN 8 ESSAY

Essays earning an 8 are extremely well-written and demonstrate considerable mastery of written English. They meet all the criteria for essays earning a 9, but fall just slightly short of distinction.

A 7 ESSAY

Essays scored 7 competently analyze rhetorical strategies. They often use specific examples from the text and discuss, directly or indirectly, such matters as tone, irony, diction, and use of examples. They are reasonably well-developed and coherent, but they are less complex than essays rated 8 or 9. A few errors in word choice or sentence structure may exist, but no error is egregious enough to interfere with the clear expression of the writer's ideas.

A synthesis essay earning a score of 7 effectively supports the writer's position and appropriately incorporates at least three sources into the discussion of the issue. The overall argument may be less developed or less precise than arguments presented in essays that earn an 8 or a 9.

A 6 ESSAY

Essays earning a 6 are generally the same as those receiving a 7 except that the prose style may be less mature, or lapses in diction, syntax or clarity may be more serious or occur more often.

A 5 ESSAY

Essays given a grade of 5 adequately answer the question but may lack full development. Ideas may be presented clearly but remain unsupported and relatively superficial. The essay may be well organized and convey the writer's ideas, but lapses in diction or syntax weaken the impact of the essay and suggest that the writer is not fully in control of effective writing techniques.

The position taken in the synthesis essay is supported by incorporating and citing at least three sources, but the arguments and the use of citations is somewhat limited, inconsistent, or questionable.

A 4 ESSAY

An essay earning a 4 responds inadequately to the question. It may miss the point of the question or analyze secondary stylistic or rhetorical strategies. It may be superficial, or its ideas may be developed incoherently—jumping from topic to topic. Although the point of the essay may be clear, the prose is immature, showing the writer's lack of control over organization, word choice, or syntax.

A synthesis essay deserving a score of 4 makes a relatively weak or incomplete argument related to the topic. It may use too few sources or misapply or misrepresent material from the sources.

A 3 ESSAY

Essays deserving a score of 3 are similar to essays scored 4 except the analysis is even less astute or is seriously flawed. The prose demonstrates that the writer has difficulty controlling organization, developing ideas, choosing the correct words, or using standard English syntax to convey ideas.

In citing sources in the synthesis essay, the writer demonstrates a weak understanding of the meaning or function of sources.

A 2 ESSAY

An essay earning a score of 2 demonstrates the writer's inability to analyze the passage. It may wander off the topic or substitute a simpler task than that assigned by the question. The prose often reveals weaknesses in organizing material, in expressing ideas clearly, and in writing grammatically.

A score of 2 on the synthesis essay suggests that the writer has failed to address the issue, has improperly used or cited sources, or has responded to the issue largely by summarizing material in the sources.

A 1 ESSAY

An essay deserving a 1 may be similar to an essay scored 2, but the ideas are more simplistic and the expression flawed, perhaps bordering on the incomprehensible.

In the synthesis essay, the writer may have neglected to cite or even to allude to any sources.

A 0 ESSAY

A 0 score indicates a blank paper, an essay not on the assigned topic, or a piece of writing that merely paraphrases the prompt.

You've no doubt noticed that the foregoing descriptions lack precision. It's no secret that grading essays is far from an exact science. But the readers are expected to be fair and to focus their attention on an essay's strengths rather than its weaknesses.

Diagnostic Test

2

→ **TAKING A FULL-LENGTH AP EXAM**
→ **FINDING THE *BEST* ANSWERS**
→ **CHECKING YOUR ANSWERS**
→ **HOW TO SCORE YOUR OWN ESSAYS**
→ **WHAT THE NUMBERS TELL YOU**
→ **CALCULATING YOUR AP TEST SCORE**

INTRODUCTION

This self-assessment test is similar in length and format to the AP exam. Use it to determine your readiness to take the actual exam, administered in May of each year.

Take the test as though it were the real thing. Set aside three hours and 15 minutes. Be sure you are wide awake and your mind is fresh. Remove all distractions, sharpen your pencil, read the directions, and go to work.

Allow yourself one hour to answer the multiple-choice questions. Use the answer sheet provided. At the end of the hour take a five-minute break and then tackle the essay questions. Write your essays on standard 8½" × 11" composition paper, the approximate size of an official AP essay response sheet. For the first essay, the synthesis essay, allot 15 minutes to read the sources and 40 minutes to write the essay. Then, allow 40 minutes each for essays 2 and 3.

When you have finished, check your answers with the Answer Key on page 71. Then read the Answer Explanations. Spend some time analyzing your wrong answers. Try to identify the reason you missed each question: Did you misinterpret the question? Was your choice too specific or too general? Did you misread the passage? Did you base your answer on the wrong material in the passage? Did you jump to a conclusion that led you astray? Knowing why you stumbled can help you avoid similar errors on future tests.

At the same time, don't ignore the questions you got right. Check all the answer explanations. Do they coincide with your reasons for making the correct choices? If so, give yourself a pat on the back for nailing the reasoning techniques you're expected to employ while answering these questions. If your rationale for choosing the answer differs from the given explanation, however, don't fret. On the contrary, rejoice, because, unless your choice was only a stab in the dark, you may have devised a functional new tactic for answering multiple-choice questions that even the professionals who wrote the test hadn't considered.

Although it is hard to evaluate your own essays, don't shy away from trying. Let the essays cool off for a while—maybe even for a day or two—and then, insofar as possible, reread them with an open mind and a fresh pair of eyes. Rate your essays using the Self-Scoring Guide on page 82.

Finally, using data from the Answer Key and the Self-Scoring Guide, calculate the grade you earned on this test.

ANSWER SHEET
Diagnostic Test

Multiple-Choice Questions

Time—1 hour

1. Ⓐ Ⓑ Ⓒ Ⓓ Ⓔ   16. Ⓐ Ⓑ Ⓒ Ⓓ Ⓔ   31. Ⓐ Ⓑ Ⓒ Ⓓ Ⓔ   46. Ⓐ Ⓑ Ⓒ Ⓓ Ⓔ
2. Ⓐ Ⓑ Ⓒ Ⓓ Ⓔ   17. Ⓐ Ⓑ Ⓒ Ⓓ Ⓔ   32. Ⓐ Ⓑ Ⓒ Ⓓ Ⓔ   47. Ⓐ Ⓑ Ⓒ Ⓓ Ⓔ
3. Ⓐ Ⓑ Ⓒ Ⓓ Ⓔ   18. Ⓐ Ⓑ Ⓒ Ⓓ Ⓔ   33. Ⓐ Ⓑ Ⓒ Ⓓ Ⓔ   48. Ⓐ Ⓑ Ⓒ Ⓓ Ⓔ
4. Ⓐ Ⓑ Ⓒ Ⓓ Ⓔ   19. Ⓐ Ⓑ Ⓒ Ⓓ Ⓔ   34. Ⓐ Ⓑ Ⓒ Ⓓ Ⓔ   49. Ⓐ Ⓑ Ⓒ Ⓓ Ⓔ
5. Ⓐ Ⓑ Ⓒ Ⓓ Ⓔ   20. Ⓐ Ⓑ Ⓒ Ⓓ Ⓔ   35. Ⓐ Ⓑ Ⓒ Ⓓ Ⓔ   50. Ⓐ Ⓑ Ⓒ Ⓓ Ⓔ
6. Ⓐ Ⓑ Ⓒ Ⓓ Ⓔ   21. Ⓐ Ⓑ Ⓒ Ⓓ Ⓔ   36. Ⓐ Ⓑ Ⓒ Ⓓ Ⓔ   51. Ⓐ Ⓑ Ⓒ Ⓓ Ⓔ
7. Ⓐ Ⓑ Ⓒ Ⓓ Ⓔ   22. Ⓐ Ⓑ Ⓒ Ⓓ Ⓔ   37. Ⓐ Ⓑ Ⓒ Ⓓ Ⓔ   52. Ⓐ Ⓑ Ⓒ Ⓓ Ⓔ
8. Ⓐ Ⓑ Ⓒ Ⓓ Ⓔ   23. Ⓐ Ⓑ Ⓒ Ⓓ Ⓔ   38. Ⓐ Ⓑ Ⓒ Ⓓ Ⓔ   53. Ⓐ Ⓑ Ⓒ Ⓓ Ⓔ
9. Ⓐ Ⓑ Ⓒ Ⓓ Ⓔ   24. Ⓐ Ⓑ Ⓒ Ⓓ Ⓔ   39. Ⓐ Ⓑ Ⓒ Ⓓ Ⓔ   54. Ⓐ Ⓑ Ⓒ Ⓓ Ⓔ
10. Ⓐ Ⓑ Ⓒ Ⓓ Ⓔ   25. Ⓐ Ⓑ Ⓒ Ⓓ Ⓔ   40. Ⓐ Ⓑ Ⓒ Ⓓ Ⓔ   55. Ⓐ Ⓑ Ⓒ Ⓓ Ⓔ
11. Ⓐ Ⓑ Ⓒ Ⓓ Ⓔ   26. Ⓐ Ⓑ Ⓒ Ⓓ Ⓔ   41. Ⓐ Ⓑ Ⓒ Ⓓ Ⓔ
12. Ⓐ Ⓑ Ⓒ Ⓓ Ⓔ   27. Ⓐ Ⓑ Ⓒ Ⓓ Ⓔ   42. Ⓐ Ⓑ Ⓒ Ⓓ Ⓔ
13. Ⓐ Ⓑ Ⓒ Ⓓ Ⓔ   28. Ⓐ Ⓑ Ⓒ Ⓓ Ⓔ   43. Ⓐ Ⓑ Ⓒ Ⓓ Ⓔ
14. Ⓐ Ⓑ Ⓒ Ⓓ Ⓔ   29. Ⓐ Ⓑ Ⓒ Ⓓ Ⓔ   44. Ⓐ Ⓑ Ⓒ Ⓓ Ⓔ
15. Ⓐ Ⓑ Ⓒ Ⓓ Ⓔ   30. Ⓐ Ⓑ Ⓒ Ⓓ Ⓔ   45. Ⓐ Ⓑ Ⓒ Ⓓ Ⓔ

SECTION I

TIME: 1 HOUR

> **Directions:** *Questions 1–12.* Carefully read the following passage and answer the accompanying questions.

The passage below is an excerpt from an essay on violence in America, written by a contemporary historian.

PASSAGE 1

On September 26, 1872, three mounted men rode up to the gate of the Kansas City Fair, which was enjoying a huge crowd of perhaps 10,000 people. The bandits shot at the ticket seller, hit a small girl in the leg, and made off for the woods with some-
Line thing less than a thousand dollars. It was highhanded, and it endangered the lives of
(5) a whole host of holiday-minded people for comparatively little reward.

What makes the robbery and the violence notable is not the crime itself but the way it was reported in the Kansas City *Times* by one John N. Edwards. In his front-page story he branded the robbery "so diabolically daring and so utterly in contempt of fear that we are bound to admire it and revere its perpetrators."

(10) Two days later the outlaws were being compared by the *Times* with knights of King Arthur's Round Table:

"It was as though three bandits had come to us from storied Odenwald, with the halo of medieval chivalry upon their garments and shown us how the things were done that poets sing of. Nowhere else in the United States or in the civilized world,
(15) probably, could this thing have been done."

Quite likely this deed was perpetrated by the James brothers: Jesse and Frank, and a confederate. The details really do not matter. What pertains is the attitude of the innocent toward the uncertainly identified guilty. The act had been perpetrated by violent, lawless men. If the *Times* is any indication, a respectable section of people
(20) approved of their action. No one, of course, thought to ask the little girl with the shattered leg how she felt about such courage. Nearly 17 months later, Edwards was quoted in the St. Louis *Dispatch* as preferring the Western highwayman to the Eastern, for "he has more qualities that attract admiration and win respect . . . . This comes from locality . . . which breeds strong, hardy men—men who risk much, who
(25) have friends in high places, and who go riding over the land, taking all chances that come in the way." The purpose here is not to belabor one reasonably anonymous newspaperman of nearly a century ago, but merely to point up a fact—and a problem—of the American frontier.

The frontier placed a premium on independent action and individual reliance.
(30) The whole history of the American frontier is a narrative of taking what was there to be taken. The timid never gathered riches, the polite nearly never. The men who first carved the wilderness into land claims and town lots were the men who moved in the face of dangers, gathering as they progressed. The emphasis naturally came to be placed on gathering and not on procedures. Great tales of gigantic attainments
(35) abound in this frontier story; equally adventurous tales of creative plundering mark the march from Jamestown to the Pacific. It was a period peopled by giants, tow-

ers of audacity with insatiable appetites. The heroes are not the men of moderate attitudes, not the town planners and commercial builders, not the farmers nor the ministers nor the teachers. The heroes of the period, handed along to us with all the

(40) luster of a golden baton, are the mighty runners from Mt. Olympus who ran without looking back, without concern about social values or anywhere they might be going except onward.

We revere these heroes because they were men of vast imagination and daring. We have also inherited their blindness and their excesses.

1. It can be inferred that the speaker knows the facts about the incident in Kansas City on September 26, 1872, because he

   (A) was an eyewitness to the events described.
   (B) happened to be a visitor to the fair.
   (C) interviewed the ticket seller.
   (D) read about it in a newspaper.
   (E) was related to the girl who got shot.

2. In which of the following ways does the sentence that starts "It was highhanded . . ." (line 4) differ from the other sentences in the first paragraph?

   I. It is a compound sentence.
   II. It expresses the opinion of the speaker.
   III. It employs alliterative language.

   (A) I only
   (B) III only
   (C) I and II only
   (D) II and III only
   (E) I, II, and III

3. In lines 6–7 "the way it was reported" refers to

   (A) the appearance of the story on the front page.
   (B) John N. Edwards's qualifications to write the story.
   (C) the reporter's praise of the bandits.
   (D) the flowery language used by the reporter.
   (E) the matter-of-fact tone in which the story was written.

4. In lines 6–15, the speaker's attitude toward John N. Edwards and his newspaper can best be described as one of

   (A) outright scorn.
   (B) profound disillusion.
   (C) extreme hatred.
   (D) honest skepticism.
   (E) exaggerated uneasiness.

5. Which of the following rhetorical devices is most in evidence in lines 10–15?

   (A) An inspiring myth
   (B) An analogy
   (C) A parable
   (D) A caricature
   (E) An annotation

6. Which of the following best describes the rhetorical effect of the sentence beginning "Quite likely . . ." (line 16)?

   (A) To restate the main idea of the passage
   (B) To reinforce a theory stated earlier in the passage
   (C) To shift the focus of the passage to an entirely new topic
   (D) To emphasize the foolishness of the preceding quotation
   (E) To endorse the position taken by the Kansas City newspaper

7. The phrase "such courage" (line 21) can best be described as an example of

   (A) a subtle use of irony.
   (B) a metaphorical allusion.
   (C) a witty analogy.
   (D) a paradox.
   (E) an oxymoron.

8. In the context of the passage, the word "innocent" (line 18) can be interpreted to mean all of the following EXCEPT

   (A) gullible people.
   (B) those who cannot make up their minds.
   (C) individuals who don't know right from wrong.
   (D) uncritical readers.
   (E) simple-minded people.

9. The quotation from the St. Louis newspaper (lines 23–26) serves the author's purposes in which of the following ways?

   (A) It makes a case for more accuracy in newspaper writing.
   (B) It makes clear the author's intention to destroy Edwards's career as a reporter.
   (C) It further illustrates the thinking of many Americans.
   (D) It reinforces the author's view expressed earlier that the bandits were "violent" and "lawless."
   (E) It provides a generalization on which the author will comment in the next paragraph.

10. Which of the following quotes from the passage best supports the author's claim that frontier men valued "independent action and individual reliance" (line 29)?

(A) "the James brothers" (line 16)
(B) "a problem—of the American frontier" (lines 27–28)
(C) "... timid never gathered riches" (line 31)
(D) "creative plundering" (line 35)
(E) "march from Jamestown to the Pacific" (line 36)

11. The conclusions drawn in the last paragraph (lines 43–44) contribute to the unity of the passage in which of the following ways?

(A) They reiterate a similar idea stated early in the passage.
(B) They justify the lawlessness that dominated the frontier.
(C) They indicate the similarity between frontier people and the knights of King Arthur.
(D) They explain why the bandits in Kansas City were admired instead of condemned.
(E) They mock the values of the frontier just as the author has mocked John N. Edwards.

12. As described in the passage, the bandits, the Knights of the Round Table, and the people of the frontier all share which of the following?

(A) A concern for upholding their reputations
(B) An intense commitment to strive for their goals
(C) Uncertainty about their position in society
(D) A sentimental attachment to the past
(E) A reckless disregard of the truth

Directions: *Questions 13–23.* Carefully read the following passage and answer the accompanying questions.

This passage is a speech delivered in 1873 by the renowned social reformer and advocate for women's suffrage, Susan B. Anthony.

PASSAGE 2

Friends and fellow citizens:

I stand before you tonight under indictment for the alleged crime of having voted in the last presidential election, without having a lawful right to vote. It shall be my
Line work this evening to prove to you that in thus voting, I not only committed no crime,
(5) but, instead, simply exercised my *citizen's rights*, guaranteed to me and all United States citizens by the National Constitution, beyond the power of any State to deny
.... The preamble of the Federal Constitution says:

"We, the people of the United States, in order to form a more perfect union, establish justice, insure *domestic* tranquillity, provide for the common defense, promote

(10)   the general welfare, and secure the blessings of liberty to ourselves and our posterity, do ordain and establish this Constitution for the United States of America."

   It was we, the people; not we, the white male citizens; nor yet we, the male citizens; but we, the whole people, who formed the Union. And we formed it, not to give the blessings of liberty, but to secure them; not the half of ourselves and the half of

(15)   our posterity, but to the whole people—women as well as men. And it is downright mockery to talk to women of their enjoyment of the blessings of liberty while they are denied the use of the only means of securing them provided by this democratic-republican government—the ballot.

   For any state to make sex a qualification that must ever result in the disenfran-

(20)   chisement of one entire half of the people is to pass a bill of attainder,[1] or an *ex post facto* law,[2] and is therefore a violation of the supreme law of the land. By it the blessings of liberty are forever withheld from women and their female posterity. To them this government has no just powers derived from the consent of the governed. To them this government is not a democracy. It is not a republic. It is an odious aris-

(25)   tocracy; a hateful oligarchy[3] of sex; the most hateful aristocracy ever established on the face of the globe; an oligarchy of wealth, where the rich govern the poor. An oligarchy of learning, where the educated govern the ignorant, or even an oligarchy of race, where the Saxon rules the African, might be endured; but this oligarchy of sex, which makes father, brothers, husbands, sons, the oligarchs over the mother and sis-

(30)   ters, the wife and daughters of every household—which ordains all men sovereign, all women subjects, carries dissension, discord and rebellion into every home of the nation.

   Webster, Worcester and Bouvier all define a citizen to be a person in the United States, entitled to vote and to hold office. The only question left to be settled now is:

(35)   Are women persons? And I hardly believe any of our opponents will have the hardihood to say they are not. Being persons, then, women are citizens; and no State has a right to make any law, or to enforce an old law, that shall abridge their privileges or immunities. Hence, every discrimination against women in the constitutions and laws of the several States is today null and void, precisely as in every one against

(40)   negroes.

---

[1] *An act that takes away one's civil rights.*
[2] *A law that imposes punishment for an act not punishable when it was committed.*
[3] *The exercise of power in the hands of a privileged few.*

13. The opening sentence of the passage (lines 2–3) performs which of the following rhetorical functions?

   I. It states the main idea of the passage.
  II. It provides a reason for delivering the speech.
 III. It reveals the speaker's mood.

  (A) I only
  (B) III only
  (C) I and II only
  (Đ) II and III only
  (E) I, II, and III

14. Which of the following phrases does the author use to support her claim that she is innocent of committing a crime?

    (A) "under indictment" (line 2)
    (B) "the last presidential election" (line 3)
    (C) "exercised my *citizen's rights*" (line 5)
    (D) "form a more perfect union" (line 8)
    (E) "establish justice" (lines 8–9)

15. The primary rhetorical purpose of quoting the Federal Constitution can best be described as

    (A) an emotional appeal.
    (B) evidence to support an earlier assertion.
    (C) a use of elegant words to earn the good will of the audience.
    (D) up-to-date background information.
    (E) an opportunity to weigh both sides of the argument.

16. In the preamble (lines 8–11), which of the following words is parallel in function to "establish" (lines 8–9)?

    (A) "union" (line 8)
    (B) *"domestic"* (line 9)
    (C) "promote" (line 9)
    (D) "general" (line 10)
    (E) "ordain" (line 11)

17. Throughout the second paragraph (lines 12–18), the rhetorical strategy most in evidence is

    (A) antithesis.
    (B) abstract allusion.
    (C) sentimentality.
    (D) euphemism.
    (E) extended metaphor.

18. The phrase "downright mockery" (lines 15–16) is reinforced by the author's later reference to

    (A) "this democratic-republican government" (lines 17–18).
    (B) "*ex post facto* law" (lines 20–21).
    (C) "supreme law of the land" (line 21).
    (D) "blessings of liberty are forever withheld" (lines 21–22).
    (E) "female posterity" (line 22).

19. Lines 19–21 contain which of the following?

(A) Two independent clauses
(B) A single periodic sentence
(C) An analogy
(D) Understatement
(E) A rhetorical question

20. By comparing an "oligarchy of sex" (line 28) with an "oligarchy of race" (lines 27–28) the speaker primarily means to suggest that

(A) racial discrimination is tolerable; sexual discrimination isn't.
(B) racism needs to be abolished.
(C) America has a long tradition of discriminatory practices against minorities.
(D) our country's democracy is being torn apart.
(E) equality in America is a myth, not a reality.

21. Whose point of view is expressed in "It is an odious . . . the poor" (lines 24–26)?

(A) The framers of the Constitution
(B) Political scientists
(C) Citizens who exercise their right to vote
(D) All present-day and future women
(E) The author

22. The organization of the last paragraph (lines 33–40) can best be described as a

(A) question followed by several possible answers.
(B) series of premises leading to a logical conclusion.
(C) generalization supported by illustrative details.
(D) hypothesis proven by factual data.
(E) sequence of truths from which it may be possible to draw an inference.

23. The tone of the passage as a whole can best be described as

(A) proud and idealistic.
(B) petty and inflexible.
(C) pompous but generally cautious.
(D) embarrassed but self-righteous.
(E) angry and resentful.

Directions: *Questions 24–34.* Carefully read the following passage and answer the accompanying questions.

This passage is taken from a 20th-century book on the history and culture of the Kiowa Indians.

PASSAGE 3

Yellowstone, it seemed to me, was the top of the world, a region of deep lakes and dark timber, canyons and waterfalls. But, beautiful as it is, one might have the sense of confinement there. The skyline in all directions is close at hand, the high wall of
Line the woods and deep cleavages of shade. There is a perfect freedom in the mountains,
(5) but it belongs to the eagle and the elk, the badger and the bear. The Kiowas reckoned their stature by the distance they could see, and they were bent and blind in the wilderness.

Descending eastward, the highland meadows are a stairway to the plain. In July the inland slope of the Rockies is luxuriant with flax and buckwheat, stonecrop
(10) and larkspur. The earth unfolds and the limit of the land recedes. Clusters of trees, and animals grazing far in the distance, cause the vision to reach away and wonder to build upon the mind. The sun follows a longer course in the day, and the sky is immense beyond all comparison. The great billowing clouds that sail upon it are shadows that move upon the grain like water, dividing light. Farther down, in the
(15) land of the Crows and Blackfeet, the plain is yellow. Sweet clover takes hold of the hills and bends upon itself to cover and seal the soil. There the Kiowas paused on the way; they had come to the place where they must change their lives. The sun is at home on the plains. Precisely there does it have the certain character of a god. When the Kiowas came to the land of the Crows, they could see the dark lees of the hills at
(20) dawn across the Bighorn River, the profusion of light on the grain shelves, the oldest deity ranging after the solstices. Not yet would they veer southward to the caldron of the land that lay below; they must wean their blood from the northern winter and hold the mountains a while longer in their view. . . .

A dark mist lay over the Black Hills, and the land was like iron. At the top of a ridge
(25) I caught sight of Devil's Tower upthrust against the gray sky as if in the birth of time the core of the earth had broken through its crust and the motion of the world was begun.

24. The diction and content of the passage suggest that the speaker is most likely

   (A) a tourist on an Indian reservation.
   (B) a botanist studying plant life in Yellowstone.
   (C) a Native American visiting the land of his ancestors.
   (D) a student of Indian customs and traditions.
   (E) a historian returning to a familiar place.

25. The main rhetorical function of the last sentence in paragraph 1 (lines 5–7) is

    (A) to provide a transition to the next paragraph.
    (B) to support the main idea of the passage.
    (C) to introduce a contradiction that needs to be explained later.
    (D) to illustrate an idea presented earlier in the paragraph.
    (E) to present a thesis that will be developed later in the passage.

26. In line 8, "Descending" modifies

    (A) "highland" (line 8).
    (B) "meadows" (line 8).
    (C) "stairway" (line 8).
    (D) "plain" (line 8).
    (E) "slope" (line 9).

27. Which of the following best describes the rhetorical function of the first sentence of the second paragraph (line 8)?

    (A) It shifts the focus of the passage.
    (B) It reiterates the main idea of the preceding paragraph.
    (C) It is meant to emphasize the speaker's feelings about being in the wilderness.
    (D) It dismisses the first paragraph as unimportant to the development of the thesis.
    (E) It emphasizes the speaker's profound understanding of his subject.

28. Lines 12–14 contain which of the following rhetorical devices?

    (A) Onomatopoeia and hyperbole
    (B) Personification and euphemism
    (C) Paradox and ambiguity
    (D) Synecdoche and rhyme
    (E) Metaphor and simile

29. The principal contrast employed by the author of the passage is between

    (A) Kiowas and Crows.
    (B) winter and summer.
    (C) light plains and dark mountains.
    (D) the past and the present.
    (E) near and far.

30. The speaker's tone throughout the passage is best described as

    (A) earnest and profound.
    (B) reverent and poetic.
    (C) sensible and scholarly.
    (D) exotic and sentimental.
    (E) sober and philosophical.

31. The sentences in lines 17–21 contain all of the following EXCEPT

    (A) elaborate personification.
    (B) parallel syntax.
    (C) a subordinate clause.
    (D) direct comparison.
    (E) a balance of overstatement and understatement.

32. In context, the phrase "wean their blood" (line 22) is referred to elsewhere as

    (A) "reckoned their stature" (lines 5–6).
    (B) "bent and blind in the wilderness" (lines 6–7).
    (C) "wonder to build upon the mind" (lines 11–12).
    (D) "paused on the way" (lines 16–17).
    (E) "change their lives" (line 17).

33. The rhetorical style of the passage is best described as

    (A) wordy and pedantic.
    (B) ornate and flowery.
    (C) graphic and graceful.
    (D) terse and didactic.
    (E) severe and classic.

34. The last paragraph (lines 24–27) contributes to the overall unity of the passage in which of the following ways?

    I.   It echoes the sense of darkness that dominated the first paragraph.
    II. It describes the land in ways that recall earlier descriptions.
    III. It brings the speaker's perspective back into the narrative.

    (A) II only
    (B) III only
    (C) I and II only
    (D) I and III only
    (E) I, II, and III

Directions: *Questions 35–45.* Carefully read the following passage and answer the accompanying questions.

This passage is an excerpt from a book about the world's black people written in the mid-20th century.

PASSAGE 4

Let's imagine a mammoth flying saucer from Mars landing, say, in a peasant Swiss village and debouching swarms of fierce-looking men whose skins are blue and whose red eyes flash lightning bolts that deal instant death. The inhabitants are all
Line
(5) the more terrified because the arrival of these men had been predicted. The religious myths of the Western world—the Second Coming of Christ, the Last Judgment, etc., have conditioned Europeans for just such an improbable event. Hence, those Swiss natives will feel that resistance is useless for a while. As long as the blue strangers are casually kind, they are obeyed and served. They become the Fathers of the people. Is this a fragment of paperback science fiction? No. It's more prosaic than that. The
(10) image I've sketched above is the manner, by and large, in which white Europe overran Asia and Africa.

But why did Europe do this? Did it only want gold, power, women, raw materials? It was more complicated than that. The fifteenth-, sixteenth-, and seventeenth-century neurotic European, sick of his thwarted instincts, restless, filled with self-disgust, was
(15) looking for not only spices and gold and slaves when he set out; he was looking for an Arcadia, a Land's End, a Shangri-la, a world peopled by shadow men, a world that would permit free play for his repressed instincts. Stripped of tradition, these misfits, adventurers, indentured servants, convicts and freebooters were the most advanced individualists of their time. Rendered socially superfluous by the stifling weight of the
(20) Church and nobility, buttressed by the influence of the ideas of Hume and Descartes, they had been brutally molded toward attitudes of emotional independence and could doff the cloying ties of custom, tradition, and family. The Asian-African native, anchored in family-dependence systems of life, could not imagine why or how these men had left their homelands, could not conceive of the cold, arid emotions sustain-
(25) ing them. . . .

Living in a waking dream, generations of emotionally impoverished colonial European whites wallowed in the quick gratification of greed, reveled in the cheap superiority of racial domination, slaked their sensual thirst in illicit sexuality, draining off the dammed-up libido[1] that European morality had condemned, amassing
(30) through trade a vast reservoir of economic fat, thereby establishing vast accumulations of capital which spurred the industrialization of the West. Asia and Africa thus became a neurotic habit that Europeans could forgo only at the cost of a powerful psychic wound, for this emotionally crippled Europe had, through the centuries, grown used to leaning upon this black crutch. But what of the impact of those white
(35) faces upon the personalities of the native? Steeped in dependence systems of family life and anchored in ancestor-worshiping religions, the native was prone to identify

---

[1] *sexual drive*

those powerful white faces falling athwart his existence with the potency of his dead father who has sustained him in the past. Temporarily accepting the invasion, he transferred his loyalties to those white faces, but, because of the psychological, racial, (40) and economic luxury which those faces derived from their denomination, the native was kept at bay.

35. The subject of the passage is introduced in the first paragraph by means of

   (A) an exposé.
   (B) an allusion.
   (C) a parable.
   (D) an exposition.
   (E) a saga.

36. In context, the word "Fathers" (line 8) is best interpreted as having which of the following meanings?

   (A) Role-models
   (B) Ruthless tyrants
   (C) Priests
   (D) Masters
   (E) Representatives

37. Which of the following words is grammatically and thematically parallel to "restless" (line 14)?

   (A) "neurotic" (line 14)
   (B) "sick" (line 14)
   (C) "thwarted" (line 14)
   (D) "self-disgust" (line 14)
   (E) "looking" (line 15)

38. The speaker mentions Arcadia, a Land's End, Shangri-la (line 16) as examples of which of the following?

   (A) Destinations for wealthy European travelers of the 15th–17th centuries
   (B) Places where slaves, spices, and gold could be traded for goods to take back to Europe
   (C) Utopian societies where people could be free and happy
   (D) Lost civilizations that disappeared centuries ago
   (E) Exotic places that attracted explorers and adventurers

39. The phrase "advanced individualists" (lines 18–19) is best described as an example of

   (A) irony.
   (B) hyperbole.
   (C) an oxymoron.
   (D) understatement.
   (E) parody.

40. The characteristics of the colonial European described in the clause beginning on line 21 ("they had been . . .") is referred to elsewhere in all of the following phrases EXCEPT

   (A) "filled with self-disgust" (line 14).
   (B) "socially superfluous" (line 19).
   (C) "Stripped of tradition" (line 17).
   (D) "cold, arid emotions" (line 24).
   (E) "emotionally impoverished" (line 26).

41. Which rhetorical device is most evident in line 28: "slaked their sensual thirst in illicit sexuality"?

   (A) Onomatopoeia
   (B) A metaphor
   (C) Assonance
   (D) Allegory
   (E) Alliteration

42. Which of the following best describes the prevailing tone of the passage?

   (A) Objective and impartial
   (B) Irate and contentious
   (C) Pedantic and nitpicking
   (D) Restrained and thoughtful
   (E) Moralistic and circumspect

43. Throughout the passage, the speaker contrasts the European colonists and the Asian-African natives on the basis of

   (A) their economic wealth.
   (B) the strength of their belief in God.
   (C) their attitude toward family life.
   (D) their desire to own property.
   (E) their attachment to the land.

44. The speaker's repeated use of questions (lines 9, 12, and 34–35) serves which of the following rhetorical purposes?

   (A) To raise issues that would not otherwise be raised
   (B) To discuss the issue from a new, totally different, point of view
   (C) To provide a quick transition from one topic to a different but related one
   (D) To anticipate objections that readers may have in mind
   (E) To establish the speaker as an authority on the subject

45. Throughout the passage, which of the following rhetorical strategies is most in evidence?

(A) Specific examples and anecdotes to illustrate the main idea
(B) The testimony of experts on the subject of European colonialism
(C) Well-reasoned logical argumentation in support of a thesis
(D) The use of highly-charged, emotional language to create an effect
(E) The testing of a hypothesis using observation and the massing of data

Directions: *Questions 46–55.* Carefully read the following passage and answer the accompanying questions.

This passage is taken from a book written in the late 20th century.

PASSAGE 5

Gary infuriated his fiancée, Ellen, because even though he was intelligent, thoughtful, and a successful surgeon, Gary was emotionally flat, completely unresponsive to any and all shows of feeling. While Gary could speak brilliantly of science and art,
Line when it came to his feelings—even for Ellen—he fell silent. Try as she might to elicit
(5) some passion from him, Gary was impassive, oblivious. "I don't naturally express my feelings," Gary told the therapist he saw at Ellen's insistence. When it came to emotional life, he added, "I don't know what to talk about; I have no strong feelings, either positive or negative."

Ellen was not alone in being frustrated by Gary's aloofness; as he confided to his
(10) therapist, he was unable to speak openly about his feelings with anyone in his life. The reason: He did not know what he felt in the first place. So far as he could tell he had no angers, no sadness, no joys.[1]

As his own therapist observes, this emotional blankness makes Gary and others like him colorless, bland: "They bore everybody. That's why their wives send them into
(15) treatment." Gary's emotional flatness exemplifies what psychiatrists call *alexithymia*, from the Greek *a* for "lack," *lexis* for "word," and *thymos* for "emotion." Such people lack words for their feelings. Indeed, they seem to lack feelings altogether, although this may actually be because of their inability to *express* emotion rather than from an absence of emotion altogether. Such people were first noticed by psychoanalysts puz-
(20) zled by a class of patients who were untreatable by that method because they reported no feelings, no fantasies, and colorless dreams—in short, no inner emotional life to talk about at all.[2] The clinical features that mark alexithymics include having difficulty describing feelings—their own or anyone else's—and a sharply limited emotional vocabulary.[3] What's more, they have trouble discriminating among emotions as well

---

[1] *Larry Cahill et al., "Beta-adrenergic activations and memory for emotional events,"* Nature *(Oct. 20, 1994).*

[2] *Psychoanalytic theory and brain maturation: the most detailed discussion of the early years and the emotional consequences of brain development is by Allan Schore,* Affect Regulation and the Origin of Self *(Hillsdale, NJ: Lawrence Erlbaum Associates, 1994).*

[3] *Dangerous, even if you don't know what it is; Joseph LeDoux, quoted in "How Scary Things Got That Way,"* Science *(Nov. 6, 1992), p. 887.*

(25)   as between emotions and bodily sensation, so that they might tell of having butterflies
        in the stomach, palpitations, sweating, and dizziness—but they would not know they
        are feeling anxious.

            "They give the impression of being different, alien beings, having come from an
        entirely different world, living in the midst of a society which is dominated by feel-
(30)   ings," is the description given by Dr. Peter Sifneos, the Harvard psychiatrist who
        in 1972 coined the term *alexithymia*.[4] Alexithymics rarely cry, for example, but if
        they do their tears are copious. Still, they are bewildered if asked what the tears
        are all about. One patient with alexithymia was so upset after seeing a movie about
        a woman with eight children who was dying of cancer that she cried herself to
(35)   sleep. When her therapist suggested that perhaps she was upset because the movie
        reminded her of her own mother, who was in actuality dying of cancer, the woman
        sat motionless, bewildered, and silent. When her therapist then asked her how she
        felt at that moment, she said she felt "awful," but couldn't clarify her feelings beyond
        that. And, she added, from time to time she found herself crying, but never knew
(40)   exactly what she was crying about.[5]

———————

[4]*Much of this speculation about the fine-tuning of emotional response by the neocortex comes from
Ned Kalin, M.D., Departments of Psychology and Psychiatry, University of Wisconsin, prepared for
the MacArthur Affective Neuroscience Meeting, Nov., 1992.*
[5]*See Ned Kalin, Departments of Psychology and Psychiatry, University of Wisconsin, "Aspects
of Emotion Conserved Across Species," an unpublished manuscript presented at the MacArthur
Affective Neuroscience Meeting, Nov., 1992; and Alan Schore,* Affect Regulation and the Origin of Self
(Hillsdale, NJ: Lawrence Erlbaum Associates, 1994).

46. Which of the following best states the main subject of the passage?

    (A) The difficulties of treating alexithymia
    (B) Research in alexithymia
    (C) Symptoms of alexithymia
    (D) A puzzling psychological disorder of modern times
    (E) The causes of alexithymia

47. Which of the following best explains the function of the passage's first sentence?

    (A) It introduces a conflict to be resolved by the end of the passage.
    (B) It defines the limits of the discussion that follows.
    (C) It establishes the author as an expert on the subject of the passage.
    (D) It makes a claim that the author will try to prove in the remainder of the passage.
    (E) It describes a situation that illustrates the central concern of the passage.

48. The structure of the footnoted paragraph (lines 9–12) can best be described as

    (A) a statement describing a situation followed by an explanation of its cause.
    (B) movement from particular details to generalizations.
    (C) a series of controversial ideas unrelated to the preceding paragraph.
    (D) the introduction and definition of an abstract psychological term.
    (E) the presentation of a hypothesis that will be proved later in the passage.

49. Which of the following best explains why the word *express* in line 18 is italicized?

   (A) To differentiate between the expression of emotion and the feeling of emotion
   (B) To emphasize that in order to talk about emotions you must feel them
   (C) To indicate that those suffering from alexithymia never have emotions to express
   (D) To alert the reader that the word is being used ironically
   (E) To suggest that the author has borrowed the word from one of the passage's footnoted sources

50. In context, the word "colorless" (line 21) is best interpreted to mean

   (A) humdrum and routine.
   (B) silent but full of action.
   (C) vague but creative.
   (D) crazy but meaningful.
   (E) gray and impressionistic.

51. The primary purpose of footnote 3 (line 24) is to inform readers that

   (A) Joseph LeDoux's main academic interest is "emotional vocabulary."
   (B) Joseph LeDoux wrote an article published in a science periodical.
   (C) Joseph LeDoux is the author of a book named *Science.*
   (D) the footnoted material has been adapted from words written by Joseph LeDoux.
   (E) lines 22–24 were originally published in an article entitled "How Scary Things Got That Way."

52. The author includes footnote 4 (line 31) in the text of the passage mainly to

   (A) inform readers where the term *alexithymia* originated.
   (B) specify where the quotation in lines 28–30 can be found in print.
   (C) establish the academic credentials of an authority on the subject of emotional responses.
   (D) suggest that several researchers have contributed to an understanding of emotional responses.
   (E) indicate that alexithymia came into existence in 1972.

53. Which of the following is an inference that can be drawn based on information in footnote 5 (line 40)?

   (A) An article by Ned Kalin was published after November, 1992.
   (B) The University of Wisconsin sponsored a meeting on affective neuroscience.
   (C) Both Ned Kalin and Alan Schore have written about alexithymia.
   (D) "Aspects of Emotion Conserved Across Species" was published in New Jersey.
   (E) In his book, Alan Schore cited words spoken by Ned Kalin at the meeting on affective neuroscience.

54. The development of the passage can best be described as

   (A) a discussion of physical symptoms related to a psychological problem.
   (B) the explanation of a psychological condition illustrated by specific cases.
   (C) an argument for employing therapy in order to overcome a psychological disorder.
   (D) the outline of a procedure for treating a 20th-century mental disease.
   (E) an analysis of consequences stemming from a widespread mental deficiency.

55. The attitude of the author toward people suffering from alexithymia is primarily one of

   (A) indifference.
   (B) awe.
   (C) puzzlement.
   (D) compassion.
   (E) respect.

SECTION II

Three Essay Questions

TIME: 2 HOURS AND 15 MINUTES

Write your essays on standard 8½" × 11" composition paper. At the exam you will be given a bound booklet containing 12 lined pages.

Essay Question 1

SUGGESTED TIME:
15 MINUTES FOR READING THE QUESTION AND SOURCES
40 MINUTES FOR WRITING AN ESSAY

Because an educated population generally enjoys levels of prosperity, culture, and well-being unavailable to many individuals who don't continue their education after high school, some people argue that all students, regardless of their ability to pay, should go to college—or at least be pushed hard in that direction.

Carefully read the following six sources, including the material that introduces each source. Then, in an essay that synthesizes at least three of the sources, take a position on the claim that all students should attend college.

Don't simply summarize the sources. Instead, weigh evidence from the sources to support and illustrate your position on the issue. You may paraphrase, review, and quote relevant material directly and indirectly from the sources. Be sure to indicate in your essay which sources you use. Refer to them as Source A, Source B, and so on, or by the key words in the parentheses below. In making your argument, you may, of course, also include any ideas of your own.

Source A (Hansen)

Source B (Kurtzman)

Source C (Banya)

Source D (Herbig)

Source E (Toppo and DeBarros)

Source F (Rob)

Katherine Hansen, "What Good Is a College Education Anyway?" Quintessential Careers, *www.quintcareers.com*. Accessed August 7, 2006.

The following passage is excerpted from an online article describing the value of a college education, and was written by an authority on career management.

Research shows that children of college-educated parents are healthier, perform better academically, and are more likely to attend college themselves than children of those with lower educational attainment.

Your education builds a foundation for your children—for our nation's children, and for the children of our global community—which leads to the last point: Education is the cornerstone of public progress.

Education is the essence of the democratic ideals that have elevated the United States from a backward land of rebellious colonists to the greatest, most spirited, powerful and successful nation in the world.

. . . And the relationship between a college education and success will become more and more significant in our information-driven global economy. Higher education will be increasingly important for landing high-paying jobs. Technology and the information age are not the only reasons to be well educated; the trend is toward multiple jobs and even multiple careers, and higher education prepares you to make the transition to new fields.

So what more could you ask of your investment in higher education than prosperity, quality of life, the knowledge that bolsters social change, a legacy for your children, and the means to ensure the continuing success of the American dream?

Lori Kurtzman, "Remedial Classes Teach Freshmen What They Should Already Know," *The Cincinnati Enquirer*, July 30, 2006.

Of the thousands of freshmen entering Ohio colleges and universities this fall, it's a safe bet that more than one-third won't be completely ready for the next level of their education. Recent figures show that 41 percent of newly minted Ohio high school graduates who went to Ohio public colleges enrolled in remedial math or reading courses during their freshman year. . . .

. . . So why be concerned over some students playing a little bit of catch-up? Education experts say this isn't just about a student taking a few extra classes. Remediation, which often affects minorities from poor families in low-income public districts, has an impact that stretches from families to schools to taxpayers.

Remedial needs strain the student, who might pay hundreds or thousands of dollars for classes that don't count toward a degree.

. . . They strain colleges, too, which devote instructors, classrooms and supplies to classes that ideally wouldn't be necessary.

And they strain the state—in essence, taxpayers—to the tune of about $30 million a year in remedial costs. . . .

But perhaps the greatest problem is what so often happens to students who require remediation: They struggle. They fail. They drop out. They lose the earning power of a college degree. The state tracked a group of students for six years and found that among the remedial students, only 15 percent earned a bachelor's degree in that time; nearly three times as many nonremedial students received their degrees. . . .

The following excerpt comes from "College Education Provides Intangibles to Student, Society," by Dr. Kingsley Banya, Chair of Department of Teacher Education at Misericordia University, *Education News*, September 2011.

Why is a college education important?

At face value, that appears to be a simple question to answer. More opportunities, better job security and advanced critical-thinking skills are just a few of the advantages college graduates enjoy. One of the major benefits of the college experience is the intangible impact college-educated individuals have in our society. Cultural enrichment that occurs from interacting with individuals from all over the world is immeasurable. In today's multicultural and complex world, understanding the cultures of other nations and individuals is invaluable. Many of society's prejudices and stereotypes come from the lack of understanding of other cultures and how that impacts behavior at global, national, and individual levels.

The appreciation of a work of art, a painting and, yes, a piece of music is a byproduct of culture. College endeavors to teach students to appreciate these cultural artifacts in addition to whatever field of study a student may be interested in studying. Higher education also imbues students with a sense of service to others. Indeed, many academic classes have service-learning components to them. Graduates often say that their introduction to new cultures was the highlight of their college experience and has prepared them to contribute to society in a myriad of positive ways. One cannot put a price tag on such learning.

Many such people, having left college as cultured individuals, will eventually work for non-governmental organizations and community agencies because they take pride in helping others less fortunate in society. They are more likely to vote and participate in civic society, and for many of them, the environment will become a major concern.

Another aspect of the intangible impact of a college education is the camaraderie among students that is promoted through sports, club activities, and other related outlets. Many residential colleges have athletic complexes and special activities for students that teach the value of teamwork, healthy living, and leadership. These opportunities contribute to making society more productive, help to reduce health care costs, and also produce more well-rounded individuals.

The concept of lifelong learning that society is promoting is best exemplified in a collegiate setting. The chances are that a good number of college graduates will continue to want to learn during their lifetime. Having been exposed to the joy and beauty of learning and the possibilities that follow, college graduates will not be content with their current knowledge and skill set. More and more people are returning to college—not necessarily to get a degree—but to learn new skills and improve on their hobbies or interests, be it painting or their appreciation of music. These are byproducts of a college education that cannot be easily quantified financially.

The graph below appeared in *The Quick and the Ed*, an online publication of the Education Sector of the American Institute for Research, August 2011.

Survey conducted by Shawn Herbig, IQS Research, among residents of Louisville, Kentucky, 2010.

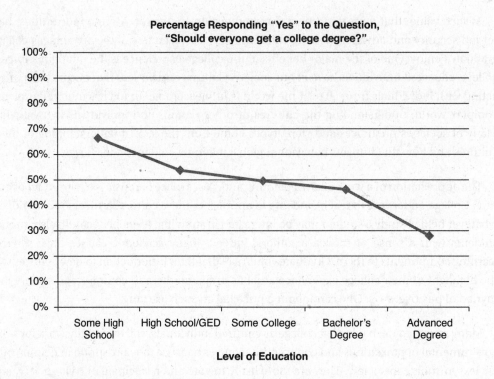

Percentage Responding "Yes" to the Question, "Should everyone get a college degree?"

Source: *Community Perceptions of Higher Education: How Does Greater Louisville Perceive the Value of Higher Education?* (Louisville, KY: IQS Research, 2010).

SOURCE E

Gregg Toppo and Anthony DeBarros, "Reality Weighs Down Dreams of College," *USA Today*, posted online February 2, 2005.

What follows is part of a newspaper article that describes the trend toward increased college enrollment.

New research reveals a huge gap between aspirations and reality, especially for poor and minority students. For them, high school dropout rates remain high and college graduation rates low.

. . . Recent studies also show that many low-income and minority students who aspire to college are poorly served by their schools and their families, arriving at college unprepared and forcing colleges and universities to spend an estimated $1 billion a year on remediation.

"There is a real gap between the aspirations teenagers have and the realities of what happens to them," says Christopher Swanson of the Urban Institute, a think tank in Washington, D.C. "Teenagers grow up hearing these 'college for all' expectations, and they internalize this. While rhetorically it makes sense, in reality all students are not going to go to college."

". . . We're not being honest with a lot of kids today," says Thomas Toch, author of *High Schools on a Human Scale*. "We're telling kids that they can do it, when we're not giving them the academic tools to be successful. We're not giving them an education that will truly prepare them to be successful in college."

Nudged by economic trends showing manufacturing, farming and other blue-collar jobs disappearing or being shipped overseas, public schools are telling students—even low-income and underperforming students—that they need college degrees.

"Rob," Declining College Standards, "Say Anything," an online blog, posted January 3, 2006.

In the following passage, a blogger identified as "Rob" makes observations about what it means to go to college.

I can't speak for other places in this country, but my experience in my community during my post high-school days (which weren't just a few years ago) was one where college was "just something you do" after high school. Kids who didn't plan to go to college were considered "lazy" or "unambitious," while those who did go to college usually didn't even know what they wanted to do with their careers. I often wondered if a lot of the kids who decided to hold off on college weren't making the wiser decision. After all, drifting through a couple of years of classes with no real career direction was a good way to waste many thousands of dollars.

But not a lot of kids do this, mostly because I think kids go off to college seeking the "college experience" rather than a real education for a specific career. They go off looking for the frat parties, sporting events, campus life and activism, all of which is commonly associated with higher education. What many of them don't understand is that while all that stuff has its place it doesn't exactly translate into a lot of intellectual capital for the business market. I don't know how many acquaintances of mine have graduated from college with a "business" or "criminal justice" degree and absolutely no idea how to get a job with it. Most of them end up starting on the bottom rung of some company, about where they would have started without a degree, only now with a degree and thousands of dollars of debt.

(This question counts as one third of the total score for Section II.)

> **Directions:** The passage below, adapted from an essay written in 1920 by A. A. Milne, is a mock-serious reflection on the passing of summer. Read it carefully. Then, in a well-written essay, analyze how the rhetorical strategies that Milne uses reveal the speaker's personality and values.

Last night the waiter put the celery on with the cheese, and I knew that summer was indeed dead. Other signs of autumn there may be—the reddening of the leaf, the chill in the early-morning air, the misty evenings—but none of these comes home to
Line me so truly. There may be cool mornings in July; in a year of drought the leaves may
(5) change before their time; it is only with the first celery that summer is over. . . .

There is a crispness about celery that is the essence of October. It is as fresh and clean as a rainy day after a spell of heat. It crackles pleasantly in the mouth. Moreover, it is excellent, I am told, for the complexion. One is always hearing of things which are good for the complexion, but there is no doubt that celery stands
(10) high on the list. After the burns and freckles of summer one is in need of something. How good that celery should be there at one's elbow. . . .

"Season of mists and mellow fruitfulness," said Keats, not actually picking out celery in so many words, but plainly including it in the general blessings of autumn. Yet, what an opportunity he missed by not concentrating on that precious root.
(15) Apples, grapes, and nuts he mentions specially—how poor a selection! For apples and grapes are not typical of any month, so ubiquitous are they, while as for nuts, have we not a national song which asserts distinctly, "Here we go gathering nuts in May"? Season of mists and mellow celery, then let it be. A pat of butter underneath the bough, a wedge of cheese, a loaf of bread and—Thou.
(20) How delicate are the tender shoots that unfold layer by layer. Of what a whiteness is the last baby one of all, of what a sweetness his flavor. It is well that this should be the last rite of the meal so that we may go straight on to the business of the pipe. Celery demands a pipe rather than a cigar, and it can be eaten better in an inn or a London tavern than in the home.
(25) Yes, and it should be eaten alone, for it is the only food which one really wants to hear oneself eat. Besides, in company one may have to consider the wants of others. Celery is not a thing to share with any man. Alone in your country inn you may call for celery; but if you are wise you will see that no other traveler wanders into the room. Take warning from one who has learnt a lesson. One day I lunched alone at
(30) an inn, finishing with cheese and celery. Another traveler came in and lunched too. We did not speak—I was busy with my celery. From the other end of the table he reached across for the cheese. That was all right! It was the public cheese. But he also reached across for the celery—my private celery for which I owed. Foolishly—you

(35) know how one does—I had left the sweetest and crispest shoots till the last, tantalizing myself pleasantly with the thought of them. Horror! To see them snatched from me by a stranger. He realized later what he had done and apologized, but of what good is an apology under such circumstances? Yet at least the tragedy was not without its value. Now one remembers to lock the door.

(40) I can face the winter with calm. I suppose I had forgotten what it was really like. I had been thinking of the winter as a horrid, wet, dreary time fit only for professional football. Now I can see other things—crisp and sparkling days, long pleasant evenings, cheery fires. Good work shall be done this winter. Life shall be lived well, The end of the summer is not the end of the world. Here's to October—and, waiter, some more celery.

Essay Question 3

SUGGESTED TIME: 40 MINUTES

(This question counts as one third of the total score for Section II.)

> **Directions:** The paragraph below comments on the issue of second chances. After reading it, write a well-organized essay that develops your position on the phenomenon of giving people second chances. Use appropriate evidence from your reading, experience, or observations to support your argument.

At one time or other, we all do or say things that we regret and would like to do over or take back. Most of the time we must live with our mistakes, but sometimes, we get a second chance. Some people take a dim view of second chances, claiming
Line that second chances not only foster irresponsible behavior but also weaken our
(5) character. Others see value in second chances. They say that second chances help us learn and permit us to take intellectual, creative, and other kinds of risks instead of always playing it safe. In your opinion, are second chances desirable, or not?

ANSWER KEY
Diagnostic Test

Answers to Multiple-Choice Questions

1	**D**	16.	**C**	31.	**E**	46.	**C**
2.	**E**	17.	**A**	32.	**E**	47.	**E**
3.	**C**	18.	**D**	33.	**C**	48.	**A**
4.	**A**	19.	**C**	34.	**D**	49.	**A**
5.	**B**	20.	**A**	35.	**C**	50.	**A**
6.	**D**	21.	**D**	36.	**D**	51.	**D**
7.	**A**	22.	**B**	37.	**B**	52.	**D**
8.	**B**	23.	**E**	38.	**C**	53.	**C**
9.	**C**	24.	**C**	39.	**A**	54.	**B**
10.	**D**	25.	**D**	40.	**A**	55.	**D**
11.	**D**	26.	**B**	41.	**E**		
12.	**B**	27.	**A**	42.	**B**		
13.	**D**	28.	**E**	43.	**C**		
14.	**C**	29.	**C**	44.	**C**		
15.	**B**	30.	**B**	45.	**D**		

Summary of Answers in Section I (Multiple Choice)

Number of correct answers _____

Use this information when you calculate your score for this exam. See page 84.

ANSWER EXPLANATIONS

Passage 1—An excerpt from Richard Maxwell Brown, *Historical Patterns of Violence in America*

1. **(D)** Much of the passage is devoted to the newspaper coverage of the event, especially the work of John N. Edwards, a "reasonably anonymous newspaperman of nearly a century ago" (lines 26–27). Because the incident took place long ago, the likely source of information is old newspapers. (A), (B), and (C) are wrong choices because the robbery probably occurred before the speaker was born. (E) is neither mentioned nor implied in the passage.

2. **(E)** Unlike the others, it is a compound sentence containing two independent clauses joined by the conjunction "*and.*" It also expresses the speaker's opinion that the robbery was "highhanded" and dangerous. Finally, it uses alliteration: "<u>h</u>igh<u>h</u>anded . . . <u>wh</u>ole <u>h</u>ost of <u>h</u>oliday-minded people."

3. **(C)** The speaker is referring to the sentiment expressed by the reporter in lines 8–9. Eliminate (A) as an answer because the speaker has no argument with the placement of the story, only with its contents. (B) is incorrect because the speaker has no reason to question Edwards' qualifications to report on the incident. (D) may be referring to quoted material that appeared in the newspaper two days later, but in line 8 he means the report written immediately after the crime. (E) does not accurately describe the tone of the story.

4. **(A)** The speaker finds it hard to believe and accept reportage that praises "violent, lawless men" who "endangered the lives" of innocent people.

5. **(B)** The lines compare the bandits to medieval knights. (A) comes close to a correct answer, but in the context, the reference to King Arthur's knights is not meant to be inspiring. (C) may be a tempting answer because a parable is a kind of story, but its purpose—to reveal moral or spiritual truths—does not apply here. (D) is not a bad choice, but a caricature points out grotesque likenesses, not complimentary ones. (E) refers to notes made while analyzing or explaining a written work, and so does not apply here.

6. **(D)** The sentence in question is written like an offhand remark that contrasts with the overblown passage comparing outlaws to the legendary Knights of the Round Table. (A) is incorrect because the main idea of the passage has not yet been stated or established. (B) is wrong because no particular theory has been stated earlier. (C) is a promising answer, but the discussion of the newpaper's coverage of the event continues into the next paragraph. (E) is contrary to fact; the speaker is criticizing the newspaper's position.

7. **(A)** The phrase is used ironically. In lines 12–14, the bandits are compared to noble and courageous knights. Here the author pokes fun at the comparison with a wry comment on the "courage" it took to shoot a little girl. (B) is incorrect because the phrase is not a figure of speech referring metaphorically to a particular place, person, or thing. The other choices don't apply. (C) is a humorous comparison of two unlike things, (D) a self-contradictory statement that is nevertheless valid, and (E) is a term consisting of contradictory elements that create a paradoxical effect.

8. **(B)** In the context "innocent" refers to gullible readers who embrace, or at least, simple-mindedly and uncritically accept, the newspapers's glorification of the bandits. Because people who are undecided fall into a different category, (B) is the correct answer.

9. **(C)** The quotation exemplifies a mentality prevalent in parts of America—a way of thinking that, as the author goes on to explain, originated on the frontier. (A) is irrelevant in the context. (B) is not accurate because the author specifically denies in lines 26–27 that he is out to "belabor one reasonably anonymous newspaperman"—i.e., Edwards. (D) does not apply in the context. (E) has some merit because the author discusses frontier mentality in the next paragraph, but in the context (E) does not accurately describe the author's purpose.

10. **(D)** The phrase "creative plundering" describes an action that most clearly exemplifies "independent action and self-reliance." (A) names two infamous outlaws who did not represent frontier values. (B) and (C) represent values contrary to "independent action," etc. (E) describes the frontier's movement, not a characteristic value of frontier life.

11. **(D)** The conclusions reveal the ambiguity of the entire passage. At first, the author objects to the glorification of the bandits. Then, he acknowledges the impulse—inherited from the frontier—to admire men of "imagination and daring." In the end, though, he regards the legacy of the frontier a "problem" (lines 27–28) that has left us with a kind of "blindness" (line 44). (A) and (B) are irrelevant to the conclusions in the last paragraph. (C) misses the point. Where similarities exist, they describe frontier people such as those who came to admire the bandits. (E) inaccurately describes the author's attitude toward both the frontier and Mr. Edwards.

12. **(B)** All three groups are marked by their drive to carry out their goals: the bandits aimed to rob and hurt others, the knights strove to be chivalrous, and the frontier people did all they could to thrive in a rugged and often hostile environment. (A) has no validity because they didn't care what others thought. What counted was self-satisfaction. (C) was of little or no concern to any of the groups, although one might argue that knights probably devoted considerable effort to improve their standing in King Arthur's court. Neither (D) nor (E) is discussed in the passage.

Passage 2—Speech by Susan B. Anthony

13. **(D)** The opening creates the context for the speech—the speaker's indictment for an alleged crime. In just a few words, the speaker also reveals her anger and indignity. The sentence does not state the main idea, which comes just afterward.

14. **(C)** In the speaker's view, the act of voting is not a crime. Rather it is only an "alleged crime" and a right guaranteed to her by the Constitution. (A) cannot be the answer because the term "under indictment," in and of itself, doesn't suggest innocence or guilt. The same holds for the other incorrect choices. A sense of a wrongful accusation is not associated with any of them.

15. **(B)** Just prior to the quotation, the speaker claims that voting is a right guaranteed by the Federal Constitution. To prove her point, she quotes the preamble of the Constitution. (A) is a possible answer because the Constitution is an inspiring document to which Americans are emotionally attached, but it doesn't accurately describe Anthony's reason

for including an excerpt from the document's preamble in the passage. (C), (D), and (E) fail to explain the rhetorical purpose of quoting the preamble.

16. **(C)** For sentence elements to be parallel, they must be grammatical equivalents. The word *establish* appears in a series of phrases, each using the infinitive form of a verb: *to form, to insure, to provide*, etc. None of the other choices except (E) is a verb, but *ordain* is used not in its infinitive form but as a verb in the present tense.

17. **(A)** An antithesis sets up an opposition or contrast of ideas. This paragraph is dominated by contrasts between conditions as they exist and conditions as they should be, according to the Constitution. (B) is a tempting answer because the paragraph alludes to the language of the Constitution, but by no means are the allusions abstract. (C) does not apply. If anything, the language in the paragraph is direct and down-to-earth. (D) is not in the speaker's repertoire—just the opposite, in fact, because she describes the unjust treatment of women in vivid terms. (E) is not a good answer because the speaker's words are to be taken literally.

18. **(D)** The author used the phrase "downright mockery" to describe the empty promise of the blessings of liberty for women. The idea is echoed by the sentence that begins in line 21. None of the other choices suggests a false promise or the lack of women's rights.

19. **(C)** The author uses an analogy to compare two things: using gender to determine eligibility to vote, and passing a bill of attainder. Both actions violate the law by depriving people of their civil rights. (A) is incorrect. A sentence containing two independent clauses needs two separate subjects. This sentence has just one, the infinitive phrase *to make sex a qualification.* (B) is wrong because the main thought of periodic sentences is completed only at the end of the sentence. Neither (D) nor (E) appear in the sentence.

20. **(A)** The message contained in the whole sentence that begins in line 24 is that the oligarchy of race "might be endured," while the oligarchy of sex has dire consequences. (B) is just the opposite of what the speaker is saying. (C) and (E) are vaguely implied, but those ideas do not reflect the speaker's main purpose. (D) refers only to what may happen if the oligarchy of sex is permitted to continue.

21. **(D)** The ideas in the sentence are attributed to "women and their female posterity" (line 22). As the passage says, *To them,* the government is an "odious aristocracy," etc. Everyone named in choices (A), (B), and (C) might agree with the sentiment expressed in lines 24–26, but they play no role in the passage. (E) certainly has merit as the answer because the author speaks the words, but she gives credit for the ideas to "women and their female posterity" (line 22).

22. **(B)** Using logic, the author lists several truths from which she has drawn the only possible conclusion: that laws disenfranchising women are "null and void." (A) is valid only to the extent that the author includes a question (line 35), but asking whether women are "persons" is only one step in the development of the paragraph. (C) and (D) don't apply to this paragraph. (E) comes close to describing how the final paragraph is developed, but the author's inference, or conclusion, is clearly spelled out in the last sentence of the passage.

23. **(E)** The passage is full of strong language that reflects the speaker's bitterness about women being deprived of their rights. (A) is not accurate because the speaker's ideas

are based in reality, not idealism. That is, she doesn't dream of a better tomorrow, she demands it based on what the Constitution says. (B) ignores the fact that the speaker is concerned about big issues, not petty ones. (C) cannot characterize a speech that includes a number of bold statements, including the accusation that the government is the "most hateful aristocracy . . . on the face of the globe." (D) may be half right, for the speaker is justifiably self-righteous, but she is not at all embarrassed by her strong convictions.

Passage 3—An excerpt from N. Scott Momaday, *The Way to Rainy Mountain*

24. **(C)** The speaker's obvious reverence for the land implies that he has strong ties to Yellowstone. To him, it is almost sacred. (A) indicates that the speaker is a casual visitor, but considering his feeling for the place, he most certainly is not. (B) overlooks the fact that the plant life is almost totally ignored in the description of the land. (D) is incorrect because the passage contains no evidence to support it. (E) is disqualified because the awe that the speaker feels about the scenery strongly suggests that he is a first-time visitor to Yellowstone. Someone returning to a place repeatedly is more likely to use rhetoric couched in the present tense rather than in the past, as in "seemed" (line 1).

25. **(D)** The sentence shows the effect of the "sense of confinement" mentioned earlier in the paragraph. (A) is not the answer because the discussion of the Kiowas is not immediately picked up in paragraph 2. (B) is incorrect because the sentence merely adds detail to the portrait of the Kiowas. (C) is wrong because the sentence fails to contradict other material in the paragraph. (E) cannot be the answer because the notion of the Kiowas' freedom/confinement is dropped after the first paragraph.

26. **(B)** "Descending" is a verbal that functions like an adjective. It describes (i.e., modifies) the noun "meadows," the subject of the sentence.

27. **(A)** The sentence takes the reader from the high country down the "stairway to the plain." Choice (B) is wrong because the sentence adds new information to the passage. (C) is not the best answer because the speaker's purpose is to impart information, not to express feelings. (D) is incorrect because the author needs the first paragraph to tell the full story of the Kiowas' migration southward from the mountains to the plains. (E) is partly correct because the speaker has observed the terrain very closely. But it is not his main intent to show off his knowledge.

28. **(E)** The lines contain examples of metaphor—"clouds . . . are shadows," and of simile—"move upon the grain like water." To answer this question correctly, you should be familiar with all the rhetorical terms. Turn to the Glossary, page 389.

29. **(C)** In the passage, the mountainous Yellowstone area is characterized by darkness, as in "dark timber" (line 2) and "deep cleavages of shade" (line 4), while the sun-filled plains are "yellow" (line 15) and marked by a "profusion of light" (line 20). The other choices are either incidental or irrelevant to the passage.

30. **(B)** The passage is filled with poetic images and reflects the speaker's sense of wonder and pleasure over the changing beauty of the land across which the Kiowas once passed. (A) may be partly correct; the speaker is earnest but not noticeably profound. (C) is not correct; the passage is not at all scholarly but rather impressionistic. In (D) *exotic* does

not accurately describe either the land or the speaker's state of mind. (E) is not a good choice because the passage is not philosophical. Rather, much of it is down to earth—literally.

31. **(E)** Choices (A) and (D) are found in the extended comparison between the sun and a god, including the phrase "the oldest deity." (B) is exemplified by the series of phrases beginning with "dark lees . . . ." (C) is present in the clause that begins "When the Kiowas . . ."

32. **(E)** The phrase refers to the Kiowas' need to accustom themselves to their new surroundings. Choice (D) comes close to the correct answer, but it fails to suggest the reason for the Kiowas' break in their southward journey. The other choices don't apply.

33. **(C)** The language is fluent, rhythmic, and poetic. The speaker portrays the land in vivid images. No pair of adjectives in the four other choices accurately describes the style of the passage.

34. **(D)** The last paragraph, like the first, is filled with images of darkness. In both paragraphs, too, the speaker puts himself into the narrative: "it seemed to me" in the first paragraph and "I caught sight" in the last. What differs between the two paragraphs is the style of description. In the first, the speaker tells what he sees and how he reacted to it. In the other, the speaker's impression of the landscape is literally earth-shattering.

Passage 4—An excerpt from Richard Wright, *White Man, Listen!*

35. **(C)** The imaginative account of Martians conquering a Swiss village is a parable—a short, fictitious story that illustrates a moral attitude or religious principle. In this case, the story represents European seizures of Asian and African communities. None of the other choices apply: (A) is a factual revelation of something discreditable. (B) is a reference to a familiar person, place, or thing. (D) explains the background or situation in a story or play. (E) is a literary form that consists of a long, historical, episodic narrative that follows the fortunes of a hero, a family, or a group of heroic people.

36. **(D)** According to line 8, the invaders are "obeyed and served," a description that implies that "Fathers" is another name for "Masters." (A), (C), and (E) are inappropriate in the context of the passage. (B) is a possibility, although the passage says that the strangers, unlike tyrants, are "casually kind" (line 8)—at least for a while.

37. **(B)** The adjective "restless" comes after "European," the noun it modifies. "Sick" is parallel to "restless" because it is an adjective that both modifies and comes after the very same noun. Also, because both adjectives have unfavorable connotations, they are linked thematically.

38. **(C)** Arcadia, Land's End, and Shangri-la are not real places but metaphors for idealized places, unlike Europe, where men would be free to do as they wished.

39. **(A)** Ordinarily the phrase might have a positive connotation. In this context, however, the phrase is ironic because the speaker's point is that those "advanced individualists" behaved like destructive barbarians. (B) may seem like a possible answer because much of the passage may seem exaggerated, but in this context, irony is more pronounced than hyperbole. One could argue for (C) as the answer because in the context the phrase seems contrary to truth. But an oxymoron must itself contain contradictory terms. (D)

is wrong because there is nothing understated in the passage. (E) cannot be correct because there is no suggestion of ridicule in the phrase.

40. **(A)** Except for (A), each choice reiterates a quality of the colonial European individualist not bound by emotional ties to custom, tradition, the church, or the family.

41. **(E)** Alliteration is the repetition of initial consonant sounds. Note the prevalence of the *s* sound in the words in question. (A) applies to words that imitate sounds. (B) is a figurative comparison without using *like* or *as*. (C) is the repetition of vowel sounds without the repetition of consonants. (D) is a type of story in which people, things, and actions represent an idea or generalization about life.

42. **(B)** The speaker vigorously condemns Europeans who cruelly exploited others for material gain. No other pair of adjectives applies.

43. **(C)** The most obvious contrast is the two groups' loyalty to family life. The speaker says of the colonists that they had cast off the "ties . . . of family" (line 22). The natives, on the other hand, were "[s]teeped in dependence systems of family life" (lines 35–36). No other choice plays a significant role in the passage.

44. **(C)** Questions like those used in the passage are a rhetorical device that allows the speaker to add new ideas to a discussion, move a discussion along quickly, or to rapidly change the subject. They also serve to involve the reader because the questions serve as a kind of conversation between the author and reader. None of the other choices apply.

45. **(D)** From the opening scenario in which "fierce-looking men whose skins are blue and whose red eyes flash lightning bolts" (lines 2–3) to the image of an "emotionally crippled Europe . . . leaning upon this black crutch" (lines 33–34), powerful, almost inflammatory language dominates the passage. All the other choices describe a more sedate and conventional passage.

Passage 5—An excerpt from Daniel Goleman, "The Man Without Feelings," *Emotional Intelligence*

46. **(C)** The passage concentrates on the typical symptoms of alexithymia. All the other choices are mentioned only in passing.

47. **(E)** The opening sentence introduces a person with a problem: an inability to express emotion. That is the main concern of the passage. (A) alludes to a conflict—the anger that Ellen felt toward Gary—but the passage discusses neither how, or whether, the conflict was resolved. (B), (C), and (D) list functions of some introductory sentences, but not this one.

48. **(A)** The paragraph states the effect of Gary's behavior on Ellen, then explains the cause of her frustration. (B) is a poor choice, for the paragraph moves in the opposite direction—from the general to the specific. (C) represents a misreading of the paragraph. If anything, lines 9–12 continue to develop ideas presented earlier. (D) is wrong. Although "frustrated" is a psychological term, it is hardly abstract, and it is not defined in the rest of the paragraph. (E) does not apply. No hypothesis is presented in the paragraph.

49. **(A)** In context, the phrase "to express" is meant to contrast with the phrase "to lack feelings" (line 17). In other words, the inability to *express* emotion does not mean the inability to *feel* emotion.

50. **(A)** In the context, the phrase "colorless dreams" is paired with "no feelings, no fantasies," suggesting that the dreams are dull. This interpretation is supported by the author's use of the same word, "colorless," in line 14 as a synonym for dull and boring.

51. **(D)** Because the footnoted lines of the passage are presented without quotation marks, they have been paraphrased or otherwise adapted by the author of the passage. (A) draws an inference unjustified by either the footnote or anything else in the passage. (B) is incorrect because the footnote says that LeDoux is quoted in the article, not that he wrote it. (C) *Science* is the name of a periodical, as indicated by the volume number following the title. (E) is incorrect because the lines, based on an idea expressed by LeDoux, were composed by the author of this passage.

52. **(D)** Unlike most footnotes, this one does not pertain directly to the text of the passage. Rather, it serves as a supplement to the previous paragraph, which alludes generally to psychiatrists puzzling over patients who lack an inner emotional life. (A) is stated in the text of the passage (lines 15–16), making a footnote superfluous. (B) is not a likely answer because the footnote does not say where Dr. Sifneos' words can be found. (C) The "authority," Ned Kalin, has impressive credentials, but that is incidental to the purpose of the footnote. (E) is faulty conjecture. Although alexithymia was named in 1972, it cannot be assumed to have suddenly made its appearance in that year.

53. **(C)** The two works cited in footnote 5 pertain to aspects of alexithymia. (A) is incorrect because the footnote fails to say whether the manuscript had been published. (B) is possible but the meeting place is not mentioned. (D) is incorrect because that information is not given. (E) is a possibility, but the footnote doesn't contain that information.

54. **(B)** The passage explains alexithymia and provides two illustrative case studies, one at the beginning and the other at the end. (A) is partly right; the passage mentions physical symptoms but not extensively. (C) may be a tempting choice because therapists do treat alexithymics. The passage doesn't take a position on the use of therapists, however. (D) is incorrect because no procedure is discussed in the passage. (E) has some validity, although the passage never mentions the incidence of alexithymia.

55. **(D)** The author doesn't come right out and say how he feels about alexithymics. Yet, he stresses their anguish throughout the passage, suggesting that he is sympathetic to their plight. (A) reflects an inaccurate reading of the passage. (B), (C), and (E) may be somewhat valid, but they do not describe the author's primary attitude toward alexithymics.

Answers to Essay Questions

For an overview of how essays are graded, turn to "How Essays Are Scored," pages 36–37.

Although answers to essay questions will vary greatly, the following descriptions suggest a possible approach to each question and contain ideas that could be used in responding to the question.

ESSAY QUESTION 1, BASED ON THE TOPIC: "COLLEGE FOR ALL"

As an AP student on the verge of college, you're likely to hold some strong views on the issue of college for all. Your opinions can serve as the core of your essay, but the sources offer a number of ideas on both sides of the question that you may not have considered before.

Arguments in favor of college for all may include:

- Education is the key to progress and prosperity. (Source A)
- Education is the essence of democracy; it gives everyone an equal chance to succeed. (Source A)
- Investment in education has long-lasting personal and financial benefits. (Source A)
- Graduates' understanding of other cultures helps them to contribute to society in countless ways. (Source C)
- People lacking a college degree know how hard it is to find good jobs. (Source D)
  Note: This is one interpretation of the graph in Source D. See below for another view.
- A college degree is necessary for jobs that formerly required less education. (Source E)

Arguments against college for all may include:

- Many students are not academically prepared for college work. (Source B)
- The cost of remedial work for unprepared students strains resources. (Source B)
- The drop-out rate for remedial students is very high. (Source B)
- Many people with college and graduate degrees doubt the true value of a degree in an uncertain economy. (Source D)
  Note: This is one interpretation of the graph in Source D. See above for another view.
- Many graduates find themselves working in jobs that don't require a college degree. (Source F)
- Students with unreal aspirations are doomed to be disappointed and disillusioned by the reality of college. (Source E)

ESSAY QUESTION 2, BASED ON "A WORD FOR AUTUMN" BY A. A. MILNE

Most readers are likely to find Milne's mock-serious essay witty, lighthearted, urbane—not to be taken seriously. Some, however, may legitimately see a solemn purpose behind Milne's musings on celery. Both responses are valid, provided that readers can support their views with evidence from the passage.

Those in the first group might immediately point out that assigning significance of any kind to something as inconsequential as celery is just plain silly. Yes, silly it is, and that is just the point. Milne is out to entertain his readers by playing with a ridiculous idea, exaggerating the importance of celery beyond all reason: Celery marks the change of seasons, it enhances the complexion, it is an excellent end to a meal, and is a prelude to smoking a pipe rather than a cigar.

What sort of person would actually put such ideas on paper? Well, the sort that is the speaker in the passage. Presumably, he is a man of independent means who dines out a lot and takes himself to be a gentleman. He is cultured enough to quote Keats, but he seems to take no interest in the affairs of the world. His main concerns are being comfortable, feeling good, enjoying the benefits of his station in life, and enjoying "crisp and sparkling days, long pleasant evenings, cheery fires." Then he adds, toward the end of the passage, "Life shall be lived well."

Other readers, searching between the lines, may find the essay as a piece of social criticism. A case can be made that the speaker represents an egocentric, hedonistic, empty-headed class of people, whose existence serves no useful purpose. Milne uses celery as a symbol to represent the trivialities that dominate the speaker's life. Not only is the man out of touch with the real world but he contributes nothing to it. That Milne chose celery as the speaker's concern merely emphasizes the speaker's shallowness. The anecdote about lunch at the inn reinforces the point. "Horror!" says the speaker about having his celery snatched, an event he also terms a "tragedy," as though the stranger had done something truly horrendous. Although Milne chose celery as the subject, anything of equal insignificance could have served his purpose.

ESSAY QUESTION BASED ON THE ISSUE OF "SECOND CHANCES"

Theoretically, an argument that either supports or is dead set against the principle of second chances in every imaginable circumstance might be made, but a moderate stance—one that leans in one direction or the other—is likely to be far more rational and convincing.

Once you've pondered the issue, you could begin your essay by describing a real or imagined scenario in which someone has erred. After revealing the circumstances surrounding the misstep, discuss why the perpetrator should or should not be granted a second chance.

In developing your essay, you might take into account the nature of the mistake, the offender's age and position in life, the time and place of the offense, and what occurred as a consequence of the transgression. Consider such matters as whether the perpetrator should have known better, or whether there were mitigating conditions beyond his or her control. You might also question whether the action was self-motivated or whether the individual may have been in uenced by others. Was the action impulsive or had it been thought out beforehand? What, if any, significant harm was done, and especially what might be gained or lost as a result of offering a second chance? In effect, your essay would explore relevant variables used to determine whether people ought to be held accountable for certain actions.

Another way to approach this topic is to base your decision mainly on the seriousness of the offense. Did it ignore standards that govern day-to-day social behavior, such as being unkind to others, telling lies, making threats, deceiving others, disturbing the peace, and so forth? Or did the mistake literally violate laws against, say, theft, underage drinking, texting while driving, physically damaging property, injuring people, and many, many others? Because not every offense is equally serious, weigh the appropriateness of granting second chances in a variety of circumstances.

A third approach might be to analyze a specific experience in which a second chance should have been granted but wasn't, or a time when granting a second chance backfired in some way. Rather than simply write a narrative of what happened, analyze the reasons why the decision was faulty and what conclusions might be drawn from the results.

In a way, this essay topic obliges you to confront and explain aspects of who you are and what you value. By addressing the topic thoughtfully, you'll not only inform AP readers about your ability to write a perceptive analytical essay, you could also learn something important about yourself.

Before scoring your essays, carefully review "How Essays Are Scored" (pages 36–37), a guide meant to help you judge as objectively as possible the quality of your writing.

Use the criteria listed below to evaluate each of your essays. Because it's tough to be totally impartial about your own writing, you may get a more accurate score by asking a well-informed friend, teacher, or counselor to rate your essays for you.

On the following Rating Chart, enter a number (from 1 to 6) that you think represents your level of performance in each category (A–F).

CATEGORY A: OVERALL PURPOSE/MAIN IDEA
6   extremely well-defined and insightful
5   clearly defined and generally insightful
4   mostly clear
3   somewhat clear but occasionally confusing
2   generally unclear and confusing
1   mostly incomprehensible or simplistic

CATEGORY B: HANDLING OF THE PROMPT
6   self-evident or extremely clear throughout
5   mostly clear
4   somewhat clear
3   somewhat unclear
2   generally unclear or ambiguous
1   confusing or nonexistent

CATEGORY C: ORGANIZATION AND DEVELOPMENT
6   insightfully organized; fully developed with excellent supporting evidence
5   reasonably well organized; developed with appropriate supporting material
4   appropriately organized; developed with some relevant material
3   inconsistent organization; weak development
2   poorly organized; little or no development
1   no discernible organization or development

CATEGORY D: SENTENCE STRUCTURE
6   varied and engaging
5   sufficiently varied to create interest
4   some variety
3   little variety; minor sentence errors
2   frequent sentence errors that interfere with meaning
1   serious sentence errors that obscure meaning

CATEGORY E: USE OF LANGUAGE
6   precise and effective word choice
5   competent word choice
4   conventional word choice; mostly correct
3   some errors in diction or idiom
2   frequent lapses in diction or idiom
1   meaning obscured by word choice

CATEGORY F: GRAMMAR AND USAGE
6   error-free or virtually error-free
5   occasional minor errors
4   basically correct but with several minor errors
3   meaning somewhat obscured by errors
2   meaning frequently obscured by errors
1   meaning blocked by several major errors

RATING CHART

Rate your essay	Essay 1	Essay 2	Essay 3
Overall Purpose/Main Idea			
Handling of the Prompt			
Organization and Development			
Sentence Structure			
Use of Language			
Grammar and Usage			
Composite Scores (sum of each column)			

By using the following scale, in which composite scores are converted to the nine-point AP rating scale, you may determine the final score for each essay:

Composite Score	AP Essay Score
33–36	9
29–32	8
25–28	7
21–24	6
18–20	5
15–17	4
10–14	3
7–9	2
6 or below	1

AP Essay Scores Essay 1 _____ Essay 2 _____ Essay 3 _____

TEST SCORE WORKSHEET

The scores you have earned on the multiple-choice and essay sections of the exam may now be converted to the AP five-point scale by performing the following calculations:

I. Determine Your Score for Section I (Multiple-Choice)

(STEP A) Number of correct answers _____

(STEP B) Multiply the figure in Step A by 1.2272 to find your
Multiple-Choice Score _____. (Do not round.)

II. Determine Your Score for Section II (Essays)

(STEP A) Enter your score for Essay 1 (out of 9) _____

(STEP B) Enter your score for Essay 2 (out of 9) _____

(STEP C) Enter your score for Essay 3 (out of 9) _____

(STEP D) Add the figures in Steps A, B, and C _____

(STEP E) Multiply the figure in Step D by 3.0556 _____ (Do not round.)
This is your Essay Score.

III. Determine Your Total Score

Add the scores for I and II to find your composite score _____.
(Round to nearest whole number.)

To convert your composite score to the AP five-point scale, use the chart below. The range of scores only approximates what you would earn on the actual test because the exact figures may vary from test to test. Be aware, therefore, that your score on this test, as well as on other tests in this book, may differ slightly from your score on an actual AP exam.

Composite Score	AP Grade
114–150	5
98–113	4
81–97	3
53–80	2
0–52	1

AP essays are ordinarily judged in relation to other essays written on the same topic at the same time. Therefore, the scores you assign yourself for these essays may not be the same as the scores you would earn on an actual exam.

Mastering
Multiple-Choice Questions

3

→ **SIX ROUTES TO CORRECT ANSWERS**

→ **WHAT YOU NEED TO KNOW ABOUT:**

■ **GRAMMAR**

■ **RHETORIC**

■ **SENTENCES**

→ **WORD CHOICE AND DETAILS OF DICTION**

→ **UNDERSTANDING FOOTNOTES**

→ **PASSAGES AND SAMPLE QUESTIONS FOR PRACTICE**

The Diagnostic Test has given you a taste of the types of questions that are coming your way on the AP exam. Whether you breezed through the Diagnostic Test or struggled with every question, it's worth your while to look at the following tried-and-true techniques for answering multiple-choice questions:

Untold numbers of students have relied on the following rules of thumb. You should, too.

FIVE RULES OF THUMB

1. Read each question carefully. To be sure you understand what a question asks, put it into your own words. Then reread the question to be sure you haven't misread it.

2. Read the five choices. Remember that you must select the *best* choice, which could mean that one or more of the incorrect choices may be partially valid. With a stroke of your pencil or an "X" in the margin, eliminate all the choices that are obviously wrong. Then concentrate on the others. Examine each remaining choice for irrelevancies, for absolute words such as *always* and *never*, and for meanings that merely approximate what the passage says. If a question refers you to a specific line or lines in the passage, reread not only those lines but the two or three lines that come both before and after the designated lines. Knowing the context in which the lines appear can lead you to the correct answer.

3. After you've made your choice, scan the passage for evidence to support your decision. Just before filling the space on your answer sheet, be sure the question number is correct, and re-read the question to check whether you've interpreted every word correctly.

4. If you're stumped by a question, make a tentative guess and put a "?" in the margin. Come back to it later, if you can. Return visits often provide a new perspective that helps you find the answer. Also mark any questions about which you have any doubts.

5. If time remains after you've filled in all the blanks, review your answers, especially those, if any, that gave you trouble. Oh, yes, one more thing: Ridiculous as it may sound, make sure you've put your answers in the right places. Don't blacken a space for question 12 in a space for question 11, etc. (Please don't snicker; it's been done, and not just once.)

TIP

Before choosing your answer, eliminate the other choices.

While taking the model exams in this book, practice these five guidelines. At first, they may seem cumbersome, even nitpicky. But as you grow accustomed to using them, your pace will pick up, and you'll answer questions more quickly and efficiently. That's a promise.

But remember, mastery of test-taking techniques can take you only so far toward earning a top score on the AP exam. What will take you the rest of the way is your knowledge of language and rhetoric.

LANGUAGE AND RHETORIC

All the question-answering techniques in the world won't do you much good without knowledge of the subject matter covered by the exam. Moreover, a book like this can't tell you everything you need to know or should have remembered from years of English classes. But it can hit some of the highlights. That is, it can call your attention to matters regularly included in past AP exams. That's what the following pages aim to do.

English Grammar Questions

Three or four multiple-choice grammar questions customarily turn up on the test. Typically, they ask how a certain grammatical structure, such as a series of compound sentences or a list of adjectives, has been used in a passage to convey meaning or create certain effects.

For example, the following paragraph by the American author Washington Irving is tailor-made for a question about sentence structure—particularly the use of parallelism.

> Her mighty lakes, like oceans of liquid silver; her mountains, with their bright aerial tints; her valleys, teeming with wild fertility; her tremendous cataracts, thundering in their solitudes; her boundless plains, waving with spontaneous verdure; her broad deep rivers, rolling in the solemn silence to the ocean; her trackless forests, where vegetation puts forth all its magnificence; her skies, kindling with the magic of summer clouds and glorious sunshine;—no, never need an American look beyond his own country for the sublime and beautiful of natural scenery.

Notice that the paragraph—except for the clause after the dash—consists of a single sentence composed of a series of nouns and modifiers, most followed by a participle phrase. The effect of this pattern is cumulative. It creates an image of the vastness of America, an idea aided not only by the piling up of visual images but by the repeated used of adjectives such as "tremendous," "boundless," and "broad."

Another type of grammar question asks about the function of certain words. You may, for example, find a question that requires you to know about modifiers, as in

In line 34, the word "moral" modifies

(A) crowd.
(B) demands.
(C) persuasion.
(D) leadership.
(E) rectitude.

Grammar questions sometimes focus on grammatical terms, as in

The opening sentence of the passage includes all of the following EXCEPT

(A) an analogy.
(B) irony.
(C) a coordinate clause.
(D) conjunctions.
(E) parallel structure.

TIP

To do well, you should be familiar with everyday grammatical terms and concepts.

The most important terms to know pertain to types of sentences (*simple, compound, complex;* also *periodic* and *loose* sentences), the parts of speech (*noun, pronoun, verb, adjective, adverb, conjunction, preposition, exclamation*), and parts of sentences (*subject, predicate, object, clauses*).

Chapter 4 (pages 115–222) reviews several grammatical principles related to questions asked on past AP exams. A full treatment of English grammar, however, lies beyond the scope of this book. So, if your grammar skills are rusty, spend time with a comprehensive guide to grammar. Check your local bookstore, borrow one from your English teacher, or just Google "English grammar," and you'll find enough material to keep you busy for the rest of the century.

Comprehension Questions

The exam may include perhaps a half-dozen comprehension questions that ask not how a passage is composed but rather what it says. Some questions may refer to the meaning of the passage as a whole. Others pinpoint particular words in context, and still others may ask about the meaning or significance of certain details. Such questions require you to read closely, of course, but they also serve as a springboard to answering the majority of the questions, which have to do with rhetoric.

Questions About Rhetoric

Questions about rhetoric test your understanding of such concepts as tone, diction, syntax, imagery, irony, figures of speech, theme, point of view, and many other rhetorical concepts. Also, you'll most certainly have a chance to demonstrate your awareness of how certain kinds of sentences reveal an author's intent and convey meaning.

Rhetoric is a broad term. Having come this far in your education, you are already acquainted with many of its varieties. Everything you have ever written or read—from a movie review to a college application—is subject to analysis in rhetorical terms.

Everything you've ever written can be analyzed in rhetorical terms.

In fact, virtually all writing has a rhetorical purpose. If authors aim to describe a place, person, or object, they try to recreate the look, the sound, the smell, the taste, and the feel of things. If their purpose is to tell a story, they narrate an event or a sequence of events by selecting and arranging particulars, usually in the order they occurred. An author with a point to make may take a position and offer reasons to support it. Whatever the mode, the author's choice of words, syntax (order of words and phrases), sentence sound and structure, the sequence of ideas, the selection of details—all these elements and more are meant to serve the purpose of the whole.

The purpose is often more complex than simply conveying an experience or telling a story. Authors may, for example, want to stimulate certain responses in their readers, who may react to a vivid re-creation of an experience as though they themselves had the experience: they may laugh out loud, become tense or frightened, weep, grow angry. A biographer may want to communicate the facts of his subject's life. A. Scott Berg, for instance, wrote a prize-winning biography of Charles Lindbergh. In doing so, Berg established a tone that revealed his own thoughts about Lindbergh. In laying out the facts about the individual, he also meant to convince the reader that Lindbergh was both an admirable and a reprehensible figure. He wants us to admire and despise the man at the same time, just as he, the biographer, does. Notice how the rhetoric used by a reviewer of Berg's book highlights both sides of Lindbergh, the man:

> Charles Lindbergh's one-man flight from New York to Paris in 1927 made him the most admired man on earth, and the kidnapping and death of his firstborn son won him the world's sympathy in 1932. But after Pearl Harbor, memories of his obdurate opposition to American intervention in the war against Hitler caused millions to see him as a Nazi sympathizer, a defeatist, perhaps even a traitor. "Imagine," his sister-in-law wrote, "in just 15 years he had gone from Jesus to Judas."

Language molds the reader's attitude toward the subject discussed. And tone determines precisely what that attitude will be.

Of course, a writer's attitude toward the subject is not necessarily identical with the response of the reader. An advertising copywriter for Nike may be totally indifferent to the shoes he crows about, but since his job is to make readers feel a certain way, he purposefully uses words to produce a particular response—namely, to turn readers into consumers of Nike products.

Tone

In the multiple-choice section of the exam, you will certainly need to deal with tone. One of the most common questions asks you to identify the tone of a passage, a sentence, or even a single word or phrase. To answer the question you will need a sense of the narrator's or speaker's attitude toward the subject of the passage. This may differ from the author's attitude, of course. An author may portray a scoundrel in a favorable way, but that doesn't necessarily mean the author has a soft spot in his heart for scoundrels.

Because an author's tone may be complex or may shift part way through a passage or poem, it can be described in innumerable ways, often by one or more adjectives. For example,

Negative

bitter	facetious	patronizing	scornful
condescending	flippant	pedantic	teasing
contemptuous	indignant	petty	threatening
disdainful	irreverent	sarcastic	
disgusted	mocking	satiric	

Positive

benevolent	ecstatic	enthusiastic	learned
compassionate	effusive	hopeful	supportive
determined	elegiac	laudatory	sympathetic

Neutral

bantering	detached	informal	scholarly
colloquial	didactic	objective	
confident	factual	restrained	

Words themselves and the manner in which they are expressed work together to establish the tone. Consider the simple question, "Who are you?" Depending on the tone in which the words are expressed, the question may be funny, sassy, inquisitive, challenging. Because the inflection of the speaker's voice is not available to writers, they must rely more on diction—the writer's choice of words, including figures of speech—to establish a tone. The differences between "Shut your mouth," "Please keep still," and "Would you be kind enough not to talk now?" are apparent. In a general sense the three sentences mean the same thing. The tone in each, however, could hardly differ more, because the words chosen to convey the meaning evoke very different feelings.

While the form of sentences significantly influences tone, other rhetorical elements also play a major part, especially diction, metaphors, and other figures of speech such as symbols and allusions. One way an author reveals tone is by the form of sentences.

In essence, tone is the psychological quality of the words.

EXCLAMATORY SENTENCES

An exclamatory sentence expresses a wish, a desire, a command—and is often, but not always, indicated with an exclamation point:

> Heads up!
>
> May the Force be with you!
>
> Have a nice day!

Such sentences can express various gradations of begging, beseeching, praying, imploring, apologizing, requesting, advising, commanding, persuading, and so on. "Let the word go forth," intoned John F. Kennedy in his inauguration address, "that the torch has been passed to a new generation . . . ." Kennedy's inspirational tone is initiated by the use of the imperative verb *let*. The highsounding verb *go forth* and the metaphorical use of *torch* also contribute a sense of mission to the mood of the occasion.

INTERROGATIVE SENTENCES

An *interrogative* sentence also offers a writer a variety of tones. Questions are usually asked in order to obtain information: "When is the next train to Mount Kisco?" But the tone of a question can also be:

> A CHALLENGE: Who are you calling a nerd, Mac?
> A DENIAL: Do you actually think that I'm capable of such a thing?
> DISBELIEF: Can you believe the nerve of that driver?
> HESITATION: Do you really think I should step off the edge of the cliff?

and so on.

On the AP exam, you're also likely to be asked about rhetorical questions—questions whose answers are implied by the questions themselves. Used in an argument, a rhetorical question calls attention to an obvious proposition—or it can be used to make an argument more dramatic and convincing. The author of the following uses a series of questions and answers, structured somewhat like a dialogue:

When our ancestors condemned a woman for one crime, they considered that by this single judgment she was convicted of many transgressions. How so? Judged unchaste, she was also deemed guilty of poisoning. Why? Because, having sold her body to the basest passion, she had to live in fear of many persons. Who are these? Her husband, her parents, and the others . . . .

DECLARATIVE SENTENCES

A *declarative* sentence, the most common form of sentence, makes a factual statement. Unlike exclamatory and interrogative sentences, the declarative sentence does not blatantly reveal its tone. Much of the time, the tone of a declarative sentence is neutral. It merely states information in a matter-of-fact way:

In 1897, Columbia University moved from 49th Street and Madison Avenue, where it had stood for 40 years, to its present location on Morningside Heights at 116th Street and Broadway.

While this matter-of-fact tone is prevalent in scientific and other informational prose, declarative sentences can also be highly charged with emotion:

People who knew the American novelist Thomas Wolfe recall that he habitually roamed down the long aisles of the library stacks, grabbing one book after the other from the shelves and devouring its contents as if he were a starving man suddenly let loose in an immense storehouse of food. He wrote with abandon, turning out incredible quantities of manuscript, filling whole packing cases with the product of his frenzied pen.

On the surface, this may seem like a factual description of Thomas Wolfe. The writer is informing us that Wolfe read many books and wrote prodigiously. But the words create a portrait of an awe-inspiring, larger-than-life figure. The simile, "as if he were a starving man suddenly let loose in an immense storehouse of food," while possibly overstating Wolfe's behavior in the library, does not exaggerate the passion Wolfe evidently felt for reading books.

SENTENCE LENGTH

Sentences can vary in length between one word ("Walk!") and hundreds, even thousands, of words. Usually, the complexity of an idea determines sentence length, but not always. Profound ideas can also be expressed in very few words: "I think, therefore I am."

On the AP exam you could be asked why an author may have chosen to write very long sentences or why the author put a short sentence in a particular place or wrote a whole string of very short sentences. In general, long sentences allow authors to differentiate important ideas from less important ideas. Material in subordinate clauses, appositives, or any other secondary sentence element receives less emphasis than an idea expressed in the main clause. On the other hand, when an author uses several brief sentences in a row, no one sentence stands out. All are equally emphatic, and a thoughtful author most likely has a rhetorical reason for structuring a passage that way.

Short sentences are easier to grasp. A short sentence makes its point quickly and often with considerable force, as in this sample passage about authors and critics:

> A person who pries into the private lives of others, with no other motive but to discover their faults and tell the world about them, deserves a name that can't be published here, just like a reviewer who reads books with an eye toward destroying the reputation of the author. Both are odious vermin.

The blunt closing sentence produces a mild jolt, especially because it sits next to a windy 50-word sentence. The effect is intentional.

SENTENCE STRUCTURE

Experienced writers know how sentence parts should be arranged to convey meaning and affect a reader's response to the sentence. Of the three main sections of a sentence—the beginning, the middle, and the end—the end is the best place for emphasizing an idea. Why? Because the reader comes to a very brief stop at the end of a sentence—brief, but still long enough for the last idea to sink in.

TIP

To emphasize an idea, save it for the end of a sentence.

This principle underlies the use of so-called *periodic* sentences—sentences that save the most important idea for the end. Compare these two sentences:

1. A harmful economic system develops when a worker cannot get a job that pays a enough to support a family
2. When a worker cannot get a job that pays enough to support a family, a harmful economic system develops.

Both sentences state their point clearly, but if the writer wanted to stress that certain conditions lead to a destructive economic system, the second sentence does it more emphatically. In sentence 1, the main point is stated first but is then pushed into the background by the example of the underpaid worker.

What distinguishes a periodic sentence from its opposite, the *loose* sentence, is that its thought is not completed until the end. In a way, the reader is held in suspense. The loose sentence, in contrast, gives away its "secret" at the start. It follows the most common structure of English sentences: subject-verb, as in *Geraldo texted*, or subject-verb-object: *Geraldo used his new iPhone.*

As you probably know, every sentence has a main clause consisting of at least a subject and a verb. That's all a *simple* sentence needs to be complete—a subject and a verb. Even if many modifiers and objects are added, it still remains a *simple* sentence.

For example, both of the following sentences, despite the disparity in their length, are *simple* sentences:

Berkeley admitted Freda.

Situated on the eastern side of San Francisco Bay, Berkeley, the University of California's flagship institution, admitted Freda as a freshman in the class of 2021, to the delight not only of Freda herself but to the satisfaction of her family, teachers, and friends.

Leaving aside the wordiness and wisdom of including so much miscellaneous information in the second sentence, you still find a simple declarative sentence—*Berkeley admitted Freda*—lurking within its jumble of modifiers, participles, prepositional phrases, and appositives.

To turn a *simple* sentence into a *compound* sentence, add a conjunction, a word like *and* or *but,* as in

Berkeley admitted Freda and she was delighted.

You can infer from this example that a *compound* sentence is made up of at least two simple sentences joined by a conjunction. What is rhetorically noteworthy about a compound sentence is that the author gives more or less equal emphasis to the information in each of the clauses. Clauses of equal rank and structure are called *coordinate clauses* and are joined by *coordinating conjunctions* (*and, but, or, nor, yet, so*) and sometimes by a semicolon with connective words like *however, moreover, nevertheless, otherwise, therefore, consequently,* and others. In this case, whether logical or not, Freda's acceptance has been given equal importance to her reaction to the news.

If the author's intent, however, is to emphasize Sarah's state of mind, the sentence might best be turned into a *complex* sentence—that is, a sentence that contains both a subordinate and a main clause:

TIP

By carefully structuring sentences, you can emphasize some ideas and de-emphasize others.

Because Berkeley admitted her, Freda was delighted. (Subordinate clause italicized)

Here, the cause-and-effect relationship between the two ideas is made clearer. The addition of a subordinating conjunction *because* gives prominence to the information in the main, or independent, clause. (Other widely used subordinating conjunctions include *although, before, even though, while, unless, if,* and *when.*)

THE SOUND OF SENTENCES

Some AP exam questions may well ask you to consider the sounds found in a passage. For one, you should recognize **onomatopoeia**—words that imitate the sound they describe. Is there a more expressive word than *moan*, for example, to make the sound of . . . well, a moan? Similarly, *murmur* resembles the sound of a murmur. And other words, too—*boom, buzz, clang, crack,* and so on—all echo their sense.

You should also be attuned to **alliteration,** the repetition of initial sounds in words and syllables, as in *Peter Piper picked a peck of pickled peppers.* Sometimes such repetition is for ornament, but authors sometimes use it for emphasis as in such words as *flim-flam* and phrases such as *fickle fortune* and *bed and breakfast.* (*Turn to the Glossary, page 389, for definitions of other terms related to sound:* assonance, consonance, *and* rhyme.)

Unlike rhythm in music, the **rhythm** of prose is more subtle. Rhythmic sentences don't have a foot-tapping beat, but they often possess a graceful combination of sounds, accents, phrases, and pauses. Authors intentionally use rhythm to arouse emotions. In fact, rhythm can have at least as much power as well-chosen words to create an emotional effect. A passage that is meant to create a sense of peace and calm demands a slow, even rhythm, as in this sample of prose from the pen of the American naturalist/writer Edward Abbey. Describing early morning in the desert, he writes:

> The sun is not yet in sight but signs of the advent are plain to see. Lavender clouds sail like a fleet of ships across the pale green dawn; each cloud, planed flat on the wind, has a base of fiery gold. Southeast, twenty miles by line of sight, stand the peaks of the Sierra La Sal, twelve to thirteen thousand feet above sea level, all covered with snow and rosy in the morning sunlight. The air is dry and clear as well as cold; the last fogbanks left over from last night's storm are scudding away like ghosts, fading into nothing before the wind and the sunrise.

In an entirely different mood, Abbey writes on the topic "Transcendence":

It is this which haunts me night and day. The desire to transcend my own limits, to exceed myself, to become more than I am. How? I don't know. To transcend this job, this work, this place, this kind of life—for the sake of something superlative, supreme, exalting. But where? Again, how? Don't know. It will come of itself . . . like lightning, like rain, like God's gift of grace, in its own good time. (If it comes at all.)

In this passage, the inner turmoil Abbey feels about himself is revealed in the short, choppy phrases, the combination of questions and fragmentary sentences, and the clipped rhythm of his thoughts.

A typical question on the exam may ask about the effects of rhythm in a passage. Perhaps the author intentionally used it to arouse emotions.

Diction

Diction, or word choice, is one of the elements of style that gives each person's writing a quality that is is uniquely his or her own. Diction determines whether an author has succeeded in communicating a particular message to a particular audience. In the following passage, from an article titled "Fenimore Cooper's Literary Offenses," Mark Twain comments on the diction of a well-regarded American writer.

> An author's diction, or word choice, is crucial. It determines tone, creates effects, and ultimately conveys meaning for the reader.

Cooper's word sense was singularly dull. When a person has a poor ear for music, he will flat and sharp right along without knowing it. He keeps near the tune, but it is not the tune. When a person has a poor ear for words, the result is a literary flatting and sharping; you perceive what he is intending to say, but you also perceive that he doesn't say it. This is Cooper. He was not a word musician. His ear was satisfied with the approximate word. I will furnish some circumstantial evidence in support of this charge. My instances are gathered from half a dozen pages of the tale called Deerslayer. He used "verbal" for "oral"; "precision" for "facility"; "phenomena" for "marvels"; "necessary" for "predetermined"; "unsophisticated" for "primitive"; "preparation" for "expectancy"; "rebuked" for "subdued"; "dependent on" for "resulting from"; "fact" for "condition"; . . . "brevity" for "celerity"; "distrusted" for "suspicious"; "mental imbecility" for "imbecility"; "eyes" for "sight"; "counteracting" for "opposing"; . . . . There have been daring people in the world who claimed that Cooper could write English, but they're all dead now.

Apparently, Cooper's diction left much to be desired. In Twain's view, Cooper was insensitive to the connotation of many, many words. "The difference between the right word and the approximate word," wrote Twain, "is the difference between 'lightning' and 'lightning bug.'" Presumably, Cooper's prose is full of bugs. He may well have known the definitions of words, but he had a so-called tin ear when it came to understanding the words in context. He seems deaf to the feelings that words represent, and, therefore, chose his words badly.

Authors usually can select from several possibilities words that are best suited to their purposes. For instance:

insult/slur, spit/expectorate, complain/gripe, excellent/superior, eat/stuff one's face

The words in each pair mean more or less the same thing, but none is a perfect synonym for another. Some are plain, others are fancy. Some are clinical, euphemistic, or slang; each has a distinct connotation.

Connotation

Words derive their connotation from two sources: people's common experience and an individual's personal experience. Words represent not only ideas, events, and objects, but also the feelings we attach to ideas, events, and objects. Thus, the word *rat* represents a certain kind of rodent—among other things. That is its *denotative* meaning. But a rat also evokes in us feelings of fear and disgust—its *connotation*. What is true of *rat* is also true of countless other words: *mother, home, candy, money, grease, America, dog,* and so on. They all evoke feelings and ideas.

Connotations may change over time, and our personal experience often adds connotative value to words that may at first mean nothing beyond their definition. Scientific words that at one time merely named physical phenomena or technical achievements—*cloning, abortion, www.com*—have since acquired rich connotative meanings.

Really good descriptive writing often gets its power from the author's choice of connotative words. The more closely you read a passage, the more you may enjoy it. Notice how the following passage employs connotation to create a graphic impression of a very agreeable place:

> There couldn't be a more idyllic spot in May than Albion, on the Mendocino coast. The land, strung between redwood groves and sea, is lush with flowers. Summer crowds are weeks away, and it's still possible to find a quiet beach or stroll the cliffs above the ocean without seeing another soul. Four miles from the coastal highway, the road narrows, loses its paving, and curves into the woods. A graveled driveway winds to a graceful country house close to a pond and surrounded by park-like grounds. A trellis of interlocking timbers draped with vines leads to the front door of the house. A Chinese lantern hangs overhead. From high on a post a clay mask stares at passersby. Pieces of driftwood lie on a wooden bench weathered to a silver-grey. Attention has been paid to make visitors feel welcome.

In familiar but carefully chosen words the author of the passage has conveyed the pleasure of visiting Albion—a feeling he wants his readers to share. References to things that most people enjoy and value—redwood groves, flowers, a quiet beach, a country house—create a sense of peace and contentment.

Metaphorical Language

Because figures of speech often reveal an author's tone, be prepared to deal with questions that refer to the most common figures of speech found in non-fiction prose:

- ✔ Metaphor
- ✔ Simile
- ✔ Allusion
- ✔ Analogy
- ✔ Metonymy
- ✔ Synecdoche

As a group, these figures of speech constitute what might be called generally *metaphorical language.*

Metaphorical language functions as a means of making comparisons.

When an author can't find the exact words to describe a feeling or to capture experiences that seem almost inexpressible, a metaphor may come to the rescue: "She has a voice of gold," says the music critic, using a metaphor to express not only the beauty of her voice but also its value. Indeed, in a particular context the metaphor could mean that the singer makes big money with her voice. Figures of speech are economical. They condense a lot of thought and feeling into a few words. Ernie Pyle, a famous World War II war correspondent, reported his stories as though they were being told by the average GI lying in a foxhole. He said, "I write from a worm's eye point of view." The idea gives a fresh slant to an old expression and cogently fixes Pyle's position on the battlefield.

Because metaphorical language evokes mental images, it has a good deal to do with the emotional content of a piece of writing. An author relying on trite, second-hand expressions to convey an idea, using such metaphors as *walking on air* or *life in the fast lane*, apparently has nothing new or surprising to say. On the other hand, an author who fills a passage with fresh metaphorical language may give readers rich new insights and understandings.

ALLUSION

An allusion—an implied or direct reference to something in history or culture—is, like a richly connotative word, a means to suggest far more than it says. An allusion of a single word or phrase can expand the reader's understanding more completely than a long, discursive comparison. Take, for example, Robert Frost's poem "Out, Out . . .," a narrative poem that recounts a farmyard accident that kills a young boy. A theme of the poem, the uncertainty and unpredictability of life, is alluded to in the title, which you may know comes from Macbeth's soliloquy upon hearing of his wife's death: "Out, out, brief candle./Life's but a walking shadow, . . ." Macbeth's speech is a reflection on both the tragedy of a premature death and the impermanence of life. While readers unfamiliar with *Macbeth* might read "Out, Out . . ." with insight and empathy, understanding the allusion to Shakespeare's play enriches the experience.

Literature isn't the only source of allusions. History, religion, politics, sports—almost every human endeavor can spawn allusions. Think of the origin and implications of such metaphorical allusions as a football team that "sinks like the *Titanic*," your "hitting a homerun" on a math test, a scandal termed "Irangate," and and nicknaming a malevolent and tyrannical school principal "Lord Voltemart."

Such metaphors are potent when used well, but metaphorical language that seems inappropriate to the general tone and purpose of the passage will grate on readers and weaken the overall effect that the author has in mind. It also suggests that the author lacks a clear sense of purpose or just doesn't know how to achieve a particular purpose. Take, for example, this attempt to describe how memories of childhood fade with the passing of time:

> As you grow older, your memory of childhood is obliterated like a bus blown to bits by a terrorist.

Isn't it obvious that the author missed the point? After all, memories fade slowly, not cataclysmically. Whatever tone the author may have intended is lost in the incongruity of the simile. A more appropriate way to capture the idea that memories erode gradually might be:

> As you grow older, memories of childhood vanish like sand dunes at the edge of the sea.

Of course, there may be another possibility. Perhaps the author wrote an incongruous metaphor for a particular purpose. To heighten interest, authors often try to surprise their readers. They introduce an inappropriate or contradictory metaphor, for instance, for the sake

Figures of speech have the power to make something clearer or more vivid, or to turn a vague impression into something concrete.

TIP

Good writers choose metaphors carefully.

of contrast. They invent a figure of speech with a connotation that is off kilter in order to create a kind of tension or to make an ironic or amusing comment.

During the Spanish Civil War, Ernest Hemingway, writing a dispatch from the front lines, said of the enemy planes, "If their orders are to strafe the road on their way home, you will get it [be wounded or killed]. Otherwise, when they are finished with their jobs on a particular objective, they go off like bank clerks, flying home." The comparison of deadly fighters and bank clerks may seem frivolous, but it does make the point effectively. Both are eager to scurry away from their jobs as quickly as possible. Moreover, by contrasting bank clerks—generally harmless, well-meaning functionaries—with ruthless fighters, Hemingway heightens the viciousness of the enemy aircraft strafing the people on the road.

ANALOGY

Another form of comparison is the *analogy*, usually defined in words like these: *A comparison of two objects or situations that have several common characteristics*. An extended analogy, showing parallels between two unlike things, can simplify a complicated idea and leave a powerful impression on a reader. Consider the tone established in the following excerpt from a speech by President Woodrow Wilson:

> I had a couple of friends who were in the habit of losing their tempers, and when they lost their tempers they were in the habit of using very unparliamentary language. Some of their friends induced them to make a promise that they never would swear inside the town limits. When the impulse next came upon them, they took a street car to go out of town to swear, and by the time they got out of town they did not want to swear . . . . Now, illustrating the great by the small, that is true of the passions of nations.

Wilson used this analogy in support of his position that a country must not jump into a war in the heat of passion. By using colloquial words (e.g., "a couple of friends") and telling a personal anecdote, Wilson established a folksy tone. The analogy, which would be accessible to every listener, draws on everyday experience, and makes good common sense. Wilson, in effect, has taken on the persona of one of the guys. Neither moralistic nor panicky, he creates the image of a fellow whose judgment the country can trust in a crisis.

METONYMY

An author's use of metonymy and synecdoche also contributes to the establishment of tone. Unlike metaphors, which make comparisons, these two figures of speech make substitutions—usually something abstract for something concrete (or vice versa), a container for the thing contained (or vice versa), a part for the whole, a cause for the effect, and so on.

In the statement, "Gilberto has a good head," the word *head* has been substituted for *brain* (the container for the thing contained). But *head* also means "IQ" or "intelligence"—both abstract concepts that are made more tangible by the use of *head*. To some degree, metonymy can simplify an idea—unlike a metaphor, which tends to complicate a thought—particularly when a concrete substitution is made for an abstraction, as in "Your hands made you rich," in which the word *hands* means occupation, trade, or line of work.

TIP

In general, metonymy tends to bring a kind of vitality to a phrase or idea.

SYNECDOCHE

Synecdoche is a type of metonymy, in which a part is substituted for the whole, or vice versa. Any time you use the word *sail* for ship ("A fleet of a hundred sails"), or call a truck an *eighteen-wheeler,* you are using synecdoche. When Hamlet is about to remove the body of Polonius from Gertrude's bedchamber, he says, "I'll lug the guts into the neighbor room." His synecdoche *guts* clearly stands for corpse, but its connotation also suggests the disdain that Hamlet felt for Polonius. Indeed, both metonymy and synecdoche can be rich with implied meaning.

As you consider the metaphorical language in passages on the AP exam, keep in mind the passages' purpose and tone. Ask yourself whether each figure of speech is appropriate, and how it contributes to or detracts from the reader's response.

Footnotes

Three or four questions on the exam ask you to interpret information found in the footnotes and/or a bibliography that accompanies one of the passages. Footnoting is basically a shorthand method for giving readers detailed information about where the author found specific material used in the passage. A bibliography is more general. It lists the works the author cited or consulted while doing research. Not every system presents information in exactly the same format, but they all give readers essentially the same information.

For example, here are **standard forms for citing books**:

Author's Name, Title of Book (Place of Publication: Publisher, Year), Page Number.

Michael André Bernstein, Conspirators (New York: Picador, 2014), p. 223.

The same form is used for **a book with two or more authors**. The authors' names are listed in the same order as on the book's title page:

Richard Polay and Mark Restaino, Wines of the World (Sacramento: Prima, 2011), p. 76.

If a book has four or more authors, however, only the first author is named. The co-authors are listed as "*et al.,*" meaning *and others.*

Dick Burns, et al., Old Kew Gardens: A History (New York: Metro Avenue Press, 2012).

In a **book with an editor but no author**, the name of the editor is listed first and is followed by *(ed.)* as in

Matthew Speier (ed.), Fighting for Peace (Vancouver: Alt Green Press, 2006).

In a **book with an editor and an author**, the author's name is listed first, as in

Miles Hochman, Soap, Ed. Robert Moseman (Ossining, NY, 2002), p. 50.

Some books—as well as shorter works—are published without saying who wrote it. Such a work is cited this way:

Atlas of the World's Biggest Harbors (New York: Allison Press 2004).

Sometimes a corporation or organization takes credit for writing a work, as in

League of Veterans, The March of Patriots (Gettysburg, PA, 2013).

For a work published in an anthology or other book:

Author's Name, "Title of Article," Title of Book, Name of Editor (Place of Publication: Publisher, Year), Page Number.

Lucinda Goo, "Spectral Realities," Nineteenth Century Plein Air Painting, ed. P. J. Steadman (White Plains, NY: Windmill Books, 2013), p. 333.

A passage may use material from a book's introduction, preface, forward, or an afterword written by someone other than the author of the book:

Kenneth Iverson, preface to Safe No More by Walter Lipow (New York: Victory Press, 2003), p. xi.

For material that comes from a multi-volume work, the number of the volume must be included, as in

Alberto Gilbert, The Rise and Fall of Ancient Rome (Chicago: Lakeshore Press, 2006), Vol. 3, p. 332.

Writers sometime refer to material they found printed in a second-hand source. Say, for example, that Book A contains an excerpt from Book B, and a writer quotes part of the excerpt in a passage. Because the writer didn't get the material directly from Book B, a footnote must cite both Book A and Book B. The excerpt is listed first, its source second.

Margorie Mottus, The Cliff Walker, as published in Rudolph Schmidt, Dangerous Pursuits (New York: Beverly Publishers, 1999), p. 56.

For articles printed in magazines, newspapers, and other periodicals:

Author's Name, "Title of Article," Title of Periodical, Volume Number and/or (Date), Page Number.

Lilah Collins, "The Fairyland Myth," The Montclarion (June 5, 2006), p. 60.

If you run into a footnote that seems incomplete—the author's name may be omitted, for example—the writer of the passage may have cited the name in the text, and there is no need to repeat it in a footnote. Likewise, you may occasionally run into a footnote consisting only of the author's last name and a page number, as in

Altick, p. 35.

An abbreviated note often signifies that information about Altick's work was given earlier in the article or chapter. Therefore, it's pointless to repeat it. If, however, the writer of the passage has used more than one of Altick's works, the footnote needs to specify which title is now being referred to, as in

Altick, Preface to Critical Reading, p. 43.

Occasionally, you may encounter a footnote containing multiple titles. This tells you that the writer of the passage probably found two or more sources containing similar, if not identical, material:

Micaela DiGennaro, "Teaching Wharton's The Age of Innocence," Modern Literary Studies, Vol 16 (2014), p. 455.

Joseph Downey, "Wharton's Age of Anxiety," Guide to Literary Theory, November 14, 2010, Columbia University, accessed March 18, 2006, *http://apps.columbia.edu/resource/library/5589*

Documentation of scholarly journals, such as those named in the previous footnote, usually include a volume number and/or issue number. Page numbers may also be cumulative, so that the first issue in a calendar year may contain pages 1–200, the next issue starts on page 201, etc.

ELECTRONIC SOURCES

Contemporary passages often cite electronic sources—e-mails, social networks, YouTube, texts, and especially the Internet. Because websites don't always publish complete information about themselves, citations will vary, but you're apt to find at least a few of the following:

- Name of website
- Name of author and/or editor
- Title of article
- Title of online publication
- Institution/organization sponsoring site
- The date material was posted on the web/date of revisions
- Date that the author of the passage accessed the material
- URL

For example:

"Find the Right College for You," CollegeBoard.com, posted March 2014; accessed March 28, 2014, http://apps.collegeboard.com/search/index/jsp.

TECHNIQUES FOR TACKLING READING PASSAGES

Directions: *Questions 1–8.* Carefully read the following passage and answer the accompanying questions.

This passage comes from the autobiography of Edward Bok, an American journalist. In 1870, at age seven, Bok emigrated to the United States from Holland. He and his family settled in Brooklyn. This excerpt recounts boyhood experiences.

PASSAGE 1

The elder Bok did not find his "lines cast in pleasant places" in the United States. He found himself, professionally, unable to adjust the methods of his own land and of a lifetime to those of a new country. As a result the fortunes of the transplanted
Line family did not flourish, and Edward soon saw his mother physically failing under
(5) burdens to which her nature was not accustomed nor her hands trained. Then he and his brother decided to relieve their mother in the housework by rising early in the morning, building the fire, preparing breakfast, and washing the dishes before they went to school. After school they gave up their play hours, and swept and scrubbed, and helped their mother to prepare the evening meal and wash the dishes
(10) afterward. It was a curious coincidence that it should fall upon Edward thus to get a first-hand knowledge of woman's housework which was to stand him in such practical stead in later years.

It was not easy for the parents to see their boys thus forced to do work which only a short while before had been done by servants. And the capstone of humiliation (15) seemed to be when Edward and his brother, after having for several mornings found no kindling wood or coal to build a fire, decided to go out evenings with a basket and pick up what would they could find in neighboring lots, and the bits of coal spilled from the coal-bin of the grocery store, or left on the curbs before houses where coal had been delivered. The mother remonstrated with the boys, although in her heart (20) she knew that the necessity was upon them. But Edward had been started upon his Americanization career, and answered: "This is America, where one can do anything if it is honest. So long as we don't steal wood or coal, why shouldn't we get it?" And, turning away, the saddened mother said nothing.

But while doing these homely chores was very effective in relieving the untrained (25) and tired mother, it added little to the family income. Edward looked about and decided that the time had come for him, young as he was, to begin some sort of wage-earning. But how and where? The answer he found one afternoon when he was standing before the shop-window of a baker in the neighborhood. The owner of the bakery, who had just placed in the window a series of trays filled with buns, tarts, and (30) pies, came outside to look at the display. He found the hungry boy wistfully regarding the tempting-looking wares.

"Look pretty good, don't they?" asked the baker.

"They would," answered the Dutch boy with his national passion for cleanliness, "if your window were clean."

(35) "That's so, too," mused the baker. "Perhaps you'll clean it."

"I will," was the laconic reply. And Edward Bok, there and then, got his first job. He went in, found a step-ladder, and put so much Dutch energy into the cleaning of the large shop-window that the baker immediately arranged with him to clean it every Tuesday and Friday afternoon after school. The salary was to be fifty cents per week!

1. The events described in the passage are narrated by

   (A) one of Edward's parents.
   (B) Edward himself.
   (C) Edward's brother.
   (D) a participant in the events.
   (E) an outside observer.

Explanation

Questions that ask you to identify or characterize the speaker in a passage appear regularly on the AP exam. To determine the identity of the speaker in any passage, look first for pronoun usage. A passage written in the first person—that is, using "*I*" or "*we*"—clearly indicates that the speaker is writing from his or her own point of view. (Note that the speaker may or may not be be the same person as the author; authors often invent speakers whose words are used in the passage.)

In this case, the author has chosen a narrator who speaks with the voice of someone who knows all the details but plays no part in the events—in other words, an omniscient observer. When you consider that the passage is autobiographical, Bok has made an unusual choice: By using the third person ("*he*") he writes as though Edward were someone other than himself.

Choice (E) is the best answer.

2. Which of the following phrases does the author use to illustrate that the elder Bok failed to find his "lines cast in pleasant places" (line 1)?

    (A) "professionally, unable to adjust" (line 2)
    (B) "transplanted family" (lines 3–4)
    (C) "physically failing" (line 4)
    (D) "her nature was not accustomed" (line 5)
    (E) "capstone of humiliation" (line 14)

Explanation

Because the phrase "lines cast in pleasant places" is a quotation, it is safe to assume that it refers to something that was said or something that occurred earlier in the story. It might have been used, for example, when the family arrived in America and Mr. Bok optimistically began searching for a job. Regardless of its precise context, the opening sentence of the passage implies that Mr. Bok experienced some sort of disappointment. Two reasons are given to explain the cause: (1) the family's fortunes "did not flourish," and (2) Mr. Bok's old-world professional methods were incompatible with his new environment.

(A) therefore, is the best answer.

(B) is not related to Mr. Bok's discontent.

(C) and (D) refer only to Mrs. Bok.

(E) relates to both of Edward's parents, not only to Mr. Bok.

3. Which of the following best describes the rhetorical function of the last sentence of the first paragraph (lines 10–12)?

    (A) It changes the tone of the passage from serious to lighthearted.
    (B) It contrasts the personalities of Edward and his brother.
    (C) It explains the general significance of the details contained in the paragraph.
    (D) It describes the state of the family's poverty.
    (E) It hints at a dilemma that will become important later in the story.

Explanation

To answer a question about the *rhetorical function* of a sentence, you must try to define what that sentence contributes to the passage. Also ask what it adds to the meaning of the passage and whether it affects the author's tone. Does it help to develop the purpose of the passage, or does the sentence help the author achieve a particular effect? In short, you must analyze the role that the sentence plays in the passage.

Much of the first paragraph details the chores performed by Edward and his brother. The last sentence draws a conclusion about the boys' efforts, saying, in effect, that Edward's work was preparing him for the future.

(A) is incorrect because the tone of the passage remains consistent.

(B) doesn't apply because we don't learn much about the brother except that he worked alongside Edward.

(D) should be rejected because the sentence has no relevance to the poverty of the family.

(E) may be a tempting answer because of the phrase "later years," but the sentence contains no hint of a dilemma.

(C) is the best answer.

4. In line 13, "work" refers to which of the following?

    I. fixing breakfast before school (line 7)
    II. washing the dinner dishes (line 9)
    III. picking up bits of spilled coal (lines 16–19)

    (A) I only
    (B) III only
    (C) I and III only
    (D) I and II only
    (E) I, II, and III

Explanation

Before answering this question you should read the entire sentence in which the word "work" appears. Note that the work in question had once been done by servants—presumably the servants who worked for the family back in Holland. Nothing in the passage, however, suggests that the servants went out looking for coal. Note also that the sentence contains the phrase "thus forced," indicating that *work* refers to something stated earlier in the passage. Because the boys' decision to go out looking for pieces of coal comes later (lines 16–19), the *work* alluded to does not include item III.

5. In context, the expression "necessity was upon them" (line 20) is best interpreted as having which of the following meanings?

    (A) It didn't matter.
    (B) Things would never be the same.
    (C) The time had come to meet the challenge.
    (D) It was all in a day's work.
    (E) It could not be helped.

Explanation

Mrs. Bok found it difficult to permit her sons to scour the neighborhood for scraps of wood and coal, but circumstances prevented her from doing anything about it.

Only (E) expresses the idea that she had no choice but to accept the boys' decision.

6. Edward can best be described as a person who

    (A) is determined to go into business for himself.
    (B) has made up his mind not to follow in his father's footsteps.
    (C) believes that honesty is the best policy.
    (D) is quick to seize opportunities that come his way.
    (E) can be counted on to keep his word.

Explanation

Much of the passage is devoted to a description of Edward's energy and initiative. Whether he is out scrounging for bits of coal and wood or talking his way into a part-time job as a window washer, he uses his quick mind to get ahead.

    (A) cannot be the correct answer. Even though Edward seems to be very ambitious, the passage does not contain enough information to support it.

    (B) is not mentioned in the passage.

    (C) is probably true, but Edward's honesty is not emphasized in the passage.

    (D) accurately describes one of Edward's most important traits.

    (E) may also be valid, but Edward's integrity is not discussed.

7. Which of the following themes best serves to unify the passage?

    (A) The rundown neighborhood in which the Boks lived
    (B) A passion for cleanliness
    (C) A closely-knit family
    (D) The difficulty of assimilating into American life
    (E) The generation gap between the Bok parents and children

Explanation

    (A) is not a valid choice because the passage does not describe the neighborhood.

    (C) is implied, but is not significant enough to contribute to the unity of the passage.

    (D) and (E) are not discussed in the passage.

    (B) is the best choice. Edward's "passion for cleanliness" is suggested by his after-school sweeping and scrubbing of the house (lines 8–10), by the fact that his knowledge of housework will "stand him in such practical stead in later years" (lines 11–12), and by his acquisition of a job as the bakery's window cleaner.

8. The style of the passage as a whole can best be characterized as

    (A) descriptive and informal.
    (B) abstract and profound.
    (C) plain and analytical.
    (D) subtle and inspirational.
    (E) symbolic and sentimental.

Explanation

Each choice consists of two adjectives. For a choice to be correct, both adjectives must accurately describe the style of the passage.

(B) is an unlikely choice because the passage is full of concrete detail. Nor does it contains profound thoughts and ideas.

(C), (D), and (E) all contain adjectives that characterize the passage: plain, inspirational, and sentimental. But the other adjective in each pair does not apply.

(A) is the best choice, for the author takes pains to describe the plight of the Bok family and what Edward and his brother do to help. The last section of the passage describes what Edward does and says while looking for a job. The story is told in a friendly, casual manner. Note, for example, that several sentences start with "But" and "And"—just one characteristic of informal, conversational prose.

Directions: *Questions 9–17.* Carefully read the following passage and answer the accompanying questions.

This passage, written in the 1960s, is from an anthology on the history of violence in America.

PASSAGE 2

Unquestionably the longest and most remorseless war in American history was the one between whites and Indians that began in Tidewater, Virginia, in 1607 and continued with only temporary truces for nearly 300 years down to the final mas-
Line sacre at Wounded Knee, South Dakota in 1890. The implacable hostility that came to
(5) rule white-Indian relations was by no means inevitable. The small Indian population that existed in the continental United States allowed plenty of room for expansion of white settlement. The economic resources of the white settlers were such that the Indians could have been easily and fairly reimbursed for the land needed for occupation by the whites. In fact, a model of peaceful white-Indian relations was
(10) developed in 17th-century New England by John Eliot, Roger Williams, and other Puritan statesmen. The same was true in 18th-century Pennsylvania, where William Penn's humane and equitable policy toward the Indians brought that colony decades of white-Indian amity.[1] Racial prejudice and greed in the mass of New England whites finally reaped the whirlwind in King Phillip's War of 1675–76, which shattered
(15) the peaceful New England model.[2] Much later the same sort of thing happened in Pennsylvania in 1763 when Pontiac's Rebellion (preceded by increasing tensions) ended the era of amicable white-Indian relations in the Keystone colony.

Other Indian wars proliferated during the 17th and 18th centuries, nor did the pace of the conflict slacken in the 19th century. It is possible that no other factor has
(20) exercised a more brutalizing influence on the American character than the Indian

---

[1] *Douglas E. Leach,* The Northern Colonial Frontier, 1607–1763 *(New York et al.: Holt, Rinehart & Winston, [1966]). See also Alden T. Vaughan,* New England Frontier: Puritans and Indians, 1620–1675 *(Boston and Toronto: Little, Brown [1965]).*
[2] *Douglas E. Leach,* Flintlocks and Tomahawk: New England in King Phillip's War *(New York: W. W. Norton paperback, 1966).*

wars. The struggles with the Indians have sometimes been represented as being "just" wars in the interest of promoting superior Western civilization at the expense of the crude stone-age culture of the Indians. The recent ethnohistorical approach to the interpretation of white-Indian relations has given us a more balanced under-
(25) standing of the relative merits of white and Indian civilizations. The norms of Indian warfare were, however, at a more barbaric level than those of Western Europe. Among the Indians of Eastern America torture was an accepted and customary part of warmaking.[3] In their violent encounters with Indians, the white settlers brought themselves down to the barbaric level of Indian warfare. Scalping was adopted by
(30) white men,[4] and down to the very last battle at Wounded Knee, lifting the hair of an Indian opponent was the usual practice among experienced white fighters. Broken treaties, unkept promises, and the slaughter of defenseless women and children, along with the un-European atrocity of taking scalps, continues to characterize the white American's mode of dealing with the Indians. The effect on our national
(35) character has not been a healthy one; it has done much to shape our proclivity to violence.

---

[3] *Leach*, Northern Colonial Frontier, *pp. 12–13.*
[4] *Leach*, Northern Colonial Frontier, *p. 112. William T. Hagan, American Indians (Chicago: University of Chicago Press, 1961) is a general history in which the major Indian wars are duly treated.*

9. Which of the following best states the main subject of the passage?

   (A) A tragedy that should never have happened
   (B) Problems of colonial America
   (C) The long-term effects of conflict between whites and Indians
   (D) The history of violence in America
   (E) Consequences of racial prejudice and greed

Explanation

To find the main subject you must read the whole passage, then step back from its many details in order to determine what the author is really saying. Because this particular passage tells of horrific events in American history, you might be distracted from its true subject. Don't let that happen to you. Instead, look for general statements that capture the essence of the passage.

(A) is a reasonable inference to draw from the passage, but the passage contains little evidence to support it as the primary subject.

(B), (D), and (E) are broad subjects, far too general to be the subject of a short passage.

(C) is the best answer. In one way or other, the author reiterates the idea that Americans tend toward violence, a characteristic with roots in the long history of white-Indian conflict. See lines 21–24 and 31–36.

10. In which of the following did the author most likely stretch the truth for the purpose of creating a rhetorical effect?

  (A) "Unquestionably the longest and most remorseless war in American history" (line 1)
  (B) "hostility . . . was by no means inevitable" (lines 4–5)
  (C) "William Penn's humane and equitable policy . . . brought . . . decades of white-Indian amity" (lines 11–13)
  (D) "The norms of Indian warfare were . . . at a more barbaric level than those of Western Europe" (lines 25–26)
  (E) "The effect on our national character has not been a healthy one" (lines 34–35)

Explanation

Authors use rhetorical effects for numerous reasons: to emphasize ideas, to provoke thought, to arouse readers' emotions, etc. Your task now is to decide which of the choices contains *hyperbole*—an overstatement or exaggeration used to create an effect.

All the choices with the exception of (C) contain provocative ideas. But the one that exaggerates the truth more than any other is (A), a statement containing such extreme words as "*Unquestionably*," "*longest*," and "*most remorseless*"—words that are meant to surprise, if not shock, the reader. Appearing at the start of the passage, those words serve the author's purpose—to capture the reader's attention. Once you've read the sentence, it is hard to resist reading the next one, and perhaps the next one after that, in order to understand what lies behind the author's startling assertion.

11. Which of the following is an accurate reading of footnote 1 (line 13)?

  (A) In his book *The Northern Colonial Frontier, 1607–1763*, Douglas E. Leach cites the work of Alden T. Vaughan.
  (B) A passage by Vaughan is quoted in Leach's book.
  (C) Leach's book deals with some of the same matters discussed in Vaughan's book.
  (D) Holt, Rinehart and Winston are the editors of Leach's book.
  (E) *The Northern Colonial Frontier, 1607–1763* deals with the history of New York and other states.

Explanation

This question is strictly about footnotes and can be answered even if you haven't read a word of the passage. Familiarity with details of documentation will lead you to the correct answer (*see pages 97–98*). Footnote 1 cites two different books. Your job is to explain why.

(A) is wrong because the footnote gives no indication that one author quoted another. Had Leach quoted Vaughan, part of the footnote would read "cited by Leach," or something to that effect.

(B) is the same as (A).

(C) accurately explains the reason that both titles appear in the same footnote. It is the correct answer.

(D) Holt, Rinehart and Winston are the publishers of the book, not its editors. In footnotes editors are always identified by "*eds.*" or a similar notation.

(E) New York is the place of publication and is unrelated to the book's contents.

12. The primary function of lines 4–13 is to support which of the following ideas?

    (A) The war between whites and Indians lasted longer than any other.

    (B) The white-Indian hostility was resolved at Wounded Knee.

    (C) Conflict between whites and Indians could have been avoided.

    (D) Whites and Indians should share the blame equally for years of conflict.

    (E) Whites and Indians fought constantly from 1607 to 1890.

Explanation

Each sentence from lines 4–13 develops the statement in lines 4–5 that hostility between whites and Indians "was by no means inevitable." Putting it another way, the author asserts that white-Indian relations didn't have to be hostile, and devotes lines 4–13 to explain why.

    (C) is the only choice that correctly identifies the idea supported by lines 4–13.

13. Taken altogether, the footnotes in this passage suggest that

    (A) historians should rely only on recent works.

    (B) the author wants his work to seem scholarly.

    (C) for historical background information, the author depended heavily on the work of others.

    (D) the author wrote this passage to appeal to an audience of historians.

    (E) almost nothing was published about antagonism between whites and Indians prior to the 1960s.

Explanation

Authors generally use footnotes for no other reason than to give credit to others for ideas and quotations. It's possible of course to guess that an author has other motives, too, such as to flatter a colleague who has written on the same subject or to show the breadth of his own research. But the footnotes themselves reveal nothing about an author's hidden agenda.

    For that reason, eliminate (B) and (D).

    (A) seems like a valid point but the footnotes fail to suggest that historians ought to rely solely on recent works. Recent books may contain the latest information and up-to-date interpretations of history, but they're not necessarily more relevant or more informative than works of the past.

    (E) is almost absurd. To be sure, the works cited all come from the 1960s (when the passage was written), but that alone is not sufficient evidence to infer that three hundred years of white-Indian conflict had been ignored until then.

    (C) is the best answer. The passage contains many of the author's own opinions, but for background, the author went to the works of others.

14. The organization of the passage can best be described as

    (A) an interpretation of the past supported by published documentation.

    (B) a chronological account of a historical situation and its influence today.

    (C) the presentation of a problem and several possible solutions.

    (D) an examination of historical events from two different perspectives.

    (E) the refutation of a thesis using evidence arranged chronologically.

Explanation

The passage opens with a generalization about the extended war between whites and Indians. Employing a chronological approach, the passage then lists several events in the centuries-long struggle. Emphasizing the brutality used by both sides, the author argues that this history of bloodshed and violence has left an unhealthy mark on the American character.

(A) has some merit because the passage is an interpretation of a certain historical condition. The second part of the description disqualifies it as the answer, however, because the author supports his views not with published documentation but with his own opinions.

(C) is only partly accurate. The passage discusses a long-standing problem but offers no solutions.

Neither (D) nor (E) comes close to describing the passage accurately.

(B) is the best answer.

15. Footnote 4 (line 30) has been included in the passage to tell readers that the information in lines 28–29

    (A)   was revealed for the first time in 1961.
    (B)   appears in an article entitled *American Indians* written by William T. Hagan.
    (C)   was found by a researcher at the University of Chicago.
    (D)   describes a practice that probably began between 1607 and 1763.
    (E)   came from the paperback edition of a book written by Douglas E. Leach.

Explanation

To answer this question, you must read not only footnote 4 but others, too, because one of the works listed in footnote 4—a book by Leach—is also cited in footnotes 1 and 3.

(A) cannot be confirmed by the footnotes. It's true that a book published in 1961 discusses the footnoted information but there's no way to tell whether it originated in Hagan's book.

(B) is incorrect because book titles are italicized and the names of articles appear inside quotation marks.

(C) is nonsense. Although the University of Chicago Press published Hagan's book, it's impossible to tell from the footnote where the research was done.

(D) According to the footnote, the information came from Leach's book, *The Northern Colonial Frontier, 1607–1763*. Although one can't be absolutely sure, whites probably began taking scalps at some point during those 150 years. (D) is the best answer.

(E) represents a misreading of the footnotes. The only paperback cited is another title by Leach, in footnote 2.

16. According to the speaker, white settlers engaged in all of the following practices EXCEPT

    (A)   paying Indians for the use of their land for settlement.
    (B)   treating native Americans humanely.
    (C)   failing to abide by treaties and bargains.
    (D)   taking the lives of innocent people.
    (E)   believing that whites were superior to Indians.

Explanation

To answer this question you must search the passage for references to each of the choices. The one you don't find is the correct answer.

(A) is the correct answer. It names a practice avoided by white settlers. In fact, the author makes the point (lines 7–9) that the whites could have reimbursed the Indians for their land but didn't.

(B) is discussed in lines 9–13.

(C) and (D) are mentioned in the last paragraph, lines 31–33.

(E) is dealt with by the sentence beginning "The struggles with" (line 21).

17. The speaker's tone at the end of the passage (lines 34–36) can best be described as

    (A) agitated.
    (B) remorseful.
    (C) pessimistic.
    (D) fussy.
    (E) devastated.

Explanation

Whenever you see the word *tone* on the AP exam, think of the speaker's attitude or state of mind. Ask yourself: "What does the passage reveal about the speaker's head and heart?"

When the speaker, at the end of this passage reflects on the national character of Americans, the tone is dark, disapproving, almost sad. The choice that best captures that feeling is (C).

Directions: *Questions 18–27.* Carefully read the following passage and answer the accompanying questions.

This passage is an excerpt from a book written early in the twentieth century.

PASSAGE 3

"Do you wiz zo haut can be?"

That was what the guide asked, when we were looking up at the bronze horses on the Arch of Peace. It meant, *Do you wish to go up there?* I give it as a specimen
Line of guide-English. These are the people that make life a burden to the tourist. Their
(5)   tongues are never still. They talk forever and forever, and that is the kind of bil-
lingsgate[1] they use. Inspiration itself could hardly comprehend them. If they would
only show you a masterpiece of art, or a venerable tomb, or a prison-house, or a
battlefield, hallowed by touching memories, or historical reminiscences, or grand
traditions, and then step aside and hold still for ten minutes and let you think, it
(10) would not be so bad. But they interrupt every dream, every pleasant train of thought,
with their tiresome cackling. Sometimes when I have been standing before some

---

[1] *coarse or offensive language*

cherished old idol of mine that I remembered years and years ago in pictures in the geography at school, I have thought I would give a whole world if the human parrot at my side would suddenly perish where he stood and leave me gaze, and ponder, (15) and worship.

No, we did not "wiz zo haut can be." We wished to go to La Scala, the largest theater in the world, I think they call it. We did so. It was a large place. Seven separate and distinct masses of humanity—six great circles and a monster parquette.[2]

We wished to go to the Ambrosian Library, and we did that also. We saw a manu-(20) script of Virgil, with annotations in the handwriting of Petrarch, the gentleman who loved another man's Laura, and lavished upon her all through life a love which was clear waste of the raw material. It was sound sentiment, but bad judgment. It brought both parties fame, and created a fountain of commiseration for them in sentimental breasts that is running yet. But who says a word in behalf of poor Mr. Laura? (25) (I do not know his other name.) Who glorifies him? Who bedews him with tears? Who writes poetry about him? Nobody. How do you suppose *he* liked the state of things that has given the world so much pleasure? How did he enjoy having another man following his wife everywhere and making her name a familiar word in every garlic-exterminating mouth in Italy with his sonnets to her preempted eyebrows? *They* got (30) fame and sympathy—he got neither. This is a peculiarly felicitous instance of what is called poetical justice. It is all very fine; but it does not chime with my notions of right. It is too one-sided—too ungenerous. Let the world go on fretting about Laura and Petrarch if it will; but as for me, my tears and lamentations shall be lavished upon the unsung defendant.

---

[2]*the lowest floor of a theater; the orchestra section*

18. The opening sentence of the first main paragraph (lines 2–3) contains all of the following EXCEPT

(A) a proper noun.
(B) a personal pronoun.
(C) a dependent clause.
(D) prepositional phrases.
(E) parallelism.

Explanation

This is one of the few grammar questions you'll find on the AP exam. To answer the question you need to know about sentence structure and be familiar with basic grammatical terminology.

Examine the sentence in the passage. Look for the features listed in the five choices. The one feature that doesn't appear is the correct answer. (NOTE: The exam usually contains two or three questions that ask you to identify the **exception**, or to name which of several choices apply—as in question 19.)

(A) is not a good choice because the *Arch of Peace* is a proper noun.

(B) is incorrect because *we* is a personal pronoun.

(C) is not the correct choice because the sentence contains a subordinate clause (*when we were looking*).

(D) is wrong because the sentence contains two prepositional phrases: *at the bronze horses* and *on the Arch of Peace.*

(E) is the best answer, determined by the process of elimination.

19. In line 11, the word "cackling" derives its effect from

     I. its use as a description of human speech
     II. its position as the last word in the sentence
     III. the sound of the word

    (A) I only
    (B) I and II only
    (C) I and III only
    (D) II and III only
    (E) I, II, and III

Explanation

The question implies that readers will find the word "cackling" unusual in some way. Your job is to determine why.

It goes without saying that chickens, turkeys, and other fowl are known to cackle—not humans. Therefore, Roman numeral I is a good choice. What about the position of "cackling" in the sentence? Beginnings and endings are often places of prominence in a sentence. Knowing that, writers make an impact on a reader by saving a catchy or unusual word for the end. Roman numeral II, therefore, is also a valid answer.

As for Roman numeral III, you must ask yourself whether the sound of the word "cackling" has a particular force. It probably does because it is somewhat onomatopoeic—that is, it sounds like the action it describes. Because all three descriptions fit, (E) is the best answer to this question.

20. The guide's question (line 1) is written in nonsensical language because the narrator

    (A) disapproves of guides who talk too much.
    (B) does not speak Italian.
    (C) cannot understand what the guide is saying.
    (D) would rather be at home where English is spoken.
    (E) would prefer that the guide keep his mouth shut.

Explanation

Look for the answer to this question in lines 2–15, which provide a context for the statement and also reveal the narrator's state of mind.

Several of the choices seem to be potential answers because they accurately describe the narrator's opinions. But don't be misled. These so-called distractors are meant to draw unwary students away from the question being asked.

(A) is a tempting answer because the narrator disapproves of guides whose "tongues are never still." But remember that the question is about those opening words, and there is no clear link between the nonsense syllables that the narrator hears and the amount of talking done by the guide.

(B) may seem valid because it's quite possible that the narrator doesn't speak Italian. But that fact is not related to the opening words, which are meant to represent the sounds that the narrator hears.

(D) may also be true, but the narrator's longing for home is not evident anywhere in the passage.

(E) resembles (A). It may accurately convey the narrator's feelings but is unrelated to the use of nonsensical language.

That leaves choice (C). Because the narrator cannot understand the guide's words, he mocks them. Indeed, later he adds, "Inspiration itself could hardly comprehend them" (line 6). (C) is the best answer.

21. The sights listed in lines 6–9 are things and places that

(A) tourists favor.
(B) Italy has in great abundance.
(C) inspire dreams.
(D) demand visitors respect.
(E) provoke emotions.

Explanation

The answer to the question is found in the overall context and tone of the passage.

(B) should be eliminated because the passage contains no evidence that Italy is abundantly endowed with masterpieces of art, venerable tombs, and so forth. (Italy, in fact, has plenty of art and tombs, but the passage doesn't imply that.)

(C), (D), and (E) are all partly true, but not all the places listed inspire dreams, demand respect, or provoke emotions. Some do, some don't.

(A), being the most inclusive choice, is the best answer.

22. The tone in the clause "and we did that also" (line 19) suggests that the narrator

(A) relishes seeing all the sights.
(B) is tired of traveling in Italy.
(C) remembers seeing a photo of the Ambrosian Library in a geography schoolbook
(D) is an indifferent tourist.
(E) dutifully follows the guide from place to place.

Explanation

To answer this question, you must know the definition of tone—the author's attitude toward his subject. If you re-read the previous paragraph (lines 16–18), you'll find that the narrator could hardly care less about the opera house and the library—at least until he lays eyes on the Virgil manuscript.

(A) is highly unlikely, considering the totality of the narrator's account of his time in Italy.

(B) may be valid to a point, although the narrator never states outright that he'd like to go home.

(C) has no basis in fact.

(D) the correct answer, is evident in the narrator's account of La Scala and of his visit to the Ambrosian Library.

(E) seems reasonable except that the narrator twice says, "we wished to go . . .," implying an act of volition that is contrary to following the guide around from place to place.

23. Upon seeing Petrarch's handwriting on the Virgil manuscript (lines 19–20), the narrator

    (A) reflects on the nature of the love between Petrarch and Laura.
    (B) understands why tourists are drawn to the Ambrosian Library.
    (C) realizes that he's in the presence of a rare literary masterpiece.
    (D) wonders why Petrarch got away with defacing the manuscript.
    (E) imagines the consequences of Petrarch's love for Laura.

Explanation

In the last paragraph of the passage, the narrator focuses not on the Virgil manuscript *per se* but on Petrarch's annotations. Petrarch's handwritten notes inspire the narrator to reflect on Petrarch's relationship with Laura. Rather than sentimentalize Petrarch's love, the narrator thinks about "Mr. Laura," the "wronged" husband. In that sense, choice (E) most accurately describes the narrator's response to the Virgil manuscript.

24. In line 22, "a clear waste of raw material" is best interpreted to mean that

    (A) Petrarch's love of Laura was unrequited.
    (B) Petrarch should have loved another woman.
    (C) Petrarch's sonnets were of poor quality.
    (D) Petrarch's annotations on Virgil's manuscript were pointless.
    (E) Too many tears have been spilled over the sad story of Petrarch and Laura.

Explanation

Questions that ask you to interpret the meaning of a sample of figurative language are popular on AP exams.

The metaphor "clear waste of raw material" refers to "a love" that evidently was unhappy, making choice (A) the best answer. If you piece together the story from hints in the passage, it seems that Petrarch loved Laura, who was married to another man. His love lasted a long time ("lavished upon her all through life"), and brought the pair not only fame but sympathy ("created a fountain of commiseration"). Hindsight suggests that Petrarch might have been better off loving another woman—Choice (B)—but then his famous love sonnets might never have been written. Neither (C) nor (D) are not supported by material in the passage. (E) is suggested by line 32 ("Let the world go on fretting . . ."), but there is no obvious connection to the phrase "a clear waste of raw material."

25. In which of the following sentences does the narrator use hyperbole to convey the intensity of his feelings?

    (A) "These are the people . . ." (line 4)
    (B) "Sometimes when I . . ." (line 11)
    (C) "We wished to go . . ." (line 16)
    (D) "But who says a word . . ." (line 24)
    (E) "It is all very fine . . ." (lines 31–32)

Explanation

To find the answer to this question you must recognize *hyperbole,* or overstatement.

Read all the sentences indicated by choices (A)–(E). Look for an exaggeration meant to achieve a rhetorical effect.

(B) contains such an overstatement: "I would give the whole world if the human parrot at my side would suddenly perish . . . ." The "whole world" is a lot to give to be rid of the guide. Moreover, the author's wish that the guide "would suddenly perish" is an extreme measure that overstates his desire to be rid of the man.

26. Which of the following best describes the narrator's overall tone?

   (A) Admiring and respectful
   (B) Hostile and condescending
   (C) Contemptuous and hateful
   (D) Satirical and ironic
   (E) Moralistic and solemn

Explanation

For a choice to be correct, *both* the adjectives listed must accurately describe the narrator's tone.

In (A) neither adjective seems to apply.

(B) contains one appropriate adjective, *condescending.* From the outset, the narrator assumes an air of superiority toward the tour guide. But he is never *hostile.*

(C) overstates the narrator's attitude. While his words border on the *contemptuous,* they don't cross the line into hatefulness.

(E) is wrong because the passage is full of humor.

(D) is the best answer. Throughout the passage the narrator pokes fun not only at the hapless guide but to his own situation as a tourist in Italy. What's more, in sympathizing with Laura's husband, "Mr. Laura," the narrator's tongue is lodged firmly in his cheek. In other words, the passage reeks of irony.

27. The structure of the sentences in lines 24–26 does all of the following EXCEPT

   (A) create suspense.
   (B) express a mock indignation.
   (C) provoke amusement.
   (D) vary the rhythm of the prose.
   (E) add a touch of playfulness.

Explanation

This question asks you to determine the effect of a series of short questions all answered by a single word—"Nobody." The writing in the passage is informal, its tone more lighthearted than ponderous. A series of terse questions can suggest anger, but the subject matter (the long-ignored husband of the famous Laura) is far from somber. Thus, choices (B), (C), and (E) accurately describe the passage. Choice (D) is also valid because the rest of the passage is made up predominantly of longer, complex, and compound sentences. Only choice (A) does not apply.

Mastering
Essay Questions

4

▰▰▰▰▰▰▰▰▰▰▰▰▰▰▰

→ **REACHING YOUR GOAL: THREE ESSAYS IN 135 MINUTES**
→ **TWO ANALYTICAL ESSAYS: WHAT AP READERS LOOK FOR**
→ **CHOOSING AND NARROWING A TOPIC**
→ **ARRANGING IDEAS PURPOSEFULLY**
→ **A WRITING STYLE THAT WORKS**
→ **POLISHING YOUR ESSAYS FOR A TOP SCORE**
→ **SAMPLE QUESTIONS AND STUDENT RESPONSES**

Just as you don't learn to play the piano, twirl a baton, or dance hip-hop by reading books on music, baton-twirling, or dancing, you're not likely to become a better writer of essays by reading about essay writing. The best this book can do is to lay out some basic principles of essay writing for you to contemplate and incorporate into the writing you do every day. The more experience you have, the more control you'll have, and the better you'll perform not only on the AP exam, but also in future college courses and whatever work you do afterwards.

Our language contains many adjectives that describe good writing: *eloquent, well-written, lively, stylish, polished, descriptive, honed, vivid, engaging,* and countless others. On the AP exam you're instructed to write "well-organized" or "carefully reasoned" or "effective" essays—directions that mean, in effect, that your writing should be:

1. **CLEAR**, or easy to follow, because your ideas need to be clear to you before you can make them clear to others.
2. **INTERESTING**, or expressed in economical, entertaining language, because readers are put off by dull and lifeless prose.
3. **CORRECT**, because you and your work will inevitably be judged according to how well you demonstrate the conventions of writing.

If your ideas are expressed clearly, interestingly, and correctly, there is no reason that you can't expect to write three winning essays on the exam.

STEPS FOR WRITING THE PERFECT ESSAY

You won't have time to invent an essay-writing process during the exam. So, it pays to have a process in mind ahead of time, one that helps you to work rapidly and efficiently. Try to map out ahead of time the steps to take during each stage of the writing process. The plan that follows is a place to start. Use it while writing a few practice essays, but alter it in any way that helps you produce the best essays you can.

FIRST STAGE **PREWRITING**

Prewriting consists of the planning that needs to be done before you actually start writing an essay:

- ☑ Reading and analyzing the question, or prompt
- ☑ Choosing a main idea, or thesis for your essay
- ☑ Gathering and arranging supporting ideas

SECOND STAGE **COMPOSING**

- ☑ Introducing the thesis
- ☑ Developing paragraphs
- ☑ Choosing the best words for expressing your ideas
- ☑ Structuring sentences for variety and coherence
- ☑ Writing a conclusion

THIRD STAGE **EDITING and PROOFREADING**

- ☑ Editing for clarity and coherence
- ☑ Editing to create interest
- ☑ Checking for standard usage and mechanical errors, including spelling, punctuation, and capitalization

How Long Does Each Stage Last?

The truth is that the three stages overlap and blend. Writers compose, revise, and proofread simultaneously. They jot down sentences during pre-writing, and even late in the process may weave new ideas into their text. In fact, no stage really ends until the final period of the last sentence is put in place—or until the AP proctor calls "Time!"

No book can tell you how to divide up the 40 minutes recommended for each essay. What works for you may be different from what works for others. But most students get good results by devoting between 25 and 30 minutes to composing and roughly 5–10 minutes each to prewriting and editing/proofreading.

How to Prepare

During the weeks before the exam, or even sooner, write an essay a day for several days in a row, until you get the feel of 40 minutes' writing time. Pace yourself and keep track of how much time you spend thinking about the topic, how many minutes you devote to composing the essay, and how long it takes you to proofread and edit.

TIP

Once you've developed a pattern that works, stick to it, and practice, practice, practice until it becomes second nature.

To make every second count, don't waste time inventing titles for your essays (no titles are needed on the exam). Don't count words, and don't expect to re-copy your first drafts. Because AP readers understand that the essays are first drafts, feel free to cross out, insert words using carets (^), and move blocks of text with neatly drawn arrows. If necessary, number the sentences to make their sequence clear. You won't be penalized for sloppy looking essays. Just be sure they're legible.

Don't waste time inventing titles; you don't need them.

POINTERS FOR WRITING THE SYNTHESIS ESSAY

- ☑ Writing a synthesis essay
- ☑ Using sources to your advantage
- ☑ Developing a persuasive argument
- ☑ Pitfalls to avoid
- ☑ Integrating sources into your essay
- ☑ Sample question and student responses

The first essay question on the exam calls for a synthesis essay—an essay that argues your point of view on a given issue. Along with a prompt that describes the issue, you are given several sources related to the issue. One of the sources is an image, such as a photo, chart, graph, or cartoon. From at least three of the sources you are to draw facts, ideas, information—any relevant evidence you can use to bolster your argument.

A 15-minute reading period is built into the test before you start writing. How you fill the time is up to you, but you'll make the most productive use of those fifteen minutes by first focusing on the prompt. Read it carefully, with pencil in hand. Underline the words that tell you exactly what you must do. Then, think hard about the issue and jot down a tentative thesis for your essay. With a main idea in mind, search the sources for ideas to incorporate into your essay and prepare a working outline. In other words, use the time to get ready to write.

A MESSAGE FROM THE AUTHOR

The following pages are full of pointers for writing the synthesis essay. But many of the guidelines also apply to writing the analytical essays required for essay questions 2 and 3 on the exam.

(Turn to page 144 for details on writing analytical essays.)

A Typical Prompt for the Synthesis Essay

In many high schools students are threatened with suspension or worse for wearing T-shirts or other clothing printed with obscenities, inflammatory language, X-rated content, and messages that may be offensive to ethnic, racial, LGBT, religious, or other groups. School officials have implemented this policy because, among other reasons, offensive messages undermine the learning environment necessary for an educational institution to do its job effectively. Free-speech advocates and civil-liberties organizations disagree, claiming that a ban on controversial clothing violates students' constitutional rights and is inconsistent with the mission of schools to teach and to show by example the values of a free society.

The prompt contains the topic for the synthesis essay. Be sure you understand it before you begin to write your essay.

Carefully read the following six sources, including the material that introduces each source. Then, in an essay that synthesizes at least three of the sources, take a position on the claim that schools should not allow students to wear clothing that may be objectionable to some members of the school population.

Be sure to focus the essay on your point of view and use the sources to support and illustrate your position. Don't simply summarize the sources. You may paraphrase, adapt, and quote material directly and indirectly from the sources. In your essay be sure to indicate which sources you use. Refer to them as Source A, Source B, and so on, or by the key words in the parentheses below.

The first paragraph of the prompt does little more than introduce the topic. It may stir up your thinking, but it doesn't tell you how to proceed. The next two paragraphs do that by spelling out the instructions: *read the sources and write an essay*—not just any essay but one that *takes a position* that agrees or disagrees with the assertion that schools should prohibit students from wearing clothing that may be objectionable to some members of the school population. Remember that you're not required to defend or oppose the assertion. Instead, you can take a position that falls somewhere in between.

What It's About

A synthesis essay is basically an **argumentative** essay. At the heart of the essay lies a claim, or statement of opinion. Call it a *main idea* or a *thesis statement*. The main idea spells out the overall purpose of the essay. Once you've made clear where you stand on the issue, the rest of the essay should back up your claim. To do that, you need to present a variety of supporting evidence.

The evidence you present is likely to make or break your argument. Solid evidence consists of facts, observations, statistics, the opinions of experts, relevant anecdotes, and more. But you'll get the most mileage from a series of logically presented ideas. No doubt you've had experience trying to convince someone to agree with you—to see an issue your way. Maybe you've tried to talk a teacher into raising a grade. Or how about the time you wanted to drive with your friends to a rap concert 200 miles away, and you had to persuade your parents to let you go? You probably cited reasons why you thought it was a good idea, gave examples of your maturity, reminded them of past instances when you acted responsibly, cited the fact that Scott's and Chris' parents have already given their consent, and so on. In short, you chose and shaped the most convincing evidence you could think of to fit the audience—your parents.

When you write the synthesis essay, you are faced with a similar task. Your audience, of course, will be AP essay readers, and your task is to convince them first, that you understand the essay assignment and second, that you can apply both your own ideas and other ideas you've found in the sources to build a persuasive argument.

Before you begin to write, however, you must read the sources.

Reading the Sources

Some students are blessed with lightning-quick minds that can instantly analyze an issue and articulate a thoughtful position on it. If you happen to be one of them, you're lightyears ahead of the pack. Enjoy your head start and plunge right into the sources to look for the evidence with which to build your case.

The rest of us, unless we happen to have thought about the issue in the past, will start from scratch. We'll begin reading sources with relatively open minds and will weigh all the evidence we can find before making up our minds.

The sources will offer a variety of interpretations and points of view for you to consider. Don't be satisfied that you know what any individual source is all about until you've analyzed it thoroughly and can say clearly what it contributes to the discussion of the issue. If you think it's okay to read only some of the sources in order to find enough ideas for your essay, please think again. In other words, read every source from start to finish before you start to write. After all, the most irresistible idea could pop up in the final paragraph of the last source.

As you read the sources, keep in mind the following purposes:

- **READ TO UNDERSTAND WHAT THE SOURCE HAS TO SAY.** Quickly underline or circle striking ideas, topic sentences, and other key words and phrases. Use your pencil sparingly, though, or you may end up with most of each passage marked up. A note or two scribbled in the margin can serve later as shorthand reminders of what the passage says.

- **READ TO ANALYZE THE AUTHOR'S POSITION ON THE ISSUE.** Read each source to determine where the author stands on the issue. Where the author presents evidence in favor of the claim, put a check in the margin. Where the evidence opposes it, write an X. Later, when you've decided on your own position, these notations will lead you quickly to ideas you may wish to include in your essay.

- **READ FOR EVIDENCE AND DATA THAT HELP DEFINE YOUR POSITION ON THE ISSUE.** The position to choose should be the one about which you have the most compelling things to say. The sources will offer a variety of perspectives. Read them in search of evidence that makes the most sense to you. The sooner you know where you stand, the better. If you've read the sources and still can't decide what position to take, make two lists, one for arguments in favor of the issue, one for those opposed. With any luck, the arguments on one side will speak to you more forcefully than those on the other.

  You won't be penalized for taking an unpopular or politically incorrect stance, but you'll get little credit for promoting an unrealistic or illogical position. If you wish, you can straddle the fence on the issue with the "it-all-depends" argument. That approach is safe but not too exciting. But if your judgment tells you that the question warrants a middle-of-the-road response, don't hesitate to write one. In the end, readers will be less impressed by your position than by the potency of your presentation.

- **INTERPRET THE VISUAL SOURCE.** The visual source won't require much reading, but it still must be analyzed for what it communicates. Your job is to interpret the graph, the chart, the image, the cartoon, or whatever, and determine its relationship to the other sources. Ask yourself what relevant information it contributes to the discussion of the issue. Once you understand its point, you can use it as evidence in your essay.

  Because visual sources often convey a large amount of information, they can be interpreted in various ways. It all depends on your perspective. Take, for example, the following line graph that comes from a recent census:

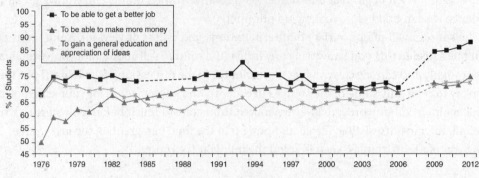

Trends of Reasons in Deciding to Go to College
(% Indicating "Very Important")

Source: Los Angeles: Higher Education Research Institute, UCLA.

Analyze what the graph tells you about why American students decided to attend college. In the spaces below, write three different conclusions that can be drawn from the graph.

1. _____

2. _____

3. _____

One of the more obvious conclusions shown by the graph is that students persist in putting a premium on job-related reasons to go to college. The graph also tells you that between 2006 and 2012, getting a better job jumped significantly higher than the other reasons for attending college.

If you were writing an essay on an issue related to, say, how the state of the economy affects choices made by college-bound students, you might focus on long-term trends, especially on students' relative indifference toward making money in 1976 compared with their eagerness in 2012 to attend college mainly to boost their future income.

Based on one interpretation of the graph, you might conclude:

American students are becoming increasingly materialistic and money hungry.

Another writer, taking a different point of view, might say:

Knowing that a college education is the key to financial security, students are likely to work harder and take their studies more seriously.

In other words, what you make of a visual source while writing your synthesis essay depends greatly on the topic and your point of view on the issue.

Assessing the Validity of Sources

Because not all sources are equally reliable, it pays to think about their validity before tapping them for evidence to include in your essay. For each source, determine insofar as possible:

- ☑ When it was published
- ☑ Where it came from
- ☑ Who its readers were likely to be
- ☑ What its purpose was
- ☑ How objectively it was written

DATE OF PUBLICATION

The date of the piece is important because facts, ideas, what we know, how we think, what we do—almost everything—is perpetually changing. Consequently, information can become obsolete almost before we know it. A source written, say, in 1990 on a scientific subject, such as climate change or human genetics, cannot be trusted to be up-to-date. The same holds true for discussions of the media, the economy, lifestyles, and many other topics. On the other hand, observations of the American system of government written in 1837 may be just as valid today as when they were written.

Some sources will seem more reliable than others. But always be cautious. Don't believe everything you read, and don't depend too heavily on any single source in your essay.

 TIP

A passage from a blogger's website can't be completely trusted.

PLACE OF PUBLICATION

A passage that comes from, say, a blogger's website, a supermarket tabloid, or the pen of a politician with an axe to grind can't be completely trusted. On the other hand, a passage taken from a scholarly journal, a report published by a foundation, a government document, a popular mass magazine, or a book written by a reputable author is likely to be more reliable. But frankly, there are no guarantees.

THE INTENDED AUDIENCE

Authors almost always slant their writing to appeal to certain audiences. An article on children's health meant for a mass audience, for example, will be different from an article directed at subscribers to a pediatrics journal. Likewise, an author writing for an audience of nursing home residents will include certain material that would be inappropriate in a publication read mostly by college students. Knowing the intended audience, then, can help you weigh the validity of any source.

AUTHOR'S PURPOSE

An essay you write for school will be different from an email letter you write to a friend, mainly because the reason for writing is different. Every piece of writing has one or more purposes. Think of all the possibilities: to inform, to entertain, to anger, to provoke, to inspire, to move, to convince, to calm down, to compliment, to declare love, and on and on. Knowing why an author has written a particular passage helps you figure out how trustworthy it is.

TONE AND LANGUAGE

Check the source for objectivity. If the author expresses a view in rational terms and supports the idea with sound evidence—even if you don't agree with it—you can pretty well count on the reliability of the material. A source full of excessively passionate and inflammatory language, on the other hand, should not be accepted at face value.

For example, which of the following reports of a fire is a more reliable source of information?

#1: At 3:30 P.M. on September 21, the Bedford Fire Department received a call that a residence at 330 Holly Road was on fire. Ten minutes later, the first fire truck arrived at the site and found a conflagration on an unfinished porch. Firemen promptly extinguished the fire. Damage was limited to the wood frame of the unfinished structure. The cause of the fire is yet to be determined.

#2: Charlotte Robbins, a 36-year-old widow and mother of four young children wept profusely as she surveyed the charred ruins of the unfinished porch outside her Bedford home last weekend.

"Poor Fred, he would have been devastated," she sobbed, referring to her husband, a disabled mechanic, dead only three weeks, whose dream had long been to build a porch for his loving family. "Why, oh, why did this happen to me?" Charlotte asked, but no one could answer. The cause of the fire remains a mystery, but the misery and heartbreak it caused for Fred's survivors is readily apparent.

The contrast between these two passages is easy to detect. The first account states just the facts; the second gushes with emotion. Sources used for the synthesis essay won't often be as extreme as these sample passages. But you can be sure that analyzing the tone and language of the sources will help you determine their validity.

HOW TO WRITE A SYNTHESIS ESSAY

Don't be misled by the heading of this section. It promises more than it can deliver. The reason is that no one learns to master essay writing by reading about how to do it. You learn to write masterful essays by writing essays, by messing around with ideas and words, by experimenting, practicing, and doing. Many of the essays you've written in English, social studies, and other classes have probably been good practice for writing a synthesis essay. And if you've ever written a research paper containing a thesis you had to prove, you've already done it.

In a sense, this AP essay is a mini-research paper. You are given a topic and sources to study. You must devise a thesis and bring in evidence to support it. The AP guidelines require that in one way or other you refer to **at least three** of the sources. In addition, you may use your own knowledge, observations, and experience to support your point of view. In fact, you shouldn't rely solely on the sources. An essay derived partly from your own thinking about the issue stands a greater chance for a top score because your own ideas add a layer of depth that would be absent from an essay drawn completely from the sources.

Writing an Argument

To write an argumentative essay, follow the same steps recommended for writing analytical essays: prewriting, composing, editing, and proofreading—all discussed earlier in this book (*page 116*). But take note: The process may be similar, but argumentative essays also impose a

TIP

Use your own experience and the sources in your essay.

unique set of demands, because you are making a claim that you want your readers to accept. And they're more likely to accept it if you take steps to prove its validity.

The odds of writing a convincing argument grow exponentially with a good solid position statement. When composing your statement, beware of hyperbole. That is, avoid overemphasizing the truth of your claim. Dogmatism has its place, but absolute statements can often be discredited. Therefore, don't hesitate to qualify your claim with words such as *often, usually, most,* and *sometimes.* As a case in point, which of the following claims has greater validity?

1. **Video games turn children violent.**
2. **Excessive use of video games often turns children violent.**

It's obvious, isn't it, that sentence 1 exaggerates the effect of video games, and sentence 2 makes a claim that is beyond dispute?

An argumentative essay requires evidence, or grounds, on which to base your claim. Nothing is more persuasive than factual information and data that support your claim. Expert testimony drawn from several of the sources that accompany the essay question also adds credence to your argument. Emotion appeals to many readers, too. Use it freely to support your point of view, but don't overdo it. To legitimize your claim, balance emotion with rational evidence.

Finally, an effective argument may not be complete without a rebuttal of some kind. Regardless of how thoroughly you've built your argument, a counterclaim may still be possible. Your job as an essayist is to anticipate the counterclaim and preempt it by pointing out its flaws.

Keeping in mind these basic principles of constructing a persuasive essay, use the following pages as a step-by-step guide through the composition of a first-rate synthesis essay.

Introducing Your Position

Avoid writing a fuzzy, overly complicated position statement. Make your position crystal clear with precise, unambiguous language. No rule says that a position statement is limited to a single sentence, although that's not a bad idea. A concise declarative sentence that focuses the reader on the issue may do the trick.

TIP

State your position with precise, unambiguous words.

For example, let's assume that a synthesis essay topic deals with the effects of gambling. The issue is whether positive aspects of gambling outweigh its harmful effects, or whether the reverse is true—that gambling causes more harm than good. After weighing the evidence, a student claims:

Gambling is an activity that affects the lives of millions of Americans.

Well . . . the problems with that statement nearly jump off the page. Just count its flaws:

1. It's too broad.
2. It fails to state a position or express the writer's opinion.
3. It's not arguable (no reasonable person would disagree with it).
4. It ignores the issue raised by the question.

In short, its weaknesses disqualify it as a viable claim.

Now, look at another position statement on the same topic:

The economic effects of gambling are generally positive.

This position statement works. Why?

1. It's specific enough to be the topic of a short paper.
2. It expresses the writer's opinion.
3. Its controversial—worthy of an argument.
4. It addresses the issue raised by the question.

USE OF QUALIFYING WORDS

Notice the word *generally* in the position statement, "The economic effects of gambling are generally positive."

Generally is a qualifying term that makes the statement less dogmatic. Without the word, the statement implies that gambling *always* has a positive effect on the economy, a claim that is hard to defend and nearly impossible to prove. Just a single exception would destroy its credibility. When you write a position statement, therefore, consider making the claim more difficult to challenge by including an appropriate qualifier, such as *almost*, *frequently*, *generally*, *in most cases*, *likely*, *often*, *might*, *maybe*, *probably*, *sometimes*, *customarily*, and so forth.

Where to Put Your Position Statement

Ordinarily, an essay's thesis or main idea is stated early in the essay. How early? It can be the first sentence, or part of the first sentence, although creating a context for the thesis is often a desirable thing to do. That is, before stating your thesis, search through the sources for interesting ideas that you can adapt for an opening that will draw readers into your essay. Then, consider any of the following introductory techniques, or use one that you've invented.

1. Begin with a brief incident or anecdote related to the point you plan to make in your essay:

   Until Harrah's introduced casino gambling, Joliet, an Illinois steel town 40 miles from Chicago, was a depressed place, with high unemployment, low wages, and slum conditions. With the coming of the casino, the city enjoyed a remarkable economic rebirth. Jobs were created, opportunities for businesses multiplied, and the place became a magnet for investment in new housing, businesses, restaurants, and motels. While gambling is known to harm millions of Americans, the revitalization of Joliet demonstrates that its overall effect on a community can nevertheless be positive. (Thesis statement is underlined.)

2. State a provocative idea in an ordinary way or an ordinary idea worded in a provocative way:

   Gambling casinos pay higher wages to their employees than almost any other businesses except salmon fisheries in Alaska. In spite of its potential for positive economic effects, however, the gambling industry harms American society more than it helps. (Thesis statement is underlined.)

3. Use a quotation from the prompt, from one of the sources, or from your reading, your experience, your grandmother:

> "All you need is a dollar and a dream." These catchy words have enticed millions of gullible New Yorkers into throwing their money away with the hope that they'll win the state lottery. <u>Because low-income people play the Lottery more often than well-off people, the lure of gambling harms them more than it does others.</u> (Thesis statement is underlined.)

4. Knock down a commonly held assumption, or define a word in a startling new way:

> Last February, when Sophie Whittaker, a waitress in St. Louis, Missouri, eagerly boarded a Mississippi River boat for an evening of playing slot machines, she had no idea that <u>winning</u> really meant <u>losing</u>. She won five hundred dollars that night and came back the next weekend to win some more. But the gambling gods had other ideas. Sophie lost, and lost big. To make up for losing nearly a thousand dollars, she returned a few nights later. Two days later she went back once more, and then again and again, sometimes calling in sick to her boss in order to spend the evening hoping for a jackpot. She won a few dollars now and then but slid ever deeper into debt, pulled down by her new-found addiction. Sophie's experience is not unique. Hers is but one of countless similar stories about Americans who have <u>surrendered to the gambling habit, an unquestionable plague on American society.</u> (Thesis is underlined.)

5. Ask an interesting question or two that you'll answer in the essay:

> Why have Native Americans fought so hard in Washington for the right to run casinos on their tribal lands? The answer is simple. Casinos make their owners rich. In addition, gambling profits can pay the bills for schools, hospitals, roads, and other needs. In effect, <u>in the right circumstances gambling does more good than harm.</u> (Thesis is underlined.)

An introduction invites your readers into the essay. It enriches the essay and adds a layer of depth, suggesting that your essay hasn't been written merely to fulfill the assignment, but that it has been prepared with care and thought.

But if none of these techniques for writing introductions works for you, or you don't have the time to devise another, just state your position up front. Don't phrase your position like an announcement, however, as in, "In this essay, I am going to prove that gambling does greater harm than good." State your point, as in "Gambling does greater harm than good," and go from there.

Supporting Your Position with Appropriate Evidence

Each paragraph in your essay should contribute to the development of the main idea. It should contain facts, data, examples—reasons of all kinds to corroborate the thesis and to convince readers to agree with you. If you reread what you've written and find that the evidence fails to support the thesis, cross it out or revise it. Be ruthless! Even though you may admire your own words, give them the boot if they don't help to strengthen your case.

How Much Evidence to Include

A rule of thumb is that three distinct and relevant reasons will usually suffice to prove a point. But essay writing is far from an exact science. Three or more is usually better than one or two, but which works best depends largely on the issue, the potency of the reasons, and the skill and grace with which the essay is written.

Regardless of how many ideas you present, each one may not require an equal amount of emphasis. You might dispose of the weakest ideas in just a few sentences, while the others require at least a paragraph or more. But whatever you emphasize, be sure that each idea is separate and distinct. Don't disappoint your readers with an idea that rehashes an earlier one in different words. But whatever the number of reasons, the argument will be weak if the reasons themselves are weak.

TIP

Find at least three separate and distinct ideas to support your thesis.

Here's an outline written by a student using three reasons in support of a thesis that said *the effects of gambling on the economy are generally positive:*

Reason 1: Gambling occurs in many places, including the Internet.
Reason 2: If you can't afford to lose money, you shouldn't gamble.
Reason 3: The money you lose goes into someone else's pocket.

The outline consists of reasons that are trite and largely irrelevant to the writer's position statement. Only Reason 3 vaguely refers to the economic consequences of gambling. On the whole, evidence of this caliber would fail to make a sufficient case.

In contrast, check these reasons:

Reason 1: Gambling casinos create jobs, especially in rural areas.
Reason 2: Taxed at a high rate, casinos serve as a rich source of revenue for the states in which they operate.
Reason 3: Casinos attract tourists who spend money for food, lodging, and services.

Using these distinct and relevant reasons, a writer could construct a sturdy argument, especially if the reasons are sensibly arranged.

The arrangement of ideas recommended for an analytical essay (*see page 144*) applies equally to the synthesis essay: Sort through your reasons, pick the best ones, and put them in order of importance. Then decide which reason provides the strongest evidence. That reason may be listed first in your outline, but save it for last in your essay. Giving it away too soon diminishes the impact of the less important reasons. In other words, it will help you work toward your best point, not away from it. By no means is this the only way to structure an argument, but it's one that works.

TIP

Save your best idea for last.

Refuting Opposing Viewpoints

Another decision you must make in writing a synthesis essay is whether to include a counterargument, or refutation—a paragraph or more that points out weaknesses in the evidence likely to be used by someone who disagrees with you. In order to write a counterargument, you must, of course, anticipate the arguments that a prospective opponent might use. A counterargument isn't essential, but it's highly desirable because it weakens your opponent's position while strengthening yours. In fact, it can add potency to an essay that can't be achieved in any other way.

To illustrate how to refute an argument, let's return briefly to the claim that the negative economic effects of gambling outweigh its positive effects. Here are three reasons that could be used to support that point of view:

Reason 1: Gamblers squander money that has better uses, such as education, housing, family life, donations to charity, etc.
Reason 2: Compulsive gambling is a disease that requires costly treatment to cure.
Reason 3: Gambling drains community resources, such as the extra amount spent for law enforcement.

TIP

A counterargument adds punch to your argument.

All three reasons sound valid enough, so how can they be refuted? Well, if you focus on Reason 3, you might begin by saying that it makes a good point, but it's not foolproof. You could argue that casinos generate considerable tax revenue that pays for additional law enforcement, or point out that gambling facilities tend to increase the price of nearby housing, thereby raising the standard of living in a community. Since wealthier people usually pay higher property taxes, the community should have no trouble raising money to pay for a larger police force. While refuting claims made by your opposition, it's important to resist the temptation of tearing to shreds every one of their arguments. Your essay will seem far more rational and circumspect if you concede the possibility that one or two of the reasons offered by the opposition may at least be somewhat valid.

Where to Put a Counterargument

There's no rule that tells you where in your essay to put a counterarguments. Sometimes it fits best near the end of an essay, just before the conclusion. At other times it should be stated early in the essay. A counterargument can also be discussed briefly in each paragraph. As you develop your case, anticipate opposing arguments and refute them then and there. In the end, the location of your counterargument is less important than the message it delivers: that your evidence is superior to that of your adversary.

Avoiding Faulty Reasoning

Evidence must logically support your essay's main idea. As a case in point, let's consider a synthesis essay question on the issue of tracking, or ability grouping, a longtime controversy in high school education. Some educators argue that students make greater educational gains when they are grouped according to ability. Others claim that ability grouping does more harm than good.

To judge the quality of evidence, let's examine an argument that comes from an essay written in favor of ability grouping. The topic sentence of one of its paragraphs reads:

Intelligent and capable students are often bored in mixed classes.

What would you expect the writer of this statement to say next? From the following list, choose the sentence that provides the most logical and appropriate evidence in support of the topic sentence:

☐ **1.** The quality of education improves when students are homogeneously grouped.

☐ **2.** Bright students in mixed classes are often left waiting for slow students to catch up.

☐ **3.** Pity the poor teachers tearing their hair out while trying to teach those godawful mixed classes.

☐ **4.** No one with his head on straight supports mixed classes.

☐ **5.** Homogeneous classes usually offer more intellectual stimulation.

All five sentences more or less relate to the subject of the essay. But not all of them offer a logical follow-up to the claim that mixed classes bore smart students.

1. In Sentence 1, the broad generalization raises issues far beyond the topic sentence.

2. Sentence 2 works well; it provides a relevant detail that supports the writer's view.

3. Sentence 3 is an emotional outburst that has no place in a rational discussion of the topic.

4. Sentence 4 contains inappropriate language that diverts the discussion away from the topic.

5. Sentence 5 provides a point that follows logically from the topic sentence.

TIP

Beware of over-generalizations, emotionalism, and inappropriate language.

Sentences 1, 3, and 4 illustrate three types of faulty reasoning that inevitably weakens an essay: overgeneralization, emotionalism, and distracting language. In your thinking and writing, try to avoid such pitfalls as well as these other types of faulty reasoning:

1. IRRELEVANT TESTIMONY:

Former New York Yankee shortstop Derek Jeter says, "I hated mixed classes in high school."

Is it logical to cite the classroom experience of a professional ex-baseball player (or any other celebrity) in a serious educational argument?

2. **SNOB APPEAL:**

> The best AP English students everywhere agree that ability grouping is the way to go.

There's nothing logical about this statement. It is a crude appeal to readers who think they are or wish to be part of an elite group. It adds nothing to a discussion of the pros or cons of ability grouping.

3. **CIRCULAR REASONING:**

> I favor ability grouping because it separates students with different skills and interests.

The fallacy here is that the writer has tried to justified a bias toward ability grouping simply by defining the term. Precisely why the writer prefers ability grouping remains unclear.

4. **ABSENCE OF PROOF:**

> Grouping has been studied time and again, but I have never seen proof that mixed grouping is educationally superior to ability grouping.

A writer's admitted lack of knowledge can never be logically used as evidence to support a claim.

5. **OVERSIMPLIFICATION:**

> When you get right down to it, ability grouping is like life; people prefer to be with others like themselves.

It's neither logical nor helpful to reduce a controversial and complex issue to a simple platitude.

6. **TELLING ONLY HALF THE STORY:**

> Ability grouping is better because it serves the educational needs of both the smartest and the slowest students.

The writer has ignored the mass of students in the middle.

7. **GOING TO EXTREMES:**

> If ability grouping were abolished, the system of American education as we know it would no longer exist.

This sort of thinking suggests desperation. By offering only the most extreme position, the writer ignores all other possibilities.

Incorporating Sources

Instructions for the synthesis essay tell you to incorporate **at least three** sources into your essay. You won't earn extra credit for citing more than three, but neither will it hurt to refer to four or more if the additional citations bolster your position on the issue.

The simplest and most obvious way to use a source in your essay is to state your position and back it up with evidence pulled from the source. Suppose, for instance, that the essay question relates to the effects of the digital media on young people. You plan to make the point that it's virtually impossible to escape from the influence of electronic communication.

One of the sources—let's call it *Source A*—discusses the pervasiveness of digital technology in 21st-century America and contains this paragraph:

> The most important and most multidimensional of the forces shaping youth culture is electronic communication. Smart phones, iPads, texting, Twitter, e-books, and especially the all-consuming substitute environment, the Internet, have enveloped today's youth in a cocoon of sensory information. I think it is doubtful that anyone who grew up before the turn of the last century can appreciate how much the senses of the young are being bombarded, even tyrannized, by electronic communication. Indeed, the digital media—in the broadest sense of the word—are not only influencing a whole environment. To those coming of age at the present time, they *are* the environment.

Ideas from this paragraph can be woven into an essay using any of the following techniques:

- Direct Quotes
- Indirect Quotes
- Paraphrasing
- Commentary

TIP

Learn to use both direct and indirect quotes.

DIRECT QUOTES

Direct quotes are word-for-word reproductions of material found in a source. Everything—grammar, spelling, capitalization—must duplicate the original exactly, and the words must be enclosed in quotation marks:

> For most young people, the digital media have permanently altered the environment. In fact, according to the author of Source A, "To those coming of age at the present time, they are the environment."

If you wish to omit words from the original for grammatical or other reasons, use an ellipsis (. . .) consisting of three periods to mark the place where material has been deleted.

> The author of Source A writes," I think it is doubtful that anyone who grew up before the turn of the last century can appreciate how much the senses of the young are being bombarded . . . by electronic communication."

If you find it necessary to add words for clarity or any other reason, enclose the words in brackets [like this]. Brackets inform readers that the bracketed words are not part of the original quotation.

> Source A sums up the situation by saying, "To those coming of age at the present time, they [the media] *are* the environment."

INDIRECT QUOTES

An indirect quote reports an idea without quoting it word-for-word. No quotation marks are needed.

> Most young people accept digital communication as a fundamental part of their environment. In fact, Source A claims that it virtually *is* the environment to those coming of age at the present time.

A WORD OF CAUTION

In your essay, use direct and indirect quotations sparingly and only as illustrative material. Use them to support ideas that you have first stated in your own words. Although you may be tempted to use lots of quoted material to make your case, don't do it. Don't let quotes dominate your essay. After all, the AP exam is a test of your writing ability, not of your ability to quote others.

Notice how the author of the following paragraph relied too heavily on quotations:

Even though most young people accept almost without question the use of electronic communication, it profoundly influences their environment. *"Smartphones, iPads, texting, Twitter, e-books, and especially the all-consuming substitute environment, the Internet, have enveloped today's youth in a cocoon of sensory information."* It is clear that for anyone *"coming of age at the present time,"* the digital media *"are the environment."*

PARAPHRASING

Paraphrasing is restating someone else's idea in your own words. A paraphrase contains the same information and should be roughly the same length as the original.

Today's teens are creatures of the digital age. Most of them remain unimpressed by how completely surrounded they have become by electronic communication. Yet it has had an unbelievably profound influence on their environment. *In fact, the author of Source A says that digital media actually have become the environment for young people coming of age now or in the near future.*

COMMENTARY

The sources provided on the exam are meant to give you information and to stimulate your thinking about the issue. They also give you ideas to discuss in your essay. With a little practice, you can learn to pick material from a source, transfer it verbatim to your essay, adapt it, or shape it any way you want to build your main idea. But to write a more distinctive essay, one that reveals your ability to interpret and analyze source material, try not only to draw from the sources but also to comment on them. Think of the sources as a one-sided conversation with the authors. Once the authors have their say, it's your turn to respond by commenting on their ideas, their reasoning, their points of view.

Thus, it would be perfectly appropriate to incorporate sources with such comments as:

"The author of Source B offers a short-sighted view of . . . ."

"To a point I agree with the author of Source B, although he doesn't carry the argument far enough. To strengthen his case, he should have included . . . ."

"In Source B, the author says that . . . , an assertion that supports my own views. I would add, however, that . . . ."

"Clearly, the author of Source B has a bias against . . ., a failing that weakens her argument."

TIP

Comment on some of the material in the sources.

Notice that you need not comment only on sources with which you agree. Feel free to quarrel with authors who ideas differ from yours. Show that they are all wet, out to lunch, or have loose screws—but please use more refined language than that. Avoid name-calling (*moron, airhead, ignoramus*, etc.) and exclamations such as, "That's the dumbest idea I've ever heard!" Refuting the opinions of others can bolster an argument, but treat even wrongheaded opinions with respect.

Citing Sources

In your essay, you must acknowledge the source of all direct and indirect quotations. Custom also requires you to give credit to any source from which you borrow, paraphrase, or adapt ideas.

Don't bother to cite the source of everyday factual material that's known by most literate, reasonably alert people. No citation is needed, for example, if you draw from the sources the information that the United States is a republic, that Thanksgiving falls on the fourth Thursday in November, or that most kids like to stay up late at night.

Many different formats exist for acknowledging sources, but on the AP exam you need no more than a brief parenthetical reference within the text of your essay, as in:

> According to a school psychologist, "Some children may be better off if they escape their parents' grip, healthier if they grow up wild and free and sort things out on their own" (Source A).

Instead of writing *Source A* inside the parentheses, you may insert the last name of the author, as in:

> One panel member summed up the conflict by saying, "Young people want a larger share in the decision-making about their lives" (Collins).

(Note that the end punctuation comes after the close of the parentheses and outside the quotation marks.)

Another technique for naming sources is to integrate the information more fully into the text, as in

> Dean Marcy Denby argues that "the basic purpose of a university education has always been . . . etc."

Which method you use to cite sources on the AP exam is up to you. It's probably better to choose one method and stick to it. Using a variety can make you appear indecisive, maybe even confused.

THE PROBLEM OF PLAGIARISM

The one basic rule about plagiarism is this: **Don't do it!**

Why? For one thing, it's dishonest, immoral, and it can get you into a whole mess of trouble. Intentional or not, plagiarism is theft. Stealing someone else's words or ideas and passing them off as your own is, to put it bluntly, a stupid thing to do.

To avoid even the slightest hint of plagiarism on the AP exam, give credit to your sources. It's simple: Whenever you take words or ideas from a source, identify their origin inside a pair of parentheses: (*Source B*), (*Jones*), or ("*Title*"). If you forget, your essay score will suffer. Even a brilliant essay that might otherwise earn an 8 or 9 may receive a score of 2 or 3 if you fail to document sources. When in doubt about the need to document a particular idea in your essay, play it safe and smart. Err on the side of inclusion, not exclusion.

SAMPLE SYNTHESIS ESSAY QUESTION

What follows is a sample synthesis essay question. It is followed by the essays of three students. The essays were handwritten under AP testing conditions: 15 minutes to read the sources and 40 minutes to write the essay, with no access to a computer, a dictionary, or any other book. By reading the essays you'll see what it takes to earn a high score. Read the comments, too. They'll alert you to some pitfalls to avoid when you write a synthesis essay of your own.

SUGGESTED TIME:

15 MINUTES FOR READING THE QUESTION AND SOURCES

40 MINUTES FOR WRITING AN ESSAY

The U.S. Constitution makes no explicit mention of the right to privacy. The courts, however, have recognized that privacy is a fundamental right in a free society. Yet, public figures—from politicians to athletes to entertainers—often have their private lives revealed by the media. Is this fair? Shouldn't celebrities enjoy as much privacy as ordinary citizens? Or should they expect to pay a price for fame by having details of their private lives made public? Is the public's right to know stronger than the right of celebrities to maintain their privacy?

Carefully read the following six sources, including the material that introduces each source. Then, in an essay that synthesizes at least three of the sources, take a position on the claim that celebrities have the same right to privacy enjoyed by other citizens.

Don't simply summarize the sources. Instead, weigh evidence from the sources to support and illustrate your position on the issue. You may paraphrase, review, and quote relevant material directly and indirectly from the sources. Be sure to indicate in your essay which sources you use. Refer to them as Source A, Source B, and so on, or by the key words in the parentheses below. In making your argument, you may, of course, also include any ideas of your own.

Source A (Hilden)
Source B (jenblacksheep)
Source C (DeGrandpré)
Source D (Graph)
Source E (GNL)
Source F (Nordhaus)

Julie Hilden, *Does Celebrity Destroy Privacy?* published by FindLaw, an online legal news and commentary site for lawyers, businesses, students, and consumers.

The passage below is an excerpt from an article entitled "Is Disclosure of Private Facts About Celebrities Justified?" written in 2002 by Julie Hilden, an attorney and columnist.

Often, it is the intensely private aspects of a celebrity's life—involving drugs, sex, or sexual orientation, marital discord, issues with children or other family members, or similar topics— that the public and the media deem newsworthy. (Illegality only ratchets up the stakes, and increases interest in the story.) But is the public entitled to know such private details about a celebrity, just because that person is a public figure?

Two basic theories are used to justify the exposure of celebrity privacy. One is the "waiver theory," which holds that celebrities have given up their privacy by choosing to appear in the public eye. Those who believe in this theory see celebrities as having made a sort of Faustian bargain: lifelong fame in exchange for the lifelong loss of privacy.

Another widely cited argument for celebrities having forfeited their privacy is what I will call the "hypocrisy theory." It holds that celebrities who, in their statements to the public, have lied about or deceptively omitted a private fact about themselves cannot then complain when the truth becomes known.

Neither of these theories is entirely valid, but the "waiver" theory is by far the weaker of the two. It seems somewhat unfair to say that because a person's gift lies in acting, basketball, or singing, rather than, for example, engineering, architecture, or computer science, that he or she has somehow "chosen" to give up all of his or her privacy.

"jenblacksheep," "Do Public Figures Have Privacy Rights?" Hubpages.com, 2010

The passage below is an excerpt from an article posted on a British website that publishes opinion pieces related to issues of politics, social conditions, and human rights.

The definition of privacy (according to the OED) states that people should be "free from public attention, as a matter of choice or right." In my opinion, taking a position of power takes away from this area of privacy.

It seems obvious that there are areas of one's life that someone would wish to keep private but would be in the public's interest to disclose. There are some cases of media invasion that are completely justified. The public needs to know if a politician is abusing his position, accepting bribes, or has a hidden agenda that could lead him to act in his own interests rather than the national interest.

In 2005, it was reported that the current UK Prime Minister David Cameron had taken drugs at school. He refused to comment until 2007 when he admitted to it, but defended himself saying, "I didn't spend the early years of my life thinking: "I better not do anything because one day I might be a politician." It is my opinion that events occurring in someone's past should remain there, as they are not a realistic reflection of what that person is now.

. . . Although public figures have no legal rights to privacy from the media, there are an increasing number of cases where it seems justified for privacy to be overridden. The most obvious of these is when a person of responsibility is abusing a position of power. The thought here is that in fact they don't really have the right to privacy in this area, even if they wish a deed to remain private. If a public figure has a personal problem that is affecting his or her ability to do the job, then it seems that it is in the public's interest to divulge this.

Vincent M. DeGrandpré, "Understanding the Market for Celebrity: An Economic Analysis of the Right of Publicity," published online by Simpson, Thacher & Bartlett, LLP, September 15, 2001.

The following passage is an excerpt from a monograph prepared by a New York law firm.

. . . What explains the public's interest in celebrities?

In his provocative work *Life: The Movie*, Neal Gabler argues that entertainment, and the movies in particular, have become so important to our individual existence that American public life itself has evolved to resemble the movies. Gabler argues that this trend has reshaped every sphere of human activity from politics to religion to the arts, all because of the need for these activities to rival readily available entertainment in keeping public attention. Not only have moving pictures become the central metaphor for understanding American public life, they have changed our epistemology, the very understanding of the world in which we live. According to Gabler, we now live in the "lifies." This "lifies" metaphor not only captures the reality that Americans use a significant portion of their income to be entertained; it conveys the idea that we have populated our lives with celebrities, those lead actors whose stories we eagerly watch and weave into our lives.

Our urge to know and associate with celebrities is not only motivated by our desire to be entertained, however. As one author notes, "celebrities have become, in recent decades, the chief agents of moral change in the United States." They have come to embody abstract issues of points of view, and are shorthand forms for ideals or expertise. Theorists have also argued that celebrities attract us because we see them as individuals who stand out in our anonymous, mass society. We seek them because they make us feel in-the-know or on the inside; in our mass society, they humanize our lives. "Stars" attract us because they seem to be free, on-the-go and liberated from the constraints of daily life.

Entertainment to Environment Headlines of Prominent News Sources (Ratio of 5 to 1 or Greater), from Pew Research Center's Project for Excellence in Journalism, 2013

The graph below shows the frequency of reporting on environmental issues compared with reporting on celebrities or entertainment-related topics.

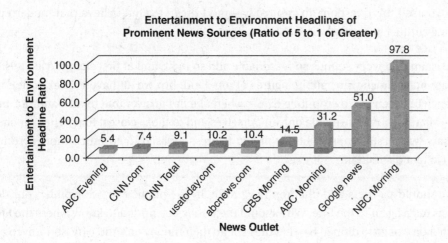

GNL, "For Today's Public Figures, Private Lives Really Matter," *Buzzle.com., Intelligent Life on the Web*, November 30, 2004.

The passage below is adapted from an article published in an online British periodical, of general interest to contemporary readers.

Ask yourself this question: do you really—and I mean really—believe that modern politicians are entitled to a private life?

The claim to privacy sounds so reasonable and so right, and at first sight indeed it is. Most of us are not politicians or public figures of any kind, but we all have a clear notion of the difference between our own public lives—where we are answerable to all—and our private ones—where we are answerable only to ourselves and to those closest to us. How much more necessary, we reason, must it be for public figures, exposed to so much more scrutiny, to maintain that distinction?

Why should partners and children have to be in the public eye, we wonder, our decent instincts once again to the fore. Why should the public be entitled to know where the famous go on holiday, or go to dinner, or what they spend their money on? And why, some even assert, do we have any right to know about their private mistakes and their sexual secrets? Nobody denies that such things are often interesting, but surely that is not the point. Would we not all be happier people living in a better society if we drew the line?

Jamie Nordhaus, "Celebrities' Rights to Privacy: How Far Should the Paparazzi Be Allowed to Go?" University of Texas School of Law, *Review of Litigation*, Volume 18, 1999.

The excerpt below comes from an article written in a journal read by law school students, practicing attorneys, judges, and others interested in matters pertaining to the individual rights of citizens.

Celebrities are entitled to the same general rights of privacy that extends to all individuals. However, the degree to which that right is protected is much narrower for public figures. . . . As a result, a broad spectrum of information concerning celebrities is transferred from the protective shield of privacy into the realm of the public interest.

Various rationales exist for affording a smaller degree of protection to the private lives of public figures than to private figures . . . . The first rationale is that most public figures seek and consent to publicity. Actors and actresses strive to be stars who are known and recognized worldwide. The same holds true for politicians striving to attain higher positions, as well as other individuals who relish their moments in the spotlight.

. . . Second, the personalities and affairs of celebrities are viewed as inherently "public." In this sense, the public nature of celebrities' occupations is construed as waiving their rights to privacy. This waiver should be regarded, however, as a limited waiver, restricting the press to examining and exposing only that information that has some bearing on the individual's position in society.

. . . Finally, the press has a right to inform the public about matters of public interest. As celebrities cultivate their positions in the public spotlight, they generate continued interest in their activities. The public begins to feel as if they "know" the individual and are thus entitled to be privy to their private lives.

Sample Student Responses

Whitney's Response

(Printed as it was written)

In dentists waiting rooms and magazine racks all across the United States is People Magazine, one of the most popular magazines in America. The public likes to read about famous people. They are curious about who is going out with who and who is getting divorced or having children. They enjoy photos of movie stars going shopping at the Safeway or visiting Disney World or just walking down the street or washing dishes. That helps them identify with the stars who do the everyday activities of life. It makes them think that being famous is not that big of a deal because even celebrities have to take out the garbage once in a while. In addition when we think of celebrities as just plain folks like us, we "feel in-the-know or on the inside." (Source C) In a way, imagining that we really "know" famous people, the writer of Source C says, in our mass society, celebrities "humanize our lives" by making us feel important.

A problem takes place when the famous person wants to maintain privacy. He or she has the right to do that but the public also has the right to try to find out as much as they want about celebrities. The case of Ray Rice is a good example. Rice was a member of the Baltimore Ravens football team and was caught on camera beating up his fiancé late one night in the elevator of a hotel in Atlantic City, NJ. A hotel security guard sold the video to TMZ, the notorious website that is all gossip about celebrities all the time. The video went viral and afterwards, the National Football League suspended Rice indefinitely from his football career. If Rice had been just an ordinary person, the incident would probably have been ignored and soon forgotten. But it wasn't and he paid a huge price for being famous.

Once a person such as Rice and other stars start to make headlines, they give up their rights of privacy. Julie Helden, the author of Source A calls this the "waiver theory." It says that when someone makes the choice to become a public figure, they trade privacy for fame. Although Helden doesn't agree that it is right, it is inevitable.

If a famous person wants privacy, they have to take steps to get it. Take J.D. Salinger, the author of Catcher in the Rye, as an example. For many years he escaped in the mountains of Vermont since he wanted no part of public life. He gave no interviews and refused to show his face in public.

Politicians are a different story. They may want to keep their lives private, but the actions of people in powerful positions, as Source B says, "will necessarily be of public attention" and they have no legal rights to privacy. This often happens when the politicians abuse power. As an example, the Chicago, Illinois, congressman Jesse Jackson, Jr., was sent to prison recently for using nearly a million dollars in campaign contributions to pay for expensive vacations, antiques, fur coats, and clothing that once belonged to Michael Jackson. The people who supported him were misled and had every right to know that he illegally used his political power. The author of Source E sums up the situation very well: "The way people live their private lives does tell us things that can help to make judgments about them as public people."

It's less important to know facts about singers and other stars. Yet, many of them deliberately let themselves be photographed and encourage reporters to write stories about them. They even hire publicists whose job is to make them famous. When Britney Spears goes to the grocery store, her agent alerts the press. Many ordinary people crave a few minutes of fame. Some of them put themselves through degrading and humiliating experiences on reality television, all for the chance to be noticed or considered out of the ordinary. Some people say that the desire to be different or nonconforming is part of human nature. However, once they make a name for themselves, they often find that fame is not that great after all. Since nobody forces them to make this "Faustian bargain" (Source A), they have to accept that the eye of the people will be on them from then on, and they have no right to complain.

Your impressions: _____

_____

_____

_____

Comment to Whitney from an AP Reader

You engage your reader immediately by showing that the issue of your essay is current and widespread. By explaining both the desire and the rewards of knowing about famous people, you provide a context for your thesis statement at the beginning of the second paragraph. To support your point of view, you cite examples not only from the sources but from your own fund of knowledge, and set up a particularly apt contrast between the behavior of J.D. Salinger and Jesse Jackson, Jr. In various ways throughout your essay, you emphasize the psychological need of the public to know details about the lives of famous figures. That emphasis leaves unaddressed the issue of the public's right to know, although you imply that a *need* to know is tantamount to the *right* to know.

Let me commend you for making the most of your references. You not only cite the source of the ideas, but you also enter into a kind of dialogue with some of the authors. For example, you openly agree with Source B and state that the "waiver theory" espoused by Source A "makes sense." These references integrate the sources into the text of your essay and help the authors of the sources, in effect, participate in the development of your main point.

Another strength of your essay is that it discusses issues surrounding the pursuit of fame, including some people's extraordinary efforts to achieve it. The examples you chose—such as those about Ray Rice and Britney Spears—are quite startling and lead seamlessly and convincingly to your conclusion that those who have sought fame have no right to complain when their privacy is violated.

Overall, the essay demonstrates your maturity as a thinker. The writing, however, contains a number of sentence errors and a few awkward uses of language. Also, the point of the para-

graph about people's craving for fame wanders away from the essay's main idea. These flaws are relatively minor but they keep the essay from earning the highest possible score.
SCORE: 8

Sonya's Response

(Printed as it was written)

The right to privacy is important. If you know that everthing you do is being watched, you can't be free to do what you like. It is like you are a prisoner which is not right in a free country like ours. This affects especially famous people because they are the ones most watched and put under a microscope by photographers, fans, and reporters.

Source A says, "It seems unfair to say that because a person's gift lies in acting, basketball, or singing, rather than, for example, engineering, architecture, or computer science, that he or she has somehow "chosen" to give up all of his or her privacy." I believe that a person should be free. A person who is a celebrity is entitled to the same freedom as everyone else. Just because a person is a fashion model or a baseball player doesn't mean they should not have the freedom to do what they choose to do.

Source C says that "Stars attract us because they seem to be free, on-the-go and liberated from the constraints of daily life." That statement is not true for many stars. They can't go out without being surrounded by crowds of people. Just to go out of the house requires a plan to trick the photographers and the people who write gossip columns. Just to go to the store for a loaf of bread means avoiding cameras and microphones waiting outside. This is not being free. Its more like an animal trapped inside in a cage in my opinion.

If you study the graph in Source D, it reveals that entertainment news about celebrities is many times more popular than news about serious issues like the environment. Celebrity news is gathered basically by professional stalkers. An ordinary person can keep their lives private if they want to. Movie stars and other celebrities don't have that right, and that's wrong. In our country everybody is supposed to be equal. I wouldn't go so far as to say that famous people are not equal, but with little right to privacy, equality is much harder to achieve for them.

In conclusion, it is easy for someone to look up to a famous person with envy of their money, looks, house, car, and their lifestyle. But the next time you are tempted to do that, imagine that you are walking in their shoes and you will see that privacy is too valuable to give up.

Your impressions: _____

_____

_____

_____

Comment to Sonya from an AP Reader

By stating your thesis early and often, you leave no doubt about where you stand on the issue of privacy for celebrities. Your essay's unity, therefore, is one of its obvious strengths, and perhaps a weakness, too. Each paragraph restates the notion that lack of privacy leads to lack of freedom, unquestionably a thoughtful idea. But by limiting yourself to that single notion, you oversimplify the whole right-to-privacy issue and miss a chance to discuss it in depth.

The sources you cite are closely linked to your thesis, but they shape your argument. By leaning on them too heavily, you have abandoned control of the discussion. It would have been preferable to state your positions and then integrate source material as supporting evidence instead of relying on sources for the topic and the starting point of each paragraph.

Your essay follows the popular five-paragraph structure. For that you cannot be faulted, although it turns what could be a fresh and scintillating essay into something more conventional. As it should, the final paragraph brings closure to the essay, but at the same time it raises a new issue—that privacy is too precious to give up for the trappings of celebrity. This is an observation worth pondering, but is only tangentially related to your essay's main concern, the right to privacy.

SCORE: 5

Ricky's Response

(Printed as it was written)

People like Justin Timberlake, Beyoncé and the Kardashians are celebrities always on TV and in the newspaper. But who cares about their drug habit, sex life, marriage problems, issues with children or other family members, or similar topics? I know I don't. If I asked my friends they would not care either.

When Cameron the prime minister of England was a young man he took drugs. He defended himself by saying that everybody did it in those days. It does not matter whether he did it or not. It is none of anybody's business but his own, and who really cares?

Brad Pitt's romance with ---- (I forgot her first name) Jolie is also no one else's business and Brad Pitt is less important than England's prime minister. If people cared about Cameron's drug use they did not have to vote for him.

The question I ask is what explains the public's interest celebrities? The author Neal Galber says that movies are so important that our lives resemble movies, so naturally we are interested in celebrities. We see them as outstanding individuals and so we want to know how they got that way. One author said, they humanize our lives, which means they make us more human. Even so their privacy is not our business so we should stay away from them. When they want to become more popular, some do outrageous things and want their photographs in the paper. Sometimes they put their home addresses on the web. Most of the time they are just regluar people trying to get along, so we should leave them alone.

Your impressions: _____

_____

_____

_____

Comment to Ricky from an AP Reader

Your essay deserves a low score mainly because it lacks unity and fails to synthesize any of the sources. To be sure, you clearly make the point that the private lives of celebrities don't matter to you. Yet, you explain that we are curious about celebrities because they are outstanding in some way. At the end you contradict yourself again by declaring that celebrities are "just regular people." Despite the overall incoherence of these and other ideas, the essay contains occasional insights—your discussion of Neal Gabler's theory, for example. But they remain under-developed and get lost in the confusion.

Your failure to synthesize sources is a particular shortcoming. Synthesis requires documentation of the sources cited. Although some of your ideas are drawn from the sources, you give them no credit. Using others' ideas without acknowledgment is unacceptable in an AP essay.
Score: 2

POINTERS FOR WRITING AN ANALYTICAL ESSAY

An analytical essay examines the purpose, content, structure, and rhetoric of a passage.

☑ Writing an analytical essay
☑ Picking "rhetorical strategies" to write about
☑ Reading the passage with eyes wide open
☑ Arranging ideas pragmatically
☑ Using a down-to-earth writing style
☑ The nuts and bolts of polishing an essay
☑ Sample questions and student responses

For the analytical essay, you must read a passage and **analyze** it. (A question sometimes contains two short passages to be analyzed and compared.) To start you off in the right direction, you're often given the author, date, and context of the passage.

The prompt usually instructs you to write about the author's use of "rhetorical strategies." In other words, you are expected to analyze how the passage conveys its meaning, achieves its purpose, or creates an effect. Your job is to break the passage into its component parts in order to explain how the author put it together.

Reading and Analyzing the Topic

At the risk of stating the obvious, read the question, or prompt, very, very carefully. Read it twice or three times, if necessary, underlining important ideas and words until you know *exactly* what you are being asked to write about.

Here is a recent AP analytical essay question. As you read it, underline the words that tell you precisely what to do:

Read carefully the following autobiographical narrative by Gary Soto. Then, in a well-written essay, analyze some of the ways in which Soto recreates the experience of being six years old and feeling guilty about something he did. You might consider such devices as contrast, repetition, pacing, diction, and imagery.

You're on the right track if you underlined <u>analyze</u>, the key word in the instructions. It means that your job is to disassemble the passage, looking at how the author recreated the experience of his childhood guilt.

The question also says that you "*might consider* such devices as contrast, repetition, pacing, diction, and imagery." Hey, have you noticed that the AP test writers have just given you a gift? The phrase *might consider* has just turned a requirement into a suggestion, a suggestion that you may accept or reject. It's your choice. Consider not taking the suggestion because AP essay readers, who read scores of similar essays a day, often look kindly on essays that break the mold, that show a spark of originality.

Practice in Reading and Analyzing Questions

Read the following pair of AP questions carefully. Underline the key words that define the task to be performed. Then, write your interpretation of the task in the blank spaces provided.

Question A   Carefully read the following excerpt from an essay by the columnist Charles Donahue entitled "People With Noses in the Air." Then write an essay in which you define Donahue's attitude toward snobs and analyze the rhetorical strategies the writer uses to communicate that attitude.

Required task: _____

_____

_____

Explanation

Question A doesn't include the word *tone* but instead refers to the author's attitude toward a subject, which amounts to pretty much the same thing. (Incidentally, in AP lingo, the term *rhetorical stance* is sometimes used in place of *tone*.) In this instance, Donahue may employ a sarcastic tone to ridicule snobbish behavior, or he may convey resentment or envy or disbelief or any number of other feelings about snobs.

An essay responding to the question must contain at least two things: (1) a definition of Donahue's attitude toward snobs, and (2) a discussion of how Donahue communicated that attitude—that is, what rhetorical methods he used to achieve his goal.

The essay might discuss these two concerns separately, or it might deal with both issues simultaneously. However the material is organized, though, it must address both concerns.

TIP

Don't get bogged down in every rhetorical detail. Focus only on those that help shape the author's point and purpose.

Question B   Carefully read the following passage from _____(Title)_____ written by _____(Author)_____. Then write an essay on the given passage analyzing the rhetorical strategies the author used to achieve her purpose.

Required task: _____

_____

_____

Explanation

This question gives you the chance to write about virtually any rhetorical technique that you can find in the passage. You may think that's easy because the choice is completely yours. But be careful. It may be a challenge to find rhetorical techniques that help shape the author's purpose. Because you happen to locate a metaphor or an example of personification doesn't necessarily make figurative language significant to the passage. To be important, figures of speech must seriously contribute to the overall impact that the passage leaves on its readers. In other words, this open-ended question forces you to scrutinize the passage with great care in order to locate rhetorical devices that have helped the author to achieve her goal.

Reading the Passage

Reading a passage to analyze it in an essay differs little from reading a passage in order to answer multiple-choice questions. If anything, the approach is somewhat simpler because you need not zero in on every tiny detail but only on the rhetorical strategies specified by the question.

If the prompt instructs you to discuss figurative language, search the passage for metaphors, symbols, analogies, samples of irony and imagery, and so forth. If you're told to analyze diction, look for words and phrases that serve as clues to the author's background, personality, and especially the author's tone and purpose.

TIP

Depend on the prompt to tell you what to search for while reading the passage.

Read the passage at least twice—first for an overview of its point and purpose and then to track down examples of rhetorical devices. Mark up the page with underscoring, asterisks, circles, and arrows, highlighting only those features of the passage you might use in your essay. Scribble notes in the margin. Jot down thoughts and ideas that occur to you as you read. Your notes may well serve as an outline of an essay.

Regardless of the question, an understanding of the content of the passage is crucial. That means reading *every word*, not just enough of it to give you a vague sense of the passage's main idea. By the time you've finished reading you ought to be able to complete the following statement in 10 or fewer well-chosen words:

This passage is about _____.

Everything you discuss in your essay must be tied to your understanding of the passage's content. It won't be enough simply to identify examples of highly-charged words or figures of speech, or to say the tone is nostalgic or the writing style is sophisticated. What counts is your analysis of the author's rhetorical choices—or how the purpose of the passage was achieved.

PLANNING YOUR ANALYTICAL ESSAY

Preparing an Outline

Spend a few minutes outlining your essay before writing your opening sentence. You don't need a formal outline, but just a list of ideas arranged in the order that you'll use them in your essay. It speaks well of you as a writer when you present ideas in a well-thought-out sequence instead of spilling them onto the page in the order they happened to pop into your head. Since time is short on the AP exam, your outline may consist of no more than scrawled words or phrases that tell you what each paragraph will be about.

After reading the following passage, Bridget B, a high school senior, prepared an outline for an essay that analyzed the author's use of rhetorical devices.

This passage by Laura Eirmann appeared on the website of the Cornell University Pet Loss Hotline.

STRATEGY

In general, an essay outlined in advance is likely to be clearer and more coherent than one thrown together willy-nilly.

PASSAGE

When an owner and veterinarian decide that a pet is suffering or unlikely to make a recovery, euthanasia offers a way to end a pet's pain. The decision is difficult for both the owner and the veterinarian, but we should recognize that sometimes this
Line is the kindest thing we can do in the final stage of a pet's life.
(5)   Understanding how the procedure is performed may help an owner in this decision. It may also help an owner decide whether they wish to be present during the euthanasia. Initially, a pet is made as comfortable as possible. Some veterinarians will perform the procedure in a pet's home. If the animal is brought to the hospital, veterinarians often choose a quiet room where the pet will feel at ease. Sometimes a
(10) mild sedative or tranquilizer is first given if the animal appears anxious or painful. Frequently an indwelling catheter is placed in the pet's vein to ensure that the euthanasia solution is delivered quickly. The euthanasia solution is usually a barbiturate—the same class of drugs used for general anesthesia. At a much higher dose, this solution provides not only the same effects as general anesthesia (loss of conscious-
(15) ness, loss of pain sensation), but suppresses the cardiovascular and respiratory systems. As the solution is injected, the animal loses consciousness and within minutes the heart and lungs stop functioning. Since the pet is not conscious, they do not feel anything. Most times, the animal passes away so smoothly, that it is difficult to tell until the veterinarian listens for absence of a heartbeat. The eyes remain open
(20) in most cases. Sometimes, the last few breaths are what's termed "agonal," meaning involuntary muscle contractions, but again, the pet is not aware at this point. After the animal dies, there is complete muscle relaxation, often accompanied by urination and defecation. This is completely normal and is something an owner should expect. In addition, after death, chemicals normally stored in nerve endings
(25) are released causing occasional muscle twitching in the early post-mortem period.

Many owners who choose to stay with their pets are surprised how quickly and easily the pet is put to rest.

The decision to stay or not stay with a pet is a very personal one. Some owners feel they could comfort their pet in its final minutes. Others feel their emotional upset *(30)* would only upset their pet. Those who choose not to stay may wish to view the pet's body after the procedure is complete. Euthanasia is emotional for veterinarians as well. Sometimes, the veterinarian has known the pet for a long time or has tried very hard to make the animal well again. James Herriot stated the view of most veterinarians in *All Things Wise and Wonderful:* "Like all vets I hated doing this, painless *(35)* though it was, but to me there has always been a comfort in the knowledge that the last thing these helpless animals knew was the sound of a friendly voice and the touch of a gentle hand."

After reading the passage carefully, Bridget jotted down her impressions of the passage and its author:

1. The author of the passage is a veterinarian.

2. The passage was written for an audience of pet owners.

3. The passage reflects the writer's concern for the well-being of animals.

4. The writer is trying to help pet owners make decisions about taking the life of their terminally ill pets.

5. The writer describes the process of pet euthanasia unemotionally.

Using these thoughts as a springboard, Bridget prepared an outline for an essay on the author's rhetorical strategies.

(For the record, Bridget's outline below is far more detailed than an outline hurriedly written during an AP test.)

<u>Point of passage</u>: to help pet owners deal with euthanasia

Main idea: Author's tone, point of view and diction comfort pet owners, put them at ease about making a difficult decision.

1. Tone: Uses compassionate tone
   Avoids harsh words—e.g., kill, destroy, put to death, deathly ill.
   Uses euphemisms and soft words: "euthanasia," (line 2) "end a pet's pain," (2) "put to rest," (27) final stage of . . . life" (4)

2. Point of view: Author identifies with pet owner, maybe to help relieve owner's guilt about killing a pet.
   (Implication: We're in this together, so don't blame yourself.)
   - - difficult decision for both owner and vet (2–3)
   - - emotional for vets (31)
   - - - quote by J. Herriot (34–37)

3. Dicton (word choice)
        Plenty of repetition of words with connotations that stress
        painlessness, ease, and speed of the euthanasia "procedure"
        Painless: "Pet is made . . .comfortable"(7)
                    Quiet room where pet feels "at ease" (9)
                    "sedative," "tranquillizer," "same as general anesthesia,"
                    "loss of pain," etc.
        Ease of process: "animal passes away so smoothly" (18)
        Speed of process: "solution delivered quickly" (11-12)
                    Owner's surprise at "how quickly and easily the
                    pet is put to rest" (22-27)
Possible conclusion: Author covers process thoroughly from start to finish;
thoroughness shows respect for pet owner, causing pet owner to feel confident
in the vet.

As you prepare for the AP exam, get into the habit of writing outlines. If you're not accustomed to outlining before you write, it may take a while to get into the groove. But once in, the rewards may astound you.

TIP

Get into the habit of writing outlines.

Choosing a Main Idea

The purpose, or point, of any essay is its **main idea**, also called its **thesis**. Essays may be written with beautiful words, contain profound thoughts, and make readers laugh or weep. But without a main idea, an essay remains just words in search of a meaning, causing readers to scratch their heads and ask, "Huh? What's the point?"

Open-ended essay questions on general topics invite you to range far and wide in search of a main idea. Not on the AP exam, however. Because the analytical essay question asks you to perform a specific writing task, devising a main idea is reasonably simple: Just identify the relationship between the rhetorical strategies used in a passage and the point or purpose of the passage. In fact, a main idea may include the actual words or a paraphrase of the question itself. For example:

> Laura Eirmann, the author of the passage, makes use of such rhetorical devices as a sympathetic tone, a friendly point of view, and a soothing choice of words to achieve her purpose.

This opening sentence won't win a prize for originality but it gets the job done. It shows that the writer understands the question and it suggests that the essay to follow will contain a three-part analysis of Eirmann's writing style.

It's not essential, nor is it particularly desirable to state the main idea at the essay's outset. In fact, it's often preferable to lead up to your main idea with a general discussion of the context in which the passage was written. For instance,

> Pet owners, experiencing great anxiety when their pets develop incurable illnesses, often face the terrible decision of whether to let their pets suffer until they die or to "put them to sleep." Knowing that pet owners agonize over what to do, Laura Eirmann carefully constructed an essay intended to help pet owners make an informed, guilt-free decision about euthanizing their pets. *To make readers feel comfortable, Eirmann uses a sympathetic tone, a friendly point of view, and a soothing choice of words.*

TIP

State your essay's main idea at the beginning, middle, or end— wherever it works best.

Still another approach is to save the thesis statement for your conclusion. Instead of giving away your main idea at the start, let it emerge naturally and inevitably from evidence presented in all the prior paragraphs.

The guidelines for placing main ideas in analytical essays are no different from those for persuasive essays, although it may often be advantageous to make clear your position early on in a persuasive essay. By stating your opinion at the outset, you can build a strong argument step-by-step through the remainder of the essay. On the other hand, an essay that makes its main point less overtly, or one that uses suspense to frame an argument leading to an incisive conclusion, may engage a reader more fully—always a desirable outcome on an AP essay.

WRITING A PERSUASIVE ESSAY

The third essay on the exam requires you to respond to an idea contained in a short statement or paragraph. Your response must be written as an argument that either supports or refutes a writer's views on a particular subject. Or, if you prefer not to take an either/or position, you can adopt a stance somewhere in between the two.

Writing a persuasive essay involves more than simply expressing your opinion on an issue. The validity of your position must be based on sound evidence. Passion alone won't do it. You need to corral evidence from your experience, reading, studies, and observation in order to prove that your opinion has merit.

To argue in behalf of your position, find at least two (three is even better) distinct arguments to support it. It helps, too, to develop a counterargument—an argument most likely to be used by someone who opposes your views—that you can refute in order to persuade readers that you are right and your opponent is not.

TIP

Back up your opinion with solid evidence.

Because topics for AP persuasive essays are unpredictable, it makes sense to arm yourself with a ready-to-use essay-writing strategy—one that, regardless of the topic, lays out the steps to take during the approximately forty minutes it takes to complete the essay. Chances are that you've written reams of essays during your school career. Over the years, you may have developed a method for writing blue-ribbon essays. But in case you haven't, here is a list of steps you can count on. Follow them while you write essays for practice. Then, based on the results you get, amend the list in ways that enable you to write the best essays you can.

✔ Read and analyze the prompt.

✔ Jot down ideas that might be used to argue both sides of the issue.

✔ Review the ideas and choose a position on the issue.

✔ Articulate a main idea, or thesis, for your essay.

✔ Arrange supporting ideas purposefully—not simply in the order they occurred to you.

✔ Introduce the main idea of your essay.

✔ Develop unified paragraphs in support of your main idea.

✔ Devote at least part of your essay to refute an argument likely to be used by someone whose opinion differs from yours.

✔ Choose words and structure sentences that concisely convey your thoughts.

✔ Write a memorable conclusion but not a brief summary of your essay.

✔ Edit your essay for clarity, interest, and correctness.

Writing an essay in 40 minutes

• 5–10 minutes to plan
• 20–25 minutes for composing
• 5–10 minutes to polish your essay

Experience shows that these steps do not need be taken in the order presented, nor is each step discrete. Rather, they often overlap and blend into each other. While composing your essay, for example, you may also be revising and proofreading. Late in the process, you may weave new ideas into your text or shift the location of ideas. In short, no step really ends until the final period is put into place or the AP proctor calls "Time!"

This book can't tell you exactly how much of the suggested 40-minute writing period to devote to each step. A plan that works for other students may not work for you. In general, however, you won't go wrong by devoting more than half the time—about 25–30 minutes—to composing an essay and no more than 5–10 minutes planning and polishing it.

By now you may have noticed that the basic process of writing a persuasive essay hardly differs at all from that used in writing synthesis or analytical essays. All three require you to read the prompt over and over until you are absolutely sure of what it says and what you are expected to do. The prompt may not turn you on right away, but if you really concentrate on the issue, you may soon be bursting with ideas for your essay.

PERSUASIVE ESSAY TOPICS FOR PRACTICE

SUGGESTED TIME FOR EACH—40 MINUTES

1. *The following statement comes from the writings of the Roman emperor Marcus Aurelius. Read it carefully, and then write an essay that agrees with, modifies, or opposes the author's description of the nature of humankind. Use evidence from your observation, reading, studies, or experience to support your position.*

    We are made for co-operation, like feet, like hands, like eyelids, like rows of the upper and lower teeth. To act against one another, then, is contrary to nature; and it is action against one another to be vexed and to turn away.

2. *The paragraph that follows has been adapted from an article about pressures felt by young American women in the middle of the twentieth century. Read it carefully, and then write an essay that examines the extent to which the author's characterization of the relationship between young American men and women is valid today. Support your views with appropriate evidence.*

    The relations between college [-bound] boys and girls are a tender subject, seldom discussed between the generations. The contemporary sexual mores of young people are so different from those which governed their parents' or teachers' lives that a common meeting ground between them scarcely exists. (It is possible that their parents have forgotten some of the details of their own past experiences.) Girls seldom, if ever, discuss their sexual experiences with their parents, and when they do—unless they are facing a crisis—one cannot escape the impression that the parent-child relationship is a little unhealthy. To be sure, girls often come to college with standards handed to them by their mothers and tacitly upheld by their fathers. Letting a boy kiss you good night, for example, is all right, but preferably not on the first date. Here is where conflict often begins. If the girl is standoffish and stiff, the chances are she will not see the boy again. But this is just what she wants to forestall unless he is a "jerk," and so, partly to secure her aim and partly because she is moved and flattered, she accepts his kisses, and soon after, if she has not already learned, she is taught to "kiss back."

3. *What follows is a well known passage by the seventeenth-century British poet John Donne. Read it carefully, and then write an essay that agrees with, modifies, or opposes Donne's view of man's place in the world. Use appropriate evidence to support your argument.*

No man is an island entire of itself; every man is a piece of the continent, a part of the main. If a clod be washed away by the sea, Europe is the less, as well as if a promontory were, as well as if a manor or thy friend's or of thine own were. Any man's death diminishes me, because I am involved in mankind, and therefore never send to know for whom the bell tolls; it tolls for thee.

4. *To explain why many dramatists and authors of fiction tend to fill their works with disturbed, problem-plagued, and disaffected characters, essayist Roger Rosenblatt said "because defects make for better reading than virtues."*

After considering Rosenblatt's assertion, write an essay that agrees with, modifies, or opposes his explanation for the presence of troubled characters in works of literature. Use appropriate evidence to support your argument.

5. *In a letter to Chuck Klosterman, a newspaper columnist known as "The Ethicist," a reader questioned the validity of the so-called Golden Rule, the common principle of ethical behavior, that says you and I should treat others as we would like to be treated.*

   The reader challenged the rule on the grounds that it imposes one person's values and preferences on other people. That is to say, why should it be assumed that others want to be treated as we do? Wouldn't it be far better if the rule said to treat others as they want to be treated?

What is your opinion? Write an essay that either agrees with the reader's view or one that modifies or disagrees with the reader's point of view. Use evidence from your observation, studies, reading, or experience to support your position.

ARRANGING IDEAS

The best order is the clearest order.

The words you've underlined while reading a passage, or prompt, the notes you've written in the margins, the items listed in your outline—these are the raw materials of an essay. Before you begin composing, select the details that will best support your main idea. Discard the others, or better, hold them in reserve—to be used in case one of your selections turns out to be a dud.

Then, arrange those materials. Decide what comes first, second, and third. The best order is the clearest order, the one your reader can follow with the least effort. But, just as a highway map may show several routes from one place to another, there is no single way to get from the beginning to the end of an essay.

No plan is superior to another provided there's a valid reason for using it. The plan that fails is the aimless one, the one in which ideas are presented solely according to when they occurred to you. To guard against aimlessness, rank the ideas in your outline in order of importance. Then work toward your best point, not away from it. Giving away your *pièce de resistance* at the start is self-defeating. Therefore, if you've identified, say, three good rhetorical strategies, save the best one for the end of the essay. Start with your second best, and sandwich your least favorite between the other two. A solid opening draws readers into the essay and creates that all-important first impression, but a memorable ending is even more important. Coming last, it is what readers have fresh in their minds when they assign the essay a grade.

THE FORMULA

The five-paragraph essay formula is a fundamental, all-purpose plan for arranging ideas into clear, easy-to-follow order. It's a technique you can rely on any time you need to set ideas in order. Its greatest virtue is clarity. Each part has its place and purpose.

THE FORMULA

Introductory paragraph	Point 1
Body consisting of three paragraphs	Point 2
Concluding paragraph	Point 3

You needn't follow the formula slavishly. In fact, professionally written essays rarely adhere to this five-paragraph arrangement. Yet, many essay writers, even those who take a circuitous path between the beginning and end, use some version of it.

But here's a word of caution: The five-paragraph essay is taught so widely in schools that it has almost become a cliché. AP readers will recognize it instantly and may grade it accordingly. The highest scores are usually reserved for essays that demonstrate a particularly strong command of essay-writing techniques. Essays that rely on an obvious organizational formula may not reach that lofty level.

AP ESSAY WRITING STYLE

Choose your words carefully, of course, and try to adopt a plain, natural style. Don't drag out your SAT vocabulary in an attempt to snow your readers. AP readers won't be impressed by formal, pompous, or elegant writing. Think of them as everyday folks who appreciate straight, plain, everyday language. You have a natural voice. Use it.

Don't be pretentious. Use your natural voice.

AP essays are likely to be more formal than informal. It's inappropriate to be casual when you are analyzing a text, providing quotes, paraphrasing others' words, using the terminology of literary criticism and scholarship. At the same time, though, don't be stuffy or pompous. AP essay readers are old hands at spotting pretense in students' writing.

Just let your genuine voice ring out, although the way you speak is not necessarily the way you should write. Spoken language is often vague, clumsy, repetitive, confused, wordy. Adopt a writing style not unlike the everyday speech of someone who speaks grammatical English, free of the latest cool or hip expressions and clichés. Think of it as the kind of mature speech expected of you in serious conversation, say, during a college interview. Or maybe even the way this paragraph sounds. You could do a lot worse!

Use plain and precise language. Fortunately, English is loaded with simple words that can express the most profound ideas. A sign that says STOP! conveys its message more clearly than CEASE AND DESIST. When a dentist pokes at your teeth, it *hurts*, even if dentists call it "experiencing discomfort." Simple doesn't necessarily mean short, however. It's true that plain words tend to be the short ones, but not always. The word *fid* is short, but it's not plain unless you are a sailor, in which case you'd know that a fid supports the mast on a boat. On the other hand, *spontaneously* is five syllables long. Yet it is a plain and simple word because of its frequent use.

Simple ideas dressed up in ornate words not only obscure meaning but make writers sound phony, as in:

Fancy: The epistle states that politicians have a proclivity toward prevarication.
Plain: The letter says that politicians often lie.

Ernest Hemingway called a writer's greatest gift a "built-in, shock-proof crap detector." Hemingway's own detector worked well. He produced about the leanest, plainest writing in the English language—not that you should try to emulate Hemingway. (That's already been done by countless imitators.) But an efficient "crap detector" of your own will encourage you to choose words only because they express exactly what you mean.

> ## EUPHEMISMS
>
> Of course, there are occasions when the plainest words won't do. When you wish to soften or mitigate painful, unsavory, or objectionable truths, our language offers innumerable euphemisms. For example, there are scores of euphemisms for the verb "to die" (*pass away*, *pass on*, *be deceased*, *rest*, *expire*, *meet one's maker*, and so on), for "bathroom" (*restroom, ladies'/men's room, W.C., lounge*), and for "drunk," "vomiting," and everything else that might upset a prissy sensibility. Pussyfooting with words has its place. We do it all the time, but in your AP essays resort to euphemisms only when you have a valid reason for doing so.

TIP

Steer clear of language and abbreviations customarily used in text messages and blogs.

Don't interpret this admonition to use plain words as *carte blanche* to use current, everyday slang or street talk in your AP essays. Spoken language, which brims with colorful words and expressions like *chill, pig out, dissed*, and *bummed* has its place, but its place is not in your AP essay unless you definitely need such lingo to create an effect that you can't produce another way. If you insist on writing like a blogger, that's fine, but don't use quotation marks to call attention to the fact that you can't think of standard or more original words. If, to make a point, you overload your essay with digital slang, such as *Facestalling, YOLO*, and *4ever*, be sure to demonstrate your mastery of conventional English, too, in at least part of the piece. After all, an AP student must be able to write good, standard prose.

Putting Yourself in the Essay

TIP

In AP essays references to yourself are not forbidden, but use them sparingly.

Although it's not forbidden in formal essays to put yourself in the spotlight, custom requires writers to focus on the subject matter, not on themselves. In other words, avoid using first-person pronouns (*I, me, we, us, our, myself, ourselves*). AP readers recognize that in certain contexts such pronouns are appropriate. When writing a personal anecdote to support a claim, for example, using *I* is often preferable to using the more impersonal *one*, as in "When *one* faces a blank page on which to write an AP essay, *one* can feel panic." If, by shunning first-person pronouns, however, your prose becomes stilted or awkward, feel free to use them. In short, use whatever words you need to make your essay interesting and readable.

Varying Sentences

When writing your essay, try to use a variety of sentences to show your awareness that the type, structure, and length of sentences help authors convey meaning and create effects on readers. It's easy to fall into a rut by using the same sentence structure over and over and over. But if you are aiming for a high AP score, vary your sentences. For one thing, variety adds vitality to your prose.

English sentences, as you probably know, are structured in three ways: ***simple, compound, and complex.***

SIMPLE: Metaphors are great.

The sentence is *simple* because it contains one grammatical subject (*Metaphors*) and one verb (*are*). It also states a single main idea.

COMPOUND: Grammar is difficult, but it helps you write well.

The sentence is *compound* because it is made up of two simple sentences joined by a coordinating conjunction (*but*). Other coordinating conjunctions used in compound sentences are *and, yet, or, for, nor,* and *so,* as in:

Grammar is difficult, *and* it drives many people up the wall.
Eliana studied hard, *for* she wanted an 5 on the AP exam.

Notice that the structure of each of these compound sentences gives roughly equal emphasis to its two main ideas.

COMPLEX: Although he's taking four AP courses, Spencer won't study.

The sentence is *complex* because it is made up two parts—a simple sentence (*Spencer won't study*) and a dependent clause (*Although he's taking four AP courses*). Because the clause begins with a subordinating conjunction (*Although*), it is called a *subordinate clause.* Subordinate clauses contain ideas related to the complete sentence (called the *independent* or *main* clause), but, compared with the main clause, are usually less important to the meaning of the sentence. Other common subordinating conjunctions include *because, after, before, though, unless, until, whenever,* and *while.*

Not every simple, compound, and complex sentence is structured in the way just described. In fact, variations abound because English is a remarkably flexible language that can be shaped in countless ways, as you'll see below.

Most simple sentences start with the grammatical subject followed by the verb:

Cats (subject) *fall* (verb) asleep in about three seconds.
They (subject) *sleep* (verb) best after eating and cleaning themselves.
I (subject) *wish* (verb) to be a cat in my next life.

A string of sentences with this subject-verb pattern resembles the prose in a grade-school primer—a style that just won't do on an AP essay. To be sure that you write in a more mature and engaging way, analyze one of your recent essays. Do several sentences begin with grammatical subjects? If so, try shifting the subject elsewhere. Try leading off with a prepositional phrase, or with an adverb, adjective, or some other grammatical unit.

The following pairs of sentences show how a subject can be shifted from its customary position:

BEFORE THE SHIFT: Ms. Santero is one of the most popular teachers in the school.
AFTER THE SHIFT: In this school Ms. Santero is one of the most popular teachers.

After a prepositional phrase was added, the subject (*Ms. Santero*) has been moved further along in the sentence.

BEFORE: She taught the novel *Beloved* to our AP English class with enthusiasm.
AFTER: Enthusiastically, she taught the novel *Beloved* to our AP English class.

Obviously, the revised sentence begins with an adverb.

BEFORE: Students were less excited about the book than she was.
AFTER: Yet, students were less excited about the book than she was.

Well, here the subject (*students*) is stated after an opening connective.

BEFORE: I loved the book, although it turned out to be an intolerable drag for most of my classmates.
AFTER: Although the book turned out to be an intolerable drag for most of my classmates, I loved it.

After introducing the sentence with a dependent clause, the writer names the subject, *I*, and then adds the rest of the sentence.

BEFORE: Santero pushed the class to find symbolic meaning in various scenes to make the book more meaningful.
AFTER: To make the book more meaningful, Ms. Santero pushed the class to find symbolic meaning is various scenes.

To revise this sentence the writer begins with a verbal, in this case "to make," the infinitive form of the verb. (Verbals look and feel much like verbs but serve a different function. Verbals, though, come from verbs. Hence, their name and their resemblance.)

BEFORE: I read the book in two days, hoping that it would never end.
AFTER: Hoping that it would never end, I read the book in two days.

Aiming to diversify sentence openings, the writer starts this sentence with another kind of verbal, known as a *participle*. The *-ing* ending often indicates that a word is a participle.

BEFORE: I was awed by the tenacity of the characters and absorbed by every soul-stirring syllable of the story.
AFTER: Awed by the tenacity of the characters, I was absorbed by every soul-stirring syllable of the story.

Determined to try something different, the writer begins the sentence with an adjective that happens to sound like a verb because of its *-ed* ending.

Still another variation to try now and then is the sentence constructed from matched ideas set in juxtaposition. President Kennedy famously used such a sentence to memorable effect in his inaugural speech:

"Ask not what your country can do for you, ask what you can do for your country."

The power of such sentences lies in the balance of parallel clauses. Each clause could stand alone, but together they express the idea more vigorously. Another example:

It wasn't that the spirit of the pioneers caught my imagination, it was my imagination that caught the pioneer spirit.

Emphasis can also come from a reversal of customary word order. Out of context, a sentence in which the predicate precedes the subject may seem awkward. But in the right spot, an inverted sentence can leave an indelible mark. "Dull the book is not" packs more wallop than "The book is not dull" or "The book is exciting." In the right context, "Perilous was the climb to the top of the cliff" sounds more ominous than, "The climb to the top of the cliff was perilous." Inverted sentences should be used rarely, however. More than once in an essay diminishes the vigor of each occurrence and may sound silly.

No rule of thumb says that a certain percentage of sentences in an essay ought to be different from the usual subject-verb structure. It really depends on the purpose and style of the essay. But if you find yourself repeating the same sentence pattern, restructure some of your sentences. Your readers are bound to reward you for the effort.

Sentence Types

Our language offers a rich menu of sentence types. Declarative sentences predominate in most essay writing. (Just to refresh your memory, a *declarative* sentence, such as the one you are now reading, simply makes a statement.) But other types of sentences can create all sorts of fascinating effects. Take interrogative sentences, for example. (Do you remember that *interrogative* sentences ask questions?) An interrogative sentence appropriately placed in an essay consisting of declarative sentences can change the pace and rhythm of the prose, underscore an idea, and promote the reader's involvement.

By varying sentences, you'll write more readable essays.

Don't forget about imperative sentences (keep in mind that *imperative* sentences make requests or give commands) and exclamatory sentences (What strong emotion an *exclamatory* sentence can express!).

Furthermore, you can write sentences interrupted at some point by a dash—although some editors and teachers claim that it's not proper to do so in formal prose. Direct and indirect quotations are useful, and on occasion you can drive home a point with a single emphatic word. Excellent!

There's peril, however, in scrambling sentence types for no other reason than to scramble sentence types, for you may end up with a mess on your hands. Be guided by what expresses your ideas most clearly and seems varied enough to interest your readers.

Repetition of Ideas

Repetition can be annoying, but, adroitly used, it adds clout to an idea. When your sweetheart says, "I love you. I love you very much," the repetition intensifies the sentiment. If a coach admonishes his team, "OK, guys, knock it off. I said knock it off," you know he really means it.

The following paragraph may suggest that the writer has a one-track mind:

In the fall Bethany will be going to college. She is psyched to get out of high school. She is psyched to break away from her small town and live in a big city. She is psyched for meeting new people from all over the country and the world, and she is psyched to get started on a program of studies that she expects will prepare her for law school. But first, she is psyched to take the AP exam.

Every sentence but the first uses the same subject/verb combination. Yet, the overall effect is anything but monotonous. What's memorable is not repetition, but relentlessness. Repeating the verb *psyched* five times emphasizes Bethany's frame of mind. The point could not have been made as emphatically using a different verb in each sentence.

Or take this passage written by an incorrigible bagel freak.

My taste for bagels knows no bounds. I stop at the bagel shop on my way to school each morning and grab an onion bagel and coffee. Lunch consists of an olive bagel and a couple of veggie bagels smeared with cream cheese. At snack time I'm not picky. Any style bagel will do, but I hate to have dinner without a buttered poppy-seed bagel. Before bed I wash down a plain toasted bagel with a glass of milk, and in case I have insomnia, I stash two or three garlic bagels on my nightstand for a tasty middle-of the-night pick-me-up.

The writer virtually beats you over the head with bagels. But the repetition won't allow you to forget the point—that the writer has eyes not for pizza, not for burritos, not for onion rings— but only for bagels.

A word of caution: Restatements of a word or phrase can also be distracting. Inadvertent repetition obstructs progress by putting useless words in the reader's path. Therefore, stay alert, for accidental repetition, as in:

In a corner of the room stood a clock. The clock said four o'clock.

Columbus made three ocean voyages. The voyages took him across the Atlantic Ocean.

Combining such sentences will keep you from ending one sentence and starting the next one with the same words:

The clock in the corner of the room said four.

Columbus made three voyages across the Atlantic.

Sentences can also be plagued with a word or a rhyme that draws attention to itself:

Maybe some people don't have as much freedom as others; but the freedom they do have is given to them for free. Therefore, freedom is proof enough that the best things in life are free.

The members of the assembly remembered that November was just around the corner.

These writers failed to listen to the sound of their words. Had they read their sentences aloud, they may have noticed that the voices were stuck in a groove. In fact, reading your words aloud allows you to step back and examine word sounds (Hold it! Those two words— *aloud* and *allows*—sound jarring and should not be allowed to stand side by side.) Hearing your written words spoken, you're more apt to notice unwanted repetition. Whenever possible, let each of your practice essays cool for a while. Then enlist a friend to read it aloud. Hearing it in another's voice lends objectivity to the process of self-evaluation.

Short and Long Sentences

TIP

To fend off monotomy, vary the length of your sentences.

Long sentences (like this one) demand greater effort from readers because they must keep track of more words, modifiers, phrases (not to speak of parenthetical asides), and clauses, without losing the writer's main thought, which may be buried amid any number of secondary, or less important, thoughts, while short sentences are usually easier to grasp. A brief sentence can make a point sharply because all its words concentrate on a single point. Take, for example, the last sentence in this passage:

> For three days, my parents and I sat in our SUV and drove from college to college to college in search of the perfect place for me to spend the next four years. For 72 hours we lived as one person, sharing thoughts and dreams, stating opinions about each campus we visited, taking guided tours, interviewing students and admissions officials, asking directions a hundred times, eating together in town after town, and even sleeping in the same motel rooms. But mostly, we fought.

A terse closing sentence following a windy, 46-word sentence produces a mild jolt. Indeed, its point is to startle the reader. The technique is easily mastered but should be used sparingly. Overuse dilutes its impact.

A series of short sentences can be as tiresome as a succession of long ones. A balance works best. If you have strung together four or five equally long (or short) sentences, try to separate, or combine, them. Here, to illustrate, is an overweight sentence that needs demolition:

> In the 1870s, the archaeologist, Heinrich Schliemann, dug in the correct spot and discovered not only one ancient city of Troy, but nine of them, one lying on top of the other, since every few centuries a new city had been built upon the ruins of the old, causing Schliemann to dig right past the layer containing the ruins of the famous city of the Trojan Horse without realizing he had done so, a mistake not corrected until almost fifty years later by Carl Blegen of the University of Cincinnati, by which time, unfortunately, it was too late for Schliemann because he had been dead for forty years.

The sentence is perfectly grammatical, but it carries a big 108-word load. Cut it down to size. Break it into pieces, rearrange it, add verbs, drop an idea or two, change the emphasis and delete words. When you're done, the restyled sentence might sound something like this:

> In the 1870s, the archaeologist, Heinrich Schliemann, dug in the correct spot and discovered not only one ancient city of Troy, but nine of them, one lying on top of the other. He figured out that every few centuries a new city had been built upon the ruins of the old. Without realizing it, he had dug right past the layer he was seeking, the layer containing the ruins of the famous city of the Trojan Horse. His mistake was corrected fifty years later by Carl Blegen of the University of Cincinnati. By then, however, it was too late for Schliemann. He had been dead for forty years.

Likewise, a string of four or five sentences of almost equal length can be combined to create a more balanced and varied paragraph. Here, for instance, is a paragraph, also about an ancient city, made up of short, choppy sentences:

> Pompeii was an ancient city. It belonged to the Roman Empire. It was near the base of Mount Vesuvius. In 79 A.D. the volcano on Vesuvius erupted. Tons of hot, wet ash fell on Pompeii. In less than a day the city was buried. It just vanished. More than seventeen centuries later an Italian peasant found Pompeii. His discovery was accidental. He was digging in a field. His shovel struck the top of a wall. That was two hundred years ago. Pompeii is still being excavated two hundred years later. About two-thirds of the city has been unearthed. It must have been a beautiful city.

With repetition eliminated and some ideas subordinated to others, here is what you get:

The ancient Roman city of Pompeii lay near the base of Mt. Vesuvius. In 79 A.D. Vesuvius erupted, burying the city with tons of hot, wet ash. In less than a day the city vanished. More than seventeen centuries later an Italian peasant digging in a field with a shovel accidentally struck the top of a wall. He had found Pompeii. Today, 200 years later, the city is still being unearthed. The excavation reveals that Pompeii must have been a beautiful city.

VARYING SENTENCES—A SUMMARY

✔ Use a variety of sentence types: *simple, compound,* and *complex.*
✔ Create variety by starting sentences with:

- A prepositional phrase: *From the start, In the first place, At the outset*
- Adverbs and adverbial phrases: *Originally, At first, Initially*
- Dependent clauses: *When you start with this, Because the opening is*
- Conjunctions: *And, But, Not only, Either, So, Yet*
- Adjectives and adjective phrases: *Fresh from, Introduced with, Headed by*
- Verbal infinitives: *To launch, To take the first step, To get going*
- Participles: *Leading off, Starting up, Commencing with*
- Inversions: *Unique is the writer who embarks . . .*

✔ Balance long and short sentences.
✔ Combine a series of very short sentences.
✔ Dismember very long sentences.

Paragraphing

Whoever invented paragraphs deserves a pat on the back because he or she devised a simple way to guide readers through a piece of writing. Each new paragraph alerts readers to get ready for a shift of some kind, just as a car's directional blinker tells other drivers that you're about to turn.

Yet, not every new paragraph signals a drastic change. The writer may simply want to nudge the discussion ahead to the next step. Some paragraphs spring directly from those that preceded them. The paragraph you are now reading, for instance, is linked to the one before by the connecting word *Yet.* The connection was meant to alert you to a change in thought, but it was also intended to remind you that the two paragraphs are related. Abrupt starts may be useful from time to time to keep readers on their toes. But good writers avoid a string of sudden turns that can transform surprise into confusion.

In an essay, paragraphs usually play a primary role and one or more secondary roles. An *introductory paragraph*, for instance, launches the essay and makes the intent of the essay clear to the reader. The *concluding paragraph* leaves the reader with a thought to remember and provides a sense of closure. The majority of paragraphs, however, are *developmental.* They carry forward the main point of the essay by performing any number of functions, among them:

- Adding new ideas to the preceding discussion
- Continuing or explaining in more detail an idea presented earlier
- Reiterating a previously stated idea
- Citing an example of a previously stated idea
- Evaluating an opinion stated earlier
- Refuting previously stated ideas
- Providing a new or contrasting point of view
- Describing the relationship between ideas presented earlier
- Providing background material
- Raising a hypothetical or rhetorical question about the topic

Whatever its functions, a paragraph should contribute to the essay's overall growth. A paragraph that fails to amplify the main idea of the essay should be revised or deleted. Similarly, any idea within a paragraph that doesn't contribute to the development of the paragraph's topic needs to be changed or eliminated.

TOPIC AND SUPPORTING SENTENCES

As you write your AP essays, be sure to include sentences that contain landmarks to help readers know where they are. Such guiding sentences differ from others because they define the paragraph's main topic, hence their name: *topic sentence*. Topic sentences come in many forms, but what they all have in common is their helpfulness. They are like landmarks that tell readers the direction they'll be going for a while.

> **Every sentence in a paragraph should help to develop the paragraph's topic.**

Most, but not all, paragraphs contain topic sentences. The topic of some paragraphs is so obvious that to state it would be redundant. For instance, a description of a fast-food restaurant might detail the crowd, the noise, the overflowing garbage cans, the smell of cooking oil, the lines of people, the crumb-strewn formica tables, and so on. A reader would certainly get the picture. To state explicitly "It was a busy day at Burger King" would serve no purpose.

No rule governs every possible use of a topic sentence. A sense of what readers need in order to understand the essay must be your guide. Let topic sentences lead the way. Consider your readers as absentminded wanderers who need frequent reminders of where they are and where they are going. If in doubt, grasp their hands too firmly rather than too loosely. Follow the principle that if there is a way to misunderstand or misinterpret your words, readers are sure to find it.

> ### Strategy for Getting on Top of Topic Sentences
>
> Print out or photocopy an essay you've written recently. On one copy underline all the topic sentences. Let a friend do the same on the second copy. Then compare your answers. If you agree, you can be pretty sure that your topic sentences are doing what they are supposed to do.

DEVELOPING PARAGRAPHS

Like essays, paragraphs should have a discernible organization. Ideas can be arranged from general to specific, or vice versa. Sequential arrangements make sense for analytical paragraphs. In a cause-and-effect paragraph, logic dictates that the cause precedes the effect, but the opposite may sometimes be preferable. As always, clarity and intent should govern the sequence of ideas.

Writers shun formulas in creating paragraphs, but they generally concur that paragraphs of only one or two sentences are too scanty. Thorough development of an idea calls for several sentences—most of the time, at least. Journalists, however, often write paragraphs consisting of one or two sentences. But most contemporary nonfiction consists of paragraphs of four to eight sentences. Recognizing that readers need frequent breaks, writers these days almost never write paragraphs of a dozen or more sentences.

Poor essays often suffer from lack of development. The writer states ideas and then drops them. You're not apt to do that, though, if you think of your readers as skeptics who doubt that you're on the level unless you prove that you know what you're talking about. An underdeveloped statement, no matter how strongly worded, usually won't do. That's why you must back up your general ideas with specifics, using illustrative material that can be in any number of forms. In an analytical essay, that means referring frequently to the passage. Paraphrase the passage or use direct quotes, but don't let the quotes constitute the bulk of your essay. Rather, state ideas in your own words, then support them with direct or indirect quotations.

The kind of analytical writing expected on the AP exam is rational discourse, not emotional ranting.

Whatever you do, your analysis must be based on something more solid than your intuition or personal preference. The left side of your brain, the logical side, is being examined along with the right, the creative, side. The best essays reveal that both sides of your brain are in good working order.

Using Transitions

Picture your readers as tourists in a foreign country and your essay as a journey they are making from one place to another. Because you can't expect strangers to find their own way, you must lead them. Tell them where they are going (the introduction) and remind them of the progress they're making (the body of the essay).

In long essays readers need more reminders than in short ones. To keep readers well informed, you don't need to repeat what you've already written but rather plant key ideas, slightly rephrased, as milestones along the way. (The sentence you just read contains just such a marker. The phrase *To keep readers well-informed* cues you to keep in mind the topic of this paragraph—helping readers find their way.) By regularly alluding to the main idea of the paragraphs, you'll keep readers focused and hold their attention from start to finish.

You can help readers along, too, by choosing words that set up relationships between one thought and the next. This can be done with such words as *this*, which actually ties the sentence you are now reading to the previous one. The word *too* in the first sentence of this paragraph serves the same function; it acts as a link between this paragraph and the one before. Fortunately, the English language is brimming with transitional words and phrases for tying sentences and ideas together.

What follows is a collection of common transitional words and phrases grouped according to their customary use. With a bit of thought, you could probably add to the list.

When you **ADD** ideas: *moreover, in addition (to), further, besides, also, and then, then too, again, next, secondly, equally important . . .*

When you make a **CONTRAST**: *however, conversely, in contrast, on the other hand, on the contrary, but, nevertheless, and yet, still, even so . . .*

When you **COMPARE** or draw a **PARALLEL**: *similarly, likewise, in comparison, in like manner, at the same time, in the same vein . . .*

When you cite an **EXAMPLE**: *for example, for instance, as when, as illustrated by . . .*

When you show **RESULTS**: *as a result, in consequence, consequently, accordingly, therefore, thus, hence . . .*

When you **REINFORCE** an idea: *indeed, in fact, as a matter of fact, to be sure, of course, in any event, by all means . . .*

When you express **SEQUENCE** or the passing of **TIME**: *soon after, then, previously, not long after, meanwhile, in the meantime, later, simultaneously, at the same time, immediately, next, at length, thereafter . . .*

When you show **PLACES**: *here, nearby, at this spot, near at hand, in proximity, on the opposite side, across from, adjacent to, underneath . . .*

When you **CONCLUDE**: *finally, in short, in other words, in a word, to sum up, in conclusion, in the end, when all is said and done . . .*

You don't need a specific transitional word or phrase to bind every sentence to another. Ideas themselves can create strong links. Notice in the paired sentences below that the underlined words in each second sentence echo an idea expressed in the first.

> (1) As a kind of universal language, music unites people from age eight to eighty. (2) <u>No matter how old they are</u>, people can lose themselves in melodies, rhythms, tempos, and endless varieties of sound.

> (1) At the heart of *Romeo and Juliet* is a long-standing feud between the Capulets and the Montagues. (2) <u>As enemies</u>, the two families always fight in the streets of Verona.

> (1) To drive nails into very hard wood without bending them, first dip the points into grease or soap. (2) <u>You can accomplish the same end</u> by moistening the points of the nails in your mouth or in a can of water.

One of your goals on the AP is to assure readers a smooth trip through your essay. Without your help—that is, unless you deliberately tie sentences together with transitions—readers may find themselves lurching from one idea to another. Before long, they'll give up or get lost like travelers on an unmarked road. While not every sentence needs a specific transition, three or four successive sentences without a link of some kind can leave readers wondering whether the trip through your essay is worth taking.

Mini-Workout: Transitions

Directions: Use as many transitions as you can while writing paragraphs on the suggested topics below.

1. Write a paragraph on how to do something—drive a car from home to school, pull a practical joke, avoid doing homework, scrub info from your Facebook page, get on the good side of a teacher, give your cat or dog a bath. Use as many SEQUENCE/TIME transitions as possible, but don't overdo it.

2. Write a paragraph detailing a cause and its effect: the cause and effect of good teaching, of a new fad, of stress in high school students, of taking risks, of lying, of a close friendship. Use as many RESULT transitions as you can, but don't go overboard.

3. Write a paragraph that makes a comparison and contrast—the way people respond to pressure, groups in your school, two athletes, then and now, boredom and laziness, two books, a friend who turned into an enemy, an enemy who became a friend. Use as many COMPARISON/CONTRAST transitions as you can, but don't get carried away.

4. Write a paragraph in which you argue for or against an issue—electronic eavesdropping, school dress codes, educational vouchers, censoring the Internet, dieting, restrictions on smoking. Use as many ADDITION transitions as you can, but only where they make sense.

Concluding Your Analytical Essay

Stay away from summary endings. They insult your reader's intelligence.

At the end of your essay, you can lift your pen off the paper and be done with it. Or, if you have the time, you can present your readers with a little gift to remember you by—perhaps a surprising insight, a bit of wisdom, a catchy phrase—something likely to tease the readers' brains, tickle their funny bones, or make them feel smart.

Choose the gift carefully. It should fit the content, style, and mood of your essay and spring naturally from its contents. Because it comes last, the final paragraph leaves an enduring impression. A weak, apologetic, or irrelevant conclusion may dilute or even obliterate the effect you tried so hard to create. Above all, *stay away from summary endings*. When an essay is short to begin with, it's insulting to review for readers what is evident on the page in front of them. Readers are intelligent people. Trust them to remember what your essay says.

A catchy conclusion isn't always necessary, but even a short ending may be preferable to none at all. Effective endings leave readers fulfilled, satisfied that they have arrived somewhere. A judiciously chosen ending may sway AP readers to judge your essay somewhat more leniently than otherwise. There are no guarantees, of course, but readers are bound to be touched by a memento of your thinking, your sense of humor, or your vision. Even an ordinary thought, uniquely expressed, will leave an agreeable afterglow.

You might try any one of these common techniques:

- Have a little fun with your conclusion; try to put a smile on your reader's face.
- End with an apt quotation drawn from the essay itself, from the prompt, or from another source.
- Finish by clearly re-stating your essay's main point but using new words. Changing the wording, in fact, may shed new light on the main idea—a gesture that your readers will appreciate. If appropriate, add a short tag line, a brief sentence that creates a dramatic effect.
- Bring your readers up to date or project them into the future. Say something about prospects for the months or years ahead.

Although an effective conclusion will add luster to an essay, don't feel obliged to add an ending just for the sake of form. Readers will have developed a fairly accurate sense of your writing ability before reaching your essay's last word. Rest assured that a good but incomplete piece of writing will be graded according to what you have done well instead of what you haven't done at all.

EDITING AND PROOFREADING ESSAYS

Once you've ended your essay, spend whatever time is left editing and proofreading.

Editing for Clarity

Because many words have multiple meanings, do a word-by-word check for clarity. Ask yourself whether a reader could misconstrue a word or find it ambiguous. For example, in an essay about missing teenagers, Paula S. wrote, "The last thing parents should do is talk to their kids." Coming to that sentence, a reader might well wonder whether Paula meant that parents should talk to their kids as a last resort, or, that in a list of what parents ought to do, the final step is talking to their kids.

Later in the essay Paula wrote, "Raya told her friend Alexa that she had made a serious mistake by running away from home." Paula certainly understood what she intended to say, but readers can't tell whether Raya took a dim view of Alexa's actions or whether Raya herself had second thoughts about her own flight. Granted, these sentences have been quoted out of context, but the point remains: What may seem perfectly clear to a writer may send a puzzling message to the reader.

That's why you should work hard to arrange your words in the clearest order. Watch for grammatical perils that interfere with meaning, especially **1) misplaced modifiers**, **2) dangling participles**, and **3) lack of parallelism**—all discussed in the pages that follow.

MISPLACED MODIFIERS

Modifiers are words, phrases, and clauses that tell something about or limit the meaning of a particular word or statement. For example:

The bedroom had a *broken window*.

The adjective *broken* is a modifier because it tells something about the condition of the *window*. In other words, *broken* "modifies" *window*.

Modifiers must be placed so that they modify the correct words:

Luke only loves Ruby.

Here *only* modifies the verb *loves*. The modifier is appropriate if Luke feels nothing but love for Ruby—no admiration, no awe, no respect, nor any other emotion. If, however, Luke has but one love, and that love is Ruby, then *only* is misplaced. Properly placed, *only* should come either before or after *Ruby*:

Luke loves *only* Ruby.   or   **Luke loves Ruby *only*.**

Another example:

Nora decided *when she had completed her AP English homework* to watch TV.

In this sentence *when she had completed her AP English homework* is the modifier. But it is hard to tell whether it modifies *decided* or *watch*. If it modifies *decided*, Nora finished her essay and then made a decision to watch TV. If it modifies *watch*, Nora worked on her homework and decided at some point that she would watch TV when she had finished.

> **When she had finished her AP English homework, Nora decided to watch TV.**
>
> **While doing her AP English homework, Nora decided to watch TV when she had finished.**

Now the meaning of both sentences is unambiguous.

Obviously, misplaced modifiers can cloud a writer's intentions. To avoid the problem, place modifiers as close as possible to the words they modify:

> **MISPLACED: Diego donated his old car to a charity *that no longer ran well*.**

The modifier *that no longer ran well* is too far from *car*, the word it modifies.

> **CLEAR: Diego donated his old car *that no longer ran well* to a charity.**

DANGLING MODIFIERS

In a sentence words must fit together like pieces of jigsaw puzzle. Sometimes, a misplaced word looks as though it fits, but it doesn't say exactly what the writer intended.

> (1) **While running to English class, the bell rang.**
> (2) **Hammering a nail, a crack developed in the board.**
> (3) **When only eight years old, my father warned me about smoking.**

The ludicrous meaning of these sentences may not strike you immediately, but look again. Do you see that these sentences describe a surreal world in which bells run to class, cracks hammer nails, and underage fathers dispense advice? The problem is that these sentences try to mate two groups of words that can't go together. The parts are mismatched. After the comma in the first sentence, you'd expect to find out who is running, but you aren't told. Likewise, after the commas in sentences 2 and 3, you are not told who was hammering and who is only eight years old. In short, you're left dangling. Hence, the label *dangling modifier* has been given to this type of construction. To correct the error, add the noun or pronoun to be modified, as in:

> **While the boys were running to English class, the bell rang.**
>
> **Hammering a nail, Rufus cracked the board.**
>
> **When I was eight, my father warned me about smoking.**

Re-writing the whole sentence is often the best cure for a dangling modifier, as in:

> **DANGLING: While talking on the phone, the stew burned in the pot.**
>
> **CLEAR: While I talked on the phone, the stew burned in the pot.**

Mini-Workout: Misplaced and Dangling Modifiers

> **Directions:** Rewrite any of the following sentences that contain an error in modification. Corrections can be made by shifting words around or revising the whole sentence. Some may be correct.

1. The bowling alley lends out shoes to its customers of all sizes.

   _____

2. An old bike was given to a junk man we planned to put in the trash.

   _____

3. At the age of ten, my family and I emigrated from Guatemala to the U.S.

   _____

4. Still sound asleep at noon, my mother thought I was sick.

   _____

5. Totaled beyond repair, Allison knew she'd have to buy another car.

   _____

6. The coach said that canceling the swim meet was the right thing to do under the circumstances.

   _____

7. Used all night to illuminate the steps, I needed new batteries for the flashlight.

   _____

8. A report was submitted about the latest bank heist by the police.

   _____

9. Pausing for a drink of water after the hike, a grizzly bear stood in front of me.

   _____

10. After a quick breakfast, the school bus picked me up at the corner.

    _____

Answers on page 216.

PARALLELISM

Parallel structure keeps equivalent ideas in the same grammatical form. Here is a sentence that lists the contents of a student's locker:

> The locker held a down jacket, aromatic sweatpants, three sneakers, two left-handed gloves, an unused tuna sandwich, a broken ski pole, a hockey puck, six overdue library books, a disposable camera, and a hiking boot.

Every item listed is an object, each expressed in the same grammatical form: a noun preceded by one or two adjectives. When the student wrote a list of his favorite pastimes, though, the sentence lost its parallelism:

> I like skiing, hiking, to take pictures, and running.

The message is clear, but the phrase "to take pictures" is not grammatically parallel with the other phrases. To revise it, write "taking pictures":

> I like skiing, hiking, taking pictures, and running.

TIP

The key to parallelism is uniformity—expressing ideas in the same grammatical form.

When you structure the pieces of a sentence in parallel form, you put yourself in the company of world-class stylists. Abraham Lincoln, for one, used parallelism at Gettysburg: "We cannot dedicate, we cannot consecrate, we cannot hallow this ground . . . ." And later, ". . . that government of the people, by the people, and for the people shall not perish from the earth." John F. Kennedy used parallelism in his inaugural speech: "Let every nation know, whether it wishes us good or ill, that we shall pay any price, bear any burden, meet any hardship, support any friend, oppose any foe to assure the survival and the success of liberty."

To apply the essential principles of parallel construction to your prose:

- Express all ideas in a series in the same grammatical form, even when the series consists of only two items:

  > NOT PARALLEL: Her parents objected to music she played loudly and keeping late hours.

  > PARALLEL: Her parents objected to the loud music she played and the late hours she kept.

  Here, parallelism is achieved with prepositional phrases, *to the loud music* and *to the late hours*. Each phrase is followed by the pronoun *she* and the past tense of a verb.

  > After graduation she promised to turn the volume down and to come home earlier.

  Each parallel idea consists of an infinitive followed by a noun and an adverb.

- Use grammatical equivalents to make comparisons and contrasts. When comparing two ideas, for example, express both ideas in phrases, or pair an idea stated in a clause with a second idea also stated in a clause.

  > FAULTY: They are worried more about public opinion than for what the effect of the proposal may be.

  The prepositional phrase *about public opinion* may not be paired with the clause *what the effect of the proposal may be*.

  > PARALLEL: They are worried more about public opinion than about the effect of the proposal.

Parallelism is achieved by pairing two prepositional phrases.

FAULTY: Going out to eat no longer thrills me as much as to cook at home.

The gerund *going out* should not be paired with the infinitive *to cook*.

PARALLEL: Going out to eat no longer thrills me as much as cooking at home.

Parallelism is achieved by pairing two gerunds, *going* and *cooking*.

- Stay alert for pairs of words that signal the need for parallelism, such as *either/or, neither/nor, whether/or, both/and,* and *not only/but also.*

Alice will attend *neither* NYU *or* Columbia.

Revise by changing *neither* to *either,* or changing *or* to *nor.* Remember to keep the pair of words close to each other in the sentence. If they are too far apart, your sentence may be hard to follow:

Jake *both* started on the basketball and the volleyball teams.

The signal word *both* is too far removed from the parallel phrase, *basketball and volleyball teams.* Its placement misleads the reader into thinking that the verb *started* is one of the parallel ideas. Correctly worded, the sentence reads:

Jake started on *both* the basketball and the volleyball teams.

- When an article, preposition, or a conjunction appears before the first in a series of parallel items, repeat the word before the others in the series.

UNCLEAR: Our mechanic did a better job on my car than his.

Did two mechanics work on the same car or did one mechanic work on two different cars? To clear up the ambiguity, repeat the preposition *on,* as in:

CLEAR: Our mechanic did a better job on my car than *on* his.

Sometimes repeating both a preposition and an article is necessary:

UNCLEAR: Before signing the contract, Tiffany spoke with the president and treasurer of the company.

Did Tiffany speak with one person or with two? Repeating *with the* helps to clarify the meaning:

CLEAR: Before signing the contract, Tiffany spoke with the president and *with the* treasurer of the company.

- Make sure that parallel ideas are logical equivalents.

ABSURD: Tyler is six feet tall, kind, and a Texan.

Physical features, traits of character, and place of origin are not logically coordinated.

LESS ABSURD: Tyler, a six-foot Texan, is kind.

Still not terribly logical, but at least the revision emphasizes only one of Tyler's qualities—his kindness.

ILLOGICAL: San Diego's *harbor* is reported to be more polluted than any city.

This sentence is meant to compare pollution in the San Diego harbor with pollution in the harbors of other cities, but it fails to achieve its goal. Instead, it illogically compares San Diego's harbor with a city.

LOGICAL: San Diego's *harbor* is reported to be more polluted than the *harbor of any other city.*

ILLOGICAL: Unlike most *cars* on the street, *Anika* has her Subaru washed almost every week.

This sentence is intended to compare Anika's car with other cars on the street, but it manages only to compare Anika to the other cars, an illogical comparison.

LOGICAL: Anika's *Subaru*, unlike *most cars* on the street, is washed almost every week.

A lack of parallelism in phrases and clauses is not just bad form but can cause confusion. Sound parallel structure, in contrast, keeps equivalent ideas in the same grammatical form. Take, for example, a sentence that lists the characteristics of a restaurant in which to have a family birthday party:

We are looking for a place that is private, plenty of space, has a friendly staff, and that people like to look at.

The sentence makes some sense, of course, but it's awkward because the four characteristics are not expressed in parallel form. Instead, they are a mix of an adjective, a phrase, and two clauses. One way to fix the problem is to use only adjectives, as in:

We are looking for a place that is private, spacious, friendly, and attractive.

Or use a series of nouns each preceded by an adjective:

We are looking for a place with total privacy, ample space, a friendly staff, and attractive surroundings.

Mini-Workout: Parallel Structure

> **Directions:** Look for faulty parallel structure in the following sentences. Write the correct version of the offending word or phrase in the space provided. Some sentences may be correct.

1. This book not only shows what happens to mentally depressed people but it's all right to seek help.

   _____

2. A more easier and direct route exist between Oakland and San Raphael than the one we took.

   _____

3. Jim is tall, kind, and forward on the basketball team.

   _____

4. Emmett prefers to cook at home rather than going out to eat.

   _____

5. Both angry and disappointment at the team's dismal performance, the coach resigned.

   _____

6. The men haven't decided whether canoeing across the lake would better than a sailboat.

   _____

7. The wind had not only knocked down the tree but the electric lines came down, too.

   _____

8. After finding a job, she'll get an apartment, continue playing the guitar, and friends will party with her.

   _____

9. Either the mouse will find a quick way into the attic or will gnaw at the siding for days.

   _____

10. City living is exciting, convenient, and provides amazing entertainment.

    _____

Answers on page 217.

Editing for Interest

Your essay will be read by people—real people who know that essays can be lively and interesting. Like readers everywhere, they'll be bored by writing that is dull.

Therefore, try to enliven your prose by:

✔ Using *active* instead of *passive* verbs
✔ Writing *active* instead of *passive* sentences
✔ Omitting needless words
✔ Using specific language

ACTIVE VERBS

TIP

Use active verbs whenever you can.

Because *active* verbs describe or show movement, they excel all other words in pumping vitality into your prose. *Being* verbs, in contrast, have almost no life in them. Their lifelessness is apparent in the common forms of the verb *to be*:

is	are	was
were	am	has been
had been	have been	will be

Being verbs ordinarily join the subject of a sentence to a predicate. They function much like an equal sign in an equation: "Five minus two *is* three" (5 – 2 = 3), or "Helena *was* happy" (Helena = happy), or "Your AP score *will be* 5" (That = good news!). Because being verbs (and equal signs) lack energy, use active verbs whenever you can.

Yes, it's hard to get along in speech and writing without *being* verbs. But be stingy with them. Check a few of your most recent essays. If more than, say, one out of four sentences uses a form of *to be* as its main verb, try the following revision techniques.

1. **SUBSTITUTE A NEW ACTIVE VERB FOR THE *BEING* VERB:**

   BEING VERB: It is not easy for most students to write immortal essays.

   ACTIVE VERB: Most students struggle to write immortal essays.

2. **EXTRACT AN ACTIVE VERB FROM A NOUN IN THE SENTENCE:**

   BEING VERB: Keizo was the winner of the essay contest.

   ACTIVE VERB: Keizo won the essay contest.

3. **EXTRACT AN ACTIVE VERB FROM AN ADJECTIVE:**

   BEING VERB: My weekend at the beach was enjoyable.

   ACTIVE VERB: I enjoyed my weekend at the beach.

As you delete *being* verbs, you'll probably notice that some sentences resist change. When that happens, turn subjects into verbs and verbs into nouns. Try also to eliminate unnecessary phrases. Full-scale sentence revisions can result in sentences bearing little resemblance to the originals, but verb-swapping often roots out excess verbiage and improves an essay's readability.

Being verbs are not the only verbs that sap the life out of sentences. They share that distinction with several other verbs, including forms of *to have, to come, to go, to make, to move*, and *to get*—verbs with so many different uses that they creep into our speech and writing virtually unnoticed. *Webster's International Dictionary* lists 16 different meanings for the verb *get* and a dozen more for *make* and *move*. It's true that we can hardly get by without these verbs, but use them only if you can swear that no other words will do. Otherwise, trade them in for more vivid verbs, as in:

DULL: The line to the box office *moved* very slowly.
LIVELIER: The line *crept* (*crawled*, *inched*, *poked*) to the box office.

Note that by using a more animated verb, you eliminate the need for "very slowly," which has suddenly become redundant.

DULL: The police officer *gave* drivers permission to turn left on red.
LIVELIER: The police officer *permitted* drivers to turn left on red.

Note that this revision has led not just to a more active sentence but one that contains fewer words—always a stylistic plus.

Mini-Workout: Active Verbs

Directions: Revise each of the following sentences by substituting active verbs for "being" verbs, but try not to change the meaning of the original.

1. Mariana and Leonardo were the highest scorers on the practice AP exam.

   _____

2. Cost is the determining factor in choosing a rug for my bedroom.

   _____

3. It is logical that admission to college is the result of a student's effort and achievement.

   _____

4. The monarchy was over after the Revolutionary War.

   _____

5. Since 9/11 there have been many more terrorist threats.

   _____

6. Chaos is a word that is relevant to my math class.

   _____

7. Everyone is scared of Mr. Gill.

   _____

8. The way to the principal's office is down the next corridor.

_____

9. There are students who are excellent in chemistry but not in physics.

_____

10. This novel was the one recommended by the librarian.

_____

Answers on page 217.

ACTIVE AND PASSIVE SENTENCES

TIP

Never use passive where you can use active.

Why?

Active sentences strengthen prose; passive sentences weaken it.

To write lively prose, keep in mind the difference between *active* and *passive* sentences. In an active sentence the person or thing performing an action is usually mentioned early in a sentence, so readers know right away who or what you are talking about. In passive sentences the performer of an action is not named or gets less notice than either the receiver of the action or the action itself. For example:

Two months were spent rehearsing for the concert.

This sentence fails to tell who performed the action—that is, who rehearsed for the concert. The following revision clears up the uncertainty:

Two months were spent rehearsing for the concert by the marching band.

This version transforms the original, but it still emphasizes the action instead of the performer of the action. To complete the transformation, say something like:

For two months the marching band rehearsed for the concert.

In the active voice, the performers of the action receive top billing.

Why is the active voice preferable? Mainly because most events in life don't just occur by themselves. Burgers don't just get eaten; people cook and devour them. Marriages don't just happen; couples deliberately go out and marry each other. Goals don't get scored, salmon don't get caught, wallets don't get lost all by themselves. People do these things.

Good essay writers, taking advantage of readers' natural curiosity about others, often strive to make the performer of the action the grammatical subject of their sentences:

PASSIVE: The award was presented to Hildie by the Art Club.

ACTIVE: The Art Club presented the award to Hildie.

PASSIVE: Ohio State was attended by my brother, my cousin, and three of my uncles.

ACTIVE: My brother, my cousin, and three uncles went to Ohio State.

In some contexts, of course, the actor is unknown or irrelevant. That's when a passive sentence works best. For example:

PASSIVE: The curtain was raised at 8:30 sharp.
ACTIVE: At 8:30 sharp, a stagehand (or Maryanne, the production assistant) raised the curtain.

In the passive version, curtain time is the important fact. Who pulled the rope or pushed the button doesn't matter.

Transforming a passive sentence to an active one takes a bit of editing. As you prepare for the AP, examine your essays for passive sentences. Change them to active sentences unless you have a very good reason not to.

Mini-Workout: Revising Passive Sentences

Directions: Put each of the following sentences into active voice:

1. The backyard was covered by dead leaves.

   _____

2. The situation in Syria was discussed by us.

   _____

3. Friday's quiz was failed because I had been at a play rehearsal every night that week.

   _____

4. Portland was flown to at the start of our weeklong vacation in Oregon.

   _____

5. The Golden Fleece was pursued by Jason and the Argonauts.

   _____

6. The newspaper was fetched by Rex every morning.

   _____

7. The decision to build a fence on the border was made by immigration officials.

   _____

8. Pizza was ordered by more than twenty diners on Saturday night.

   _____

9. Five of Shakespeare's plays were seen by our group in three days.

_____

10. The voters were urged by the candidate to throw the old mayor out of office.

_____

Answers on pages 217–218.

CUTTING NEEDLESS WORDS

Never use two words when one will do. If it's possible to cut a word out, always cut it out. Tell your readers quickly and directly what you have to say. Brevity works best. Cut out verbiage. Readers value economy.

Stop! Have you noticed that the previous paragraph disregards the very advice it dispenses? Do you see repetition and redundancy? Couldn't the point have been made more succinctly?

Here's a word to the wise:

You should work through all of the sentences you write by examining each one and crossing out all the words you don't definitely need.

To be precise, that's twenty-four words to the wise—many more than are needed.

Go through every sentence you write and cross out unnecessary words.

That's better—eleven words of free advice, but still too many. The sentence could be trimmed still further:

Trim unnecessary words out of every sentence.

This seven-word model is less than a third of the original twenty-four-word clunker. But it can be pared even more:

Omit needless words.

And still more:

Cut verbosity.

To make every word count, wring your sentences through this four-step word trimmer:

STEP 1 Look for repetition.

WORDY: Elena took Jesse to the movies. Jesse is Elena's brother. (10 words)
TRIMMED: Elena took her brother Jesse to the movies. (8 words)

Granted, cutting 10 words to 8 is not much. But consider that it's a 20 percent reduction, and in a 500-word essay, a 20 percent reduction amounts to 100 words—the equivalent of a whole paragraph.

WORDY: When Hannah was sixteen years of age she accepted a position at the Moraga Nursery. In this position she learned about plants and about how to handle customers. (28)
TRIMMED: At sixteen years old, Hannah accepted a position at the Moraga Nursery, where she learned about plants and handling customers. (20)
RE-TRIMMED: Working at the Moraga Nursery at age sixteen, Hannah learned to handle both plants and customers. (16)

TIP

Never use two words when one will do.

STEP 2 Hunt for phrases that add words but no meaning, such as *the fact that, due to the fact that, at this point in time, at the present time, that being said,* and comparable usages.

WORDY: Hamlet returned home as a result of his father's death. (10)

TRIMMED: Hamlet returned home because his father died. (7).

WORDY: The troops were in danger due to the fact that mines had been planted in the field. (16)

TRIMMED: The mine field endangered the troops. (6)

Wordy Phrases	Trimmed
what I mean is	I mean
on account of, as a result of	because
in the final analysis	finally
few and far between	few
each and every one	each
this is a subject that	this subject
ten in number	ten
at the age of six years old	at age six
most unique	unique
true fact	fact
biography of her life	biography
in regard to, with regard to, in relation to, with respect to	about

STEP 3 Search for redundancies. Innumerable words are wasted on reiteration of what has already been stated, on repeating the obvious, on restating ideas, on saying the same thing again and again and over, driving readers to the brink of madness.

WORDY: A cloud of black soot rose up to the sky. (10)

Soot, by definition, is black, and rising clouds can only go up.

TRIMMED: A cloud of soot rose to the sky. (8)

WORDY: He had a smile on his face. (7)

Where else but on a face would a smile appear?

TRIMMED: He wore a smile. (4)

WORDY: After carefully scrutinizing the X-ray, Dr. Jackson seemed fully engrossed in her own train of thought. (16)

Scrutinize means "to study carefully," and engrossed means "to think fully." Also, *her own train of thought* is nonsensical because no one can think others' thoughts.

TRIMMED: After scrutinizing the X-ray, Dr. Jackson seemed engrossed in thought. (10)

After you have pared your sentences to the bone, re-read what remains and discard still more by tracking down little words like *the, a, an, up, down, its,* and *and.* Even though it may hurt to take out what you worked hard to put in, don't whine. Just grit your teeth and be tough!

STEP 4 Look for telltale words like *which, who, that, thing,* and *all.* They often signify excess verbiage.

WORDY: Tesla was a man who was obsessed by the wonders of electricity. (12)

TRIMMED: The wonders of electricity obsessed Tesla. (6)

Changing the grammatical subject and replacing *was* with an active verb halved the word count.

WORDY: What he most wanted was that the terrorists would release the hostages. (12)

TRIMMED: He most wanted the terrorists to release the hostages. (9)

Mini-Workout: Cutting Needless Words

PART A

> **Directions:** Tighten these sentences, but preserve their meaning.

1. The biker, a woman named Mary Roe, wrote a book with the title *A Ride Across America,* about biking across America, which she accomplished after riding 90 miles a day in order to prepare for her ride across America.

   _____

   _____

2. There is no reason for the chairperson of the committee, who is Carolyn Welles, to take offense at my suggestion, which is aimed at trying to make the meetings more productive and useful to the entire student body at large.

   _____

   _____

3. Mr. Evans was appointed to be the treasurer of the group in spite of fact that he had once been arrested and tried and sent to jail for a period of six months for embezzling some money from the business he worked for.

   _____

   _____

4. Harmful criticism is criticism that tears a person down instead of helping the person overcome or deal with a problem.

   _____

   _____

5. All Americans should try to save gasoline, and the best way they can save gasoline all across the country is to cut down on the number of miles they drive when it's really not necessary to drive.

_____

_____

PART B

> **Directions:** The following paragraph comes from an essay that advocated gaining weight. Please trim its fat.

Such weight-gaining ideas can be used to good advantage by each and every man, woman, and child who is interested in adding pounds of weight to his or her body. They are the latest, most up-to-date set of procedures available anywhere. Owing to the fact that health experts and authorities believe that it is better to be underweight than it is to be overweight, ideas for putting on weight are generally thought to be jokes not taken seriously, which is the reason why such ideas are kept under wraps and not publicized very widely or broadly. Yet, there are many people of all kinds who need to gain weight for a variety of diverse reasons. Here is a quotation that Slim Snyder, who is a graduate of Stanford University, stated during a speech he gave at a meeting of people gathered together at a health conference recently: "Lean people are victims of discrimination, just as obese people are."

_____

_____

_____

_____

_____

_____

_____

_____

Answers on page 218.

BEING SPECIFIC

Specific words are memorable, while hazy words fade quickly away. Tell your garage mechanic vaguely, "This car is broken," and he'll ask for more information. If a patient in the E.R. says, "I feel pain," a doctor wants to know exactly where it hurts.

In the first draft of an essay for his AP English class, Maccabee S. wrote the following about a day he'd like to forget:

> It was an awful day outside. Everything was going wrong. I felt terrible. Things weren't going well in school. I got a below-par grade on a paper, and I was sure that I had failed my Chem quiz. I also had lots of things to do at home and no time to do them. My mother was in a bad mood, too. She yelled at me for all kinds of things. Then Penny called, and we got into a disagreement. I had trouble with my iPhone, and I couldn't fix it. I went to bed early, hoping that tomorrow would be better.

Reviewing this paragraph a few days later, Maccabee realized the writing begged for more specificity. Yes, the day had been dreadful, but his account needed specific language to prove it. The next draft took care of that:

> On a cold and rainy November day, my life was as miserable as the weather. I felt chills all day, and my throat was sore. In school I got a D on a history paper about the Bubonic Plague, and I was sure that I had failed the chemistry quiz on molecular modeling. The homework was piling up: two lab reports, more than 150 pages to read in Wuthering Heights, a chapter in the history text, and about a hundred new vocabulary words in Spanish. I didn't have time or energy to do it all, especially when my mother started to pick at me about my messy room and the thank you letters I'm supposed to write to my grandparents. Just as she was reminding me that my SAT registration was overdue, Penny called to say that she couldn't come for Thanksgiving after all, so we argued about loyalty and trust and keeping promises. Then she hung up on me. Half an hour later I tried to text her, but my phone was frozen. I tried changing the battery, forcing it into recovery mode, but got nothing but a blank screen. Disgusted, I threw the damn thing across the room. By 9:30 P.M. I fell into bed, hoping that tomorrow would be better.

This version includes many specific details that vividly illustrate the wretchedness of Maccabee's miserable day. Not every paragraph of every essay calls for such detail, but an essay consisting solely of generalities will leave readers at sea.

It's true that vague, shadowy words are easier to think of. But they're often used as a smoke screen to cover up the absence of thought. For example, it's easy to pass judgment on a book by calling it "good" or "interesting." But what readers should be told is precisely why you think so. It's simple to call someone "old" without bothering to show the reader a "round-shouldered, white-haired man hunched in a wheelchair." A student who calls her teacher "ugly" sends a different image of ugliness to each reader. But if the teacher is a "shifty-eyed tyrant who spits when she talks," the specific details create a vivid image. Or if the teacher's personality is ugly, show her cruelly insulting her hapless students.

Of course, it's not essential to back up every generalization with specific details. An essay bogged down in detail can be tedious both to read and to write. Every time you mention *dinner*, you don't have to recite the menu. Excessive analysis is boring, but so is too little. A balance is best. No one can tell you precisely how to achieve that balance. To develop the feel of what seems right takes time and practice, like riding a bike or doing a back flip. In the end, the content and purpose of an essay will have to determine how specific it needs to be.

Context determines how abstract your essay should be. Ask yourself what is most important—giving readers a more detailed account of a general idea or pushing on to other more vital matters. Just keep in mind that nobody likes reading essays that fail to deal concretely with anything.

Mini-Workout: Writing Specifically

STRATEGY

To develop the knack of writing specifically, study a written passage that you admire. Pick out both details and broad statements. For practice, use the passage as a model for writing a paragraph of your own.

> **Directions:** The following sentences desperately need more specific wording. Please provide the verbal antidote to their vagueness.

1. Missy's score on the AP English exam was high.

   _____

2. Mr. Guzman possesses a variety of values.

   _____

3. Ms. Cronin could care less about my problem doing homework.

   _____

4. Sort of violently, Carrie expressed her anger at the other team's player.

   _____

5. Mitchell studied hard, but to no avail.

   _____

6. Winning the overwhelming approval of the people gave the candidate great satisfaction.

   _____

7. People don't care about pollution in the ocean.

   _____

8. My science class is pretty useless.

   _____

9. The twins were very poor when they were growing up.

_____

10. My parents were happy when I got accepted in college.

_____

Answers on pages 218–219.

Editing for Standard Usage and Mechanics

Save some editing time to proofread your essays for proper spelling, punctuation, and grammar. You won't be penalized for one or two isolated errors, but AP readers are required to deduct credit from papers crowded with mechanical mistakes.

HANDWRITING MATTERS

Don't be like the would-be bank robber in Antioch, California, who recently handed a teller an unreadable note and fled the bank empty-handed. Sloppy, hard-to-read handwriting is not supposed to count against you on the AP exam, but think of your readers: Bogged down in a barely legible essay, they can grow impatient and irritable.

Whether you plan to rob banks or boost your AP score, write legibly. Get into the habit of scrutinizing your penmanship for every letter that doesn't look the way it should. Easier said than done, for sure. But ask a friend to read one of your handwritten essays aloud. Wherever he or she stumbles may be a place where your handwriting needs work.

To minimize writing errors:

✔ Write Correct Sentences
✔ Use the Correct Verbs
✔ Use Adjectives and Adverbs Correctly
✔ Choose Correct Pronouns
✔ Review Punctuation and Capitalization

WRITING CORRECT SENTENCES

Time won't permit you to meticulously analyze every sentence in your essays. But if you get into the habit of examining sentences in your practice essays and in other schoolwork, you'll soon purge from your writing the three most common sentence errors:

- **Fragments**—incomplete sentences
- **Run-ons**—two or more improperly joined sentences
- **Comma splices**—two complete sentences separated by a comma

FRAGMENTS

Sentence fragments often look remarkably like complete sentences. But looks can be deceptive.

The bike that Blossom often borrowed.

This fragment appears to have all the characteristics of a sentence: It starts with a capital letter and ends with a period, it conveys a complete thought (*Blossom often borrowed the bike* is a complete thought), and it seems to contain a subject (*Blossom*) and a verb (*borrowed*). What makes it a fragment, though, is that *Blossom* isn't the subject. Rather, *bike* is the subject, and the trouble is that *bike* and the verb *borrowed* don't fit together. A bike, after all, is an inanimate object and can't do any borrowing—at least not in the real world. Clearly, Blossom did the borrowing, but the noun *Blossom* cannot be the subject of the sentence because it is part of the subordinate clause, *that Blossom borrowed*. Therefore, *bike* needs a verb of its own.

The bike that Blossom often borrowed was stolen.

With the addition of *was stolen*, the sentence is now complete.

To determine whether a sentence is complete, uncover its "bare bones." That is, eliminate all its dependent clauses, phrases, and verbals. If what remains is a subject and its verb, it's a complete sentence. If not, it's probably a fragment.

To nail down the subject of long sentences may take some doing, but the bare-bones strategy usually works if you remember that grammatical subjects can never reside in prepositional phrases, dependent clauses, or phrases that interrupt the flow of the sentence.

Beware, too, of sentence fragments that can occur when you use the *-ing* form of a verb. The problem is that it cannot serve as a sentence's main verb—at least not without a helping verb.

FRAGMENT: Leah, at the box office, *selling* movie tickets to the 7:00 show.
CORRECT: Leah, at the box office, *has been selling* movie tickets to the 7:00 show.

The addition of the helping verb *has been* corrects the error. Other helping verbs include *is, was, will be,* and other forms of the verb *to be*.

TO FIND THE "BARE BONES" OF A SENTENCE

STEP 1 Cross out all prepositional phrases, such as *up the wall*, *around the corner*, *to the beach*, *over the counter*. If you eliminate all the prepositional phrases in these sentences, for instance, only the subject and the verb—the "bare bones"—will remain.

COMPLETE SENTENCE: In the middle of the night, Priscilla slept.

BARE BONES: Priscilla slept.

COMPLETE SENTENCE: One of Frieda's friends is in need of help.

BARE BONES: One is.

STEP 2 Delete all the dependent clauses—those parts of sentences which contain a noun and a verb, but which don't qualify as complete sentences because they begin with words and phrases like *although*, *as*, *as though*, *because*, *before*, *even though*, *if*, *in spite of*, *regardless of*, *since*, *so that*, *unless*, *whenever*, *whether*, and *while*. Other dependent clauses are statements (not questions) that start with when, where, which, who, and what.

Once the dependent clauses in the following sentences are gone, only the main clauses will remain. That's where to find the bare bones of each sentence.

COMPLETE SENTENCE: Because she missed the bus, Marnie wept.

BARE BONES: Marnie wept.

COMPLETE SENTENCE: While Willie waited for the bus, he studied vocabulary.

BARE BONES: He studied.

STEP 3 Delete interrupters—those parts of sentences that impede the smooth flow of the main idea. Interrupters may be just one word (*however*, *nevertheless*) or dozens. They're often set off by commas.

COMPLETE SENTENCE: Serena, regardless of the look on her face, rejoiced.

BARE BONES: Serena rejoiced.

COMPLETE SENTENCE: The boat, a sleek white catamaran, sank.

BARE BONES: Boat sank.

COMPLETE SENTENCE: Ryan, who got ticketed for doing 60 in a 30 mph zone, paid the fine.

BARE BONES: Ryan paid.

The process of identifying the bare bones of a sentence is often more complex than that suggested by these examples. But if you practice by carefully peeling away selected sentence parts, you'll eventually lay bare the subject and verb.

RUN-ON SENTENCES

A *run-on sentence* consists of two independent clauses with nothing but a blank space between them:

> Birthstones are supposed to bring good luck mine has never brought me any.

Fill the gap between *luck* and *mine* by inserting the coordinating conjunction *but*.

> Birthstones are supposed to bring good luck, *but* mine has never brought me any.

A comma has also been added because a compound sentence needs a comma between its clauses unless the clauses are very short, as in:

> Carla drove but I walked.

Another way to eliminate run-ons is to write two separate sentences:

> Birthstones are supposed to bring good luck. Mine has never brought me any.

Or you can use a semicolon, which functions like a period.

> Birthstones are supposed to bring good luck; mine has never brought me any.

Note that the initial letter of a sentence that follows a semicolon is never capitalized.

COMMA SPLICES

In a *comma splice*, a comma instead of a period or semi-colon is used to join, or splice, two independent sentences.

> Othello was fooled by a disloyal friend, he should have known better.

Replace the comma with a period and start a new sentence with *He*, or, use a semicolon:

> Othello was fooled by a disloyal friend; he should have known better.

Mini-Workout: Writing Correct Sentences

> **Directions:** Look for sentence fragments, run-ons, and comma splices. Use the spaces to identify the error and write the sentence correctly. Some items may contain no error.

1. Because Amy is stressed out about the garbage in the back yard.

   _____

2. St. Petersburg was renamed Leningrad after the Russian Revolution, its original name was restored in the 1990s.

   _____

3. My grandmother is eighty-six years old therefore she walks very slowly.

   _____

4. During the night, the stars that came out like diamonds on black velvet.

   _____

5. There is a belief among superstitious people that birthmarks are caused by influences on the mother before the child is born.

   _____

6. This year's senior class being more involved than last year's.

   _____

7. The American colonists despised the King's tax on British tea they drank Dutch tea instead.

   _____

8. Kayly found a squirrel lying dead in a ditch she didn't tell Kyle.

   _____

9. A biologist working in the field of genetic engineering; involved in the controversy surrounding human cloning.

   _____

10. Use the space below to tell one story about yourself to provide the admissions committee, either directly or indirectly, with an insight into the kind of person you are.

   _____

Answers on page 219.

USING CORRECT VERBS

Of all the parts of speech, verbs are the most apt to be used incorrectly. As you edit your AP essays, therefore, ask yourself the following three questions:

1. Do all nouns and pronouns agree in number with their verbs?
2. Is every verb in the correct tense?
3. Is every verb in the correct form?

NOUN-VERB AGREEMENT A.K.A. SUBJECT-VERB AGREEMENT

Nouns and verbs must agree in *number* and in *person*. A mismatch in number occurs when a singular noun is used with a plural verb, or vice-versa. That's why *the tiger were* and *the tigers was* are nonstandard usages.

A mismatch in *person* occurs when the subject is a pronoun and the writer uses a verb of a different person, as in *he are, you is,* and *they am*.

To avoid errors in noun-verb agreement (often called *subject-verb agreement*), it's useful to know the language constructions that most often cause problems:

TIP

Be on the lookout for words inserted between subjects and verbs.

Intervening Words Between the Subject and Verb

Few people make agreement errors when the verb comes right after the subject. But clauses and phrases that comes between the noun (i.e., the grammatical subject), or subject, and the verb can sometimes lead you astray:

Delivery (singular subject) of today's newspapers and magazines have been (plural verb) delayed.

The prepositional phrase *of today's newspapers and magazines* blurs the relationship between subject and verb, and the plural noun *magazines* can mislead you into using a plural verb. With a correctly matched subject and verb, the sentence reads:

Delivery (singular subject) of today's newspapers and magazines has been (singular verb) delayed.

In short, verbs must agree with the subject, not with words mistakenly thought to be the subject.

Take note, too, that such intervening phrases such as *in addition to, along with, as well as, including,* and other similar phrases don't influence the number of the verb.

One (singular subject) of Ikuku's stories, in addition to several of her poems, was (singular verb) chosen to be published in the school literary magazine.

Subjects Composed of More Than One Noun or Pronoun

Both singular and plural nouns, when joined by *and*, are called compound subjects and need plural verbs:

The *picture and the text* (compound subject) *go* (plural verb) inside this box. Several *locust trees and a green mailbox* (compound subject) *stand* (plural verb) outside the house.

Compound subjects thought of as a unit need singular verbs:

> Green *eggs and ham* (compound subject as a unit) is (singular verb) Fannie's favorite breakfast.

Singular nouns joined by *or* or *nor* take singular verbs.

> A Coke *or* a Pepsi (two nouns joined by *or*) is (singular verb) what I thirst for.

When a subject consists of a singular noun and a plural noun joined by *or* or *nor*, the number of the verb is determined by the noun closer to the verb.

> *Either a pineapple or some oranges are* on the table.
> *Neither the linemen nor the quarterback was* aware of the tricky play.

When a subject contains a pronoun that differs in person from a noun or another pronoun, the verb must agree with the closer subject word.

> Neither Meredith nor *you are* expected to finish the work today.
> Either he or *I am* planning to work late on Saturday.

When the subject is singular and the predicate noun is plural, or vice versa, the number of the verb is determined by the subject.

> The *bulk* of Wilkinson's work *is* two novels and a collection of stories.
> Two *novels and a story* are the bulk of Wilkinson's work.

Singular Subjects Containing Words That Sound Plural

The names of certain books (*All the King's Men*), teams (New England Patriots), diseases (mumps), course titles (Robotics), and other singular nouns may sound like plurals because they end in –*s*, but most of the time—although not always—they need a singular verb.

> The *news* is good.
> *Measles* is going around the school.

Subjects That Are Sometimes Singular and Sometimes Plural

Collective nouns sound singular but may be plural. A family, for example, is singular. But if you are referring to separate individuals, *family* takes a plural verb.

> The *family* (members) *are* arriving for the wedding at different times.

Other collective nouns include *group, crowd, team, jury, soybeans, audience, herd, public, dozen, class, band, flock, majority, committee, heap*, and *lot*. Other words and expressions governed by the same rule are units of time, money, weight, measurement, and all fractions.

> The *jury is* going to decide today.
> The *jury are* returning to their homes tomorrow.

Indefinite Pronouns Used as Subjects

Indefinite pronouns such as *everyone, both,* and *any* pose a special problem. Some indefinite pronouns must be matched with singular verbs, some with plural verbs, and some with one or the other, depending on the sense of the sentence. There's no getting around the fact that you need to know which number applies to which pronoun.

1. These words, although they sound plural, get singular verbs: *each, either, neither,* the "ones" (*anyone, no one, everyone, someone*), and the "bodies" (*anybody, everybody, nobody, somebody*).

   Each man and woman in the room **gets** only one vote.
   Everyone who works hard **is** going to earn an "A."

2. These words get plural verbs: *both, many, few, several.*

   In spite of rumors to the contrary, **both are** on the verge of a nervous breakdown.
   Several in the band **are** not going on the trip to Boston.

3. The following words require singular verbs when they refer to singular nouns but plural verbs when they refer to plural nouns: *any, none, some, all, most.*

   Some of the collection is valuable.

   In this sentence *some* is singular because it refers to *collection,* a singular noun.

   Some of the bracelets are fake.

   Here *some* is plural because it refers to *bracelets,* a plural noun.

A Subject Following the Verb

When the subject of a sentence follows the verb, the verb takes its number from the subject, as usual.

Behind the building *was* an *alley* (singular subject).
Behind the building *were* an *alley and a vacant lot* (compound subject).

Mini-Workout: Noun-Verb/Subject-Verb Agreement

> **Directions:** In some of the sentences below, verbs fail to agree with nouns. Locate the error and write the correct verb in the space provided. Some sentences may be correct.

1. A long line of cars, trucks, SUVs, and motorcycles were stuck in a traffic jam near the construction zone.

   _____

2. Either my sister or one of her boyfriends have always given me a ride to school.

   _____

3. The Board of Trustees are meeting in Springfield this year instead of in Chicago.

   _____

4. The price of gasoline, in addition to the price of home heating oil, are expected to rise this winter.

   _____

5. Lilah and Lucy started an after-school tutoring service which have more customers than they can handle.

   _____

6. There is many levels on which a reader will be able to enjoy this book.

   _____

7. Proceeds from the sale of concert tickets is going to help the victims of the hurricane.

   _____

8. The newspaper reports that a rescue team experienced in climbing rugged mountains are expected to arrive at the site of the crash tomorrow morning.

   _____

9. According to school policy, there is to be two security guards stationed in the playground during recess to protect the children.

   _____

10. Many community members say that the promises made by the principal has not brought about the changes that he predicted.

   _____

Answers on page 219.

USING CORRECT VERB TENSES

Verb tenses convey information about the relative time when an action occurred. To express past action, add *–ed* to the present form: *walk/walked, cry/cried*. To express future action, add *will* before the present tense: *will walk, will cry*. For present perfect, past perfect, and future perfect forms, add *has, have, had* or *will have*, as in *have walked, has cried, had typed, will have arrived*, and so forth.

Verb tenses permit you to indicate time sequence very precisely. But someone not attuned to distinctions between tenses may say something like this:

There was a condo where the park was.

The meaning may be clear enough, but to state the idea more accurately, it should read:

There was a condo where the park *had been*.

The original sentence states that the condo and park were in the same place at the same time—a physical impossibility. Using the past perfect verb *had been*, however, would clearly state that the condo replaced the park.

This is a subtle difference, but sensitivity to such differences helps you to convey meaning more accurately. Familarity with the following conventions governing verb tense will help you avoid errors:

Truisms Are Expressed in the Present Tense Regardless of Other Verbs in the Sentence.

Christmas *is* (present) on December 25th.

Sammy *had been taught* (past perfect) that triangles *contain* (present) 180 degrees.

In Complex Sentences, the Tense of Verbs in the Main Clause and Dependent Clause Must Be in Sequence.

They had driven (past perfect) 20 miles before Chuckie realized (past) that the gas tank was almost empty.

(Because the driving occurred before Chuckie's realization, the past perfect—not the past tense—in needed to show the sequence of events.)

Your teacher believes (present) that you will do (future) well on the AP.

In an *if* clause, don't use *would have* to express the earlier of two actions. Instead use the past perfect.

NO: If Woody *would have studied* more, he would have made the Honor Society.

YES: If Woody *had studied* (past perfect) more, he would have made the Honor Society.

NO: The party would have been better if Watu *would have played* the piano.

YES: The party would have been better if Watu *had played* (past perfect) the piano.

The Tense of Infinitives (*To Eat, To Snow, To Have Eaten, To Have Snowed*, etc.) Is Governed by the Main Verb and by the Meaning of the Sentence.

Eileen was (main verb in past tense) delighted to receive (present infinitive) the award.

(The present infinitive is used because Eileen received the award before she felt happy about getting it.)

When the infinitive refers to a time before the action described by the main verb, the perfect infinitive should be used.

Eileen is (main verb) happy to have received (perfect infinitive) the award.

Adjust Participles (Often Ending in -*ing*) According to the Tense of the Main Verb. When the Participle Describes an Action Occurring Before the Action of the Main Verb, Add *Having* and Then Adjust the Participle.

NO: Working (participle) hard on the essay, Hank opposed cutting the number of words. (Because Hank worked on the essay before he resisted cutting it, the participle needs to be revised.)

YES: *Having worked* hard on the essay, Hank opposed cutting the number of words.

Mini-Workout: Verb Tenses

> **Directions:** In these sentences, the underlined verbs may be in the wrong tense. Write the correct verbs in the spaces provided. Some sentences may contain no error.

1. When he talks with his wife, Macbeth <u>felt</u> overcome with guilt.

   _____

2. When they crossed the country by car, they <u>had visited</u> Mount Rushmore.

   _____

3. In the school parking lot, a policeman stops her and <u>asked</u> to see her driver's license.

   _____

4. <u>Writing</u> a poem every week for a year, Quinn finally got one accepted by a literary magazine.

   _____

5. In the afternoon we spotted many friends we <u>saw</u> that morning at the pancake breakfast.

   _____

6. Once the levee had broken, the streets have been flooded.

_____

7. For anyone with enough brains to have thought about the problem, now is the time to work out a solution.

_____

8. If Ariane would have stayed home, she would not have missed Eamon's visit.

_____

9. Marcy kept the promise she has given to Kendra last summer.

_____

10. The airline pilot expects to have seen the lights of the San Jose airport by now.

_____

Answers on page 220.

CHOOSING ADJECTIVES AND ADVERBS

Errors sometimes occur when an adjective is used where an adverb is required. The reverse—using an adverb in place of an adjective—occurs less often. Check your essay for the proper use of adjectives and adverbs.

Adjectives

Adjectives describe, or modify, nouns and pronouns.

Good is an adjective. Like any adjective, it can be used to descibe a noun, as in *good book, good pie, good night.* That's easy.

Good, along with some other adjectives, causes trouble when used after a verb. Because it won't work after most verbs, avoid using *talks good, sleeps good, writes good,* and so on.

Good, as well as other adjectives, however, can be used after some verbs—those called *linking verbs*, among them, *look, smell, taste, feel, appear, seem, remain,* and all forms of *to be.* So, it's perfectly correct to say *sounds good, feels good,* and *is good.*

What complicates matters is that linking verbs sometimes function as active verbs. *Look,* for instance, is a linking verb when referring to appearance, as in:

The day *looks* good for flying.

But it is an active verb when it refers to the act of looking, as in:

Lindsay *looked* sadly at her sick cat.

If you're not sure whether a verb is being used as a linking verb or an active verb, substitute a form of the verb *to be* in its place. If the sentence retains its basic meaning, the verb may well be a linking verb, as in:

The juice *tastes* good. (The juice *is* good.)

She will *stay* asleep for a century. (She *will be* asleep for a century.)

Because the second version of each sentence pretty well maintains the meaning of the original, *tastes* and *stay* are linking verbs and may be followed by any adjective you choose: *sour, sweet, tart, spoiled, inactive, torpid, somnolent*, and a zillion more.

Adverbs

Adverbs, often recognizable by their *–ly* endings, usually describe, or modify, verbs, adjectives, or other adverbs. Much of the time they supply the answer to such questions as How? When? How much? Where? In what sequence? To what exent? In what manner?

How does Brodie run? Brodie runs *well*. (The adverb *well* modifies the verb *run*.)

How did the grass look? The grass looked mostly brown. (The adverb *mostly* modifies the adjective *brown*.)

Where did Abigail sit? Abigail sat down. (The adverb *down* modifies the verb *sat*.)

In what manner did she sit down? She sat down quickly. (The adverb *quickly* modifies the verb *sat*.)

If you ever need to choose between an adjective and an adverb while writing your AP essays, follow this simple two-step procedure:

First: Find the verb and determine whether it is a linking verb.

Second: If it is, use the adjective; if not, use the adverb.

Also, if the word modifies an adjective or another adverb, remember to use the adverb. If it modifies a noun or pronoun, use the adjective.

Mini-Workout: Adjectives And Adverbs

> **Directions:** Check each of these sentences for faulty use of adjectives and adverbs. Write the correct word in the spaces provided. Some sentences may be correct.

1. Annabelle spoke sincere to Tim when she promised to marry him some day.

    _____

2. Rod always feels shyly about speaking in front of the class.

    _____

3. When the batter got hit in the head, the fans thought he had been hurt bad.

    _____

4. "No problem, Mr. Reynolds, I can do both jobs easy."

   _____

5. The audience remained calmly, even when the hall began to fill with smoke.

   _____

6. Later that day, Kirk and Eliza spoke frankly about their disagreement.

   _____

7. He walked down the corridor completely oblivious to the trail of papers he left behind.

   _____

8. Be sure to shut the door secure because it tends to swing open by itself.

   _____

9. The tyrant looked down cynical on the crowd assembled in the piazza.

   _____

10. The nurse felt bitterly that she had contracted the flu from a patient.

    _____

Answers on page 220.

USING PRONOUNS CORRECTLY

Skim your essay for pronoun errors. Faulty pronoun usage results most often:

- When pronouns in the wrong "case" are chosen
- When the pronoun reference is unclear or ambiguous
- When pronouns fail to agree in number or gender with their antecedents

Pronoun Case

Most of the time you can probably depend on your ear to tell you what's right and wrong. For example, you'd never say to the bus driver, "Let *I* off at the corner." But you can't always depend on your sense of what sounds right and wrong, especially when pronouns are paired, as in *he and I* and *me and them*. Then, it helps to know that pronouns fall into two groups:

GROUP 1: *I, he, she, they, we, you*

GROUP 2: *me, him, her, them, us, you*

The pronouns in the first group are *nominative case* pronouns and are used in grammatical subjects and predicate nominatives. The second group—*objective case* pronouns—are used everywhere else. Because pronouns, when used in pairs, must come from the same case, "*Him* and *I* went to the movies" is a nonstandard usage.

Any time you need a pair of pronouns, and you know that one of them is correct, pick the other from the same group. If you don't know either pronoun, here's a handy rule of thumb to follow: Substitute *I* or *me* for one of them. If *I* seems to fit, choose pronouns from Group 1; if *me* fits better, use Group 2.

Elvis asked that (he, him) and (she, her) practice handstands.

If you insert *me* in place of one of the pronouns, you'll get:

Elvis asked that me practice handstands.

Because no one would say that seriously, *I* must be the word that fits. So the pronouns you need come from Group 1, and the sentence should read:

Elvis asked that he and she practice handstands.

Use objective case pronouns in phrases that begin with prepositions, as in:

between *you* and *me*,
to Rhyana and *her*
among *us* women

A FEW MORE PRINCIPLES OF PRONOUN CASE

- Use objective case pronouns when the pronoun refers to a person to whom something is being done:

  Taylor invited *him* to the prom.

  The waiter gave *her* and *me* a piece of cake.

- To find the correct pronoun in a comparison, complete the comparison using the verb that would follow naturally:

  Rennie runs faster than *she* (runs).

  A woman such as *I* (am) could solve the problem.

- When a pronoun appears side by side with a noun (*we* boys, *us* women), deleting the noun will help you pick the correct pronoun:

  (*We, Us*) seniors decided to take a day off from school in late May. (Deleting *seniors* leaves <u>We</u> decided to . . .).

  This award was presented to (*we, us*) students by the faculty. (Deleting *students* leaves *award was presented to <u>us</u> by the* . . .).

- Use possessive pronouns (*my, our, your, his, her, their*) before a *gerund*, a noun that looks like a verb because of its *-ing* ending.

  Her asking the question shows that she is alert. (*Asking* is a gerund.)

  Mother was upset about *your* opening the presents too soon. (*Opening* is a gerund.)

GERUNDS

What is a gerund? It's a verb form that ends in *–ing* and is used as a noun.

Fishing is my grandpa's favorite pastime.
He started *fishing* as a boy in North Carolina.
As a result of all that *fishing* he hates to eat fish.

In all three sentences the gerund is derived from the verb *to fish*. Don't confuse gerunds with the participle form of verbs, as in:

PARTICIPLE: *Fishing* from the bank of the river, my Grandpa caught a catfish.

GERUND: *Fishing* from the bank of a river is my Grandpa's greatest pleasure.

Not every noun with an *-ing* ending is a gerund. Sometimes it's just a noun, as in *thing, ring, spring*. At other times, *-ing* words are verbs, in particular, they're participles that modify pronouns in the objective case.

I hope you don't mind *my* intruding on your conversation (Here *intruding* is a gerund.)

I hope you don't mind *me* intruding on your conversation. (Here *intruding* is a participle.)

Mini-Workout: Pronoun Choice

Directions: Find the pronoun errors in the following sentences. Write the correct pronoun in the space provided. Some sentences may be correct.

1. Josh took my brother and I to the magic show last night.

   _____

2. He said that in my pocket I would find $10 in change to split between me and Lucy.

   _____

3. The waiter promised to hold the table for we girls.

   _____

4. Him and me took turns on the treadmill.

   _____

5. They refused to let we boys into the arena without reservations.

   _____

6. When the coins fell out of his sleeve, the audience laughed even harder than us.

   _____

7. Him falling asleep at the wheel caused the accident.

   _____

8. Did you stay as long as they at the dance?

   _____

9. I never spoke with them—neither he nor his brother.

   _____

10. If I were him, I'd practice for a long time before the next performance.

   _____

Answers on page 220.

PRONOUN REFERENCES

Check the reference of every pronoun in your essay. Be certain that each refers clearly to its antecedent—usually a noun or another pronoun. Avoid the confusion that results when no clear tie exists or when a pronoun seems to refer to more than one antecedent:

The librarian told Sophia that it was *her* responsibility to shelve the books.

Who is responsible? The librarian or Sophia? It's impossible to tell because the pronoun *her* may refer to either of them. Revised, the sentence reads:

The librarian told Sophia that one of her responsibilities as a library clerk was to shelve books.

A sentence containing two or more pronouns with ambiguous references can be especially troublesome and unclear:

Mike became a good friend of Morgan's after *he* helped *him* repair *his* Toyota.

Whose car needed fixing? Who helped whom? To answer these questions, the sentence needs to be rewritten:

Mike and Morgan became good friends after Morgan helped Mike repair *his* Toyota.

This version is better, but it's still uncertain who owned the car. One way to set the meaning straight is to use more than one sentence:

When Morgan needed to repair his Toyota, Mike helped him do the job. Afterward, Mike and Morgan became good friends.

To be correct, a pronoun should refer directly and clearly to a specific noun or another pronoun, or it should refer by implication to an idea. Such implied references frequently involve the pronouns *it*, *they*, and *you*, and the relative pronouns *which*, *that*, and *this*, and cause trouble mostly when the pronoun is used to refer to rather general or ambiguous ideas, as in:

Homeless people allege that the city is indifferent to their plight, *which* has been disproved.

What has been disproved? That an allegation was made? That the city is indifferent? The intended meaning is unclear because *which* has no distinct antecedent. To clear up the uncertainty, the sentence might read:

Homeless people allege that the city is indifferent to their plight, but the allegation has been disproved.

Finally, don't use pronouns to refer to possessives, as in:

In Eminem's latest hit, he stumbles over several words.

The pronoun *he* obviously refers to Eminem, but the word *Eminem* doesn't appear in the sentence. Because the possessive noun *Eminem's* is not a grammatical equivalent to *Eminem*, the revised sentence should be:

In his latest hit, Eminem stumbles over several words.

Mini-Workout: Pronoun Reference

> **Directions:** Revise the following sentences to eliminate pronoun reference problems. Some sentences may be correct.

1. Mira loves to text and spends most of her spare time doing it.

   _____

2. Juan answered the test questions, collected his pens and pencils, and handed them in.

   _____

3. In Fitzgerald's *The Great Gatsby*, he writes about the American Dream.

   _____

4. Its economy is a mess, but Greece will weather the crisis.

   _____

5. When teens loiter outside the theater on Friday night, they give you a hard time.

_____

6. His father let him know he had only an hour to get to the airport.

_____

7. Zachary has been interested in playing major league baseball, and he aspires to be one someday.

_____

8. Rob has a part-time job at the boatyard and spends every summer on the water, which lies at the root of his interest in going to Annapolis.

_____

9. If someone buys an old used car, he better be ready to pay for repairs.

_____

10. After the interview, Alonzo told Rick that he thought Colgate University was a good place for him to spend the next four years.

_____

Answers on page 220.

Pronoun-Antecedent Agreement

Finally, take a look at the agreement between all the pronouns and their antecedents. Do they agree in gender, number, and person? Problems frequently occur with so-called *indefinite pronouns* like *everyone, anyone*, and *nobody*—singular words that should usually be followed by singular pronouns. Sometimes such words are meant as plurals, however, and should be followed by plural pronouns. (See the earlier discussion on noun-verb agreement, page 181.)

Singular pronouns should have singular antecedents; plural pronouns, plural antecedents. Note the problem of pronoun-antecedent agreement in these sentences:

Everybody is sticking to *their* side of the story
Anybody can pass this course if *they* study hard.
Neither teacher plans to change *their* policy regarding late papers.

Properly stated, the sentences should read:

Everybody is sticking to *his* side of the story.
Anybody can pass this course if *she* studies hard.
Neither teacher plans to change *his* policy regarding late papers.

Some people, objecting to the use of specific gender pronouns, prefer the cumbersome and tacky phrase "he or she," but most good writers avoid using it.

Still other words may sound singular but are plural in certain contexts:

The jury will render *its* verdict tomorrow./The jury will return to *their* homes tomorrow.

The senior class posed for *its* picture./The senior class had *their* portraits taken for the yearbook.

THE PROBLEM OF *NONE*

Heads often get scratched about the use of the indefinite pronoun *none*. Is it singular or is it plural?

Much of the time it's singular because of its meaning, *not one*, as in:

Three lost jackets were turned in, but *none* was (singular verb) Joanie's.

Every house on the block has a garage; *none* has (singular verb) a car parked inside.

When *none* is followed by a prepositional phrase with a plural meaning, however, usage varies. Some authorities claim that *none* should always be treated as singular. Others argue that it depends on the noun or pronoun the word refers to:

Sophie says she's had many boyfriends, but *none* of them *was* (singular verb) in love with her.

Here the writer has made a general statement about all of Sophie's ex-beaus. Yet, according to some experts, *none* should be followed by a singular verb. Only when it would be ridiculous to regard it as singular should it be a plural, as in:

None of the children *meet* (plural verb) in the schoolyard during lunch period.

A plural verb is used here because it makes no sense to say that one child *meets* in the schoolyard at lunch.

Similarly:

A survey of all the residents showed that *none were* (plural verb) in favor of changing the rule.

To use a singular verb would be like saying, absurdly, *all one of them.*

Mini-Workout: Pronoun Agreement

Directions: Look for errors of agreement between pronouns and antecedents in the sentences below. Use the spaces provided to write the correct pronoun or, if necessary, to revise the sentence. Alter only those sentences that contain errors.

1. The English teacher announced that everyone in the class must turn in their term papers no later than Friday.

   _____

2. The Army, which paid soldiers large bonuses to re-enlist when their tours of duty were over, changed their policy when the budget was cut.

   _____

3. The library put their collection of rare books on display.

   _____

4. Each of my sisters have their own smart phone.

   _____

5. In that class, our teacher held conferences with us once a week.

   _____

6. Everyone on the girls' field hockey team worked as hard as they could to win the championship.

   _____

7. The teacher dictates sentences in French, and each of the students write it down in English and hand it in.

   _____

8. Each horse in the procession followed their riders down to the creek.

   _____

9. The school's chess team has just won their first match.

   _____

10. The person elected to the class presidency will find that the faculty and administration will cooperate with them and help them succeed.

   _____

Answers on page 221.

PUNCTUATION AND CAPITALIZATION

There are many reasons why you should know how to punctuate and when to use capital letters. At present, one of them is that error-free AP essays tend to earn higher scores than those crowded with mistakes. The next few pages cover the basics of everyday punctuation and capitalization.

Apostrophes

Apostrophes are used in only three places:

1. **Contractions** such as *won't, it's, could've,* and *where's.* Apostrophes mark places where letters have been omitted.

2. In **plurals** of letters, signs, or numbers, as in *A's* and *B's,* the *1960's,* and *10's* and *20's,* although many experts simplify matters by writing *1960s, Ps* and *Qs,* and so forth.

3. In **possessive nouns** such as the *student's class, women's room,* and in indefinite pronouns such as *anybody's guess.* When the noun is plural and ends in *s,* put the apostrophe after the *s,* as in *leaves' color* and *horses' stable.* Some possessive forms use both an apostrophe and *of,* as in *a friend of the family's;* some others that specify time, space, value, or quantity also require apostrophes, as in a *week's time, a dollar's worth, at my wit's end.*

Commas

Commas divide sentences into parts, clarify meaning, and prevent confusion.

1. Use a comma to signal a **pause,** as in:

    NO PAUSE: After brushing his teeth gleamed.

    PAUSE: After brushing, his teeth gleamed.

    Commas are needed after some introductory words and in forms of address:

    Well, you can open it whenever it's convenient.

    The letter will be waiting for you at home, *Jimmy*.

2. Commas set off words that **interrupt the flow** of a sentence, as in

    Izzie, *regrettably*, was omitted from the roster.

    Linh, *on the other hand*, was included.

    Commas separate information not essential to the meaning of the sentence:

    The lost hikers, *who had come from New Jersey*, found shelter in a cave.

    The three bikers, *using an out-of-date road map*, arrived two hours late.

    Commas set off **appositives:**

    Samantha, *the prosecutor*, entered the courtroom.

    The judge, *Mr. Peterson*, presided at the trial.

3. Commas separate the clauses of a **compound sentence**:

    The competition is stiff, but it won't keep Rhyana from winning.

    Yamil had better call home, or he'll be in big trouble.

4. Commas separate items in a **series**:

> Rosie's car needs *new tires, a battery, a muffler, and an oil change*.

> It was a wonder that Milan could sit through the *long, boring, infantile, and ridiculous* lecture.

Some writers to prefer to skip the comma before the last item in a series, but just in case clarity may suffer, it can't hurt to put it in.

5. Commas separate parts of **addresses**, **dates**, **and place names**:

> Who lives at 627 West 115th Street, New York, NY?

> Brian was born on May 27, 2001, the same day as Maya.

> Dave has lived in Madison, Wisconsin; Seattle, Washington; and Eugene, Oregon.

Note that each location in the last example already contains a comma. So, semicolons were added between the items to avoid confusion.

6. Commas separate quotation from attributions in **dialogue**.

> John said, "Close the window."

> "I want it open," protested Ben.

Semicolons

Semicolons may be used between closely related sentences, in effect, shortening the pause that would naturally occur between two separate sentences:

> Mother was worried; her daughters never stay out this late.

> The momentum was building; she couldn't be stopped now.

A caution: Because semicolons function like periods, use them only between independent clauses or in a series in which one or more items contains a comma, as in:

> On his trek, Norwood met Noah, a carpenter from Maine; Dr. Jones, a pediatrician from St. Louis; Jonathan, an airline pilot; and me, of course.

Quotation Marks

Quotation marks usually surround direct quotations, as in:

> As the author of the passage pointed out, "George Washington, when naked, weighed at least two hundred pounds."

Quotation marks also enclose the titles of poems, stories, chapter headings, essays, magazine articles, and other short works. Don't use them for longer works. Novels, plays, films, and magazine titles should be underlined in handwritten essays and italicized when they appear in print.

Avoid calling attention to clichés, trite expressions or slang terms by using quotation marks. Rewrite instead, using fresh, original language.

Finally, quotation marks may enclose words that express the silent thoughts of a character, as in:

> Carlos glanced at his watch. "I'm going to be late," he thought.

Periods and commas are placed inside close-quotation marks. Question marks and exclamation points go outside the quotation mark unless they are part of the quote itself.

"When will the seminar start?" asked Regis.

Do you understand the meaning of the concept "The end justifies the means"?

Mini-Workout: Punctuation

PART A. POSSESSIVES

> **Directions:** Check your mastery of possessives by writing the correct possessive form of the italicized word in the space provided. Some items may be correct.

1. *Liams* reason was personal. _____

2. The future of *Americas* foreign policy is being debated. _____

3. *Teams* from all over the county have gathered at the stadium. _____

4. Luis isn't at all interested in *womens* issues. _____

5. The *girls* locker room is downstairs, but the *boys* is upstairs. _____

6. We are invited to the *Andersons* house for New *Years* Eve. _____

7. All of the *Rosses* are going out to eat. _____

8. Have you seen *Silas* iPad, which he left here yesterday? _____

9. Both of the *computers* keyboards need repair. _____

10. He'll be back in one *months* time. _____

PART B. COMMAS AND SEMICOLONS

> **Directions:** In the sentences below insert or remove commas and semicolons as necessary. Some sentences may be correct.

1. While Buddy was riding his bike got a flat tire.

2. The mail carrier did not leave the package for Valerie was not at home.

3. After doing homework Mikey as you might expect texted with friends until midnight.

4. His work criticized many commonly held beliefs however and it was strictly censored.

5. The car, that ran into mine at the intersection, was an SUV.

6. I need Google maps of Boston; and Portland, Maine.

7. The people who live by the water must be prepared for occasional flooding.

8. The boat, was 75 feet long and 18 feet wide, its mast was about 80 feet tall.

9. To anyone interested in flying planes hold endless fascination.

10. Jacob and Owen left alone for the weekend invited all their friends to a party.

Answers on page 221.

Capitalization

Capitalization isn't totally standardized, but it's not a free-for-all, either. You won't go wrong following these guidelines:

1. Capitalize the first words of sentences, direct quotations, and lines of poetry (most of the time). This includes sentences that follow colons, as in:

   He had all the symptoms of love: All day long he could think of nothing but Sherrie.

2. Capitalize proper nouns and adjectives derived from proper nouns: *Victoria, Victorian; Shakespeare, Shakespearean; France, French dressing* (but not *french fries*, which has become a generic term).

3. Capitalize place names: *North America, Lake Moosilauke, Yosemite National Park, Gobi Desert, Mount Rushmore, Panama Canal, the Arctic Ocean, Times Square, Route 66.* Don't capitalize north, east, south, and west unless you are referring to a particular region of the country, as in:

   They went camping in the West.

   Nor should you capitalize the common noun that is not part of the actual place name, as in *the canal across Panama, the city of Moline, the plains of the Midwest.*

4. Capitalize languages, races, nationalities, and religions: *the Hungarian language, Inuit, Argentinian, Hispanic, Muslim.*

5. Capitalize organizations, institutions, and brand names: *United Nations, Pittsburgh Pirates, Library of Congress, Automobile Club of America, Amtrak, Southwest Airlines, the Internet, Toyota.* Don't, however, capitalize the common noun associated with the brand name, as in *Crest toothpaste, Starbuck's coffee, or Apple computer.*

6. Capitalize titles of persons that indicate rank, office, or profession when they are used with the person's name: *Congressman Kelly, Doctor Dolittle, Coach McConnell, Judge Judy, Lieutenant Lawlor.* Also, the titles of high officials when they are used in place of the official's name, as in *the Secretary General, the Prime Minister, the Secretary of the Treasury.* Don't capitalize titles when referring generically to the position: *the superintendent of schools, the assistant librarian, the clerk of the highway department.*

7. Capitalize family relationships, but only when they are used with a person's name, as in *Uncle Wesley, Grandma Jones, Cousin Dave.*

8. Capitalize titles of books, plays, stories, articles, poems, songs, and other creative works, as in *The Grapes of Wrath, Hamlet, "An Occurrence at Owl Creek Bridge," "Ode to a Grecian Urn," "We R Who We R."* Note that articles, conjunctions and prepositions of less than five letters are not capitalized unless they appear as the last or the first words in the title.

9. Capitalize references to the Deity and religious tracts, as in *God, the Gospel, the Torah, the Koran, the Lord, the Prophet.* Also pronouns referring to *Him* or *Her.*

10. Capitalize historical names, events, documents, and periods, as in *Battle of Gettysburg, War of 1812, Bill of Rights, Middle Ages, Health Care Bill.*

11. Capitalize days of the week, months, and holidays as in *Monday, May, Mothers' Day.* The seasons are not capitalized unless given an identity such as *Old Man Winter.*

12. Capitalize the names of specific courses and schools, as in *History 101, Forensic Science, Brookvale High School, Columbia College.* While course names are capitalized, subjects are not. Therefore, you study *history* in *American History 101* and learn *forensics* in *Forensic Science.* Similarly, you attend *high school* at *Brookvale High School* and go to *college* at *Columbia.*

Mini-Workout: Capitalization

> **Directions:** Add capital letters where they are needed in the following sentences.

1. on labor day bennington county's fire department plans to hold a turkey shoot on the field at miller's pond.

2. the judge gave district attorney lipman a book entitled *the rules of evidence* and instructed her to read it before she ever dared set foot in the court of appeals of the ninth circuit again.

3. the secretary of state greeted the president of austria at the ronald reagan airport in washington, d.c.

4. the shackleton expedition nearly met its doom on georgia island in antarctica.

5. for christmas he got a black & decker table saw from the sears store next to the old bedford courthouse.

6. according to georgetown's high school principal, eugene griffiths, georgetown high school attracts students from the whole west coast. at georgetown students may major in drawing and painting, design, graphics, or sculpture. mr griffiths said, "i attended a similar high school in new england just after the vietnam war."

7. we expect to celebrate new years eve again this year by streaming an old video of an old sci-fi movie and by settling down in front of the computer with some pepsi and a box of oreos.

8. after traveling all the way to the pacific, the corps of discovery rode down the missouri river going east on their way back to st. louis.

9. This irish linen tablecloth was bought at walmart in the emeryville mall off powell street.

10. yellowstone national park is located in the northwestern corner of wyoming.

Answers on page 222.

SAMPLE ANALYTICAL ESSAYS

What follows is a typical analytical essay question along with four student responses written by hand under testing conditions: a time limit, no access to a dictionary or other book, and a certain amount of tension. By reading the essays and a reader's comments, you will see what it takes to earn an 8 or a 9, the highest scores. Read the weaker essays, too. They'll alert you to some pitfalls to avoid when you write essays of your own.

Question

SUGGESTED TIME—30 MINUTES

> **Directions:** The passage below is the complete text of a theater review by Henry James entitled "Mr. Henry Irving's Macbeth." It was published in a London newspaper in 1875. After reading it carefully, write a well-organized essay that defines James' rhetorical purpose and analyzes some of the strategies he employs to achieve it.

Mr. Henry Irving's Macbeth, which, on the actor's first appearance in the part in London some six weeks ago, produced not a little disappointment in the general public, seems to have been accepted as an interesting if not a triumphant attempt,
Line and is exhibited to audiences numerous if not overflowing, and deferential if not
(5) enthusiastic. Considering the actor's reputation, indeed, the very undemonstrative attitude of the spectators at the Lyceum is most noticeable. Mr. Irving's acting is, to my mind, not of a kind to provoke enthusiasm, and I can best describe it by saying that it strikes me as the acting of a very superior amateur. If Mr. Irving were somewhat younger, and if there existed in England any such school of dramatic training
(10) as the Conservatoire of Paris, any such exemplary stage as the Théater Français, a discriminating critic might say of him: "Here is an aspirant with the instincts of an artist, and who, with proper instruction, may become an actor." But, thanks to the

absence of a school and of any formidable competition, success has come easily
to Mr. Irving, and he has remained, as the first tragic actor in England, decidedly
(15)   incomplete and amateurish. His personal gifts—face, figure, voice, enunciation—
are rather meagre; his strong points are intellectual. He is ingenious, intelligent, and
fanciful; imaginative he can hardly be called, for he signally fails to give their great
imaginative value to many of the superb speeches he has to utter. In declamation he
is decidedly flat; his voice is without charm, and his utterance without subtlety. But
(20)   he has thought out his part, after a fashion of his own, very carefully, and in the interest of his rendering of it lies in seeing a spare, refined man, of an unhistrionic—or a
rather sedentary—aspect, and with a thick, unmodulated voice, but with a decided
sense of the picturesque, grappling in a deliberate and conscientious manner with a
series of great tragic points. This hardly gives an impression of strength, of authority,
(25)   and it is not for force and natural magic that Mr. Irving's acting is remarkable. He has
been much criticized for his conception of his part—for making Macbeth so spiritless a plotter before his crime, and so arrant a coward afterward. But in the text, as
he seeks to emphasize it, there is a fair warrant for the line he follows. Mr. Irving has
great skill in the representation of terror, and it is quite open to him to have thrown
(30)   into relief this side of his part. His best moment is his rendering of the scene with
the bloody daggers—though it must be confessed that this stupendous scene always
does much toward acting itself. Mr. Irving, however, is here altogether admirable,
and his representation of nature trembling and quaking to its innermost spiritual
recesses really excites the imagination. Only a trifle less powerful is his scene with
(35)   Banquo's ghost at the feast, and the movement with which, exhausted with vain bra-
vado, he muffles his head in his mantle and collapses beside the throne. Mr. Irving
has several points in common with Edwin Booth, and belongs to the same general
type of actor; but I may say that if, to my thinking, Edwin Booth comes nearer to
being a man of genius, I find Mr. Irving more comfortable to see. Of Miss Bateman,
(40)   who does Lady Macbeth, the less said the better. She has good-will and a certain
superficial discretion; but a piece of acting and declaiming of equal pretensions,
more charmless in an artistic way, it has not been my fortune to behold.

Lilah's Response

(Printed as it was written)

Either Henry James was depressed or trying to have fun when he wrote
this review of Macbeth with Mr. Henry Irving playing the lead. He could have
been in a cynical mood because he doesn't have a single praiseworthy thing
to say about the performance or about the audience or about Mr. Irving as
an actor. However, the review is witty in a mean sort of way and probably
caused laughter among the readers of the newspaper that printed it in 1875.
But James might have put humor into his review in order to prevent himself
from sounding like a total curmudgeon.

So how did James amuse his readers and destroyed Mr Irving at the same
time? First, he wrote the entire review in one paragraph which contains an
evaluation of five different topics with respect to the performance of Macbeth.
He covers the audience, Mr. Irving's training and acting ability, his physical

features and voice, his portrayal of Macbeth, and then at the end he writes about the performance by Miss Bateman in the role of Lady Macbeth. The last two sentences about Miss Bateman are the nastiest ones of all. After the criticism about Mr. Irving, he brings his sarcastic wit to a climax by saying "the less said the better," but then he immediately contradicts his own statement by delivering a knock-out punch with these words: "She has good will . . . but a piece of acting and declaiming of equal pretentions, more charmless in an artistic way, it has not been my fortune to behold." The other things he talks about in the review also come under his brutal criticism in a variety of ways. For example, the audience is called "deferential," implying that they are there more out of duty and respect for the lead actor than because they have any intellectual interest in seeing Macbeth. The general public says the production is "interesting," which is an "interesting" way to put it because when someone doesn't want to say something negative but can't find a positive statement to make "interesting" is the euphemism they use.

When James begins to write about Mr. Irving's acting, he says it is as good as "a very superior amateur," a devastating putdown for a professional actor. The word "amateur" has a negative connotation not only for professionals but also for amateurs because the word suggests incompetence. The insult is compounded in line 16 when James says he is "decidedly incomplete and amateurish." The reason that James gives for Irving's poor acting is related to the education received by English actors. In England there is no school or theater that trains actors the way they do in France. In a way, that excuses Mr. Irving's acting ability due to his country being unable to train him properly.

Now that James has criticized Irving's acting ability and England's deficiency in training actors, he focuses on Irving's physical features and voice and finds both unacceptable, using negative words like "meagre," "flat" and "without charm," and "without subtlety." Then he plays with the word "remarkable," saying that "Mr. Irving's acting is remarkable" (line 25). That could mean the the acting is good or even excellent, but James surprises the reader by using it ironically. What he means but doesnt' say is the acting is remarkably bad.

As he turns his attention to Irving performing Macbeth's part, James finds something good to say about the way Irving played the scene with the bloody daggers. But he undercuts his praise by adding that the scene is so stupendous that it "does much toward acting itself," meaning that the scene is so strong that it helps the actor, including one as bad as Mr. Irving, to perform well. Finally, now that he has almost destroyed Irving's acting, James can't resist one more insulting criticism by describing Irving seeing Banquo's ghost. In that scene Irving is "altogether admirable," but he is really not since he "trembles and quakes . . . muffles his head in his mantle and collapses beside the throne." (lines 33–36) What James is implying that Irving is over-acting and over-emoting; he is playing the part as if he was cast in a melodrama or TV soap.

The readers of this essay in London most likely got a laugh out of Jame's sarcastic humor, but it's a kind of negative humor because it is given at the expense of an actor whose reputation will be smeared by James's superior tone.

Your impressions: _____

_____

_____

_____

Comment to Lilah from an AP Reader

Aside from a few distracting errors in style and mechanics (more attentive proofreading would no doubt have helped), and an out-of-place allusion to a TV soap opera, your essay is a model of insight and focus. It captures the essence of James' review and analyzes in impressive detail how the author manages to be simultaneously funny and, as you say, devastating. Using apt and specific textual examples, you show how James first attacks Irving and then softens the onslaught by blaming England for the poor man's ineptitude. You also point out correctly that James saves his most brutal assault for Miss Bateman, whose performance exceeds Irving's in its deficiencies. The language in your essay not only conveys a sensitive reading of the passage but shows an awareness that diction—the use of "curmudgeon," "euphemism," and "melodrama," to cite a few well-chosen words—is essential to a mature and readable style. References to James' readers in both the opening and concluding paragraphs endow your essay with a sense of unity not always evident in AP essays.
SCORE: 9

Kevin's Response

(Printed as it was written)

Based on the theater review entitled "Mr Henry Irving's Macbeth," Henry James was a sophisticated writer and a strict judge of performers on the stage. His sophistication comes through in his diction, the syntaxes of his sentences, the structure of the passage and a use of irony. His strictness is illustrated by saying only the most critical things about two performers, one being Henry Irving and the second being Miss Bateman, who plays Lady Macbeth. He dismisses Miss Bateman with a wave of his hand by saying "the less said the better" Obviously, to write about her performance is giving it more attention than it deserves. As a matter of fact, James said that he'd never seen a more charmless piece of acting in his life.

James saves most of his abuse for Mr. Irving's Macbeth, using a whole thesaurus of negative words and phrases to describe it, including "very superior amateur," "may become an actor," "decidedly incomplete and amateurish," "fails to give great imaginative value to many of the superb speeches," "without charm," "without subtlety," and many others. He begins the review with some general commentary about the apathetic audience and about Mr. Irving's poor training as an actor. These generalizations are followed up with specific details about his looks, in particular his face and figure, and about his very poor voice, which is "thick" and "unmodulated."

By going from general to specific, he uses a very convincing structure. He introduces general ideas to the reader, getting them ready to find out more, and then wham! he provides the concrete evidence to back up his opinions. He describes Mr. Irving's weaknesses as an actor followed by an evaluation of his performance in playing the role of Macbeth. James agrees with other critics that Irving has made Macbeth a "spiritless plotter before his crime, and so arrant a coward afterward." (lines 26–27).

In terms of syntax, James likes to say things by stating the negative of the reverse of what he wants to say (litotes). For example, he uses "interesting if not triumphant" and "audiences numerous if not overflowing." This kind of sentence structure would appeal to a more sophisticated reader than if he came right out a said the performance was a flop and the audience was small.

The author's irony, however, gives the passage a tone that illustrates his opionion. He quotes an imaginary critic, who is probably James himself in disguise in lines 11–12, who might say "Here is an aspirant with the instincts of an artist, and who, with proper instruction, may become an actor." This is James's way of giving criticism. He makes a negative comment but uses words that seem positive or encouraging, but they are not. Later in the same way he gives the impression that he is praising Irving's "representation of terror," but it is really damning with faint praise because he then slaps him down by saying that any actor can make the stupendous scene with the bloody daggers exciting. Finally, there is a comparison made between Irving and an actor named Edwin Booth, who is "nearer to being a man of genius" than Irving (lines 38–39). Again, he is implying something insulting, namely that Irving is definately not a man of genius.

Your impressions: _____

_____

_____

_____

Comment to Kevin from an AP Reader

The introductory paragraph provides an accurate but conventional blueprint for the essay to follow. True to your word, you deal with each rhetorical feature in turn, and ably support your assessment of James as "a sophisticated writer and strict judge."

Your discussion of structure, complete with the dramatic "wham!" carefully explains the effects of using details to support generalizations. In addition, your analysis of James' diction, introduced with a delightful conceit ("whole thesaurus of negative words and phrases") is thorough and well documented.

Not so, however, the paragraph on syntax. Aside from misidentifying the rhetorical device—James uses antitheses, not litotes—you fail to support the dubious assertion that sophisticated readers prefer one kind of sentence structure to another. You put the essay back on track in the last paragraph, however, by serving up several astute examples of James' irony.

Although you demonstrate an ability to express ideas clearly and forcefully, the essay doesn't exhibit the level of effective writing expected of the very best papers.

SCORE: 7

Danielle's Response

(Printed as it was written)

My mother is British and so my parents go to England every year and go to plays in London. My great grandfather whose name was David Chambers was the owner of a noodle factory near London and could have read the review "Mr Henry Irving's Macbeth" in the London newspaper in 1875. (I don't know if he went to the theater, but he might of gone because he was pretty rich and dressed in elegant clothes in a photo of him and his wife (my great grandmother Jennie) that we have at home on our dining room wall.) If he saw the review by Henry James, he would not have wasted his time and money on going to see Macbeth in the theater.

So Henry James succeeded in accomplishing his purpose. He told readers not to bother with the play because it was "not a little disappointment" as he wrote in line 2.

In all ways, Macbeth was a flop. Henry James uses language that would turn anyone off to the play. For example, he writes about the "undemonstrative attitude of the spectators," meaning the audience. That means they just sat there probably bored out of their minds and maybe didn't even applaud the performance of Mr. Irving and especially Lady Macbeth played by an actress named Miss Bateman.

Mr. Irving strikes the author as "the acting of a very superior amateur," a humorous way to say it because the word amateur is as a surprise at the end of the phrase. Superior sounds like a compliment, but amateur contridicts the compliment. I suppose that readers of the newspaper would find that funny also and would probably enjoy reading the review more than going to the play because the review is filled with comments that could get readers to chuckle or maybe even laugh, while the play would put them to sleep, which I can sympathize with when we read it last year in English class.

"Here is an aspirant with the instincts of an artist, and who, with proper instruction, may become an actor." If that's not a put down, I don't know what it is. It is an awful but also funny remark to say about an actor who is trying to play the lead. Then he adds "His personal gifts—face, figure, voice, enunciation—are rather meagre." Another insult that readers would enjoy.

They'd also get a charge out of the image of a "spare, refined man, of an unhistrionic (?) or rather sedentary—aspect, and with a thick, unmodulated voice, but with a decided sense of the picturesque, grappling in a deliberate and conscientious manner with a series of great tragic points." (lines 21–24)

Henry James then delivers the final blow by saying "Mr. Irving's acting is remarkable" in line 25, but he means remarkably bad, not remarkable good.

At the end of the review James does the same thing he did before when he says that Miss Batemen acting the part of Lady Macbeth is "charmless in an artistic way." A funny phrase because charmless is negative while artistic is positive, and the contradiction is suppose to make a reader laugh. In the last line (42) Henry James concludes his irony by saying "it has not been my fortune to behold" when he really means misfortune because he is referring to Miss Batemen's terrible performance.

Obviously, I don't know if my gtreat-grandfather read this review but he would probably enjoyed it more than this performance of Macbeth.

Your impressions: _____

_____

_____

_____

Comment to Danielle from an AP Reader

The essay has a distinctive edge over most other essays written in response to this question because of the interesting link you've made with your family history. Imagining that the review may have been read by your relatives helps to make the passage a living document and serves to identify the author's purpose—to entertain readers while also encouraging them to stay away from that production of *Macbeth*.

To your credit, you point out several features of the passage that were meant to amuse readers, not an easy task when the author is Henry James, known for his elegant but convoluted style of writing. Your analysis is perceptive, although you rely on quotations rather heavily—too heavily, in fact. Quoted material is crucial in an analytical essay, but in some places, where it would have been better to use your own words, quotes dominate the text.

Your more-than-adequate analysis of the passage is limited to its humor, but the writing is marked by a rather undisciplined syntax, especially by sentences that go on and on. There are few sentence errors, to be sure, but it's a chore to wade through excessively drawn-out sentences. Marginal control of sentence structure and sentence length detracts from what could have been a more effective essay.

SCORE: 5

Franklin's Response

(Printed as it was written)

In 1875 Henry James wrote a theater review that was published in a London newspaper. It was about Macbeth, Shakespearen play with Mr. Henry Irving receiving top billing as the character Macbeth. The play opened six weeks before the review appeared in the newspaper.

The "general public" which is the name James gives to the audience thought the play was "interesting." They were probably interested in seeing the murder of the king by Macbeth and Lady Macbeth and other things like the three witches and having a whole forest move when the actors put branches in their helmets pretending to be trees.

The public also liked the scene with the bloody daggars when Macbeth came out of the king's room with them and Lady Macbeth called him a coward and takes the daggars back inside and smears blood on the two servants who are supposed to look like they killed the king. Another great scene is when Banquo's ghost comes to the bancquet. The review in line 34 says it was "powerful".

James says the interest of the play was more than what they thought about Mr. Henry Irving. They think he is a "very superior amateur" actor in line 9. James says that he is too old for the part of Macbeth, who should be younger than about 35 or 40 since he and Lady Macbeth have no children, but he should be old enough to be a general in the king's army. In the performance "his voice is without charm" meaning it is dull and flat as if he was reciting the lines from memory and doesn't have an idea of how to build them up with expression and emotion. He (line 22) also has a "think, unmodulated voice".

The performance also has some good things to it. "Mr. Irving has great skill in the presentation of terror." This is important in the play because Macbeth is fighting for his life after Lady Macbeth sleepwalks and comitts suicide. He is scared of Macduff because he has killed his wife and children and when he hears that Macduff did not have natural childbirth and was ripped out of his mother's womb instead he knows that he is soon about to meet his own doom. Macbeth also shows terror at the banquet where Banquo comes in as a ghost and only Macbeth can see him. During that scene Mr. Henry Irving "muffles his head in his mantle and collapses beside the throne (36)".

In conclusion, James is full of criticism about the acting of Mr. Henry Irving. He contradicts himself in line 39 when he says that "I find Mr. Irving more comfortable to see". So, it is like James did not really make a decision to like the play or not. The good things and the bad things cancel each other out like an acid and a base in chemistry and the end result is neutral.

Your impressions: _____

_____

_____

_____

Comment to Franklin from an AP Reader

To conclude that Henry James is "neutral" about this production of *Macbeth* suggests that you have misread the passage. Although the author manages to squeeze one or two half-hearted compliments into the review, the tone of James' remarks is mainly sarcastic and disparaging.

Your essay also suggests that you have a weak grasp of literary analysis. Although you are obviously aware of the need to paraphrase key ideas and include quotations, the essay summarizes the content of the passage more than it analyzes the author's diction, tone, imagery, and so forth.

That you are familiar with *Macbeth* is evident. Indeed, the detail with which you discuss certain events in the play demonstrates that, had you been asked to discuss the events of the play, you might have written a winning essay. But here you have overstepped the boundaries of the task and filled the essay with irrelevancies.

Your essay is competently organized, although using the opening paragraph to rephrase the prompt deprives you of an opportunity to say something fresh and appealing. The writing, while grammatically sound, is generally wordy, ungraceful, and mechanically flawed.
Score: 3

ANSWER KEY TO MINI-WORKOUTS

Misplaced and Dangling Modifiers, page 167

Answers may vary.

1. The bowling alley lends out shoes of all sizes to its customers.

2. An old bike we planned to put in the trash was given to a junk man.

3. When I was ten, my family and I emigrated from Guatemala to the United States.

4. Having found me sound asleep at noon, my mother thought I was sick.

5. After totaling the car beyond repair, Allison knew she'd have to buy another one.

6. Correct

7. Used all night to illuminate the steps, the flashlight needed new batteries.

8. A report was submitted by the police about the latest bank heist. (The original sentence is correct if the police have been busy robbing banks.)

9. Pausing for a drink of water after the hike, I found a grizzly bear standing in front of me.

10. The school bus picked me up at the corner after I had a quick breakfast.

Mini-Workout: Parallel Structure, page 171

Answers will vary.

1. but explains that it's all right to seek help

2. An easier and more direct route

3. plays forward on the basketball team

4. go out to eat

5. both angry and disappointed

6. better than taking a sailboat

7. knocked down not only the tree

8. and party with friends

9. The mouse will either find a quick way into the attic or gnaw

10. and amazingly entertaining

Active Verbs, pages 173–174

Answers will vary.

1. Mariana and Leonardo scored highest on the practice AP exam.

2. Cost determines my choice of bedroom rug.

3. Logic dictates that a student's effort and achievement govern college admission.

4. The Revolutionary War ended the monarchy.

5. Terrorist threats multiplied after 9/11.

6. The word "chaos" applies to my math class.

7. Mr. Gill scares everyone.

8. The next corridor leads to the principal's office.

9. Some students excel in chemistry but not in physics.

10. The librarian recommended this novel.

Revising Passive Sentences, pages 175–176

Answers will vary.

1. Dead leaves covered the back yard.

2. We discussed the situation in Syria.

3. Because I had been at a play rehearsal every night that week, I failed the quiz.

4. We flew to Portland at the start of our weeklong vacation in Oregon.

5. Jason and the Argonauts pursued the Golden Fleece.

6. Rex fetched the newspaper every morning.

7. Immigration officials decided to build a fence on the border.

8. More than 20 diners on Saturday night ordered pizza.

9. Our group saw five of Shakespeare's plays in three days.

10. The candidate urged the voters to throw the old mayor out of office.

Cutting Needless Words, pages 178–179

PART A

Answers may vary.

1. Mary Roe wrote *A Ride Across America*, a book about her cross-country bike ride. To train for her feat, she biked 90 miles a day.

2. My suggestion for making meetings more productive and relevant to all students needn't offend the chairperson, Carolyn Welles.

3. Even though he spent six months in prison for embezzlement, Mr. Evans was appointed treasurer of the group.

4. Harmful criticism hurts more than it helps.

5. By reducing unnecessary driving, Americans everywhere can save gasoline.

PART B

Avoiding discrimination is but one of many reasons for people to gain weight, according to Stanford University graduate Slim Snyder, who, at a recent conference on health, said, "Lean people are victims of discrimination, just as obese people are." Fortunately, many up-to-date weight-gaining procedures are widely available. But they are ridiculed and kept well hidden because health experts agree that being lean is preferable to being obese.

Writing Specifically, pages 181–182

Answers will vary.

1. Missy earned a 5 on the AP English exam.

2. Mr. Guzman insists that students study an hour every night, that they be punctual to class, and that they regard math as the epitome of logical thinking.

3. When I told Ms. Cronin that I'm kept from doing homework by driving my brother to piano lessons or Little League, by yearbook meetings on Tuesdays, by work for Peer Leaders and SADD, and by my part-time job at the florist, she muttered, "That's *your* problem."

4. "Get out of my face," Carrie snarled as she punched the Tigers' goalie in the nose.

5. Mitchell's reward for six hours at his desk studying chemistry was a big fat F on the quiz.

6. After winning by a 3 to 1 margin, the senator-elect grinned from ear to ear and told her supporters that she was ready to work in their behalf.

7. Countries bordering the Indian Ocean dump garbage, sewage, and other hazardous waste products into the sea.

8. In science we talk about experiments, but we can't do them because we don't have any equipment.

9. Joey and Teddy, the family twins, couldn't go out at the same time until they were 16 because they shared the same pair of shoes.

10. The acceptance letter thrilled my parents. Their worried looks suddenly disappeared, they stopped nagging me about homework, and because the question had been answered, they never again asked what would become of me.

Writing Correct Sentences, page 186

Answers may vary.

1. Amy is stressed out about the garbage in the back yard.

2. St. Petersburg was renamed Leningrad after the Russian Revolution. Its original name was restored in the 1990s.

3. My grandmother is 86 years old; therefore, she walks very slowly.

4. During the night, the stars came out like diamonds on black velvet.

5. Correct

6. This year's senior class is more involved than last year's.

7. The American colonists despised the king's tax on British tea; they drank Dutch tea instead.

8. Kayly found the squirrel lying dead in a ditch, but she didn't tell Kyle.

9. A biologist working in the field of genetic engineering can get involved in the controversy surrounding human cloning.

10. Correct

Noun-Verb Subject-Verb Agreement, pages 189–190

1. was stuck   The subject is *line*, a singular noun.

2. has given   The construction *either . . . or* needs a singular verb.

3. is meeting   The subject *Board* is a singular noun.

4. is expected   The subject is *price*, a singular noun.

5. which has   The pronoun *which* refers to *service*, a singular noun.

6. There are   The subject is *levels*, a plural noun.

7. are going   The subject *Proceeds* is a plural noun.

8. is expected   The noun *team* to which the verb refers is singular.

9. are to be   The subject *guards* is plural.

10. have not been   The noun *promises* is plural.

Verb Tenses, pages 192–193

1. feels
2. visited
3. asks
4. No error
5. had seen
6. were
7. No error
8. had stayed
9. had given
10. expected

Adjectives and Adverbs, pages 194–195

1. sincerely
2. shy
3. badly
4. easily
5. calm
6. Correct
7. Correct
8. securely
9. cynically
10. bitter

Pronoun Choice, pages 197–198

1. me
2. correct
3. us
4. He and I
5. us
6. we
7. His falling
8. correct
9. him
10. he

Pronoun Reference, pages 199–200

Answers will vary.

1. Mira loves texting and spends most of her spare time doing it.
2. Juan answered the test questions and handed them in. Then he collected his pens and pencils.
3. In *The Great Gatsby* Fitzgerald writes about the American Dream.
4. Correct
5. When teens loiter outside the theater on Friday night, the police give you a hard time.
6. Nate was told by his father, "I have only an hour to get to the airport?"
7. Zachary aspires to play major league baseball someday.
8. Rob wants to go to Annapolis because he has a part-time job at the boatyard and spends every summer on the water.
9. Correct
10. After the interview, Alonzo told Rick, "I think Colgate University is a good place for you to spend the next four years."

Pronoun Agreement, page 202

Answers will vary.

1. all the students in the class

2. its policy

3. its collection

4. has her own smart phone

5. Correct

6. as she could

7. write them down . . . and hand them in

8. All the horses

9. its first match.

10. will find the faculty and administration cooperative and supportive.

Punctuation, pages 205–206

A. Possessives

1. Liam's

2. America's

3. Correct

4. women's

5. girls'

6. Andersons'

7. Correct

8. Silas'

9. computers'

10. month's

B. Commas and Semicolons

1. While Buddy was riding, his bike got a flat tire.

2. The mail carrier did not leave the package, for Valerie was not at home.

3. After doing homework, Mikey, as you might expect, texted with friends until midnight.

4. His work criticized many commonly-held beliefs, however, and it was strictly censored.

5. The car that ran into mine at the intersection was an SUV.

6. I need google maps of Boston and Portland, Maine.

7. The people who live by the water must be prepared for occasional flooding.

8. The boat was 75 feet long and 18 feet wide; its mast was about 80 feet tall.

9. To anyone interested in flying, planes hold endless fascination.

10. Jacob and Owen, left alone for the weekend, invited all their friends to a party.

Capitalization, pages 207–208

1. On Labor Day Bennington County's fire department plans to hold a turkey shoot on the field at Miller's Pond.

2. The judge gave District Attorney Lipman a book entitled *The Rules of Evidence* and instructed her to read it before she ever dared set foot in the Court of Appeals of the Ninth Circuit again.

3. The secretary of state greeted the president of Austria at the Ronald Reagan Airport in Washington, D.C.

4. The Shackleton expedition nearly met its doom on Georgia Island in Antarctica.

5. For Christmas he got a Black & Decker table saw from the Sears store next to the Old Bedford Courthouse.

6. According to Georgetown's high school principal, Eugene Griffiths, Georgetown High School attracts students from the whole West Coast. At Georgetown students may major in drawing and painting, design, graphics, or sculpture. Mr. Griffiths said, "I attended a similar high school in New England just after the Vietnam War."

7. We expect to celebrate New Year's Eve again this year by streaming a video of an old sci-fi movie and by settling down in front of the computer with some Pepsi and a box of Oreos.

8. After traveling all the way to the Pacific, the Corps of Discovery rode down the Missouri River going east on their way back to St. Louis.

9. This irish linen tablecloth was bought at Walmart in the Emeryville Mall off Powell Street.

10. Yellowstone National Park is located in the northwestern corner of Wyoming.

Practice Tests

Instructions: Each test in this section lasts 3 hours and 15 minutes.

As you take each test, allow yourself one hour to answer the multiple-choice questions. Use the answer sheet provided.

Then take a five-minute break and answer the essay questions. Write your essays on standard 8½" × 11" composition paper. Before you write the essays, set aside a 15-minute reading period. During that time, you may read all the essay questions, study the sources for question 1 (the synthesis essay) and plan what you are going to say. At the end of 15 minutes take out lined paper and begin to write. The suggested writing time for each essay is 40 minutes.

When you are finished, check your answers with the Answer Key that follows each exam. Read the answer explanations for both the questions you missed and those you answered correctly.

To rate your essays, use the Self-Scoring Guide provided with each test.

Worksheets are also provided at the end of each test to help you determine your total score.

ANSWER SHEET
Practice Test A

Multiple-Choice Questions

Time—1 hour

1. Ⓐ Ⓑ Ⓒ Ⓓ Ⓔ
2. Ⓐ Ⓑ Ⓒ Ⓓ Ⓔ
3. Ⓐ Ⓑ Ⓒ Ⓓ Ⓔ
4. Ⓐ Ⓑ Ⓒ Ⓓ Ⓔ
5. Ⓐ Ⓑ Ⓒ Ⓓ Ⓔ
6. Ⓐ Ⓑ Ⓒ Ⓓ Ⓔ
7. Ⓐ Ⓑ Ⓒ Ⓓ Ⓔ
8. Ⓐ Ⓑ Ⓒ Ⓓ Ⓔ
9. Ⓐ Ⓑ Ⓒ Ⓓ Ⓔ
10. Ⓐ Ⓑ Ⓒ Ⓓ Ⓔ
11. Ⓐ Ⓑ Ⓒ Ⓓ Ⓔ
12. Ⓐ Ⓑ Ⓒ Ⓓ Ⓔ
13. Ⓐ Ⓑ Ⓒ Ⓓ Ⓔ
14. Ⓐ Ⓑ Ⓒ Ⓓ Ⓔ
15. Ⓐ Ⓑ Ⓒ Ⓓ Ⓔ

16. Ⓐ Ⓑ Ⓒ Ⓓ Ⓔ
17. Ⓐ Ⓑ Ⓒ Ⓓ Ⓔ
18. Ⓐ Ⓑ Ⓒ Ⓓ Ⓔ
19. Ⓐ Ⓑ Ⓒ Ⓓ Ⓔ
20. Ⓐ Ⓑ Ⓒ Ⓓ Ⓔ
21. Ⓐ Ⓑ Ⓒ Ⓓ Ⓔ
22. Ⓐ Ⓑ Ⓒ Ⓓ Ⓔ
23. Ⓐ Ⓑ Ⓒ Ⓓ Ⓔ
24. Ⓐ Ⓑ Ⓒ Ⓓ Ⓔ
25. Ⓐ Ⓑ Ⓒ Ⓓ Ⓔ
26. Ⓐ Ⓑ Ⓒ Ⓓ Ⓔ
27. Ⓐ Ⓑ Ⓒ Ⓓ Ⓔ
28. Ⓐ Ⓑ Ⓒ Ⓓ Ⓔ
29. Ⓐ Ⓑ Ⓒ Ⓓ Ⓔ
30. Ⓐ Ⓑ Ⓒ Ⓓ Ⓔ

31. Ⓐ Ⓑ Ⓒ Ⓓ Ⓔ
32. Ⓐ Ⓑ Ⓒ Ⓓ Ⓔ
33. Ⓐ Ⓑ Ⓒ Ⓓ Ⓔ
34. Ⓐ Ⓑ Ⓒ Ⓓ Ⓔ
35. Ⓐ Ⓑ Ⓒ Ⓓ Ⓔ
36. Ⓐ Ⓑ Ⓒ Ⓓ Ⓔ
37. Ⓐ Ⓑ Ⓒ Ⓓ Ⓔ
38. Ⓐ Ⓑ Ⓒ Ⓓ Ⓔ
39. Ⓐ Ⓑ Ⓒ Ⓓ Ⓔ
40. Ⓐ Ⓑ Ⓒ Ⓓ Ⓔ
41. Ⓐ Ⓑ Ⓒ Ⓓ Ⓔ
42. Ⓐ Ⓑ Ⓒ Ⓓ Ⓔ
43. Ⓐ Ⓑ Ⓒ Ⓓ Ⓔ
44. Ⓐ Ⓑ Ⓒ Ⓓ Ⓔ
45. Ⓐ Ⓑ Ⓒ Ⓓ Ⓔ

46. Ⓐ Ⓑ Ⓒ Ⓓ Ⓔ
47. Ⓐ Ⓑ Ⓒ Ⓓ Ⓔ
48. Ⓐ Ⓑ Ⓒ Ⓓ Ⓔ
49. Ⓐ Ⓑ Ⓒ Ⓓ Ⓔ
50. Ⓐ Ⓑ Ⓒ Ⓓ Ⓔ
51. Ⓐ Ⓑ Ⓒ Ⓓ Ⓔ
52. Ⓐ Ⓑ Ⓒ Ⓓ Ⓔ
53. Ⓐ Ⓑ Ⓒ Ⓓ Ⓔ
54. Ⓐ Ⓑ Ⓒ Ⓓ Ⓔ
55. Ⓐ Ⓑ Ⓒ Ⓓ Ⓔ

Practice Test A

SECTION I

TIME: 1 HOUR

> **Directions:** *Questions 1–13.* Carefully read the following passage and answer the accompanying questions.

The passage below is excerpted from a memoir published in the mid-20th century.

PASSAGE 1

You can live a lifetime and, at the end of it, know more about other people than
you know about yourself. You learn to watch other people, but you never watch
yourself because you strive against loneliness. If you read a book, or shuffle a deck of
Line cards, or care for a dog, you are avoiding yourself. The abhorrence of loneliness is as
(5) natural as wanting to live at all. If it were otherwise, men would never have bothered
to make an alphabet, nor to have fashioned words out of what were only animal
sounds, nor to have crossed continents—each man to see what the other looked like.

Being alone in an aeroplane even for so short a time as a night and a day, irrevo-
cably alone, with nothing to observe but your instruments and your own hands in
(10) semi-darkness, nothing to contemplate but the size of your small courage, nothing
to wonder about but the beliefs, the faces, and the hopes rooted in your mind—such
an experience can be as startling as the first awareness of a stranger walking by your
side at night. You are a stranger. It is dark already and I am over the south of Ireland.
There are the lights of Cork and the lights are wet; they are drenched with Irish rain,
(15) and I am above them and dry. I am above them and the plane roars in a sobbing
world, but it imparts no sadness to me. I feel the security of solitude, the exhilaration
of escape. So long as I can see the lights and imagine the people walking underneath
them, I feel selfishly triumphant, as if I have eluded care and left even the small sorrow of rain in other hands.

(20) It is a little over an hour now since I left Abingdon, England. Wales and the Irish
Sea are behind me like so much time used up. On a long flight distance and time are
the same. But there had been a moment when Time stopped—and Distance too. It
was the moment I lifted the blue-and-silver Gull from the aerodrome, the moment
the photographers aimed their cameras, the moment I felt the craft refuse its burden
(25) and strain toward the earth in sullen rebellion, only to listen at last to the persuasion of stick and elevators, the dogmatic argument of blueprints that said she *had*

to fly because the figures proved it. So she had flown, and once airborne, once she had yielded to the sophistry of a draughtsman's board, she had said, "There, I have lifted the weight. Now, where are we bound?"—and the question had frightened me.

(30)   We are bound for a place thirty-six hundred miles from here—two thousand miles of it unbroken ocean. Most of the way it will be night. We are flying west with the night. So there behind me is Cork; and ahead of me is Berehaven Lighthouse. It is the last light, standing on the last land. I watch it, counting the frequency of its flashes—so many to the minute. Then I pass it and fly out to sea.

(35)   The fear is gone now—not overcome nor reasoned away. It is gone because something else has taken its place; the confidence and the trust, the inherent belief in the security of land underfoot—now this faith is transferred to my plane, because land has vanished and there is no other tangible thing to fix faith upon. Flight is but momentary escape from the eternal custody of earth. . . .

(1942)

1. The rhetorical function of the first sentence (lines 1–2) is best described as

   (A) an assertion against which the entire passage argues.
   (B) a piece of common wisdom that the passage will illustrate.
   (C) a paradox that the passage will analyze and explain.
   (D) the moral of the story that the author is about to tell.
   (E) an example that supports the main idea of the passage.

2. The author uses all of the following phrases to illustrate the notion of the "abhorrence of loneliness" (line 4) EXCEPT

   (A) "live a lifetime" (line 1).
   (B) "watch other people" (line 2).
   (C) "read a book" (line 3).
   (D) "care for a dog" (line 4).
   (E) "make an alphabet" (line 6).

3. In line 8, the phrase "Being alone" is structurally parallel to the phrase

   (A) "your instruments" (line 9).
   (B) "your own hands" (line 9).
   (C) "nothing to wonder about" (lines 10–11).
   (D) "such an experience" (lines 11–12).
   (E) "the first awareness of a stranger" (line 12).

4. In lines 8–13 of the passage, the author uses an analogy between

    (A) being alone and thinking about the future.
    (B) darkness and ignorance.
    (C) being brave and contemplating one's beliefs.
    (D) flying solo and discovering yourself.
    (E) a person's hands and an airplane's instruments.

5. The rhetorical purpose of switching from second person to first person in line 13 is primarily to

    (A) explain the meaning of "You are a stranger" (line 13).
    (B) indicate that the author has not been talking about herself.
    (C) give an example of the "abhorrence of loneliness" (line 4).
    (D) show that the narrator's thoughts about flying have been based on her past experience.
    (E) prove that the narrator is an accomplished pilot.

6. In paragraph 3 (lines 20–29), which of the following rhetorical devices is most prominent?

    (A) Emphasizing sensual imagery
    (B) Using abstract generalizations
    (C) Mixing facts and impressions
    (D) Appealing to authority
    (E) Employing periodic sentences

7. The tone of the passage as a whole can best be described as

    (A) reflective and philosophical.
    (B) objective and informational.
    (C) academic and pedantic.
    (D) effusive and tumultuous.
    (E) terse and impersonal.

8. The function of the phrase "sobbing world" (lines 15–16) is primarily to

    (A) describe the rain outside the airplane.
    (B) suggest the pulsating sounds of the airplane engine.
    (C) explain the sadness of lonely people.
    (D) explain the author's affection for the Irish people far below.
    (E) indicate that flying serves as a release from everyday cares.

9. The sentence in lines 21–22 ("On a long . . . same") has all of the following functions EXCEPT

    (A) to present information about the way pilots think.
    (B) to introduce the anecdote that follows in lines 22–27.
    (C) to illustrate how pilots on long flights sometimes become disoriented.
    (D) to help to contrast the tedium of flying with the thrill of the take-off.
    (E) to explain the phrase "like so much time used up" (line 21).

10. The author's observation in line 22 that "Time stopped—and Distance too" is best described as an example of

    I. hyperbole
    II. ironic contrast
    III. mixed metaphor

(A) I only
(B) III only
(C) I and III only
(D) II and III only
(E) I, II, and III

11. In the description of the take-off (lines 22–27) the author employs all of the following EXCEPT

(A) paradox.
(B) parallel structure.
(C) personification.
(D) repetition for emphasis.
(E) shift of pronouns.

12. In context, the expression "to fix faith upon" (line 38) is best interpreted as having which of the following meanings?

(A) To be victorious
(B) To feel secure
(C) To gain a sense of direction
(D) To speed up
(E) To have the courage of one's convictions

13. The passage as a whole can best be described as

(A) an extended metaphor.
(B) a metaphysical allegory.
(C) a sentimental evocation of an episode.
(D) an objective narrative.
(E) a personal interpretation.

Directions: *Questions 14–23.* Carefully read the following passage and answer the accompanying questions.

The passage below is the text of a newspaper column published in the latter part of the 20th century.

PASSAGE 2

PARRIS ISLAND, S.C.—He is seething, he is rabid, he is wound up tight as a golf ball, with more adrenalin surging through his hypothalamus than a cornered slum rat, he is everything these Marine recruits with their heads shaved to dirty nubs have

Line ever feared or even hoped a drill instructor might be.

(5)　He is Staff Sgt. Douglas Berry and he is rushing down the squad bay of Receiving Barracks to leap onto a table and brace at parade rest in which none of the recruits, daring glances from the position of attention, can see any more of him under the rake of his campaign hat than his lipless mouth chopping at them like a disaster teletype: WHEN I GIVE YOU THE WORD YOU WILL WALK YOU WILL NOT RUN DOWN

(10)　THESE STEPS WHERE YOU WILL RUN YOU WILL NOT WALK TO THE YELLOW FOOTMARKS. . . .

Outside, Berry's two junior drill instructors, in raincoats over dress greens, sweat in a muggy February drizzle which shrinks the view down to this wooden World War II barracks, to the galvanized Butler hut across the company street, the overground

(15)　steam pipes, a couple of palmetto trees, the raindrops beading on spitshined black shoes. Sgt. Hudson mans the steps, Sgt. Burley the footmarks. They pace with a mannered strut, like men wearing white tie and tails, their hands folded behind their backs, their jaw muscles flexing. One senses that this is serious business. There's none of the smart-alecky wisecracking of TV sitcoms that portray hotshot recruits

(20)　outsmarting dumb sergeants for passes to town.

In fact, during his 63 days of training at Parris Island, unless a member of the immediate family dies, a recruit will get no liberty at all. He will also get no talking, no phone calls, no books or magazines, no television, radio or record players, no candy or gum, one movie, one newspaper a week, and three cigarettes a day. Unless

(25)　he fouls up, gets sent to the brig or to motivation platoon, and loses the cigarettes.

WHEN I GIVE YOU THE WORD TO MOVE OUT YOU WILL MOVE OUT DO YOU UNDERSTAND ME? Hudson meets the first one at the steps like a rotary mower ripping into a toad, so psyched he's actually dancing on tiptoe, with his face a choleric three-quarters of an inch from the private FASTER PRIVATE FASTER JUST TAKE

(30)　YOUR DUMB TIME SWEETHEART MOVE! MOVE! as this hog, as recruits are colloquially known, piles out of the barracks in a stumble of new boots, poncho, laundry bag and the worst trouble his young ass has ever been in, no doubt about it when Burley meets him just like Hudson, in an astonishment of rage that roars him all the way down to the right front set of yellow footprints YOU LOCK YOUR BODY AT

(35)　ATTENTION YOU LOCK YOUR BODY. . . .

Or maybe Burley writhes up around this private to hiss in his ear—and Burley is very good at this—*you hate me, don't you, you hate me, private, you'd better hate me because I hate you,* or any of the other litanies drill instructors have been barking and

hissing at their charges ever since the first of more than one million Parris Island
(40) graduates arrived on the flea-ridden sand barren in 1911.

Until there are 60 of them out there in the drizzle with the drill instructors shout-
ing themselves hoarse, 60 volunteers who had heard from countless older brothers
and street corner buddies and roommates that it would be exactly like this but they
volunteered anyhow, to be Marines.

(45) Right now, with lips trembling, eyes shuttling YOU BETTER STOP THAT EYE-
BALLING, PRIVATE! fat and forlorn, they look like 60 sex perverts trapped by a lynch
mob. They are scared. They are scared as fraternity pledges during a cleverly staged
hell week, shaking like boys about to abandon their virginity.

It's a primal dread that drill instructors invoke and exploit in eight weeks (soon to
(50) revert to the pre-Vietnam 11 weeks) of folk theater, a spectacle staged on the scale
of the Passion Play at Oberammergau, an initiation that may be the only true rite of
passage to manhood that America hasn't yet scoured away as an anthropological
anachronism.

(1972)

14. Several sections of the passage appear in capital letters and with almost no
punctuation. This can be explained by all of the following reasons EXCEPT

(A) to suggest the volume at which the words are uttered.
(B) to indicate a staccato-like manner of speech.
(C) to convey the intensity with which the words are spoken.
(D) to separate spoken words from narration and description.
(E) to heighten dramatic effect.

15. In line 7, "daring" modifies

(A) "Berry" (line 5).
(B) "squad bay" (line 5).
(C) "table" (line 6).
(D) "none" (line 6).
(E) "recruits" (line 6).

16. In paragraph 3 (lines 12–16), which of the following rhetorical devices is most in
evidence?

(A) Homily
(B) Metonymy
(C) Figures of speech
(D) Melodrama
(E) Visual imagery

17. The principal contrast employed by the author in the passage is between

(A) Sgt. Berry and Sgt. Burley.
(B) the drill instructors and the recruits.
(C) the reality of boot camp and sitcom versions of military life.
(D) modern military training and World War II training.
(E) basic training and fraternity hazing.

18. The main rhetorical function of the description of Hudson and Burley (lines 16–18) is to

(A) set the stage for material in the next paragraph (lines 21–24).
(B) reinforce a description given earlier in the passage (lines 5–11).
(C) prepare for the contrast made in the following sentence (lines 18–20).
(D) provide support for a thesis proposed in the first paragraph (lines 1–4).
(E) introduce an element of humor into the passage.

19. The point of view expressed in "In fact . . . day" (lines 21–24) is that of

(A) the author.
(B) the recruits.
(C) the Marine Corps.
(D) Sgt. Hudson.
(E) Sgt Berry.

20. To create the greatest effect, all of the following rhetorical techniques are used in lines 36–40 EXCEPT

(A) repetition.
(B) use of highly connotative verbs.
(C) evocation of historical tradition.
(D) vivid adjectives.
(E) subordinate clause set off by dashes.

21. In the last paragraph, (lines 49–53), which of the following words is parallel in function to "dread" (line 49)?

(A) "theater" (line 50)
(B) "weeks" (line 49)
(C) "initiation" (line 51)
(D) "manhood" (line 52)
(E) "anachronism" (line 53)

22. The passage as a whole might best be described as

(A) a parable of modern life.
(B) a melodramatic evocation.
(C) a parody.
(D) a dramatic monologue.
(E) an exposé.

23. Which of the following best captures the author's attitude toward the events and people described in the passage?

   (A) "Outside . . . barracks" (lines 12–14)
   (B) "One senses . . . town" (lines 18–20)
   (C) "Hudson meets . . . tiptoe" (lines 27–28)
   (D) "They are scared" (line 47)
   (E) "an initiation . . . anachronism" (lines 51–53)

Directions: *Questions 24–35.* Carefully read the following passage and answer the accompanying questions.

This is an excerpt from a speech made by a British nobleman who served in the government of Queen Victoria late in the 19th century.

PASSAGE 3

It is no doubt true that we are surrounded by advisers who tell us that all study of the past is barren except insofar as it enables us to determine the laws by which the evolution of human societies is governed. How far such an investigation has been

Line up to the present time fruitful in results I will not inquire. That it will ever enable us
(5) to trace with accuracy the course which States and nations are destined to pursue in the future, or to account in detail for their history in the past, I do not believe.

We are borne along like travelers on some unexplored stream. We may know enough of the general configuration of the globe to be sure that we are making our way toward the ocean. We may know enough by experience or theory of the laws
(10) regulating the flow of liquids, to conjecture how the river will behave under the varying influences to which it may be subject. More than this we can not know. It will depend largely upon causes which, in relation to any laws which we are ever likely to discover, may properly be called accidental, whether we are destined sluggishly to drift among fever-stricken swamps, to hurry down perilous rapids, or to glide gently
(15) through fair scenes of peaceful cultivation.

But leaving on one side ambitious sociological speculations, and even those more modest but hitherto more successful investigations into the causes which have in particular cases been principally operative in producing great political changes, there are still two modes in which we can derive what I may call "spectacular" enjoy-
(20) ment from the study of history.

There is first the pleasure which arises from the contemplation of some great historic drama, or some broad and well-marked phase of social development. The story of the rise, greatness, and decay of a nation is like some vast epic which contains as subsidiary episodes the varied stories of the rise, greatness, and decay of creeds, of
(25) parties, and of statesmen. The imagination is moved by the slow unrolling of this great picture of human mutability, as it is moved by contrasted permanence of the abiding stars. The ceaseless conflict, the strange echoes of long-forgotten controversies, the confusion of purpose, the successes which lay deep the seeds of future evils, the failures that ultimately divert the otherwise inevitable danger, the heroism which

(30)   struggles to the last for a cause foredoomed to defeat, the wickedness which sides with right, and the wisdom which huzzas at the triumph of folly—fate, meanwhile, through all this turmoil and perplexity, working silently toward the predestined end—all these form together a subject the contemplation of which we surely never weary.

(35)   But there is yet another and very different species of enjoyment to be derived from the records of the past, which require a somewhat different method of study in order that it may be fully tasted. Instead of contemplating, as it were, from a distance, the larger aspects of the human drama, we may elect to move in familiar fellowship amid the scenes and actors of special periods.

(40)   We may add to the interest we derive from the contemplation of contemporary politics, a similar interest derived from a not less minute and probably more accurate knowledge of some comparatively brief passage in the political history of the past. We may extend the social circle in which we move—a circle perhaps narrowed and restricted through circumstances beyond our control—by making intimate *(45)* acquaintances, perhaps even close friends, among a society long departed, but which, when we have once learnt the trick of it, it rests with us to revive.

    It is this kind of historical reading which is usually branded as frivolous and useless, and persons who indulge in it often delude themselves into thinking that the real motive of their investigation into bygone scenes and ancient scandals is *(50)* philosophic interest in an important historical episode, whereas in truth it is not the philosophy which glorifies the details, but the details that make tolerable the philosophy.

24. The speaker's observation in the first sentence in the passage can best be described as an example of which of the following?

    (A) A hyperbolic statement
    (B) A disdainful tone
    (C) An allusion to a well-known historical event
    (D) An objective comment
    (E) A double entendre

25. Which of the following best describes the rhetorical function of the third sentence in the passage (lines 4–6)?

    (A) It reiterates the thesis of the passage.
    (B) It explains the gap between historical theory and historical fact.
    (C) It provides evidence that supports a previous generalization.
    (D) It articulates the speaker's view on the main subject of the passage.
    (E) It confirms the speaker's authority to speak on the subject of the passage.

26. Which of the following words or phrases is grammatically and thematically parallel to "account" (line 6)?

(A) "inquire" (line 4)
(B) "enable" (line 4)
(C) "trace" (line 5)
(D) "pursue" (line 5)
(E) " believe" (line 6)

27. In lines 7–15 of the passage, the speaker uses an extended analogy that compares

(A) passengers on a boat to explorers.
(B) the behavior of people to the behavior of flowing water.
(C) the affairs of humankind to an uncharted waterway.
(D) historical events to unpredictable accidents.
(E) society's laws to the laws of physics.

28. As used in line 19, the word "spectacular" is best interpreted to mean

(A) evoking wonder and admiration.
(B) appealing to the eye.
(C) distinctly unusual or unexpected.
(D) staggering.
(E) legendary.

29. In describing the rewards of studying history (lines 21–34), the speaker emphasizes the

(A) insights gained into present conditions.
(B) inevitable surprises.
(C) challenge to determine what actually occurred.
(D) stimulation of thought.
(E) emotional excitement.

30. In paragraph 4 (lines 21–35) which of the following rhetorical devices is most in evidence?

(A) Stream of consciousness
(B) A series of factual statements
(C) Personification
(D) A buildup of suspense leading to a climax
(E) The use of poetic language

31. Lines 27–34 contain all of the following EXCEPT

    (A) parallel syntax.
    (B) a loose sentence.
    (C) prepositional phrases.
    (D) relative clauses.
    (E) a simple grammatical subject.

32. The speaker's reference to extending a "social circle" (line 43) serves primarily to

    (A) suggest that readers must seek out a variety of viewpoints on historical matters.
    (B) illustrate the "different method of study" alluded to in the previous paragraph.
    (C) persuade historians to make the acquaintance of personalities of the past.
    (D) emphasize the speaker's special interest in the sociology of groups.
    (E) encourage readers to become more knowledgeable about contemporary politics.

33. The "circumstances" referred to in line 44 can best be interpreted as

    (A) entrenched methods of historical research and scholarship that cannot be altered.
    (B) "facts" about historical periods that often change as time goes on.
    (C) historians' limited access to prominent figures of the past because they are dead.
    (D) historical records that are frequently incomplete or in disarray.
    (E) the inevitable changes that occur over time in the stature and legacy of historical figures.

34. Which of the following phrases most accurately describes the kind of reading referred to in line 47?

    (A) "contemplation of some great historic drama" (lines 21–22)
    (B) "vast epic" (line 23)
    (C) "slow unrolling of . . . human mutability" (lines 25–26)
    (D) "accurate knowledge of some . . . brief passage in the . . . history of the past" (lines 41–43)
    (E) "move in familiar fellowship amid . . . special periods" (lines 38–39)

35. The passage as a whole can best be described as

    (A) a tribute to historians.
    (B) an analysis of problems faced by serious historians.
    (C) an objective report on the value of studying history.
    (D) a reflection on the rewards of reading history.
    (E) an attack on a traditional theory of history.

Directions: *Questions 36–45*. Carefully read the following passage and answer the accompanying questions.

The passage below is an excerpt from a 20th-century book.

PASSAGE 4

Both the city and the Italian Colony were progressing steadily when the 1906 earthquake and fire struck. San Francisco had been razed by fires six times from 1849 to 1851, and each time the ruins had been swept away and the city rebuilt in a much finer fashion. This time, however, the damage was far too extensive. The
(5) tragedy was compounded by the great number of people and buildings which were concentrated along the path of the fault.

The destruction caused by the earthquake and the ensuing fire in the Italian Quarter resulted in the complete loss of the district. The Italian Quarter, as other parts of the city hit by the disaster, had been reduced to a knotted, tangled mass
(10) of bent steel frames, charred bricks, and ashes. In North Beach, only a small part of the community remained. The Italians on Telegraph Hill had been luckier than most, although they suffered losses since insurance companies were not interested in insuring remote areas of the Hill. The scattered fire hydrants and water cisterns were not to be found east of Dupont Street and the insurance companies were not
(15) willing to gamble. It was reported in the Italian press that some 20,000 Italians lost their homes in the conflagration.[1]

One of the priests from the church of Sts. Peter and Paul had managed to save the consecrated host, vestments, and holy vessels[2] and said Mass under the inflamed sky. After the fires had died, the Italians quietly returned to North Beach and tried to
(20) find the confidence to rebuild Little Italy.[3]

Approximately five to six hundred Italians had definitely left San Francisco due to this tragic event, while over six thousand new immigrants arrived and helped the survivors clear the ruins. Seven hundred building permits were granted to North Beach Italian residents and businessmen[4] to expedite the construction of the
(25) Colony. Several real estate firms, such as the J. Cuneo Company in North Beach, demonstrated their confidence in the determination of the Italians by investing $400,000 in the reconstruction of apartments, stores, flats, and business offices.[5]

Temporary buildings were cheaply erected for immediate occupancy, while the leaders of the Colony were busily engaged in drawing up plans for a modern Little
(30) Italy. The buildings would be simple, small, neat, and airy, which combined both functional and classical lines.[6] One writer described this new architecture as a reflec-

Line

---

[1] *"La Infernale Catastrofe de San Francisco,"* L'Italia, *p. 1. April 1906.*

[2] *"The Frightful Calamity on the Pacific Coast,"* Leslie's Weekly, *102:418. May 3, 1906.*

[3] *"La Riconstruzione de San Francisco,"* La Voce del Popolo, *p. 1. May 12, 1906.*

[4] *"Facts and Figures Worthy of Consideration,"* L'Italia, *p. 1. April 28, 1906.*

[5] *"J. Cuneo Co."* L'Italia, *July 2, 1906. In deposit, Bank of America NT&SA Archives, San Francisco.*

[6] *"Curious Tour of City Leaves Telegraph Hill for Fisherman's Wharf,"* San Francisco Chronicle, *p. 12. Feb. 16, 1932.*

tion of the Italian immigrants' acceptance of American ways.[7] The most picturesque features of the flats and apartments were the roof-top sun decks with flower gardens.[8] Part of the planning for the new Colony included the renaming of two of the main

(35) thoroughfares of the Italian Quarter. In 1907, one-half of Dupont Street was renamed Grant Avenue, and by the end of 1908 all of Dupont became Grant Avenue. By 1910, Montgomery Avenue was renamed Columbus Avenue and still retained its fame as "The Avenue." The changes in these street names denoted a change in the geographic character of the Italian Quarter.

---

[7] *Peixotto,* Scribner's, *48:82. July 1910.*

[8] *J.M. Scanland, "On the Roofs of the Latin Quarter,"* Overland Monthly, *57:330. March 1911.*

36. The speaker's main focus in the passage is

   (A) the effects of the 1906 San Francisco earthquake on the Italian community.
   (B) the economic consequences of the 1906 San Francisco earthquake and fire.
   (C) why Italians came to San Francisco after the 1906 earthquake.
   (D) how the San Francisco earthquake transformed the Italian Colony.
   (E) the courage and fortitude of Italians in San Francisco during the 1906 earthquake and fire.

37. Which of the following describes the rhetorical purpose of the first paragraph (lines 1–6)?

   (A) It suggests that San Franciscans were unaware of the dangers of earthquakes.
   (B) It raises questions that will be discussed in the remainder of the passage.
   (C) It provides a thesis that will be challenged later in the passage.
   (D) It explains the uniqueness of the 1906 earthquake.
   (E) It introduces the reader to the intense emotion generated by the tragic events discussed in the passage.

38. The sequence of detailed images in lines 9–10 are meant to illustrate all of the following EXCEPT

   (A) "The tragedy" (lines 4–5).
   (B) "the fault" (line 6).
   (C) "The destruction" (line 7).
   (D) "complete loss" (line 8).
   (E) "the disaster" (line 9).

39. Which of the following best describes the primary rhetorical purpose of the sentence, "The scattered . . . to gamble" (lines 13–15)?

   (A) To develop an idea presented in the previous sentence
   (B) To provide background for understanding information contained in the next sentence
   (C) To specify the location where the earthquake did the greatest damage
   (D) To clarify the author's attitude toward insurance companies
   (E) To suggest that the earthquake destroyed the hydrants and water cisterns

40. Taken as a whole, the footnotes show that

(A) it is crucial to consult published books while doing historical research.

(B) almost all news about the earthquake was reported in Italian by the Italian press.

(C) only a small amount of material about the earthquake was published after 1911.

(D) in doing historical research about an event, it is best to use work published close to the time the event occurred.

(E) the author of the passage relied heavily on sources contemporary to the earthquake.

41. Which of the following is a proper interpretation of footnote 7 (line 32)?

(A) The author found the material to be footnoted between pages 48 and 82.

(B) *Scribner's* is the name of a book published in 1910.

(C) The work by Peixotto has been cited in a previous footnote.

(D) In 1910, Scribner's published Peixotto's book.

(E) References to *Scribner's* can be found on pages 48 and 82 of an article by Peixotto.

42. The development of the passage can best be described as

(A) an analysis of how people in 1906 reacted to misfortune and tragedy.

(B) a detailed examination of a group that shared a common heritage.

(C) a compilation of information about the effects of the earthquake.

(D) a narrative of the earthquake and its aftermath.

(E) an explanation of why the earthquake had been so damaging.

43. Which of the following sources cited by footnotes 6–8 express a favorable view of the housing being planned for "a modern Little Italy" (lines 29–30)?

   I. The source cited in footnote 6

  II. The source cited in footnote 7

 III. The source cited in footnote 8

(A) I only

(B) II only

(C) I and III only

(D) II and III only

(E) I, II, and III

44. Lines 35–38 contain which of the following?

(A) An illustrative anecdote

(B) Subordinate clauses

(C) A single compound sentence

(D) Antithesis

(E) An extended metaphor

45. The tone of the passage is best described as

   (A) reverent but remorseful.
   (B) disapproving but respectful.
   (C) excited and energetic.
   (D) unemotional and informative.
   (E) admiring and awe-struck.

Directions: *Questions 46–55*. Carefully read the following passage and answer the accompanying questions.

The passage is a segment of a book written early in the 20th century.

PASSAGE 5

In a recent bulletin of the Superintendent of the Census for 1890 appear these significant words: "Up to and including 1880 the country had a frontier of settlement, but at present the unsettled area has been so broken into by isolated bodies of
Line settlement that there can hardly be said to be a frontier line. In the discussion of its
(5) extent, its westward movement, etc., it cannot, therefore, any longer have a place in the census reports." This brief official statement marks the closing of a great historic movement. Up to our own day American history has been in a large degree the history of the colonization of the Great West. The existence of an area of free land, its continuous recession, and the advance of American settlement westward, explain
(10) American development.

Behind institutions, behind constitutional forms and modifications, lie the vital forces that call these organs into life and shape them to meet changing conditions. The peculiarity of American institutions is the fact that they have been compelled to adapt themselves to the changes of an expanding people—to the changes involved in
(15) crossing a continent, in winning a wilderness, and in developing at each area of this progress out of the primitive economic and political conditions of the frontier into the complexity of city life. Said Calhoun in 1817, "We are great, and rapidly—I was about to say fearfully—growing!" So saying, he touched the distinguishing feature of American life. All peoples show development; the germ theory of politics has been
(20) sufficiently emphasized. In the case of most nations, however, the development has occurred in a limited area; and if the nation has expanded, it has met other growing peoples whom it has conquered. But in the case of the United States we have a different phenomenon. Limiting our attention to the Atlantic coast, we have the familiar phenomenon of the evolution of institutions in a limited area, such as the
(25) rise of representative government in complex organs; the progress from primitive industrial society, without division of labor, up to manufacturing civilization. But we have in addition to this a recurrence of the process of evolution in each western area reached in the process of expansion. Thus American development has exhibited not merely advance along a single line, but a return to primitive conditions on a
(30) continually advancing frontier line, and a new development for that area. American social development has been continually beginning over again on the frontier. This

perennial rebirth, this fluidity of American life, this expansion westward with its new opportunities, its continuous touch with the simplicity of primitive society, furnish the forces dominating the American character. The true point of view in the history (35) of this nation is not the Atlantic coast, it is the Great West. Even the slavery struggle, which is made so exclusive an object of attention by writers like Professor von Holst, occupies its important place in American history because of its relation to westward expansion.

In this advance, the frontier is the outer edge of the wave—the meeting point (40) between savagery and civilization. Much has been written about the frontier from the point of view of border warfare and the chase, but as a field for the serious study of the economist and the historian it has been neglected.

The American frontier is sharply distinguished from the European frontier—a fortified boundary line running through dense populations. The most significant (45) thing about the American frontier is, that it lies at the hither edge of free land. In the census reports it is treated as the margin of that settlement which has a density of two or more to the square mile. The term is an elastic one, and for our purposes does not need sharp definition.

46. In the context of the passage as a whole, the quotation from the Superintendent of the Census (lines 2–6) presents

(A) an analogy that illustrates the theme of the passage.

(B) an anecdote that introduces the main subject of the passage.

(C) a problem for which the author of the passage will offer a solution.

(D) a statement on which the passage will build.

(E) an opinion that emphasizes the gravity of the issue discussed in the rest of the passage.

47. In its context, the phrase "vital forces" (lines 11–12) refers to

(A) the Census Bureau.

(B) the U.S. Constitution.

(C) new laws and regulations passed to deal with changing social and economic conditions.

(D) the natural obstacles faced by settlers in the West.

(E) the people's urge to go west and to settle there.

48. Which of the following phrases illustrates "the germ theory of politics" (line 19)?

(A) "and rapidly—I was about to say fearfully—growing" (lines 17–18)

(B) "development . . . in a limited area" (lines 20–21)

(C) "rise of representative government" (line 25)

(D) "process of evolution" (line 27)

(E) "return to primitive conditions" (line 29)

49. The "different phenomenon" mentioned in line 23 refers to all of the following EXCEPT

    (A) a return to a primitive style of life.
    (B) new development in unsettled areas.
    (C) a recurrence of historical events.
    (D) growth within a limited geographical area.
    (E) the potential for further expansion.

50. The dominant rhetorical feature of the sentence, "This perennial . . . character" (lines 31–34) is

    (A) the use of repetition and rhythm.
    (B) alliteration.
    (C) a pronounced change in tone from the preceding sentence.
    (D) a sudden shift in the author's point of view.
    (E) a balance of overstatement and understatement.

51. In context, the word "chase" (line 41) is best interpreted to mean

    (A) the hunt for food.
    (B) survival in primitive conditions.
    (C) the question of slavery in the new territories.
    (D) the expulsion of the indigenous population.
    (E) settlers' competition for free land.

52. In the passage the author employs which of the following rhetorical strategies?

    (A) Extended analogy
    (B) Appeal to patriotism
    (C) Testimony from authority
    (D) Inspiring language
    (E) Statistical support

53. The function of the sentence in lines 43–44 ("The American frontier . . . . populations") is to

    (A) draw a contrast between American and European frontiers.
    (B) show the superiority of the American frontier.
    (C) reveal the uniqueness of the American frontier.
    (D) help summarize the passage.
    (E) present arguments in opposition to those in the previous paragraph.

54. The attitude of the author toward the closing of the frontier is primarily one of

    (A) regret.
    (B) historical interest.
    (C) disapproval.
    (D) hopefulness about the future.
    (E) satisfaction.

55. Which of the following best captures the main theme of the passage?

    (A) An industrial society has superseded a primitive society on the frontier.
    (B) America's frontier differs sharply from frontiers elsewhere.
    (C) Expansion to the West has helped to define America's character.
    (D) Criteria for taking the U.S. census must remain flexible.
    (E) America's frontier has been characterized by violence.

SECTION II

Three Essay Questions

TIME: 2 HOURS AND 15 MINUTES

Write your essays on standard 8½" × 11" composition paper. At the exam you will be given a bound booklet containing 12 lined pages.

Essay Question 1

SUGGESTED TIME:
15 MINUTES FOR READING THE QUESTION AND SOURCES
40 MINUTES FOR WRITING AN ESSAY

Many people worldwide devote huge amounts of time, money, and energy opposing the use of animals in laboratory research. Many others take the view that animals should be used in research for the overall benefit of humankind.

Carefully read the following six sources, including the material that introduces each source. Then, in an essay that synthesizes at least three of the sources, take a position on the claim that animals should be used in research for the overall benefit of humankind.

Don't simply summarize the sources. Instead, weigh evidence from the sources to support and illustrate your position on the issue. You may paraphrase, review, and quote relevant material directly and indirectly from the sources. Be sure to indicate in your essay which sources you use. Refer to them as Source A, Source B, and so on, or by the key words in the parentheses below. In making your argument, you may, of course, also include any ideas of your own.

Source A (AALAS)
Source B (PETA)
Source C (Pie graph)
Source D (Derbyshire)
Source E (Nuffield)
Source F (Haggarty)

"What Benefits Have Come from Medical Research Using Animals?" American Association for Laboratory Animal Science (AALAS), *www.foundation.aalas.org*

The following comes from the web site of a foundation that provides funding to promote awareness of research in animal care and animal contributions to biomedical research, safety testing, and education.

. . . Today's children routinely receive a vaccine that provides a lifetime of protection against polio. Children are also immunized against typhus, diphtheria, whooping cough, smallpox, and tetanus. Untold millions of people around the world are healthy because of these vaccines made possible through animal research.

Diabetes is another example of the importance of biomedical research. Approximately 6.2% of the population (17 million people) has diabetes. Nearly 1 million new cases of diabetes are diagnosed every year, and based on death certificate data, diabetes contributed to 209,664 deaths in 1999 alone. Without insulin treatments to regulate blood sugar levels, many more diabetics would die. Dogs were crucial to the research that identified the cause of diabetes, which led to the development of insulin. . . .

The importance of animal research to those suffering from heart and circulatory diseases cannot be overlooked. About 50 million Americans age six and older have high blood pressure, which can cause strokes, heart attacks, and heart disease. Research involving animals has helped identify the causes of high blood pressure and develop more effective drugs to control the problem. Other research has resulted in treatments for strokes and heart attacks that save thousands of lives and reduce recovery time. Dogs have been especially important to researchers who developed open-heart surgery, pacemakers, and heart transplants. These techniques have revolutionized therapy for people who have severe heart disease.

"Using Animals for Medical Testing Is Unethical and Unnecessary," The Ethics of Medical Testing, an online academic journal, 2012.

The following has been excerpted from an article prepared by People for the Ethical Treatment of Animals (PETA), the world's largest animal rights organization, with two million members and supporters.

Millions of animals suffer and die needlessly every year in the United States as they become subjects for medical testing and other horrible experiments. Although most people assume such activity is necessary to advance medical science, in reality it does very little to improve human health. The results of animal testing do not directly transfer to humans, and such results can be easily manipulated. . .

Diseases that are artificially induced in animals in a laboratory are never identical to those that occur naturally in humans. Because animal species differ from one another biologically in many significant ways, it becomes even more unlikely that animal experiments will yield results that will be correctly interpreted and applied to the human condition in a meaningful way.

For example, according to former National Cancer Institute director Dr. Richard Klausner, "We have cured mice of cancer for decades, and it simply didn't work in humans." And although at least 85 HIV/AIDS vaccines have been successful in nonhuman primate studies, as of 2010, every one of nearly 200 preventive and therapeutic vaccine trials has failed to demonstrate benefit to humans.

SOURCE C

"Numbers of Animals Used in Research in the United Kingdom," Home Office (2004) *Statistics of Scientific Procedures on Living Animals, Great Britain 2003.*

The pie graph below comes from a British government agency.

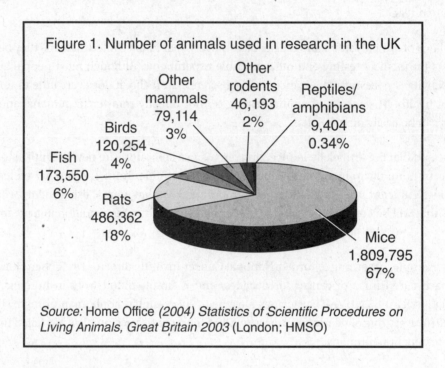

Figure 1. Number of animals used in research in the UK

Other mammals 79,114 3%

Other rodents 46,193 2%

Reptiles/ amphibians 9,404 0.34%

Birds 120,254 4%

Fish 173,550 6%

Rats 486,362 18%

Mice 1,809,795 67%

Source: Home Office *(2004) Statistics of Scientific Procedures on Living Animals, Great Britain 2003* (London; HMSO)

SOURCE D

Stuart Derbyshire, Ph.D., "Animal Experimentation," Speech at Edinburgh Book Festival, August 19, 2002.

Below are excerpts from a talk given at a book festival by a faculty member in the School of Psychology, University of Birmingham.

. . . Ongoing research with a wide variety of animals includes investigations of AIDS, cancer, heart disease, cystic fibrosis, and muscular dystrophy. The development of artificial arteries, the possibility of reversing spinal cord injury, and the aging process are all being investigated using animal models. The best hopes to cure malaria, Parkinson's and Alzheimer's diseases, epilepsy, clinical obesity, infertility, and a variety of birth defects all rely on current animal experiments.

Without doubt there are many experiments that will fail or lead to no useful therapy—such is the nature of all science. But to suggest that scientists are pointlessly pursuing experiments and models that do not work is just wrong-headed. The process of peer review and grant allocation certainly has its problems, but it is not that bad! If there were good alternatives to animals that worked better or as well, for less money and hassle, scientists would use them. We can be stubborn but we are not totally bananas.

. . . Tom Regan and Richard Ryder argue that animals are like us, that they share with us the capacity for seeing, hearing, believing, remembering, and anticipating and for experiencing pleasure and pain. They suggest that animals are "subjects of a being."

But, in every important sense, they are flat out wrong. Animals and humans do not think alike, feel alike, or experience alike. Humans and animals are not on the same scale.

"The Ethics of Research Involving Animals: A Guide to the Report," Nuffield Council on Bioethics, May 25, 2005.

The following is excerpted from a report issued by a foundation that studies and reports on ethical issues involving biological and medical research.

The question of defining the moral status of humans and animals often arises in the debate on research involving animals. Are humans morally more important than all animals? Is there a sliding scale with humans at the top and the simplest animals at the bottom? Or are humans and animals morally equal?

We suggest that the proper moral treatment of a being depends on the characteristics it possesses, rather than simply on the species to which it belongs. We identify five morally relevant features:

- Sentience (the capacity to feel pleasure and pain)
- Higher cognitive capacities (for example, the ability to use language and learn complicated tasks, such as making and using tools)
- The capacity to flourish (the ability to satisfy species—specific needs)
- Sociability (being a member of a community)
- Possession of a life (attributing value to life itself)

What weight should be given to each of the morally relevant features in considering whether or not research is acceptable? Are there factors to be weighed against human benefit? Should they be understood as absolute constraints? For example, should any use of animals that are capable of suffering be prohibited, or only the use of those that have higher cognitive capacities?

Many people seem to support a "hybrid" approach. This involves a combination of laying down definite limits for what should and should not happen (for example: "animals with higher cognitive capacities such as chimpanzees should never be used in research") and weighing up the costs and benefits of a particular action (for example, "research that causes minimum pain to a mouse is acceptable if it helps to ascertain the safety of an important and frequently used chemical").

Clare Haggarty, "Animals in Scientific Research: The Ethical Argument," National Anti-Vivisection Society, *www.navs.org*

The following comes from the website of an organization devoted to protecting animals and their rights.

The worst atrocity we inflict upon animals condemned to scientific research may be the act of removing them from the natural habitat, or breeding them in captivity, and then placing them in the artificial environment of a laboratory cage, where they have no hope of having the kind of life nature intended for them.

In the end, we as a society have a choice. Do we treat our fellow creatures with cruelty and callousness? Or with compassion, respect and justice? As humans, we have the freedom to make that choice. With this freedom comes the moral obligation to make responsible decisions.

Animals have no such choice. Because they cannot say no, they are completely vulnerable to whatever the researcher has in store for them, no matter how much pain and suffering is involved. Animals are unable to understand or claim their right to be alive, to be free from pain and suffering, and fulfill their biological potential. Therefore, it is up to humans to recognize and protect those rights for them, just as we are morally obligated to protect infants, the developmentally disabled, and the mentally ill.

It has been said that the moral progress of our society can be measured by the way it treats animals. Animal experimentation—an institutionalized form of exploitation—stands in the way of moral progress. Now is the time to extend our sphere of ethical concern to all creatures.

Essay Question 2

SUGGESTED TIME: 40 MINUTES

(This question counts as one third of the total score for Section II.)

> **Directions:** Here are two passages from the essays of the renowned physicist Albert Einstein. After reading them carefully, write an essay that analyzes and compares Einstein's use of language and rhetoric in each.

PASSAGE A

Physics deals with "events" in space and time. To each event belongs, besides its place coordinates x, y, z, a time value t. The latter was considered measurable by a clock (ideal periodic process) of negligible spatial extent. This clock C is to be *Line* considered at rest at one point of the coordinate system, e.g., at the coordinate origin (5) $(x = y = z = 0)$. The time of an event taking place at a point P (x,y,z) is then defined as the time shown on the clock C simultaneously with the event. Here the concept "simultaneous" was assumed as physically meaningful without special definition. This is a lack of exactness which seems harmless only since with the help of light (whose velocity is practically infinite from the point of view of daily experience) the (10) simultaneity of spatially distant events can apparently be decided immediately.

PASSAGE B

I am convinced there is only one way to eliminate these grave ills, namely through the establishment of a socialist economy, accompanied by an educational system which would be oriented toward social goals. In such an economy, the means of production are owned by society itself and are utilized in a planned fashion. A (15) planned economy, which adjusts production to the needs of the community, would distribute work to be done among all those able to work and would guarantee a livelihood to every man, woman and child. The education of the individual, in addition to promoting his own innate abilities, would attempt to develop in him a sense of responsibility for his fellow men in place of the glorification of power and success in (20) our present society.

Nevertheless, it is necessary to remember that a planned economy is not yet socialism. A planned economy as such may be accompanied by the complete enslavement of the individual. The achievement of socialism requires the solution of some extremely difficult socio-political problems: is it possible, in view of the far-reaching (25) centralization of political and economic power, to prevent bureaucracy from becoming all-powerful and overweening? How can the rights of the individual be protected and therewith a democratic counterweight to the power of the bureaucracy be assured?

Essay Question 3

SUGGESTED TIME: 40 MINUTES

(This question counts as one third of the total score for Section II.)

The German poet Goethe once wrote, "Treat people as if they were what they ought to be and you help them to become what they are capable of being."

Goethe's statement might be applied to schools, government, social services, business, even to families—anyplace, really, where people interact with each other. Is Goethe just expressing an unattainable principle of human behavior, or does his ideal have real-life applicability? In a well-organized essay, comment on the validity of Goethe's statement as a realistic guide to personal relationships. To support your point of view, you may draw evidence from your reading, studies, observation, and personal experience.

END OF PRACTICE TEST A

ANSWER KEY
Practice Test A

Answers to Multiple-Choice Questions

1.	**B**	16.	**E**	31.	**B**	46.	**D**
2.	**A**	17.	**B**	32.	**C**	47.	**C**
3.	**D**	18.	**C**	33.	**C**	48.	**A**
4.	**D**	19.	**C**	34.	**E**	49.	**D**
5.	**D**	20.	**E**	35.	**D**	50.	**A**
6.	**C**	21.	**C**	36.	**A**	51.	**D**
7.	**A**	22.	**B**	37.	**D**	52.	**C**
8.	**E**	23.	**E**	38.	**B**	53.	**D**
9.	**C**	24.	**B**	39.	**A**	54.	**B**
10.	**A**	25.	**D**	40.	**E**	55.	**C**
11.	**A**	26.	**C**	41.	**C**		
12.	**B**	27.	**D**	42.	**C**		
13.	**E**	28.	**A**	43.	**C**		
14.	**D**	29.	**D**	44.	**C**		
15.	**E**	30.	**E**	45.	**D**		

Summary of Answers in Section I (Multiple-Choice)

Number of correct answers _____

Use this information when you calculate your score for this exam. See page 264.

ANSWER EXPLANATIONS

Passage 1—An excerpt from Beryl Markham, *West with the Night*

1. **(B)** With such phrases as "you never watch yourself," and "avoiding yourself," the speaker grants that she is a stranger to herself. In lines 12–13, the speaker expresses surprise at meeting a "stranger" (herself) in the cockpit of her plane. Of the other choices, only (C) may be a possibility because it is somewhat paradoxical that a person may know other people better than she knows herself, but the speaker fails to analyze or explain why she feels that way.

2. **(A)** All the phrases except that in (A) identify activities that people have contrived to keep loneliness at bay.

3. **(D)** "Being alone" is a verbal phrase that starts out as the grammatical subject of the sentence. But the verb of the sentence—"can be"—does not appear until line 12, after several intervening prepositional phrases and infinitives. By that time, the speaker has chosen to recast the sentence with a new grammatical subject—"such an experience." Consequently, the two phrases together serve as the subject of the sentence.

4. **(D)** The speaker makes a specific comparison between the experience of piloting an airplane and discovering a stranger. That is, solo flying is like finding a side of yourself that you hadn't known about. The phrase "hopes rooted in your mind" (line 11) refers to thinking about the future (A) but it is not part of the speaker's analogy.

5. **(D)** Until the narration switches from second to first person, it is rooted in the past and relates to what the speaker has discovered about herself while flying. The switch in pronoun person suddenly brings the reader into the present—to the flight now in progress.

6. **(C)** After reciting the facts about where she is and what she sees, the speaker dramatizes the feelings and thoughts evoked by the experience of lifting the aircraft into the sky.

7. **(A)** During much of the passage, the speaker reflects on loneliness. She also discloses her thoughts and fears about flying.

8. **(E)** Piloting a plane provides the "security of solitude, the exhilaration of escape" (lines 16–17). These feelings contrast with those of the cares of the world below and "the small sorrow of rain" (lines 18–19). Choices (C) and (D) may be implied by the rain, but the speaker is literally and figuratively above it all and feeling "selfishly triumphant" (line 18).

9. **(C)** The sentence explains why distance is compared to "so much time used up." But it also serves all the other functions except to show that equating time and distance is an indication of pilot disorientation.

10. **(A)** The observation dramatizes a moment during the take-off—a moment so riveting that it seemed unreal. To capture that sense of unreality, the speaker uses exaggeration, or hyperbole. The notion that time and distance can stop has metaphorical implications, too, but the metaphor used here is consistent, not mixed. Choice II does not apply.

11. **(A)** A paradox is a valid statement that seems to fly in the face of logic. The lines contain no such feature. (B) and (D) are evident in the piling up of phrases beginning with "the moment." (C) can be found in lines that suggest the airplane has a will of its own,

as in "refuses its burden." (E) is seen when the speaker shifts from the impersonal "it" to "she."

12. **(B)** The speaker is describing how fear vanishes once she is airborne. Because she can no longer depend on the "security of land underfoot," security comes from the plane itself. Choice (E) alludes to courage, but only in the sense of standing up for one's beliefs, not in the sense of an absence of fear.

13. **(E)** Throughout the passage the author assigns meanings to particular moments in her flight and interprets the general experience of flying. Although a case could be made for choices (A), (B), or (C), it would be a stretch. Choice (E) is by far the best answer.

Passage 2—An excerpt from Henry Allen, "The Corps"

14. **(D)** The capitalized words convey the effect of the drill instructor's speech pattern and loudness.

15. **(E)** The phrase "daring glances" is a participial modifying the noun "recruits."

16. **(E)** The paragraph is filled with visual images, climaxed by the vivid reference to "raindrops beading on spitshined black shoes." See the Glossary (page 389) for definitions of each of the other choices.

17. **(B)** Most of the passage is devoted to describing the behavior of the omnipotent drill instructors. Their power contrasts starkly with the haplessness of the recruits. Choices (A), (C), and (E) are briefly mentioned in the passage, but each plays only a secondary role in contrasting actual drill instructors and those often portrayed in TV sitcoms.

18. **(C)** Hudson and Burley, proud, tough Marines, stand in stark contrast to the goofy, wisecracking versions of soldiers once popular on prime-time television. Choice (A) has some merit, but the description in lines 21–25 of life as a Marine Corps recruit is tied more closely to the idea that this is "serious business" (line 18).

19. **(C)** While not an exact quote from Marine Corps regulations, the material in these lines appears to be a paraphrase of the rules governing recruits during their basic training.

20. **(E)** The paragraph contains all of the techniques except a subordinate clause set off by dashes. The material between the dashes (lines 36–37) is an independent clause embedded in another independent clause.

21. **(C)** Because the word "dread" names the subject of the sentence ("It"), it is a predicate nominative. Other words in the sentence that serve the same function are "spectacle" and "initiation."

22. **(B)** Each of the choices has possibilities, but the purpose of the passage is best described as the author's attempt to recreate life at Parris Island. The extreme emotions and often inflammatory choice of words contain ample evidence of melodrama.

23. **(E)** All the choices are primarily descriptive except the last one, in which the author implies his approval of the methods used by the Marine Corps to train its recruits.

Passage 3—An excerpt from Arthur James, Earl of Balfour,
"On the Benefits of Reading" (1887)

24. **(B)** The speaker rejects the misguided opinions of his so-called "advisers." (A) and (C) are not good answers because the speaker is not exaggerating in any way, nor does he refer to a particular historical event. (D) is wrong because the statement expresses the speaker's personal opinion, and (E) is not valid because there is no evidence that the statement has a double meaning.

25. **(D)** As suggested by the first two sentences, the subject of the passage is the common theory that says the study of the past enables us to better predict the future. In the third sentence, the speaker denies the validity of that theory.

26. **(C)** The phrases, "to trace" and "to account" are parallel verb forms each referring to a step in the process of studying "the course which states and nations are destined to pursue in the future"—i.e., the unfolding of historic events.

27. **(D)** Choice (C) may seem like a reasonable answer because the waterway is "unexplored" (line 7), but the speaker claims we have only a limited vision of the future. We can guess in a very general way what the future may hold, but precisely how events will unfold depends largely on unpredictable—i.e., "accidental" (line 13)—occurrences.

28. **(A)** The paragraph that begins with line 21 enumerates many of the wondrous—i.e., "spectacular"—pleasures that await students and observers of history. Choice (B) is irrelevant. The other choices fail to capture the sense of history's grandeur that the author tries to convey to the reader.

29. **(D)** To some extent, all the choices name possible rewards of studying history. Enjoyment and the stirring of the imagination are important, but the speaker saves the greatest reward for the end of the paragraph: history serves as "a subject of contemplation" of which we never grow weary.

30. **(E)** By deliberately using poetic language, the speaker emphasizes the drama and romance of history, or, as he puts it, "The imagination is moved by the slow unrolling of this great picture of human mutability" (lines 25–26). Scan the paragraph and you will find several series of repeated sounds. Note, for example, the repetition of *hard c* and also *s, d,* and *f* in lines 25–34. These sounds serve to unify the prose.

31. **(B)** The lines consist of a single *periodic* sentence—i.e., one in which the main thought is not complete until the very end. (A *loose* sentence is the opposite—one in which the main idea is stated much earlier, often at the very beginning.)

    Parallel syntax is found in a series of phrases, some beginning with a noun (*successes, failures*), some with adjectives (*ceaseless, strange*).

    Prepositional phrases such as *of long forgotten controversies* and *of purpose* appear throughout the lines in question.

    Lines 28–29, among others, contain relative clauses: *which lay deep the seeds . . .* and *that ultimately divert . . .* and so on.

    The subject of the sentence is *those*, a single demonstrative pronoun that refers to and takes the place of the long string of nouns that came earlier in the sentence.

32. **(C)** The previous paragraph introduces the notion that increased enjoyment with the study of the past can be achieved by becoming familiar with the "scenes and actors of

special periods," in other words, by getting us to expand our "social circle." The other choices also may enhance our appreciation of history, but they pale next to the excitement of intimately knowing the figures who shaped the periods in which they lived.

33. **(C)** The speaker implies that death inevitably narrows and restricts our "social circle." Yet, he adds in lines 45–46 that there is a trick to reviving it.

34. **(E)** The sort of reading that the speaker has in mind is described in the previous paragraph. It is the kind that acquaints readers—or even allows the reader to become "close friends"—with specific individuals who lived in the past.

35. **(D)** Early in the passage the speaker rejects the notion that history is most useful as a key to predicting the future. But the bulk of the passage concentrates not on the practicality of studying history but on its joys.

Passage 4—An excerpt from Deanna Paoli Gumina, *The Italians of San Francisco*

36. **(A)** Although each of the choices is mentioned somewhere in the passage, the speaker's overall purpose in the passage is to tell the story of how the earthquake affected the Italian residents of the city.

37. **(D)** The details in the first paragraph emphasize the unusual nature of the 1906 earthquake. (E) may sound like a promising choice because the author calls the earthquake a "tragedy" (line 5). But overall, the author's rhetorical stance in the paragraph is largely straightforward and objective.

38. **(B)** The "knotted, tangled mass" of rubble depicts all the choices except the fault line— the underground crack where the earthquake was centered.

39. **(A)** The sentence is meant to explain why the people on Telegraph Hill suffered losses in spite of being "luckier than most" (lines 11–12). The text suggests the author's disdain for the insurance companies (D), but her disapproval is secondary to the main purpose of the sentence.

40. **(E)** Because five of the eight footnotes cite sources written soon after the earthquake, (E) is the only logical choice. All the other choices are assumptions based on too little evidence. All the other choices are incorrect because the numbers refer to the volume and page number of a periodical—in this case *Scribner's*, which is neither a book nor a publisher.

41. **(C)** The absence of a book title in the footnote signifies that the work by Peixotto has appeared in a previous footnote.

42. **(C)** To inform readers about the effects of the earthquake on the Italian community in San Francisco is the main purpose of the passage. (A) is too broad because the passage focuses on the Italians of San Francisco. (B) is inaccurate because the passage covers how the Italian community fared in the earthquake but does not scrutinize or examine the community in detail. (D) suggests an account of the entire event, but the passage begins only after the quake has occurred. (E) is slightly valid because the first paragraph of the passage mentions why the quake had been so deadly, but fails to take into account the rest of the passage.

43. **(C)** Sources I and II say complimentary things about the design of the buildings. The author of the remaining source (Footnote 7) neither approves or disapproves, commenting instead on what the architecture implies about Italians' experience in America.

44. **(C)** The first sentence is a compound sentence that is made up of two independent clauses joined by the conjunction *and*. None of the other features is found in these lines of the passage. For definitions of the terms listed in (A)–(D), turn to "Varying Sentences," page 155 and to the Glossary, pages 389–397.

45. **(D)** The author's intent in the passage is to write a serious, informative account of the events described. Because her approach is that of an objective historian, evidence of her personal feelings is virtually absent.

Passage 5—An excerpt from Frederick Jackson Turner, *The Frontier in American History*

46. **(D)** To answer this question you must read beyond lines 2–6, preferably to the end of the first paragraph. By then, it will be clear that all the choices except (D) fail to apply. The quotation announces a change in the manner in which census reports are made. In the remainder of the passage, the author details this change and explains its historic implications.

47. **(C)** According to the author, "vital forces" generate institutional changes. The only other possible choice is (B), but note that the phrase "vital forces" refers not to the U.S. Constitution itself but rather to "constitutional forms and modifications" (line 11). That is to say, conditions on the frontier necessitate flexibility in how the Constitution functions in American society.

48. **(A)** The author alludes to the "germ theory" in the context of a discussion about growth and development, described vividly by Calhoun's words. The quotation suggests that in 1817 the nation was expanding uncontrollably—not an altogether sanguine situation in Calhoun's words, but rather, the author believes, like a plague of "germs."

49. **(D)** According to the passage, growth in a limited geographical area is characteristic of "most nations" (line 20), including the original American settlement along the Atlantic coast. All the other choices pertain to features of the frontier in the West.

50. **(A)** The most notable feature is the rhythmic piling up of similar phrases that constitute the subject of the sentence.

51. **(D)** According to the paragraph in question, the frontier has been the "meeting point between savagery and civilization," and has been marked by "border warfare." Both phrases imply the existence of a clash between the settlers and those who interfered with their progress—namely the native inhabitants of the land. Indeed, much has been written about the conflict between settlers and the Indians.

52. **(C)** Twice in the passage, the author quotes authority figures—the Superintendent of the Census (lines 2–6) and Calhoun (lines 17–18)—and then refers to Professor von Holst (line 41). In all instances, the words serve as a springboard to further discussion. Choices (B) and (D) have potential as correct answers, but neither is as prominent as (C).

53. **(D)** While the sentence points out that the European and American frontiers differ from each other, the purpose of the entire last paragraph of the passage is to review what came before. Thus, the sentence introduces and contributes to a summary of the passage.

54. **(B)** The author analyzes the historical meaning of the end of the frontier in America. He expresses no strong feelings about it. Rather, he presents his interpretation of a great historical event.

55. **(C)** Throughout the passage, the author refers to the frontier's influence on American life. In the first paragraph he states that American development can be explained by the westward expansion. In the next paragraph, he states that America's institutions have adapted to the needs of expansion. In line 34, the author states outright that the frontier has furnished "the forces dominating the American character." Choice (B) is discussed in the passage but only as a supporting idea, not as the main theme.

Answers to Essay Questions

For an overview of how essays are graded, turn to "How Essays Are Scored," pages 36–37.

Although answers to the essay questions will vary greatly, the following descriptions suggest a possible approach to each question and contain ideas that could be used in a response to the question. Perhaps your essay contains many of the same ideas. If not, don't be alarmed. Your ideas may be at least as insightful, or even more so, as those below.

ESSAY QUESTION 1

On this issue, it's unusual to take an extreme position, although those who do probably come down on the side of animal protection. But not always.

Some Arguments In Favor of Using Animals for Research:

- Millions of people owe their good health to vaccines developed with the help of animals. (Source A)
- Many diseases, from diabetes to heart disease, can be treated with drugs developed in laboratories using animals. (Source A)
- The vast majority of animals used in research—mice and rats—are of a lower order than humans and most other mammals. (Source C)
- Animals and humans should not be equated because they are not on the same scale; humans are special. (Source D)

Some Arguments Against Using Animals for Research:

- The results of animal testing do not directly transfer to humans. (Source B)
- Literally millions of animals are used in research in just one year in just one country—England. (Source C)
- Employing animals for research should not be undertaken without considering several morally relevant features, among them the cognitive level of the animal. (Source E)
- The treatment of animals in the lab is cruel and callous. (Source F)
- The moral position of a society can be measured by the way its animals are treated. (Source F)

ESSAY QUESTION 2, BASED ON PASSAGES BY ALBERT EINSTEIN

Although the two passages were written by the same person, they are dramatically different from each other. In the first, Einstein explains a phenomenon in physics, a world in which he is very much at home. Much of the passage is factual, precise, and impersonal. He writes, for example, "The latter was considered measurable . . .," using a passive construction in order to avoid using the first person. The technical nature of the passage is evident in several symbols and formulas and in the specialized language of physics, e.g., "negligible spatial extent" and "the simultaneity of spatially distant events."

Unlike the first passage, the second is written speculatively. Gone is the voice of authority and the technical language and formulas—replaced herein by vague generalizations couched in the language of economics and sociology. Consider such phrases as "an educational system . . . oriented toward social goals," and "the education of the individual . . . would attempt to develop . . . a sense of responsibility." This sort of language may sound good, but it lacks substance. It's jargon, plain and simple. We are hearing the views of someone who may be a thoughtful human being, but the words resemble empty platitudes. Instead of stating his case forcefully, Einstein resorts to the repeated use of would, a word that suggests tentativeness. Had he been more confident and well-informed on the topic, his language would have reflected greater certainty. He would have been better served by using will, a far more decisive word.

ESSAY QUESTION 3, BASED ON A STATEMENT BY GOETHE

The task in this question is to support, challenge, or qualify Goethe's statement. If you agree with Goethe, your essay should contain examples—possibly in anecdotal form—of people living up to expectations because they were treated with respect and dignity. You may remember a time, for example, when you were treated like an adult, and so you behaved like one, or in contrast, because you were treated as a child, you acted silly or immature.

If you cannot subscribe to Goethe's point of view, you should cite examples of people being treated well but acting badly. A striking example occurred not long ago when a high school student in New York murdered his English teacher after the teacher had gone out of his way to help the student deal with both academic and personal problems. One could argue, of course, that because this case was an aberration, it cannot reasonably support a generalization about human behavior. In fact, beware of drawing any broad conclusions based on a single event or example—both in your essay writing and in life.

SCORING SECTION II ESSAYS

Before scoring your essays, carefully review "How Essays Are Scored" (pages 36–37), a guide meant to help you judge as objectively as possible the quality of your writing.

Use the criteria listed below to evaluate each of your essays. Because it's tough to be totally impartial about your own writing, you may get a more accurate score by asking a well-informed friend, teacher, or counselor to rate your essays for you.

On the following Rating Chart, enter a number (from 1 to 6) that you think represents your level of performance in each category (A–F).

CATEGORY A: OVERALL PURPOSE/MAIN IDEA
6   extremely well-defined and insightful
5   clearly defined and generally insightful
4   mostly clear
3   somewhat clear but occasionally confusing
2   generally unclear and confusing
1   mostly incomprehensible or simplistic

CATEGORY B: HANDLING OF THE PROMPT
6   self-evident or extremely clear throughout
5   mostly clear
4   somewhat clear
3   somewhat unclear
2   generally unclear or ambiguous
1   confusing or nonexistent

CATEGORY C: ORGANIZATION AND DEVELOPMENT
6   insightfully organized; fully developed with excellent supporting evidence
5   reasonably well organized; developed with appropriate supporting material
4   appropriately organized; developed with some relevant material
3   inconsistent organization; weak development
2   poorly organized; little or no development
1   no discernible organization or development

CATEGORY D: SENTENCE STRUCTURE
6   varied and engaging
5   sufficiently varied to create interest
4   some variety
3   little variety; minor sentence errors
2   frequent sentence errors that interfere with meaning
1   serious sentence errors that obscure meaning

CATEGORY E: USE OF LANGUAGE
6   precise and effective word choice
5   competent word choice
4   conventional word choice; mostly correct
3   some errors in diction or idiom
2   frequent lapses in diction or idiom
1   meaning obscured by word choice

CATEGORY F: GRAMMAR AND USAGE
6   error-free or virtually error-free
5   occasional minor errors
4   basically correct but with several minor errors
3   meaning somewhat obscured by errors
2   meaning frequently obscured by errors
1   meaning blocked by several major errors

RATING CHART

Rate your essay	Essay 1	Essay 2	Essay 3
Overall Purpose/Main Idea			
Handling of the Prompt			
Organization and Development			
Sentence Structure			
Use of Language			
Grammar and Usage			
Composite Scores (sum of each column)			

By using the following scale, in which composite scores are converted to the nine-point AP rating scale, you may determine the final score for each essay:

Composite Score	AP Essay Score
33–36	9
29–32	8
25–28	7
21–24	6
18–20	5
15–17	4
10–14	3
7–9	2
6 or below	1

AP Essay Scores Essay 1 _____ Essay 2 _____ Essay 3 _____

TEST SCORE WORKSHEET

The scores you have earned on the multiple-choice and essay sections of the exam may now be converted to the AP five-point scale by performing the following calculations:

I. Determine Your Score for Section I (Multiple-Choice)

(STEP A) Number of correct answers _____

(STEP B) Multiply the figure in Step A by 1.2272 to find your
Multiple-Choice Score _____. (Do not round.)

II. Determine Your Score for Section II (Essays)

(STEP A) Enter your score for Essay 1 (out of 9) _____

(STEP B) Enter your score for Essay 2 (out of 9) _____

(STEP C) Enter your score for Essay 3 (out of 9) _____

(STEP D) Add the figures in Steps A, B, and C _____

(STEP E) Multiply the figure in Step D by 3.0556 _____ (Do not round.)
This is your Essay Score.

III. Determine Your Total Score

Add the scores for I and II to find your composite score _____.
(Round to nearest whole number.)

To convert your composite score to the AP five-point scale, use the chart below. The range of scores only approximates what you would earn on the actual test because the exact figures may vary from test to test. Be aware, therefore, that your score on this test, as well as on other tests in this book, may differ slightly from your score on an actual AP exam.

Composite Score	AP Grade
114–150	5
98–113	4
81–97	3
53–80	2
0–52	1

AP essays are ordinarily judged in relation to other essays written on the same topic at the same time. Therefore, the scores you assign yourself for these essays may not be the same as the scores you would earn on an actual exam.

ANSWER SHEET
Practice Test B

Multiple-Choice Questions

Time—1 hour

1. Ⓐ Ⓑ Ⓒ Ⓓ Ⓔ
2. Ⓐ Ⓑ Ⓒ Ⓓ Ⓔ
3. Ⓐ Ⓑ Ⓒ Ⓓ Ⓔ
4. Ⓐ Ⓑ Ⓒ Ⓓ Ⓔ
5. Ⓐ Ⓑ Ⓒ Ⓓ Ⓔ
6. Ⓐ Ⓑ Ⓒ Ⓓ Ⓔ
7. Ⓐ Ⓑ Ⓒ Ⓓ Ⓔ
8. Ⓐ Ⓑ Ⓒ Ⓓ Ⓔ
9. Ⓐ Ⓑ Ⓒ Ⓓ Ⓔ
10. Ⓐ Ⓑ Ⓒ Ⓓ Ⓔ
11. Ⓐ Ⓑ Ⓒ Ⓓ Ⓔ
12. Ⓐ Ⓑ Ⓒ Ⓓ Ⓔ
13. Ⓐ Ⓑ Ⓒ Ⓓ Ⓔ
14. Ⓐ Ⓑ Ⓒ Ⓓ Ⓔ
15. Ⓐ Ⓑ Ⓒ Ⓓ Ⓔ

16. Ⓐ Ⓑ Ⓒ Ⓓ Ⓔ
17. Ⓐ Ⓑ Ⓒ Ⓓ Ⓔ
18. Ⓐ Ⓑ Ⓒ Ⓓ Ⓔ
19. Ⓐ Ⓑ Ⓒ Ⓓ Ⓔ
20. Ⓐ Ⓑ Ⓒ Ⓓ Ⓔ
21. Ⓐ Ⓑ Ⓒ Ⓓ Ⓔ
22. Ⓐ Ⓑ Ⓒ Ⓓ Ⓔ
23. Ⓐ Ⓑ Ⓒ Ⓓ Ⓔ
24. Ⓐ Ⓑ Ⓒ Ⓓ Ⓔ
25. Ⓐ Ⓑ Ⓒ Ⓓ Ⓔ
26. Ⓐ Ⓑ Ⓒ Ⓓ Ⓔ
27. Ⓐ Ⓑ Ⓒ Ⓓ Ⓔ
28. Ⓐ Ⓑ Ⓒ Ⓓ Ⓔ
29. Ⓐ Ⓑ Ⓒ Ⓓ Ⓔ
30. Ⓐ Ⓑ Ⓒ Ⓓ Ⓔ

31. Ⓐ Ⓑ Ⓒ Ⓓ Ⓔ
32. Ⓐ Ⓑ Ⓒ Ⓓ Ⓔ
33. Ⓐ Ⓑ Ⓒ Ⓓ Ⓔ
34. Ⓐ Ⓑ Ⓒ Ⓓ Ⓔ
35. Ⓐ Ⓑ Ⓒ Ⓓ Ⓔ
36. Ⓐ Ⓑ Ⓒ Ⓓ Ⓔ
37. Ⓐ Ⓑ Ⓒ Ⓓ Ⓔ
38. Ⓐ Ⓑ Ⓒ Ⓓ Ⓔ
39. Ⓐ Ⓑ Ⓒ Ⓓ Ⓔ
40. Ⓐ Ⓑ Ⓒ Ⓓ Ⓔ
41. Ⓐ Ⓑ Ⓒ Ⓓ Ⓔ
42. Ⓐ Ⓑ Ⓒ Ⓓ Ⓔ
43. Ⓐ Ⓑ Ⓒ Ⓓ Ⓔ
44. Ⓐ Ⓑ Ⓒ Ⓓ Ⓔ
45. Ⓐ Ⓑ Ⓒ Ⓓ Ⓔ

46. Ⓐ Ⓑ Ⓒ Ⓓ Ⓔ
47. Ⓐ Ⓑ Ⓒ Ⓓ Ⓔ
48. Ⓐ Ⓑ Ⓒ Ⓓ Ⓔ
49. Ⓐ Ⓑ Ⓒ Ⓓ Ⓔ
50. Ⓐ Ⓑ Ⓒ Ⓓ Ⓔ
51. Ⓐ Ⓑ Ⓒ Ⓓ Ⓔ
52. Ⓐ Ⓑ Ⓒ Ⓓ Ⓔ
53. Ⓐ Ⓑ Ⓒ Ⓓ Ⓔ
54. Ⓐ Ⓑ Ⓒ Ⓓ Ⓔ

Practice Test B

SECTION I

TIME: 1 HOUR

> **Directions:** *Questions 1–10.* Carefully read the following passage and answer the accompanying questions.

The passage comes from the quill of a renowned essayist of the 16th century.

PASSAGE 1

I am not excessively fond of salads or fruit, with the exception of melons. My father hated every kind of sauce; I like them all. Eating too much makes me uncomfortable; but in respect of its properties I am not yet very certain that any kind of food *Line* disagrees with me. Nor have I noticed that I am affected by full or new moons, by
(5) autumn or spring.

We are subject to fickle and inexplicable changes. For example, radishes, which I first found to agree with me, afterwards disagreed, and now they agree again. In several things I have found my stomach and palate to vary in the same way: I have changed more than once from white wine to claret, and back again from claret to
(10) white wine.

I have a dainty tooth for fish, and the meatless days are my meat-days; my fasts are my feasts. Besides, I believe that it is, as some people say, more easily digested than meat. As it goes against my conscience to eat meat on fish-days, so my taste rebels against mixing meat and fish; the difference seems to me too wide.
(15) From my youth up I have occasionally skipped a meal; either to sharpen my appetite for the next day (for, as Epicurus used to fast and make lean meals in order to accustom his greed to dispense with plenty, I do so, on the contrary, in order to train my greed to take better advantage of plenty and to enjoy it more cheerfully); or I used to fast to keep my strength for the performance of some mental or bodily action; for
(20) both my body and mind are made cruelly sluggish by repletion. . . . To cure my ailing digestion, I say that we should not so much look to what we eat as to whom we eat with.

To me no dressing is so acceptable, and no sauce so appetizing, as that derived from good company. I think it is more wholesome to eat more at leisure with a
(25) good friend, and less, and to eat oftener. But I would give hunger and appetite their due; I should take no pleasure in dragging through three or four wretched repasts a

day, restricted by doctors' orders. Who will assure me that I can recover at supper-time the good appetite I had this morning? Let us old men especially take the first opportunity that comes our way. Let us leave the making of dietaries to doctors and
(30) almanac makers . . . .

I do not cover my legs and thighs more in winter than in summer: simple silk hose. For the relief of my colds I gave way to the habit of keeping my head warmer, and my belly on account of the colic. But in a few days my ailments became accustomed to them and scorned my ordinary precautions: from a cap I advanced to a kerchief, and
(35) from a bonnet to a lined hat. The wadding of my doublet is now only ornamental. All that would be of no avail unless I added a hare's skin or a vulture's plumage, with a skull-cap for the head. Continue this gradual progress and you will go a long way. I shall take care not to do so, and would gladly go back to where I began, if I dared. "Have you developed a new ailment? Is the remedy no longer of any avail? You
(40) have grown accustomed to it? Then try another." In this way they ruin their health who allow themseves to be fettered by enforced rules, and superstitiously adhere to them; they need more and more, and after that more again. There is no end.

1. Which of the following best describes the rhetorical function of the last sentence of paragraph 1 (lines 4–5)?

   (A) It helps to establish the speaker's credentials as an expert on the topic of the passage.
   (B) It challenges a commonly held superstition to be discussed later in the passage.
   (C) It introduces a major theme of the passage.
   (D) It refers to an old saying about the consequences of overeating.
   (E) It creates a rhetorical link between paragraph 1 and the first sentence of paragraph 2.

2. The author's references to radishes and to claret (second paragraph) function in all of the following ways EXCEPT to

   (A) prove the validity of the second paragraph's topic sentence.
   (B) identify changes that the author has experienced.
   (C) define the word "fickle" (line 6).
   (D) add to the litany of the author's personal quirks.
   (E) hint that the author has switched from a serious to an ironic tone.

3. The description of the speaker's "dainty tooth for fish" (line 11) contributes to the unity of the passage by

   (A) contrasting the taste of two different foods.
   (B) adding further details to the speaker's portrait of himself.
   (C) condemning those who do not observe meatless days.
   (D) drawing a parallel between different kinds of cooking.
   (E) commenting of the absurdity of the speaker's taste in food.

4. Lines 11–14 contain all of the following EXCEPT

   (A) alliteration.
   (B) parallel syntax.
   (C) synecdoche.
   (D) a paradox.
   (E) onomatopoeia.

5. In lines 15–22, the speaker uses which of the following reasons to justify his occasional fasting?

   I. To increase his appetite
   II. To overeat without feeling guilty
   III. To derive greater enjoyment from his meals

   (A) I only
   (B) II only
   (C) I and III only
   (D) II and III only
   (E) I, II, and III

6. The passage as a whole can best be described as

   (A) a prescription for a better diet.
   (B) an anecdote about old-fashioned eating customs.
   (C) an account of one man's tastes.
   (D) a comparison of the author and his father.
   (E) a reflection on unhealthful eating habits.

7. Which of the following best describes the rhetorical function of lines 24–28 in the passage?

   (A) They serve as a transition between the paragraphs that come before and after.
   (B) They support the author's assertion that he likes all sauces (line 2).
   (C) They provide evidence contrary to material in a previous paragraph.
   (D) They reiterate an idea presented in the previous paragraph.
   (E) They state a logical conclusion based on statements in the previous paragraph.

8. The speaker's allusion to going back to "where I began" (line 38) refers to

   (A) looking for relief from a head cold.
   (B) an earlier unspecified time of life.
   (C) wearing a skull cap.
   (D) putting on a cap to keep his head warm.
   (E) covering his legs with silk hose.

9. Which of the following phrases is probably exaggerated for effect?

 (A) "from white wine to claret, and back again" (line 9)
 (B) "body and mind are made cruelly sluggish" (line 20)
 (C) "three or four wretched repasts a day" (lines 26–27)
 (D) "from a bonnet to a lined hat" (line 35)
 (E) "a hare's skin or a vulture's plumage" (line 36)

10. The principal contrast drawn by the author of the passage is between

 (A) theory and fact.
 (B) conventions and individual preferences.
 (C) old wives' tales and modern practices.
 (D) idealism and realism.
 (E) restraint and freedom.

Directions: *Questions 11–22.* Carefully read the following passage and answer the accompanying questions.

The passage below is an excerpt from a book by a 20th-century author.

PASSAGE 2

Does history repeat itself? In our Western world in the eighteenth and nineteenth centuries, this question used to be debated as an academic exercise. The spell of well-being which our civilization was enjoying at the time had dazzled our grand-

Line fathers into the quaint pharisaical notion that they were "not as other men are";

(5) they had come to believe that our Western society was exempt from the possibility of falling into those mistakes and mishaps that have been the ruin of certain other civilizations whose history, from the beginning to end, is an open book. To us, in our generation, the old question has rather suddenly taken on a new and very practical significance. We have awakened to the truth (how, one wonders, could we ever have

(10) been blind to it?) that Western man and his works are no more invulnerable than the now extinct civilizations of the Aztecs and the Incas, the Sumerians and the Hittites. So today, with some anxiety, we are searching the scriptures of the past to find out whether they contain a lesson that we can decipher. Does history give us any infor- mation about our own prospects? And, if it does, what is the burden of it? Does it

(15) spell out for us an inexorable doom, which we can merely await with folded hands— resigning ourselves, as best we may, to a fate that we cannot avert or even modify by our own efforts? Or does it inform us, not of certainties, but of probabilities, or bare possibilities, in our own future? The practical difference is vast, for, on this second alternative, so far from being stunned into passivity, we should be aroused to action.

(20) On this second alternative, the lesson of history would not be like an astrologer's horoscope; it would be like a navigator's chart, which affords the seafarer who has the intelligence to use it a much greater hope of avoiding shipwreck than when he

was sailing blind, because it gives him the means, if he has the skill and courage to use them, of steering a course between charted rocks and reefs.

(25)   It will be seen that our question needs defining before we plunge into an attempt to answer it. When we ask ourselves, "Does history repeat itself?" do we mean no more than, "Does history turn out to have repeated itself, on occasions, in the past?" Or are we asking whether history is governed by inviolable laws which have not only taken effect in every past case to which they have applied, but are also bound to take

(30)   effect in every similar situation that may arise in the future? On this second interpretation, the word "does" would mean "must"; on the other interpretation it would mean "may." On this issue, the writer of the present article may as well put his cards on the table at once. He is not a determinist in his reading of the riddle of human life. He believes that where there is life there is hope, and that, with God's help, man

(35)   is master of his own destiny, at least to some extent, in some respects.

11. The author of the passage can best be characterized as someone who

(A) is interested in theorizing about history.
(B) is critical of historical researchers.
(C) studies first-hand accounts of historical events.
(D) believes in the influence of fate in shaping human events.
(E) is not hopeful about the future of the human race.

12. In the context of the first paragraph, "grandfathers" (lines 3–4) probably refers to all of the following EXCEPT

(A) bygone observers of society.
(B) ancestors of the author.
(C) 18th- and 19th-century historians.
(D) European and American thinkers and writers of the past.
(E) scholars of previous generations.

13. In line 7, the phrase "an open book" refers to

(A) the Western world of the 18th and 19th centuries.
(B) our grandfathers' notion of history.
(C) the lessons that ancient civilizations preserved for future generations.
(D) the debates of academicians.
(E) evidence drawn from the experience of civilizations that fell into ruin.

14. Which of the following best describes a rhetorical shift that occurs in the sentence "To us, in our generation . . . ." (lines 7–9)?

(A) It wanders from the main idea of the passage.
(B) The speaker's tone changes from factual to contemplative.
(C) It introduces a contrast between past and present.
(D) It raises a new argument that the speaker will most likely refute later in the passage.
(E) It marks a transition from objective description to sympathetic narration.

15. The primary function of the author's observation made in the parentheses (lines 9–10) is

(A) to counterbalance the question asked in line 1 of the passage.
(B) to introduce an issue addressed later in the passage.
(C) to briefly inject a change in the tone of the passage.
(D) to summarize a different perspective on the topic of the passage.
(E) to imply that the passage deals with a question that cannot be adequately answered.

16. In line 12 the word "scriptures" is best interpreted to mean

(A) religious beliefs.
(B) the laws.
(C) the record.
(D) the written record.
(E) artifacts.

17. The end of the first paragraph (lines 20–24) contains all of the following rhetorical features EXCEPT

(A) an antithesis.
(B) an extended simile.
(C) a metaphor.
(D) alliteration.
(E) hyperbole.

18. The phrase "this second alternative" (line 20) refers to which of the following?

(A) History's ability to suggest what is likely to occur in the future
(B) The fate we cannot avert or modify
(C) Predictable events based on historical records
(D) The mystery of an unknown future
(E) Inferences drawn from widespread archaeological research

19. By comparing an "astrologer's horoscope" (lines 20–21) and a "navigator's chart" (line 21), the author intends to convey the idea that

(A) unlike our ancestors, we have the wherewithal to avoid mistakes of the past.
(B) our ancestors were more superstitious than we are.
(C) knowledge of navigation would have saved past civilizations.
(D) science is superior to superstition.
(E) astrology is a dying art.

20. In its context, the word "intelligence" (line 22) can best be defined as

(A) an understanding of history.
(B) probabilities.
(C) formal education.
(D) foresight and information.
(E) techniques used to solve problems.

21. For which of the following reasons does the writer use the expression, "put his cards on the table" (lines 32–33)?

    I. To win the reader's confidence
   II. To indicate that he hasn't yet made up his mind on the question
  III. To acknowledge a personal bias

(A) II only
(B) I and II
(C) II and III
(D) I and III
(E) I, II, and III

22. Which of the following most accurately describes the author's intent throughout the passage?

(A) To solve a logical problem faced by historians
(B) To refute theories espoused by other historians
(C) To speculate on the validity of a historical principle
(D) To prove an important historical theory
(E) To define several terms used by historians

Directions: *Questions 23–34.* Carefully read the following passage and answer the accompanying questions.

The passage below is taken from a work written in the 20th century.

PASSAGE 3

What are the practical results of the modern cult of beauty? The exercises and the massages, the health motors and the skin foods—to what have they led? Are women more beautiful than they were? Do they get something for the enormous expendi-
Line ture of energy, time, and money demanded of them by the beauty cult? These are
(5) questions which it is difficult to answer. For the facts seem to contradict themselves. The campaign for more physical beauty seems to be both a tremendous success and a lamentable failure. It depends how you look at the results.

It is a success insofar as more women retain their youthful appearance to a greater age than in the past. "Old ladies" are already becoming rare. In a few years, we may
(10) well believe, they will be extinct. White hair and wrinkles, a bent back and hollow cheeks will come to be regarded as medievally old-fashioned. The crone of the future will be golden, curly, and cherry-lipped, neat-ankled and slender. The Portrait of the Artist's Mother will come to be almost indistinguishable, at future picture shows, from the Portrait of the Artist's Daughter. This desirable consummation will be due
(15) in part to skin foods and injections of paraffin wax, facial surgery, mud baths, and paint, in part to improved health, due in its turn to a more rational mode of life. Ugliness is one of the symptoms of disease; beauty, of health. Insofar as the campaign for more beauty is also a campaign for more health, it is admirable and, up

to a point, genuinely successful. Beauty that is merely the artificial shadow of these
(20) symptoms of health is intrinsically of poorer quality than the genuine article. Still,
it is a sufficiently good imitation to be sometimes mistakable for the real thing. The
apparatus for mimicking the symptoms of health is now within the reach of every
moderately prosperous person; the knowledge of the way in which real health can
be achieved is growing, and will in time, no doubt, be universally acted upon. When
(25) that happy moment comes, will every woman be beautiful—as beautiful, at any rate,
as the natural shape of her features, with or without surgical and chemical aid, permits?

The answer is emphatically: No. For real beauty is as much an affair of the inner
as of the outer self. The beauty of a porcelain jar is a matter of shape, of color, of
(30) surface texture. The jar may be empty or tenanted by spiders, full of honey or stink-
ing slime—it makes no difference to its beauty or ugliness. But a woman is alive, and
her beauty is therefore not skin deep. The surface of the human vessel is affected
by the nature of its spiritual contents. I have seen women who, by the standards of
a connoisseur of porcelain, were ravishingly lovely. Their shape, their color, their
(35) surface texture were perfect. And yet they were not beautiful. For the lovely vase was
either empty or filled with some corruption. Spiritual emptiness or ugliness shows
through. And conversely, there is an interior light that can transfigure forms that the
pure aesthetician would regard as imperfect or downright ugly.

23. The word "cult" (line 1) as used in the passage means primarily

   (A) a group with a particular obsession.
   (B) a subculture dedicated to a pagan rite.
   (C) a movement sponsored by patrons of beauty salons.
   (D) the devotees of a unique ideology.
   (E) the followers of a charismatic leader.

24. The first paragraph raises expectations that the remainder of the passage
    will be

   (A) a biting indictment.
   (B) an objective description.
   (C) a "pro" and "con" kind of discussion.
   (D) praise for the perpetuation of youthfulness.
   (E) advice on maintaining good health.

25. Which of the following is most likely a deliberate exaggeration?

   (A) "tremendous success and lamentable failure" (lines 6–7)
   (B) "It is a success" (line 8)
   (C) "they will be extinct" (line 10)
   (D) "a bent back and hollow cheeks" (lines 10–11)
   (E) "old-fashioned" (line 11)

26. The primary rhetorical strategy used to develop the idea that old ladies are becoming rare is best described as

   (A) a series of metaphors.
   (B) rhetorical questions and answers.
   (C) examples with repetitive sentence structure.
   (D) parallel and periodic sentences.
   (E) allusions and analogies.

27. The speaker in the passage can be described in all of the following ways EXCEPT

   (A) probing.
   (B) intellectually curious.
   (C) somewhat condescending.
   (D) scientifically objective.
   (E) perceptive.

28. Which of the following best characterizes the tone of the phrase "crone of the future" (line 11)?

   (A) Anger
   (B) Bitterness
   (C) Sympathy
   (D) Ridicule
   (E) Irony

29. In the development of the last paragraph (lines 28–38), the rhetorical device most in evidence is

   (A) extended analogy.
   (B) compound subject.
   (C) appeal to authority.
   (D) emotional exclamation.
   (E) antithesis.

30. "The surface of the human vessel is affected by the nature of its spiritual contents" (lines 32–33) is a statement best decribed as

   (A) an epigram.
   (B) a simile.
   (C) a platitude.
   (D) a witticism.
   (E) a symbol.

31. The point at which the speaker turns to the principal theme of the passage is

   (A) at the beginning of paragraph 2.
   (B) when he refers to the Portrait of the Artist's Mother (lines 12–13).
   (C) the last sentence of paragraph 1.
   (D) the beginning of paragraph 3.
   (E) the last two sentences of paragraph 3.

32. The passage contains all of the following EXCEPT

   (A) a description of the success of the cult of beauty.
   (B) a discussion of the link between beauty and health.
   (C) a comparison of inner and outer beauty.
   (D) a sympathetic presentation of the yearning for eternal youth.
   (E) the personal feelings of the author toward the phenomena described.

33. Which of the following represents the speaker's main purpose?

   (A) To highlight the successful aspects of the beauty cult
   (B) To comment on a phase of female psychology
   (C) To describe a change of values in contemporary society
   (D) To expose the shortcomings and omissions of the beauty cult
   (E) To extol the virtues of aging

34. The principal contrast employed by the speaker of the passage is between

   (A) crones and fair ladies.
   (B) inner beauty versus outer beauty.
   (C) health and good looks.
   (D) staying young and living longer.
   (E) youth and age.

The passage below was written by a famous British playwright early in the 20th century.

PASSAGE 4

A hundred years ago a crusty old bachelor of fifty-seven, so deaf that he could not hear his own music played by a full orchestra, yet still able to hear thunder, shook his fist at the roaring heavens for the last time, and died as he had lived, challenging
Line God and defying the universe. He was Defiance Incarnate: he could not even meet
(5) a Grand Duke and his court in the street without jamming his hat tight down on his head and striding through the very middle of them. He had the manners of a dis-obliging steamroller (most steamrollers are abjectly obliging and conciliatory); and he was rather less particular about his dress than a scarecrow: in fact he was once arrested as a tramp because the police refused to believe that such a tatterdemalion
(10) could be a famous composer, much less a temple of the most turbulent spirit that ever found expression in pure sound. It was indeed a mighty spirit; but if I had writ-ten the mightiest, which would mean mightier than the spirit of Handel, Beethoven himself would have rebuked me; and what mortal man could pretend to a spirit mightier than Bach's? But that Beethoven's spirit was the most turbulent is beyond
(15) all question. The impetuous fury of his strength, which he could quite easily contain and control, but often would not, and the unroariousness of his fun, go beyond any-thing of the kind to be found in the works of other composers. Greenhorns write of syncopation now as if it were a new way of giving the utmost impetus to a musical measure; but the rowdiest jazz sounds like *The Maiden's Prayer* after Beethoven's
(20) third *Leonora* overture; and certainly no jazz ensemble that I ever heard could propel even the most eager dancer into action as the last movement of the *Seventh Symphony*. And no other composer has ever melted his hearers into complete sen-timentality by the tender beauty of his music, and then suddenly turned on them and mocked them with derisive trumpet blasts for being such fools. Nobody but
(25) Beethoven could govern Beethoven; and when, as happened when the fit was on him, he deliberately refused to govern himself, he was ungovernable.

It was this turbulence, this deliberate disorder, this mockery, this reckless and triumphant disregard of conventional manners, that set Beethoven apart from the musical geniuses of the ceremonious seventeenth and eighteenth centuries.
(30) He was a giant wave in that storm of the human spirit which produced the French Revolution. He called no man master. Mozart, his greatest predecessor in his own department, had from his childhood been washed, combed, splendidly dressed, and beautifully behaved in the presence of royal personages and peers. His childish outburst at the Pompadour, "Who is this woman who does not kiss me? The Queen
(35) kisses me," would be incredible of Beethoven, who was still an unlicked cub even when he had grown into a very grizzly bear.

35. Which of the following best describes the rhetorical function of the second sentence of the passage (lines 4–6)?

(A) It contrasts a man and the environment in which he lived.
(B) It conveys the tragic tone of the passage.
(C) It restates the main idea of the passage.
(D) It provides a specific example to illustrate the preceding generalization.
(E) It adds a new dimension to the portrait of the person being described.

36. The author uses all of the following phrases to illustrate his subject's rebellious spirit EXCEPT

(A) "old bachelor" (line 1).
(B) " shook his fist" (lines 2–3).
(C) "challenging God" (lines 3–4).
(D) "Defiance Incarnate" (line 4).
(E) "striding through . . .the very middle of them" (line 6).

37. In describing Beethoven's social behavior and appearance (lines 6–11), the author makes use of which rhetorical devices?

(A) Symbolic references
(B) Metaphors and similes
(C) Everyday clichés
(D) Caustic sarcasm
(E) Alang expressions and euphemisms

38. Which of the following words is parallel in function and theme to "fury" (line 15)?

(A) "turbulent" (line 14)
(B) "impetuous" (line 15)
(C) "strength" (line 15)
(D) "unroariousness" (line 16)
(E) "fun" (line 16)

39. In describing Beethoven's works (lines 15–24), the principal contrast employed by the author is between

(A) music played by an orchestra and music played by a jazz band.
(B) loud, vigorous music and soft, tender music.
(C) revolutionary music and conventional music.
(D) Beethoven's style and the style of other composers.
(E) formal, structured music and free-form, impressionistic music.

40. The author mentions the *Leonora* overture and the *Seventh Symphony* (lines 20–22) as examples of which of the following?

  (A) Outstanding achievements that have never been fully appreciated
  (B) Unique pieces that other composers have tried to imitate, but unsuccessfully
  (C) Well-known selections that helped Beethoven establish his reputation
  (D) Classical music that contains elements of jazz
  (E) Forceful musical compositions marked by high energy and powerful rhythm

41. In context, the expression "the fit was on him" (lines 25–26) is best interpreted to have which of the following meanings?

  (A) That he couldn't control himself
  (B) That he had a one-track mind
  (C) That he lacked faith in his ability to compose
  (D) That he was under severe pressure to write music
  (E) That he had fallen prey to his hot temper

42. The tone conveyed by the author's description of Mozart (lines 31–33) can best be described as

  (A) slightly disdainful.
  (B) mildly satirical.
  (C) astonished.
  (D) vaguely annoyed.
  (E) apprehensive.

43. The final sentence of the passage (lines 34–36) contains which of the following rhetorical devices?

   I. Paradox
   II. Metaphor
  III. Personification

  (A) I only
  (B) III only
  (C) I and II only
  (D) II and III only
  (E) I, II, and III

44. Which of the following best states the subject of the passage?

  (A) Beethoven's place in the history of music
  (B) Beethoven as a symbol of the time in which he lived
  (C) The influence of Beethoven on modern classical music
  (D) Beethoven's incomparable genius
  (E) How Beethoven the man is reflected in his music

The passage below is an excerpt from a book on world history written late in the 20th century.

PASSAGE 5

In the United States on the opening of Congress in January, 1890, a newly elected Speaker of the House of Representatives was in the Chair. A physical giant, six feet three inches tall, weighing almost three hundred pounds and dressed completely in
Line black, "out of whose collar rose an enormous clean-shaven baby face like a Casaba
(5) melon flowering from a fat black stalk, he was a subject for a Franz Hals, with long white fingers that would have enraptured Memling."*[1] Speaking in a slow drawl, he delighted to drop cool pearls of sarcasm into the most heated rhetoric and to watch the resulting fizzle with the bland gravity of a New England Buddha. When a wordy perennial, Representative Springer of Illinois, was declaiming to the House his pas-
(10) sionate preference to be right rather than President, the Speaker interjected, "The gentleman need not be disturbed; he will never be either." When another member, notorious for ill-digested opinions and a halting manner, began some remarks with, "I was thinking, Mr. Speaker, I was thinking . . ." the Chair expressed the hope that "no one will interrupt the gentleman's commendable innovation." Of two particu-
(15) larly inept speakers, he remarked, "They never open their mouths without subtract-ing from the sum of human knowledge." It was said that he would rather make an epigram than a friend. Yet among the select who were his chosen friends he was known as "one of the most genial souls that ever enlivened a company," whose con-versation, "sparkling with good nature, was better than the best champagne." He
(20) was Thomas B. Reed, Republican of Maine, aged fifty. Already acknowledged after fourteen years in Congress as "the ablest running debater the American people ever saw," he would, before the end of the session, be called "the greatest parliamentary leader of his time, . . . far and away the most brilliant figure in American politics."

Although his roots went back to the beginning of New England, Reed was not
(25) nurtured for a political career by inherited wealth, social position or landed estate. Politics in America made no use of these qualities, and men who possessed them were not in politics. Well-to-do, long-established families did not shoulder—but shunned—the responsibilities of government. Henry Adams' eldest brother, John,

Hals: Dutch painter 1582–1666; Memling: Flemish painter of 15th century. Both specialized in portraits.

[1] *DE CASSERES, BENJAMIN, "Tom Reed," American Mercury, February, 1930. The following quotations in this paragraph, in order, are from CLARK, CHAMP, My Quarter Century of American Politics, 2 vols., New York, Harper, 1920, I, 287; LEUPP, FRANCIS E., "Personal Recollections of Thomas Brackett Reed," Outlook, September 3, 1910; McCALL, SAMUEL, The Life of Thomas Brackett Reed, Boston, Houghton Mifflin, 1914, 248; DUNN, ARTHUR WALLACE, From Harrison to Harding, 2 vols. New York, Putnam's 1922, I, 165; FOULKE, WILLIAM DUDLEY, A Hoosier Autobiography, Oxford Univ. Press, 1922, 110; PORTER, ROBERT P., "Thomas Brackett Reed of Maine," McClure's, October, 1893. "The ablest running debater" was said by Rep. John Sharp Williams, Democratic Leader of the House; "the greatest parliamentary leader" by Lodge; "far and away the most brilliant" by CLARK, II, 10.*

"regarded as the most brilliant of the family and the most certain of high distinc-
(30) tion," who made a fortune in the Union Pacific Railroad, "drew himself back" from
government, according to his brother. "He had all he wanted; wealth, children,
society, consideration; and he laughed at the idea of sacrificing himself in order to
adorn a Cleveland Cabinet or get cheers from an Irish mob."[2] This attitude was not
confined to the rather worn-out Adamses. When the young Theodore Roosevelt
(35) announced his intention of entering politics in New York in 1880, he was laughed at
by the "men of cultivated and easy life" who told him politics were "low" and run by
"saloon-keepers, horse-car conductors and the like," whom he would find "rough,
brutal and unpleasant to deal with."

---

[2]*HENRY ADAMS on his brother John: Sept. 1, 1894,* Letters, *ed. Worthington Chauncey Ford, 2 vols.
Boston, Houghton Mifflin, 1930–38, II, 55.*

45. The development of the first paragraph of the passage can best be described largely as

   (A) a chronological account of a public servant's career.
   (B) a compilation of background information on the life of an influential public figure.
   (C) a report on the aspirations of a 19th-century politician.
   (D) the description of a character based on the testimony of others.
   (E) the presentation of conflicting views regarding a well-known American.

46. Which of the following rhetorical effects does the author achieve by delaying the disclosure of the Speaker's name until lines 19–20?

   (A) It emphasizes that the subject's name is irrelevant to the passage.
   (B) It creates a tentative transition from the first paragraph to the second.
   (C) It highlights a contradiction between the man's words and his actions.
   (D) It keeps the reader in suspense about the identity of an unusual man.
   (E) It illustrates the kind of rhetoric used by political figures.

47. The structure of the two sentences in lines 6–11 ("Speaking . . . either") can best be described as

   (A) a generalization followed by a specific example.
   (B) a questionable statement of fact followed by an explanation of its source.
   (C) a cause-and-effect pronouncement.
   (D) a claim followed by a qualifying statement.
   (E) an assumption followed by a conclusion based on that assumption.

48. Overall, the writers whose words are documented by footnote 1 viewed Speaker Reed as

   (A) an extraordinary political figure.
   (B) a politician who could not be corrupted.
   (C) a representative dedicated to his constituents.
   (D) a fighter for liberal causes.
   (E) the driving force behind many new laws.

49. Taken as a whole, footnote 1 suggests that the author of the passage

    (A) researched the daily newspapers published while Reed served in Congress.
    (B) relied heavily on official documents related to Reed's work.
    (C) used few sources contemporary with Reed's first term as a Congressman.
    (D) interviewed members of Congress who worked with Reed.
    (E) studied speeches delivered by Reed in the House of Representatives.

50. The author's use of the phrase "New England Buddha" (line 8) refers mainly to the man's

    (A) appearance and demeanor.
    (B) intelligence and sense of humor.
    (C) background and family history.
    (D) energy and ambition.
    (E) stubbornness and perseverance.

51. Which of Reed's characteristics does the author illustrate with the quotations in lines 10–16?

    I. Reed's quick wit
    II. Reed's fondness for sarcasm
    III. Reed's dislike of pretentiousness

    (A) I only
    (B) III only
    (C) I and II only
    (D) II and III only
    (E) I, II, and III

52. In context, the phrase "ill-digested" (line 12) is best interpreted to mean

    (A) sincere but stupid.
    (B) contradictory.
    (C) sickening.
    (D) poorly thought-out.
    (E) illogical.

53. Which of the following is an accurate reading of information in footnote 2 (line 33)?

(A) It attributes the quotations in lines 29–33 to Henry's brother, John.
(B) *Letters* was published in Boston in 1894.
(C) A letter from John Adams to Worthington Chauncey Ford was dated Sept. 1, 1894.
(D) A book published in two volumes contains the letters of Henry Adams.
(E) From 1930 to 1938, John and Henry Adams wrote letters that were published in Boston.

54. The author alludes to Roosevelt (lines 34–38) as an example of

(A) a famous government officeholder.
(B) a president with New England roots.
(C) a politician from a wealthy family.
(D) a man with great ability.
(E) a member of an American political dynasty.

SECTION II

Three Essay Questions

TIME: 2 HOURS AND 15 MINUTES

Write your essays on standard 8½" × 11" composition paper. At the exam you will be given a bound booklet containing 12 lined pages.

Essay Question 1

SUGGESTED TIME:
15 MINUTES FOR READING THE QUESTION AND SOURCES
40 MINUTES FOR WRITING AN ESSAY

According to recent polls, one out of three U.S. teenagers who use mobile devices, access the Internet, or join social networks, such as Facebook have at least once found themselves subject to insulting and potentially harmful bullying from malicious, mean-spirited schoolmates. Although most victims ignore this so-called "cyberbullying," some students experience harmful emotional reactions. They may refuse to go to school, or they feel anxiety, fear, depression, and insomnia. In a few tragic cases, teenagers have committed suicide.

Because cyberbullying usually occurs off campus during non-school hours, schools must decide whether to take action against bullies or whether to let the community handle the problem.

Carefully read the following six sources, including the material that introduces each source. Then, in an essay that synthesizes at least three of the sources, take a position on the claim that schools should track down and punish students for off-campus cyber-bullying.

Don't simply summarize the sources. Instead, weigh evidence from the sources to support and illustrate your position on the issue. You may paraphrase, review, and quote relevant material directly and indirectly from the sources. Be sure to indicate in your essay which sources you use. Refer to them as Source A, Source B, and so on, or by the key words in the parentheses below. In making your argument, you may, of course, also include any ideas of your own.

Source A (Kids)
Source B (CRF)
Source C (Kim)
Source D (Cartoon)
Source E (Willard)
Source F (Hsu)

"Stop Cyberbullying," *www.stopcyberbullying.com*, Wired Kids, accessed from the Web, July 31, 2010.

Below are excerpts from an online article published by a project that bills itself as the world's largest Internet safety, help, and education organization.

What is cyberbullying, exactly?

"Cyberbullying" is when a child, preteen or teen is tormented, threatened, harassed, humiliated, embarrassed or otherwise targeted by another child, preteen or teen using the Internet, interactive and digital technologies or mobile phones.

. . . Children have killed each other and committed suicide after having been involved in a cyberbullying incident.

. . . When schools try and get involved by disciplining the student for cyberbullying actions that took place off-campus and outside school hours, they are often sued for exceeding their authority and violating the student's free speech rights. They also often lose. . . . They can also educate the students on cyber-ethics and the law. If schools are creative, they can sometimes avoid the claim that their actions exceeded their legal authority for off-campus cyberbullying actions. We recommend that a provision is added to the school's acceptable use policy reserving the right to discipline the student for actions taken off-campus if they are intended to have an effect on a student or they adversely affect the safety and well-being of a student while in school. This makes it a contractual, not a constitutional, issue.

"The Legality of School Responses to Cyberbullying," Constitutional Rights Foundation, Chicago. Posted by *www.deliberating.org,* 2007.

The following passage comes from a document published on the website of an organization that studies issues related to education and the law.

The First Amendment to the U.S. Constutition states, "Congress shall make no law. . . abridging the freedom of speech." However, the Supreme Court has ruled in several cases that schools can limit student speech. In the 1969 Tinker decision, for example, the Court decided that schools could prohibit student speech if it "materially and substantially interfere[d] with the requirements of appropriate discipline in the operation of the school."

. . . Recent lower court decisions have addressed harassment via Internet technologies. . . . In the majority of decisions, the courts ruled that a school could not discipline a student for inappropriate off-campus e-mail unless that student brought the speech to school. Given the courts' reluctance to limit off-campus student speech, U.S. school officials, parents, and legislators have addressed cyberbullying in other ways. For example, in Vermont . . . a new state law requires that public schools establish bullying prevention procedures. Some schools have added a provision to their acceptable use policies that students must sign. These policies authorize schools to "discipline students for actions taken off campus if they are intended to have an effect on a student or they adversely affect the safety and well-being of a student while in school. . . . Additionally, some parents and students have successfully argued that cyberbullies violated civil or criminal laws by, for example, intentionally inflicting emotional distress or committing a hate crime.

Victoria Kim, "Suit Blends Internet, Free Speech, School," *Los Angeles Times*, August 3, 2008.

The following passage is excerpted from a newspaper article by a staff writer for the Los Angeles Times.

On a sunny May afternoon, teenagers dismissed from a Beverly Hills middle school gathered outside a restaurant four blocks away and gossiped about their friends.

Amid lots of giggling, the conversation among the eighth-graders . . . was dominated by an unflattering assessment of a girl at school, who was called a "spoiled brat" and a "slut."

. . . What may have been just another middle school moment became a serious headache for school officials when one of the students uploaded the conversation as a video on *YouTube.com.* Because of the Internet posting, Beverly Vista School officials found themselves grappling with their responsibility to ensure a student's well-being and the ambiguous limits of their authority on the Web.

Citing "cyber-bullying" concerns, school administrators suspended for two days the student who uploaded the video, without disciplining others in the recording. The suspended student sued the school district, saying her free-speech rights were violated.

"The speech for which the plaintiff was punished was not 'student speech' at all and cannot be regulated or controlled by the defendants," attorneys wrote in the suit.

> [The court agreed. In December 2009, the judge said that the school violated the student's First Amendment rights. He added that the girl's actions were juvenile and inappropriate, but they did not cause serious enough disruption on campus to warrant administrative action.]

In an Idaho case . . . parents sued a school district for its failure to intervene in their daughter's harassment, which included, among other things, spreading photos and rumors on the Internet about the girl's sexual orientation. The court sided with the school, saying officials did not have "substantial control" over the dissemination of the photos.

Clive Edwards, Cartoon on cyberbullying.

The image below is an unpublished cartoon created by a freelance cartoonist in 2010.

Nancy Willard, "School Response to Cyberbullying and Sexting," Center for Safe, Responsible Internet Use, August 2, 2010.

The following passage has been adapted from an article by attorney Nancy Willard, a widely recognized authority on responsible Internet use.

Jessica Logan, a senior at an Ohio high school, had sent nude photos of herself to a boyfriend. After the relationship ended, her ex-boyfriend sent the photos to other female students at Logan's school, after which the image went "viral" and was distributed to many students. This resulted in months of harassment and teasing for Logan.

Logan hanged herself one month after her graduation. Logan's parents filed suit against the high school and several other defendants, alleging that the school and local police did not do enough to protect their daughter from harassment.

A very significant challenge in this regard is what has been happening in some schools when police officers overreact. News reports of students involved in sexting who have been hauled off in handcuffs are exceptionally disturbing. The highly predictable consequence of this police overreaction is to place the student depicted at exceptionally high risk of intense harassment by peers. This could place the student at high risk of suicide. Such actions will also make it exceptionally difficult for school officials to prevent sexual harassment—for which schools could be held liable.

School officials must assert authority over actions that might take place on their campus that could cause emotional harm to students. It is entirely unnecessary, even if law enforcement response might be appropriate, to have students hauled from school in handcuffs.

Cindy Hsu, " N.J. School District Set to Battle Cyber Bullies," HD2, *wcbs.com*, August 1, 2008.

The following is adapted from a news item published on the website of CBS News.

A local school district is trying to protect its students from cyberbullies, even when they attack from home. CBS 2 HD has learned how the school is cracking down and making the bullies the target.

. . . School officials . . . now have the authority to take action, even when the cyber attacks are off school grounds.

"When a kid is at home on his home computer, then he's not totally isolated from the school," Dr. James Patterson said. "It used to be, as you know, the Internet is an area of basically free speech, but free speech has some restrictions to it.

Experts argue that the free speech argument should take a back seat to threats of physical violence. . . ."Cyber-bullying is a big deal. It's leading to significant emotional distress of young people," said Nancy Willard of the Center for Safe and Responsible Internet Use.

. . . Teachers are now obligated to report cases of cyberbullying to school officials. Students tell CBS 2 HD, they need all the help they can get.

"I think it's a good idea because if they don't take action, it's just going to keep happening and people are going to get hurt, "Montclair High School senior Carole Johnson said.

As far as the punishment for cyberbullying, school officials say bullies could face suspension or law enforcement could be called in for extreme cases.

PRACTICE TEST B

Essay Question 2

SUGGESTED TIME: 40 MINUTES

(This question counts as one third of the total score for Section II.)

> **Directions:** Read the following passage, an excerpt from an email written to friends and family by an American soldier fighting in Iraq, 2003–2004. Then write an essay in which you analyze the rhetorical strategies used by the author to explain his experience and convey his attitude toward that experience.

I know a number of you have been curious about what it's like over here, so we are going to take a small mental voyage. First off, we are going to prepare our living area. Go to your vacuum, open the canister, and pour it all over you, your bed, cloth-
Line ing, and your personal effects. Now roll in it until it's in your eyes, nose, ears, hair,
(5) and . . . well, you get the picture. You know it's just perfect when you slap your chest and cough from the dust cloud you kicked up. And so, there is no escape, trust me. You just get used to it.

OK, pitch a tent in your driveway, and mark off an area inside it along one wall about six feet by eight feet (including your bed). Now pack everything you need to
(10) live for four months—without Wal-Mart—and move in. Tear down the three walls of your tent seen from the street and you have about as much privacy as I have.

If you really want to make this accurate, bring in a kennel full of pugs; the smell, snoring, and social graces will be just like living with my nine tentmates. Also, you must never speak above a whisper because at all times at least four of your tentmates
(15) will be sleeping. That's where the flashlight comes in handy; you are going to use it to navigate a pitch-dark tent, 24 hours a day.

Time for hygiene. Walk to the nearest bathroom. In my case, it's a thousand-foot trudge over loose gravel. Ever stagger to the john at 0400? Try it in a frozen rock garden. Given the urges that woke you at this hour, taking the time to put on your
(20) thermals and jacket might not be foremost in your mind. But halfway there, it's too late. So dress warmly. It gets really freakin' cold here at night.

I don't even feel like talking about the latrine experience. All I have to say is that, after the first time, I went back to the tent and felt like either crying or lighting myself on fire to remove the filth.

Essay Question 3

(This question counts as one third of the total score for Section II.)

> **Directions:** The paragraph below comments on the tendency of human beings to think about and plan for the future. After reading it, write a well-organized essay that states and develops your views on the usefulness of planning for the future. Use appropriate evidence from your reading, experience, or observations to support your argument.

It's human nature to plan, dream, and think about the future. In fact, most students go to school and college with the presumption that they are being prepared for what lies ahead. On the other hand, some people think it's foolish and wasteful to be anything but wary about the future because our vision is limited, and unexpected events and conditions will inevitably cause us to be disappointed. Such people prefer to live for the present, to make the most of what exists here and now and to avoid wasting time with concerns about uncontrollable things to come. In your opinion, is it more worthwhile to concentrate on the present or use our energies to shape our future?

END OF PRACTICE TEST B

Answers to Multiple-Choice Questions

1.	**E**	16.	**C**	31.	**D**	46.	**D**
2.	**E**	17.	**E**	32.	**D**	47.	**A**
3.	**B**	18.	**A**	33.	**D**	48.	**A**
4.	**E**	19.	**A**	34.	**B**	49.	**C**
5.	**C**	20.	**D**	35.	**D**	50.	**A**
6.	**C**	21.	**D**	36.	**A**	51.	**E**
7.	**D**	22.	**C**	37.	**B**	52.	**D**
8.	**D**	23.	**A**	38.	**D**	53.	**D**
9.	**E**	24.	**C**	39.	**B**	54.	**C**
10.	**B**	25.	**C**	40.	**E**		
11.	**A**	26.	**C**	41.	**A**		
12.	**B**	27.	**D**	42.	**A**		
13.	**E**	28.	**E**	43.	**C**		
14.	**C**	29.	**A**	44.	**E**		
15.	**C**	30.	**A**	45.	**D**		

Summary of Answers in Section I (Multiple-Choice)

Number of correct answers _____

Use this information when you calculate your score for this exam. See page 304.

ANSWER EXPLANATIONS

Passage 1—An excerpt from Michel de Montaigne, "The Enjoyment of Living"

1. **(E)** Because it is too early in the passage to know whether (B) and (C) might be correct, search first for a rhetorical link between the first two paragraphs: Although the speaker begins by discussing his eating preferences—the ostensible subject of the passage—he adds thoughts about his father and about his indifference to changes in the phases of the moon and seasons of the year. In the second paragraph, prior to returning to his culinary preferences, he picks up where he left off—with a general statement about change. In effect, the intimate rhetorical relationship between the two sentences in question eliminates the other choices as reasonable answers.

2. **(E)** The first sentence of the paragraph is the topic sentence. The remainder of the paragraph supports the topic sentence and adds to the self-portrait of the author. There is no evidence of a change in the speaker's tone.

3. **(B)** The speaker's explanation of his preference for fish contributes to his portrait as a careful and fastidious eater. Choice (C) may be vaguely implied by the passage, but the speaker observes meatless days for one reason only—to please his taste buds.

4. **(E)** Lines 11–12 contains an alliteration ("my fasts are my feasts"). Two clauses in the last sentence of the paragraph are parallel in structure ("As it goes against . . ." and ". . . my taste rebels against . . ."). The phrase "dainty tooth" is a synecdoche—a figure of speech in which a part stands for the whole. "My fasts are my feasts" is a paradox. Only onomatopoeia is missing.

5. **(C)** The speaker skips meals to sharpen his appetite (lines 15–16). He also enjoys eating and never feels guilty about stuffing himself.

6. **(C)** The discussion of eating habits appears in the context of a description of how the author manages to lead a pleasurable life—by acceding to his whims and fancies. Allusions to the other choices appear briefly here and there in the passage, but only (C) describes the passage as a whole.

7. **(D)** According to the previous paragraph, one's dining companions at a pleasurable meal are at least as important as the quality of the food. Lines 24–25 reiterate that sentiment.

8. **(D)** To stay warm, the speaker keeps donning additional layers of clothing. His body, however, shortly craves more layers. Having grown weary of putting on more and more, the speaker would like to return to the time before he first put on a cap (line 34) to keep his head warm.

9. **(E)** In the next to last paragraph, the speaker describes the methods he uses to keep warm. He knows that it would be ridiculous to resort to "a hare's skin or a vulture's plumage." Yet he uses the terms to emphasize the lengths to which he is forced to go in order to remain comfortably warm. The other choices may slightly overstate the truth but not to the degree of choice (E).

10. **(B)** The passage is devoted to descriptions of the speaker's preferences, particularly in the domains of food and health care. In neither area do his preferences conform to conventional practices. Although other choices may be vaguely implied, they don't describe the principal contrasts drawn by the speaker.

Passage 2—An excerpt from Arnold Toynbee, "Does History Repeat Itself?"

11. **(A)** The author is a theorist. Throughout the passage, he ponders the degree to which we can intelligently use and benefit from lessons taught by history. He may well possess some or all of the qualities described by the other choices, but the passage provides no significant evidence to support them.

12. **(B)** In the context, "grandfathers" refers to 18th- and 19th-century people who may have occasionally talked over whether history repeats itself, but who deceived themselves into believing that they were unique—that is, that they were exempt from the lessons that history teaches. The passage does not mention or allude to the author's own actual grandfathers.

13. **(E)** Because the "open book" records mistakes of past civilizations, readers can infer the lessons that history teaches. The "open book" itself, however, refers to the recorded history of now extinct civilizations, especially the mistakes and mishaps that led to their downfall. Choice (A) is too limited because the passage discusses both recent and long-dead civilizations. Choice (B) refers to a "quaint" (line 4) and erroneous interpretation of history. Choice (C) hardly makes sense because our knowledge of ancient civilizations comes from inferences drawn from various sources of evidence, not from records preserved for future generations. Choice (D) fails to define "an open book."

14. **(C)** Early in the passage the author discusses our grandfathers' view of the question of whether history repeats itself. With this sentence, the author begins to present a more up-to-date perspective. None of the other choices accurately describes the rhetorical shift.

15. **(C)** By asking the question enclosed by parentheses, the author expresses an opinion that, in effect, rebukes himself and his fellow historians for their past shortsightedness. The question is different in tone—far more informal and personal—from the discussion that precedes and follows it.

16. **(C)** As we study past civilizations, we have little to go on except the ruins that have been left behind. From the ruins, we infer lessons that have the force of scripture. Choice (E) shows promise as an answer, but artifacts provide clues mainly to the civilization's character, not to the exact reasons why it failed.

17. **(E)** Lines 17–18 contain an example of an antithesis. The discussion of a navigator's chart (lines 21–24) appears in the context of an extended simile. The phrase "charted rocks and reefs" comprises a metaphor. Combinations of words such as "probabilities/possibilities" and "rocks/reefs" contain alliteration.

18. **(A)** The "second alternative" refers specifically to "probabilities, or bare possibilities" (lines 17–18) that studying history will enable us to infer what lies in store.

19. **(A)** The horoscope tells what fate has in store for us. The navigation chart, in contrast, enables us to steer "a course between charted rocks and reefs." In other words, we can learn from the mistakes of past civilizations. Because we know the perils, we can take steps to avoid them. The other choices may state truths, but they are irrelevant in the context.

20. **(D)** A seafarer with "intelligence" uses the data on the navigator's chart to avoid rocks and reefs. In other words, he realizes how the information he has before him can guide him safely into the future. Choice (E) has possibilities as an answer, but logic dictates that "foresight and information" are needed before developing strategies to solve problems.

21. **(D)** The colloquial expression tends to create the impression that the writer is going to confide his true feelings to the reader; in short, he's going to be frank and forthright. At the same time, the writer implies that he has definite views on the subject.

22. **(C)** Throughout the passage the author ruminates on the notion of history repeating itself. He contrasts current thinking about the issue with the debates of earlier times. While he does not prove the validity of the principle that history repeats itself, he is optimistic that it does.

Passage 3—An excerpt from Aldous Huxley, "Music at Night"

23. **(A)** The second sentence of the passage suggests the speaker's meaning. Those who make up a "cult" have an extreme devotion—an obsession, really—to a particular belief or set of activities; in this case it is the desire to create, preserve, or restore physical beauty. The other choices—referring to subcultures, movements, etc.—all suggest a degree of allegiance to a group, but none of them requires as strong a commitment as that demanded by a "cult."

24. **(C)** The unanswered questions and the uncertainties expressed in the first paragraph ("difficult to answer"; "It depends") prepare the reader for a discussion that weighs both sides of the issue.

25. **(C)** The notion that "old ladies" will become extinct overstates the case. In fact, the speaker retracts the idea in the next sentence by asserting that the characteristics typically attributed to aging women will become "old fashioned," but they won't altogether disappear. The exaggeration helps the speaker emphasize his point—that the cult of beauty is gradually changing women's overall appearance.

26. **(C)** Several examples of changes in women's appearance are expressed in similarly structured sentences, each beginning with the grammatical subject followed by the verb "will be." For example, see lines 11–12: "The crone . . . will be," etc.

27. **(D)** The style and content of the passage reveal that the speaker possesses all the traits listed except scientific objectivity.

28. **(E)** The dubious title "crone of the future" is meant ironically—comparable, in a way, to an accolade like "serial killer of the year" or "airhead of the month." Choice (D) isn't far off the mark because the speaker, while being ironic, gently pokes fun at unsightly old women who go to great lengths to mask their actual appearance.

29. **(A)** The paragraph is dominated by an analogy that compares beauty in a woman with the beauty of a porcelain jar.

30. **(A)** In its context, the statement is a concise, thoughtful, and memorable idea. Thus, it can be labeled an *epigram.*

31. **(D)** The speaker uses the first two paragraphs to provide a context for his main concern, which is the difference between inner and outer beauty. Therefore, paragraph 3 contains the heart of the passage.

32. **(D)** The first paragraph describes the cult of beauty; the second, the beauty/health connection. Inner and outer beauty are compared in the final paragraph. Throughout the passage, the speaker assumes a somewhat condescending attitude. What is missing from the passage, then, is a sympathetic discussion of the yearning for eternal youth.

33. **(D)** By emphasizing the differences between inner and outer beauty, the speaker makes clear his disapproval of the commercial cult of beauty, which concerns itself only with the superficial, surface appearance of its clientele.

34. **(B)** The first paragraph questions the efficacy of the "modern cult of beauty." The second paragraph discusses women's techniques for making themselves beautiful. These two paragraphs merely serve as a prelude to the final paragraph, in which the speaker raises his main concern—the difference between inner and outer beauty.

Passage 4—An excerpt from George Bernard Shaw, *Shaw on Music: A Selection from the Music Criticism of George Bernard Shaw*, 1927

35. **(D)** The opening sentences generalizes about the man's stormy, defiant personality and state of mind. The next sentence shows the man behaving defiantly in a specific situation.

36. **(A)** That Beethoven, the subject of the passage, was unmarried does not reflect his rebelliousness. All the other choices suggest feistiness, including (E), which shows Beethoven refusing to step aside to let the Grand Duke and his company pass on the street.

37. **(B)** The author compares Beethoven's manners to a steamroller (line 7), and his clothing to that of a scarecrow (line 8). The man himself is called a "temple of the most turbulent spirit" (line 10). None of the other rhetorical features apply. If you chose (A), note that a metaphor differs from a symbol, as explained in the glossary of this book.

38. **(D)** A word that is parallel to the noun "fury" must also be a noun and must precede a prepositional phrase. To be thematically parallel, it must suggest something unfriendly. The word "unroariousness" fits the bill because it is a noun preceding a prepositional phrase, and although you won't find "unroarious" in the dictionary, it is clearly meant to convey the opposite of "uproariousness"—in other words, something dark and mopey.

39. **(B)** The author contrasts the energy and power in parts of Beethoven's music with the soft sentimentality of other parts. An obvious distinction is found, for example, between music of "the tender beauty" and "derisive trumpet blasts" (lines 23–24). Choice (A) may seem like a promising answer because the author alludes to the music of a jazz band, but

his purpose is to assert that Beethoven's third *Leonora* overture is far more energizing than even the "rowdiest jazz sounds" (lines 19–20).

40. **(E)** The author's references to "syncopation" (line 18), "musical measure" (lines 18–19), and propelling an "eager dancer into action" (line 21) are clues that his concern is the foot-tapping exuberance found in some of Beethoven's most energetic music.

41. **(A)** The author is referring to Beethoven's ungovernable nature; Beethoven, in short, surrendered himself to an uncontrollable passion to compose. Choices (B) and (E) also may be clues to account for Beethoven's loss of self-control, but neither answer explains the composer's deliberate refusal to govern himself (line 26).

42. **(A)** The author clearly prefers the personality of Beethoven to the personality of Mozart, who is portrayed as an arrogant, impeccably-groomed snob.

43. **(C)** The notion that Beethoven was an "unlicked cub" and a "grizzly bear" at the same time is paradoxical. Calling him either a "cub" or a "bear" is metaphorical. There is no personification in this segment of the passage.

44. **(E)** What the author focuses on throughout the passage is Beethoven's defiance of convention, both in his personality and his music.

Passage 5—An excerpt from Barbara Tuchman, *The Proud Tower*, 1962

45. **(D)** The author's intent is to introduce Reed to the reader by means of a physical description and a sample of his spoken words, but the source of what we learn about him comes mostly from those who knew him personally or studied his work and career. The other choices are not evident in the passage.

46. **(D)** By providing several intriguing details about the man without disclosing his name, the author heightens curiosity about who this man might be. Readers presumably will keep reading to find out his identity.

47. **(A)** The author uses the first sentence to describe in general terms Reed's manner of speaking. This is followed by a sentence containing a specific example of a caustic comment directed at a long-winded congressman.

48. **(A)** Collectively, the quotations portray Reed as an exceptional man in both appearance and style.

49. **(C)** By 1890, Reed had been an ordinary member of Congress for fourteen years (line 21), but the quotations cited by the footnote come largely from his tenure as the Speaker of the House.

50. **(A)** Buddha symbolizes many different things to many different people, but in general a Buddha represents wisdom, inscrutability, contemplation, and peace of mind. The author of the passage depicts Reed sitting back rather pleased with himself after cleverly knocking a pompous speaker off his high horse. Also, Reed's physical attributes (lines 3–6) resemble those of a Buddha.

51. **(E)** The quotations show that Reed had little tolerance for long-winded, pompous, or bumbling orators. To shut them up and deflate their egos, he apparently perfected the art of the scathing and sarcastic wisecrack.

52. **(D)** The phrase is used to describe hastily-expressed opinions—that is, opinions that haven't been carefully considered or developed. Every choice in one way or other describes a flaw in the member's opinions, but (D) encompasses them all.

53. **(D)** The author of the passage drew the quotes about John from Volume II of *Letters*, a collection of the letters of Henry Adams, edited by Worthington Chauncey Ford and published by Houghton Mifflin in Boston. The first volume probably came out in 1930, and the second in 1938.

54. **(C)** The author makes the point that men with great inherited wealth did not usually go into politics. Theodore Roosevelt was an exception.

Answers to Essay Questions

For an overview of how essays are graded, turn to "How Essays Are Scored," page 36–37.

Although answers to the essay questions will vary greatly, the following descriptions suggest a possible approach to each question and contain ideas that could be used in a response to the question. Perhaps your essay contains many of the same ideas. If not, don't be alarmed. Your ideas may be no less, or even more, insightful than those presented below.

ESSAY QUESTION 1

Some Arguments <u>In Favor</u> of School-Administered Punishment for Cyberbullying:

- Schools have the authority to discipline students whose actions on or off the campus adversely affect the safety and well-being of other students. (Sources B and C)
- Schools should have the power to prevent activities that inflict emotional distress on students. (Source B)
- Giving a school the authority to punish helps to eliminate ambiguities in the law by establishing precedents for other schools to follow. (Source C)
- A school's authority to punish can serve as a warning to all students that cyberbullies will be held accountable for their actions. (Source D)
- Awareness of the school's right to punish for cyberbullying is likely to reduce the amount of cyberbullying among students. (Source F)

Some Arguments <u>Against</u> School-Administered Punishment for Cyberbullying:

- Schools may be sued for violating students' right to free speech. (Source A)
- Schools' actions should be limited to educating students on cyber-ethics and the law. (Source A)
- Schools may overstep their rightful authority to discipline students. (Sources A and B)
- Schools that punish cyberbullies may be sued if they fail to mete out penalties for every incident of harassment. (Source C)
- Doling out large numbers of penalties for cyberbullying can interfere with learning. (Source D)
- Cyberbullying in the form of sexting may require the intervention of law-enforcement authorities, which can place depicted students at a higher risk of harassment by peers. (Source E)

ESSAY QUESTION 2, BASED ON A PASSAGE BY EDWARD P. GYOKERES

The author intends to recreate his experience in Iraq for a homefront audience that he assumes has no idea what it's like being a soldier in a war zone. As he tells his story, the author addresses the reader as "you," a device that establishes intimacy between himself and the recipients of his e-mail. In addition, he speaks frankly and informally, using the common, down-to-earth parlance of a soldier—for example, "personal effects" (line 4), "0400" (line 18), "really freakin' cold" (line 21).

The author could easily have summarized his life in Iraq by stating simply, "It's wretched." Instead, however, he tries to make the account as vivid as possible by employing the rhetorical device of a "small mental voyage" (line 2). Rather than tell what he sees, feels, hears, and smells, he helps his readers recreate the experience by instructing them to do outrageous things with everyday objects: empty the contents of a vacuum cleaner bag onto yourself, tear apart the walls of a small tent you've set up on your driveway, and so forth.

Recognizing that a reader's imaginings will leave a more powerful impression than any words he can write, the author deliberately avoids going into minute detail, interjecting instead ". . .well, you get the picture" (line 5) and "trust me" (line 6). He uses a similar tactic at the end of the passage by briefly describing his nighttime "latrine experience." Again, he stops short of piling on details, saying, "I don't even feel like talking about" it (line 22). Again, he expects that a reader's imagination will fill in the blanks. But just in case, he describes what happened after returning to his tent: He feels the urge to light himself on fire, a claim that may seem like hyperbole. But everything in his existence is so dreadful that readers might well believe he means it.

ESSAY QUESTION 3, BASED ON THE CHOICE BETWEEN PREPARING FOR THE FUTURE AND LIVING FOR THE PRESENT

Should preparing for the future trump living for the here and now?

This is a question that in one form or other you probably face every day. One clear-cut response is that only an irresponsible hedonist would snub the future in favor of the present. Or you might think just the opposite: Live it up now and let the future take care of itself. A third alternative, of course, says that neither extreme works in all situations and that individuals must choose which path to follow based on various criteria applicable to themselves.

If you lean toward seizing the day, you might argue that when unique opportunities, either trifling or weighty, come along, you ought to grab them immediately rather than wait and later kick yourself for passing them by. Using a rationale such as tempus fugit (time flies. . . i.e., don't waste time), you might explain why, say, it's sometimes more important to hang out with friends than to study for tomorrow's math test. Or more consequentially, why might it be better to take time off after high school to chase your dreams rather than go directly to college? To justify such a choice you might argue that change occurs so rapidly and unpredictably that preparing for a distant goal—say, a particular job or profession—is a gamble at best because when the future comes that job or profession may have changed or even disappeared.

On the other hand, an equally compelling case could be made in support of the standard advice that success comes to those who work hard, follow the rules, and practice, practice, practice. The very fact that you are preparing for an AP exam suggests that to some extent you subscribe to those sentiments.

Whatever your position, your essay's main idea needn't be supported by your personal preferences. You might draw evidence instead from the experience of others, both real and imaginary. Take the character Macbeth, for example. Egged on by his wife, he impulsively murders the king, never bothering to contemplate the potential aftereffects. Conversely, Hamlet suffers dire consequences by ruminating too long and hard before taking steps to revenge his father's death. Even history can be instructive. Within months of testing the atom bomb during World War II, the United States dropped bombs on two Japanese cities, killing over 200,000 civilians. Days later the war came to an end. Nevertheless, the president, Harry Truman, was vilified for acting rashly—especially for failing to give the enemy a chance to surrender before unleashing the bombs' deadly power. Truman's supporters declared, however, that the bombing ultimately saved countless lives by eliminating the need to invade the Japanese homeland.

You might also tap contemporary events to support your point of view. Climate change, for instance, raises the question of whether immediate action is needed to slow it down, or whether time, being on our side, allows the world to wait for the development of new and effective technologies to help solve the problem.

Regardless of your position, be mindful of the need to include substantial, detailed evidence to support your claims, and that an in-depth discussion of the issue is far better than a broad, scatter-shot approach.

SCORING SECTION II ESSAYS

Before scoring your essays, carefully review "How Essays Are Scored" (pages 36–37), a guide meant to help you judge as objectively as possible the quality of your writing.

Use the criteria listed below to evaluate each of your essays. Because it's tough to be totally impartial about your own writing, you may get a more accurate score by asking a well-informed friend, teacher, or counselor to rate your essays for you.

On the following Rating Chart, enter a number (from 1 to 6) that you think represents your level of performance in each category (A–F).

CATEGORY A: OVERALL PURPOSE/MAIN IDEA
6   extremely well-defined and insightful
5   clearly defined and generally insightful
4   mostly clear
3   somewhat clear but occasionally confusing
2   generally unclear and confusing
1   mostly incomprehensible or simplistic

CATEGORY B: HANDLING OF THE PROMPT
6   self-evident or extremely clear throughout
5   mostly clear
4   somewhat clear
3   somewhat unclear
2   generally unclear or ambiguous
1   confusing or nonexistent

CATEGORY C: ORGANIZATION AND DEVELOPMENT
6   insightfully organized; fully developed with excellent supporting evidence
5   reasonably well organized; developed with appropriate supporting material
4   appropriately organized; developed with some relevant material
3   inconsistent organization; weak development
2   poorly organized; little or no development
1   no discernible organization or development

CATEGORY D: SENTENCE STRUCTURE
6   varied and engaging
5   sufficiently varied to create interest
4   some variety
3   little variety; minor sentence errors
2   frequent sentence errors that interfere with meaning
1   serious sentence errors that obscure meaning

CATEGORY E: USE OF LANGUAGE
6   precise and effective word choice
5   competent word choice
4   conventional word choice; mostly correct
3   some errors in diction or idiom
2   frequent lapses in diction or idiom
1   meaning obscured by word choice

CATEGORY F: GRAMMAR AND USAGE
6   error-free or virtually error-free
5   occasional minor errors
4   basically correct but with several minor errors
3   meaning somewhat obscured by errors
2   meaning frequently obscured by errors
1   meaning blocked by several major errors

RATING CHART

Rate your essay	Essay 1	Essay 2	Essay 3
Overall Purpose/Main Idea			
Handling of the Prompt			
Organization and Development			
Sentence Structure			
Use of Language			
Grammar and Usage			
Composite Scores (sum of each column)			

By using the following scale, in which composite scores are converted to the nine-point AP rating scale, you may determine the final score for each essay:

Composite Score	AP Essay Score
33–36	9
29–32	8
25–28	7
21–24	6
18–20	5
15–17	4
10–14	3
7–9	2
6 or below	1

AP Essay Scores Essay 1 _____ Essay 2 _____ Essay 3 _____

TEST SCORE WORKSHEET

The scores you have earned on the multiple-choice and essay sections of the exam may now be converted to the AP five-point scale by performing the following calculations:

I. Determine Your Score for Section I (Multiple-Choice)

(STEP A) Number of correct answers _____

(STEP B) Multiply the figure in Step A by 1.2272 to find your Multiple-Choice Score _____. (Do not round.)

II. Determine Your Score for Section II (Essays)

(STEP A) Enter your score for Essay 1 (out of 9) _____

(STEP B) Enter your score for Essay 2 (out of 9) _____

(STEP C) Enter your score for Essay 3 (out of 9) _____

(STEP D) Add the figures in Steps A, B, and C _____

(STEP E) Multiply the figure in Step D by 3.0556 _____ (Do not round.) This is your Essay Score.

III. Determine Your Total Score

Add the scores for I and II to find your composite score _____.
(Round to nearest whole number.)

To convert your composite score to the AP five-point scale, use the chart below. The range of scores only approximates what you would earn on the actual test because the exact figures may vary from test to test. Be aware, therefore, that your score on this test, as well as on other tests in this book, may differ slightly from your score on an actual AP exam.

Composite Score	AP Grade
111–150	5
97–110	4
78–96	3
51–77	2
0–50	1

AP essays are ordinarily judged in relation to other essays written on the same topic at the same time. Therefore, the scores you assign yourself for these essays may not be the same as the scores you would earn on an actual exam.

ANSWER SHEET
Practice Test C

Multiple-Choice Questions

Time—1 hour

1. Ⓐ Ⓑ Ⓒ Ⓓ Ⓔ   16. Ⓐ Ⓑ Ⓒ Ⓓ Ⓔ   31. Ⓐ Ⓑ Ⓒ Ⓓ Ⓔ   46. Ⓐ Ⓑ Ⓒ Ⓓ Ⓔ

2. Ⓐ Ⓑ Ⓒ Ⓓ Ⓔ   17. Ⓐ Ⓑ Ⓒ Ⓓ Ⓔ   32. Ⓐ Ⓑ Ⓒ Ⓓ Ⓔ   47. Ⓐ Ⓑ Ⓒ Ⓓ Ⓔ

3. Ⓐ Ⓑ Ⓒ Ⓓ Ⓔ   18. Ⓐ Ⓑ Ⓒ Ⓓ Ⓔ   33. Ⓐ Ⓑ Ⓒ Ⓓ Ⓔ   48. Ⓐ Ⓑ Ⓒ Ⓓ Ⓔ

4. Ⓐ Ⓑ Ⓒ Ⓓ Ⓔ   19. Ⓐ Ⓑ Ⓒ Ⓓ Ⓔ   34. Ⓐ Ⓑ Ⓒ Ⓓ Ⓔ   49. Ⓐ Ⓑ Ⓒ Ⓓ Ⓔ

5. Ⓐ Ⓑ Ⓒ Ⓓ Ⓔ   20. Ⓐ Ⓑ Ⓒ Ⓓ Ⓔ   35. Ⓐ Ⓑ Ⓒ Ⓓ Ⓔ   50. Ⓐ Ⓑ Ⓒ Ⓓ Ⓔ

6. Ⓐ Ⓑ Ⓒ Ⓓ Ⓔ   21. Ⓐ Ⓑ Ⓒ Ⓓ Ⓔ   36. Ⓐ Ⓑ Ⓒ Ⓓ Ⓔ   51. Ⓐ Ⓑ Ⓒ Ⓓ Ⓔ

7. Ⓐ Ⓑ Ⓒ Ⓓ Ⓔ   22. Ⓐ Ⓑ Ⓒ Ⓓ Ⓔ   37. Ⓐ Ⓑ Ⓒ Ⓓ Ⓔ   52. Ⓐ Ⓑ Ⓒ Ⓓ Ⓔ

8. Ⓐ Ⓑ Ⓒ Ⓓ Ⓔ   23. Ⓐ Ⓑ Ⓒ Ⓓ Ⓔ   38. Ⓐ Ⓑ Ⓒ Ⓓ Ⓔ   53. Ⓐ Ⓑ Ⓒ Ⓓ Ⓔ

9. Ⓐ Ⓑ Ⓒ Ⓓ Ⓔ   24. Ⓐ Ⓑ Ⓒ Ⓓ Ⓔ   39. Ⓐ Ⓑ Ⓒ Ⓓ Ⓔ

10. Ⓐ Ⓑ Ⓒ Ⓓ Ⓔ   25. Ⓐ Ⓑ Ⓒ Ⓓ Ⓔ   40. Ⓐ Ⓑ Ⓒ Ⓓ Ⓔ

11. Ⓐ Ⓑ Ⓒ Ⓓ Ⓔ   26. Ⓐ Ⓑ Ⓒ Ⓓ Ⓔ   41. Ⓐ Ⓑ Ⓒ Ⓓ Ⓔ

12. Ⓐ Ⓑ Ⓒ Ⓓ Ⓔ   27. Ⓐ Ⓑ Ⓒ Ⓓ Ⓔ   42. Ⓐ Ⓑ Ⓒ Ⓓ Ⓔ

13. Ⓐ Ⓑ Ⓒ Ⓓ Ⓔ   28. Ⓐ Ⓑ Ⓒ Ⓓ Ⓔ   43. Ⓐ Ⓑ Ⓒ Ⓓ Ⓔ

14. Ⓐ Ⓑ Ⓒ Ⓓ Ⓔ   29. Ⓐ Ⓑ Ⓒ Ⓓ Ⓔ   44. Ⓐ Ⓑ Ⓒ Ⓓ Ⓔ

15. Ⓐ Ⓑ Ⓒ Ⓓ Ⓔ   30. Ⓐ Ⓑ Ⓒ Ⓓ Ⓔ   45. Ⓐ Ⓑ Ⓒ Ⓓ Ⓔ

Practice Test C

SECTION I

TIME: 1 HOUR

> **Directions:** *Questions 1–12.* Carefully read the following passage and answer the accompanying questions.

The passage is an excerpt from an essay by a 19th-century American author.

PASSAGE 1

But it is mostly my own dreams I talk of, and that will somewhat excuse me for talking of dreams at all. Everyone knows how delightful the dreams are that one dreams one's self, and how insipid the dreams of others are. I had an illustration of
Line the fact, not many evenings ago, when a company of us got telling dreams. I had by
(5) far the best dreams of any; to be quite frank, mine were the only dreams worth listening to; they were richly imaginative, delicately fantastic, exquisitely whimsical, and humorous in the last degree; and I wondered that when the rest could have listened to them they were always eager to cut in with some silly, senseless, tasteless thing that made me sorry and ashamed for them. I shall not be going too far if I say that it
(10) was on their part the grossest betrayal of vanity that I ever witnessed.

But the egotism of some people concerning their dreams is almost incredible. They will come down to breakfast and bore everybody with a recital of the nonsense that has passed through their brains in sleep, as if they were not bad enough when they were awake; they will not spare the slightest detail; and if, by the mercy of
(15) Heaven, they have forgotten something, they will be sure to recollect it, and go back and give it all over again with added circumstance. Such people do not reflect that there is something so purely and intensely personal in dreams that they can rarely interest anyone but the dreamer, and that to the dearest friend, the closest relation or connection, they can seldom be otherwise than tedious and impertinent. The
(20) habit husbands and wives have of making each other listen to their dreams is especially cruel. They have each other quite helpless, and for this reason they should all the more carefully guard themselves from abusing their advantage. Parents should not afflict their offspring with the rehearsal of their mental maunderings in sleep, and children should learn that one of the first duties a child owes its parents is to
(25) spare them the anguish of hearing what it has dreamed about overnight. A like for-

bearance in regard to the community at large should be taught in the first trait of good manners in public schools, if we ever come to teach good manners there.

Certain exceptional dreams, however, are so imperatively significant, so vitally important, that it would be wrong to withhold them from the knowledge of those (30) who happened not to dream them, and I could scarcely forgive myself if I did not, however briefly, impart them. It was only last week, for instance, that I found myself one night in the company of the Duke of Wellington, the great Duke, the Iron one, in fact; and after a few moments of agreeable conversation on topics of interest among gentlemen, his Grace said that now, if I pleased, he would like a couple of (35) those towels. We had not been speaking of towels, that I remember, but it seemed the most natural thing in the world that he should mention them in the connection, whatever it was, and I went at once to get them for him. At the place where they gave out towels, and where I found some very civil people, they told me that what I wanted was not towels, and they gave me instead two bath-gowns, of rather scanty (40) measure, butternut in color, and Turkish in texture. The garments made somehow a very strong impression upon me, so that I could draw them now, if I could draw anything, as they looked when they were held up to me. At the same moment, for no reason that I can allege, I passed from a social to a menial relation to the Duke, and foresaw that when I went back to him with those bath-gowns he would not thank me (45) as one gentleman to another, but would offer me a tip as if I were a servant. . . .

This seemed to end the whole affair, and I passed on to other visions, which I cannot recall.

1. In the first paragraph, the primary contrast made by the speaker is between

   (A) pleasant dreams and nightmares.
   (B) his own dreams and the dreams of others.
   (C) vanity and modesty.
   (D) realistic dreams and fantastical dreams.
   (E) dreams of the past and dreams of the present.

2. Which of the following best describes the rhetorical function of the second sentence in the second paragraph (lines 12–16)?

   (A) It provides details to support the preceding generalization.
   (B) It reiterates the main idea of the passage.
   (C) It presents an alternate view of the passage's main subject.
   (D) It undercuts an assertion made in the first paragraph.
   (E) It introduces a question that will be answered later in the passage.

3. In context, the word "reflect" (line 16) is best interpreted to mean

   (A) imitate.
   (B) take into account.
   (C) show off.
   (D) mull over.
   (E) mirror.

4. The speaker in the passage can be described as a person with all of the following qualities EXCEPT

    (A) self-centered hypocrisy.

    (B) the ability to see himself as others see him.

    (C) blindness to the fact that he is the very sort of person he scorns.

    (D) a belief that he is a well-mannered gentleman.

    (E) unawareness that the more he says the more he reveals his shortcomings.

5. In line 17, "they" refers to which of the following?

    I. "people" (line 16)

    II. "dreams" (line 20)

    III. "husbands and wives" (line 20)

    (A) I only

    (B) II only

    (C) I and II only

    (D) II and III only

    (E) I, II, and III

6. The last sentence of the second paragraph (lines 25–27) can best be described as

    (A) a generalization followed by a specific example.

    (B) a suggestion followed by the reason for making it.

    (C) a statement about a cause and its effect.

    (D) a reasonable assumption and a logical conclusion.

    (E) a recommendation followed by an editorial comment.

7. That the speaker declares that some dreams "are so imperatively significant, so vitally important" (lines 28–29) is ironic mainly because

    (A) the speaker has been railing against the telling of dreams.

    (B) some dreams are "exceptional" (line 28).

    (C) the speaker has characterized dreams as "intensely personal" (line 17).

    (D) irrational events occur in dreams as well as in reality.

    (E) people rarely remember their dreams.

8. The speaker's report of his nighttime encounter with the Duke of Wellington (lines 32–45) contributes to the unity of the passage in which of the following ways?

    (A) As proof of the fleeting nature of dreams

    (B) As a deliberate example of a "silly, senseless, tasteless thing" (line 8)

    (C) As a description of the speaker's social status

    (D) As evidence that dreams leave permanent impressions on the dreamer

    (E) As an illustration of the speaker's conviction that his own dreams are "worth listening to" (lines 5–6)

9. The speaker's tone in the passage as a whole can best be described as

    (A) crude and unsentimental.
    (B) mournful and bleak.
    (C) arrogant and condescending.
    (D) grouchy and reckless.
    (E) troubled and anxious.

10. The shift in the speaker's attitude toward the Duke of Wellington (lines 42–45) is most accurately described as going from

    (A) devoted to rebellious.
    (B) friendly to violently contemptuous.
    (C) helpful to profoundly defiant.
    (D) respectful to slightly disconcerted.
    (E) courteous to angry.

11. In line 40, "Turkish" modifies

    (A) "towels" (line 39).
    (B) "bath-gowns" (line 39).
    (C) "measure" (line 40).
    (D) "color" (line 40).
    (E) "garments" (line 40).

12. The passage as a whole can best be described as

    (A) a dramatic monologue.
    (B) a statement of principles.
    (C) a soliloquy.
    (D) an expression of opinion.
    (E) an offer of advice.

Directions: *Questions 13–24.* Carefully read the following passage and answer the accompanying questions.

The passage below is part of a talk delivered by T. S. Eliot, a renowned 20th-century poet.

PASSAGE 2

I hold no diploma, certificate, or other academic document to show that I am qualified to discuss this subject. I have never taught anybody of any age how to enjoy, understand, appreciate poetry, or how to speak it. I have known a great many

Line
(5) poets, and innumerable people who wanted to be told that they were poets. I have done some teaching, but I have never "taught poetry." My excuse for taking up this subject is of wholly different origin. I know that not only young people in colleges and universities, but secondary school children also, have to study, or at least acquaint themselves with, poems by living poets; and I know that my poems are among those studied. This fact brings some welcome supplement to my income; and it also brings
(10) an increase in my correspondence, which is more or less welcome, though not all the letters get answered. These are the letters from children themselves, or more precisely, the teenagers. They live mostly in Britain, the United States, and Germany, with a sprinkling from the nations of Asia. It is in a spirit of curiosity, therefore, that I approach the subject of teaching poetry: I should like to know more about these
(15) young people and about their teachers and the methods of teaching.

For some of my young correspondents seem to be misguided. Sometimes I have been assigned to them as a "project," more often they have made the choice themselves—it is not always clear why. (There was one case, that of an Egyptian boy, who wanted to write a thesis about my work, and as none of my work was locally available
(20) and as he wanted to read it, asked me to send him all my books. That was very exceptional, however.) Very often the writers ask for information about myself, sometimes in the form of a questionnaire. I remember being asked by one child whether it was true that I only cared to associate with lords and bishops. Sometimes a photograph is asked for. Some young persons seem to want me to provide them with all the mate-
(25) rial for a potted biography, including mention of my interests, tastes, and ways of amusing myself. Are these children studying poetry, or merely studying poets? Very often they want explanations, either of a whole poem ("what does it mean") or of a particular line or phrase; and the kind of question they ask often suggests that their approach to that poem has been wrong, for they want the wrong kind of explanation,
(30) or ask questions which are simply unanswerable. Sometimes, but more rarely, they are avid for literary sources, which would seem to indicate that they have started too early on the road to Xanadu.

Now, when I was young, this sort of thing did not happen. I did study English at school, beginning, thank God, with grammar, and going on to "rhetoric"—for which
(35) also I am grateful. And we had to read a number of set books of prose and verse—mostly in school editions which made them look peculiarly unappetizing. But we never were made to read any literature which could be called "contemporary."

No. Not only were we not encouraged to take an interest in the poetry actually being written, but even had we been, I doubt whether we should have thought of
(40) entering into correspondence with the authors. Some of the juvenile correspon-

dence I receive seems to be instigated by the teachers, but the greater part does not. Indeed, some of my letters, I suspect, are inspired by a desire to score off the teacher in the hope of getting some statement from the horse's mouth which will be a direct contradiction of what has been taught. (I confess that this last type of let-
(45) ter is one which I sometimes take pleasure in answering—when the teacher seems to have been wrong.) But my point is that this pressure upon the poet from young people who have been compelled to read his work is a modern phenomenon. I don't believe that Tennyson and Browning, Longfellow and Whittier (to say nothing of Poe and Whitman, poets whose works we did not study) were embarrassed by juvenile
(50) correspondence choking up their letter boxes. The teaching of the contemporary literature, the introduction of the young to poetry by living poets, is something that came about in my time without my being aware of what was happening.

13. The rhetorical purpose of the speaker's statement that he has no experience teaching poetry (line 5) is mainly to

(A) win the audience's sympathy.
(B) highlight the division between poetic theory and practice.
(C) present a problem for which he will propose solutions.
(D) contrast his lack of expertise in one area with his profound insights in another.
(E) prepare the audience for the subject he intends to talk about.

14. The phrase "innumerable people who wanted to be told they were poets" (line 4) probably refers to

(A) aspiring poets who have asked Eliot to comment on their work.
(B) students given a class assignment to write a poem.
(C) college and university students majoring in poetry.
(D) writers who have submitted poems for publication.
(E) frustrated literary critics.

15. In line 20, the word "That" refers to

(A) the overall purpose of the Egyptian boy's letter.
(B) the fact that Eliot received a letter from Egypt.
(C) the boy's claim that he wanted to read all of Eliot's books.
(D) the unavailablity of Eliot's books in Egypt.
(E) the boy's claim that he wanted to write a thesis about Eliot's works.

16. Based on the sentence beginning in line 22 ("I remember . . . lords and bishops"), the speaker in the passage is acknowledging that

    (A) he plays an official role in church affairs.
    (B) his poetry is difficult to understand.
    (C) he has an undeserved reputation as an elitist.
    (D) he believes that schoolchildren are ignorant.
    (E) he comes from a family of nobility.

17. The tone of the second paragraph (lines 16–32) can best be described as

    (A) didactic.
    (B) amused.
    (C) resigned.
    (D) nostalgic.
    (E) confident.

18. The statement "they have started too early on the road to Xanadu" (lines 31–32) contains an example of

    (A) an epithet.
    (B) pathetic fallacy.
    (C) a metaphorical allusion.
    (D) metonymy.
    (E) hyperbole.

19. Which of the following best characterizes the rhetorical function of the first sentence of paragraph 3 (line 33)?

    (A) It provides a logical transition between the third and fourth paragraphs.
    (B) It restates the main idea of the previous paragraph.
    (C) It bolsters the main point made by the third paragraph.
    (D) It introduces a change in the speaker's attitude toward the topic of the passage.
    (E) It briefly summarizes the main idea of the passage.

20. In context, all of the following describe the speaker's rhetorical intent in using the expression "thank God" (line 34) EXCEPT

    (A) to indicate that he is a devout, God-fearing individual.
    (B) to suggest that writing letters to poets is less valuable than studying grammar.
    (C) to express skepticism about the usefulness of some current educational practices.
    (D) to imply that knowledge of grammar is essential to a good education.
    (E) to encourage his audience to master English grammar.

21. The last paragraph (lines 38–52) include all of the following rhetorical strategies EXCEPT

    (A) the use of allusion.
    (B) an interjection used for emphasis.
    (C) a metaphorical usage.
    (D) a parenthetical digression.
    (E) a rhetorical question.

22. In context, the expression "to score off" (line 42) is best interpreted to mean which of the following?

    (A) To embarrass
    (B) To take advantage of
    (C) To annoy
    (D) To slander
    (E) To scold

23. The speaker mentions Tennyson, Browning, Longfellow, and other poets (lines 48–49) as examples of which of the following?

    (A) Poets whose work is often studied in English classes
    (B) Famous writers who enjoy corresponding with their readers
    (C) Poets whose experience differs from that of the speaker
    (D) Authors whom the speaker admires
    (E) Poets who declined to answer students' letters

24. The speaker's tone in the passage as a whole can best be described as

    (A) hypercritical and agitated.
    (B) tactful and restrained.
    (C) sentimental but detached.
    (D) rigorous but sympathetic.
    (E) authoritative and demanding.

Directions: *Questions 25–40.* Carefully read the following passage and answer the accompanying questions.

The passage below comes from the pen of a well-known 19th-century writer.

PASSAGE 3

The changes wrought by death are in themselves so sharp and final, and so terrible and melancholy in their consequences, that the thing stands alone in man's experience, and has no parallel upon earth. It outdoes all other accidents because
Line it is the last of them. Sometimes it leaps suddenly upon its victims, like a Thug;
(5) sometimes it lays a regular siege and creeps upon their citadel during a score of years. And when the business is done, there is sore havoc made in other people's lives, and a pin knocked out by which many subsidiary friendships hung together. There are empty chairs, solitary walks, and single beds at night. Again, in taking away our friends, death does not take them away utterly, but leaves behind a mocking,
(10) tragical, and soon intolerable residue, which must be hurriedly concealed. Hence a whole chapter of sights and customs striking to the mind, from the pyramids of Egypt to the gallows and hanging trees of medieval Europe. The poorest persons have a bit of pageant going towards the tomb; memorial stones are set up over the least memorable; and, in order to preserve some show of respect for what remains
(15) of our old loves and friendships, we must accompany it with much grimly ludicrous ceremonial, and the hired undertaker parades before the door.

Although few things are spoken of with more fearful whisperings than this prospect of death, few have less influence on conduct under healthy circumstances. We have all heard of cities in South America built upon the side of fiery mountains,
(20) and how, in this tremendous neighbourhood, the inhabitants are not a jot more impressed by the solemnity of mortal conditions than if they were delving[1] gardens in the greenest corner of England. There are serenades and suppers and much gallantry among the myrtles overhead; and meanwhile the foundation shudders underfoot, the bowels of the mountain growl, and at any moment living ruin may leap
(25) sky-high into the moonlight, and tumble man and his merry-making in the dust. In the eyes of very young people, and very dull old ones, there is something indescribably reckless and desperate in such a picture. It seems not credible that respectable married people, with umbrellas, should find appetite for a bit of supper within quite a long distance of a fiery mountain; ordinary life begins to smell of high-handed
(30) debauch when it is carried on so close to a catastrophe; and even cheese and salad, it seems, could hardly be relished in such circumstances without something like defiance of the Creator. It should be a place for nobody but hermits dwelling in prayer and maceration, or mere born-devils drowning care in perpetual carouse.

And yet, when one comes to think upon it calmly, the situation of these South
(35) American citizens forms only a very pale figure for the state of ordinary mankind. This world itself, travelling blindly and swiftly in overcrowded space, among a million other worlds travelling blindly and swiftly in contrary directions, may very well

---

[1]*digging*

come by a knock that would set it into explosions like a penny squib.[2] And what, pathologically looked at, is the human body with all its organs, but a mere bagful
(40) of petards?[3] The least of these is as dangerous to the whole economy as the ship's powder-magazine to the ship; and with every breath we breathe, and every meal we eat, we are putting one or more of them in peril. Think with what a preparation of spirit we should affront the daily peril of the dinner table: a deadlier spot than any battlefield in history, where the far greater proportion of our ancestors have
(45) left their bones! What woman would ever be lured into marriage, so much more dangerous than the wildest sea? And what would it be to grow old? For, after a certain distance, every step we take in life we find the ice growing thinner below our feet, and all around us and behind us we see our contemporaries going through.

_____
[2]_squib: a small firecracker_
[3]_petards: a) intestinal gases; b) a case containing explosives_

25. Which of the following phrases does the speaker use to develop the notion that death "has no parallel" (line 3)?

  (A) "changes . . . are . . . sharp" (line 1)
  (B) "changes . . . are . . . terrible and melancholy" (lines 1–2)
  (C) "outdoes all other accidents" (line 3)
  (D) "leaps suddenly" (line 4)
  (E) "lays a regular siege" (line 5)

26. The primary rhetorical function of the sentence "There are . . . at night" (line 8) is to

  (A) illustrate a generalization made in the previous sentence.
  (B) contradict an assertion made in the first sentence of the paragraph.
  (C) discuss the connotation of words to be used later in the passage.
  (D) provide a brief digression from the main idea of the passage.
  (E) prove the validity of the passage's opening sentence.

27. The two sentences in lines 4–7 contain all of the following EXCEPT

  (A) simile.
  (B) dramatic irony.
  (C) personification.
  (D) unifying repetition.
  (E) metaphor.

28. In the first paragraph, the speaker's primary purpose is to

  (A) discuss the gravity and after-effects of death.
  (B) ridicule the social customs associated with dying.
  (C) propose a hypothesis about humankind's fear of death.
  (D) comfort readers who have recently lost friends or loved ones.
  (E) convince readers that death is a topic that must be discussed openly.

29. In line 5, "it" refers to

    (A) "the thing" (line 2).
    (B) "man's experience" (lines 2–3).
    (C) "no parallel" (line 3).
    (D) "earth" (line 3).
    (E) "a Thug" (line 4).

30. The speaker uses the phrase "a whole chapter of sights and customs striking to the mind" (line 11) to refer to

    (A) physical reminders of death.
    (B) lost friends.
    (C) inevitable thoughts about one's own death.
    (D) mourners.
    (E) hired undertakers.

31. Lines 17–18 contain all of the following EXCEPT

    (A) a complex sentence.
    (B) an extended analogy.
    (C) a paradoxical idea.
    (D) a subordinate clause.
    (E) parallel syntax.

32. In lines 22–23, "serenades and suppers and much gallantry among the myrtles" most directly alludes to

    (A) "fearful whisperings" (line 17).
    (B) "conduct under healthy circumstances" (line 18).
    (C) "solemnity" (line 21).
    (D) "mortal conditions" (line 21).
    (E) "gardens in . . . England" (lines 21–22).

33. The use of which rhetorical device is most in evidence in lines 22–25 ("There are serenades . . . in the dust")?

    (A) Deductive reasoning
    (B) Overdone sentimentality
    (C) Alliteration
    (D) Fantasy
    (E) Antithesis

34. The function of the sentences in lines 22–25 ("There are serenades . . . in the dust") might best be described as

    (A) presenting a problem and offering an immediate solution.
    (B) balancing an overstatement and an understatement.
    (C) citing two examples of natural perils.
    (D) contrasting man's weaknesses and nature's power.
    (E) developing in more detail the main ideas of the previous sentence.

35. Which of the following best describes how paragraph 2 (lines 17–33) is developed?

(A) With an elaborate metaphor
(B) With an abstract statement followed by a concrete explanation
(C) With a narrative about events in a South American city
(D) With factual information from which the main idea of the passage can be inferred
(E) With a series of paradoxical statements about human behavior

36. In context, the speaker uses the phrase "with umbrellas" (line 28) to suggest that

(A) it is customary for British people to carry umbrellas.
(B) keeping up an appearance of respectability is important to married couples.
(C) the people are prepared for a bit of rain but not for real disaster.
(D) umbrellas often symbolize old age.
(E) umbrellas provide a false sense of security.

37. For which of the following reasons does the speaker associate "hermits" (line 32) with "born-devils" (line 33)?

I. Neither puts value on their present existence.
II. They lead unconventional lives.
III. Both are oblivious to mortal dangers.

(A) I only
(B) III only
(C) I and II only
(D) II and III only
(E) I, II, and III

38. The pronoun "them" (line 42) refers to

(A) "South American citizens" (lines 34–35).
(B) "a million other worlds" (lines 36–37).
(C) "organs" (line 39).
(D) "petards" (line 40).
(E) "every breath" and "every meal" (line 41).

39. In the last paragraph of the passage (lines 34–48) the speaker uses all of the following rhetorical devices to characterize the perils awaiting us EXCEPT

(A) repetition for emphasis.
(B) an analogy.
(C) a rhetorical question.
(D) an anecdote.
(E) a metaphor.

40. In the passage, the speaker's primary focus is

(A) fear of violent death.

(B) the thrill of living dangerously.

(C) humanity's inability to cope with the constant threat of death.

(D) the thin dividing line between life and death.

(E) the impermanence of life.

Directions: *Questions 41–53.* Carefully read the following passage and answer the accompanying questions.

The passage below is an excerpt from a contemporary book.

PASSAGE 4

So he bought it.[1] Everyone knows that. Peter Minuit purchased Manhattan Island from a group of local Indians for sixty guilders worth of goods, or as the nineteenth-century historian Edmund O'Callaghan calculated it, twenty-four dollars. From the
Line seventeenth through the early twentieth century thousands of real estate transac-
(5) tions occurred in which native Americans sold parcels—ranging in size from a town lot to a midwestern state—to English, Dutch, French, Spanish, and other European settlers. But only one sale is legend; only one is known by everyone. Only one has had the durability to be riffed on in Broadway song ("Give It Back to the Indians," from the 1939 Rodgers and Hart musical *Too Many Girls*), and, at the end of the
(10) twentieth century, to do service as a punchline in a column by humorist Dave Barry (". . . which the Dutch settler Peter Minuit purchased from the Manhattan Indians for $24, plus $167,000 a month in maintenance fees").[2]

It's pretty clear why this particular sale lodged in the cultural memory, why it became legend: the extreme incongruity, the exquisitely absurd price. It is the most
(15) dramatic illustration of the whole long process of stripping the natives of their land. The idea that the center of world commerce, an island packed with trillions of dollars' worth of real estate, was once bought from supposedly hapless Stone Age innocents for twenty-four dollars' worth of household goods is too delicious to let slip. It speaks to our sense of early American history as the history of savvy, ruthless
(20) Europeans conniving, tricking, enslaving, and bludgeoning innocent and guileless natives out of their land and their lives. It's a neatly packed symbol of the entire conquest of the continent that was to come.

Beyond that, the purchase snippet is notable because it is virtually the only thing about Manhattan colony that has become part of history. For this reason, too, it
(25) deserves exploring.

---

[1] *The order of events is far from clear, and historians debate whether Verhulst or Minuit was the one who purchased Manhattan Island. My account is based on my own reading of all relevant primary source material, as well as arguments made by various historians. I side against those who in recent decades removed Minuit from his legendary position as purchaser of the island, and with those who reassign him to that position . . . .*

[2] *Dave Barry, "A Certified Wacko Rewrites History's Greatest Hits,"* Milwaukee Journal-Sentinel, *26 December 1999.*

So, who were the Indians who agreed to this transaction, and what did they
think it meant? The ancestors of the people whom European settlers took to calling
Indians (after Columbus, who at first thought he had arrived at the outer reaches of
India) traveled the land bridge from Siberia to Alaska that existed during the last ice
(30)   age, more than twelve thousand years ago, then spread slowly through the Americas.
They came from Asia; their genetic makeup is a close match with Siberians and
Mongolians.[3] They spread out thinly across the incomprehensible vastness of the
American continents to create a linguistic richness unparalleled in human history: it
has been estimated that at the moment Columbus arrived in the New World twenty-
(35)   five percent of all human languages were North American Indian.[4]

   There are two rival, hardened stereotypes that get in the way of understanding
these people: the one that arose from the long cultural dismissing of American Indians
as "primitive," and the modern dogma that sees them as Noble and Defenseless.
Both are cartoon images. Recent work in genetics, archaeology, anthropology,
(40)   and linguistics makes plain what should be obvious: that the Mohican, Mohawk,
Lenape, Montauk, Housatonic, and other peoples occupying the lands that for a
time were called New Netherland, as well as the Massachusett, Wampanoag, Sokoki,
Pennacook, Abenaki, Oneida, Onondaga, Susquehannock, Nanticoke, and others
who inhabited other parts of what became the states of New York, Massachusetts,
(45)   Pennsylvania, Connecticut, Vermont, New Hampshire, Maine, Delaware, Maryland,
and New Jersey, were biologically, genetically, intellectually, all but identical to the
Dutch, English, French, Swedish, and others who came in contact with them in the
beginning of the seventeenth century. The Indians were as skilled, as duplicitous, as
capable of theological rumination and technological cunning, as smart and as pig-
(50)   headed, and as curious and cruel as the Europeans who met them. The members of
the Manhattan-based colony who knew them—who spent time among them in their
villages, hunted and traded with them, learned their languages—knew this perfectly
well. It was later, after the two had separated into rival camps, that the stereotypes
set. The early seventeenth century was a much more interesting time than the Wild
(55)   West era, a time when Indians and Europeans were something like equal participants, dealing with one another as allies, competitors, partners.

---

[3]*Brian Sykes,* The Seven Daughters of Eve: The Science That Reveals Our Genetic Ancestry,
279–280.
[4]*J.C.H. King,* First People, First Contacts: Native Peoples of North America, *8.*

41.   The passage as a whole can best be described as

   (A)   the dramatization of a legendary occurrence.
   (B)   an example of an "irony of history".
   (C)   an interpretation of a historical event.
   (D)   a historical document.
   (E)   the depiction of a particular geographical place.

42. The speaker's tone of the first two sentences of the passage (line 1) is best described as

(A) scornful.
(B) confidential.
(C) undoubting.
(D) ill-tempered.
(E) argumentative.

43. Footnote 1 (line 1) suggests that

(A) the passage is hypothetical, not factual.
(B) the story of the purchase of Manhattan is most likely fictitious.
(C) information about long-ago events cannot be trusted.
(D) historians sometimes draw different conclusions from the same set of facts.
(E) the name of the buyer is historically more significant than the fact of the purchase itself.

44. The speaker's reference to a Broadway song (line 8) serves chiefly to

(A) illustrate the uniqueness of the sale of Manhattan Island.
(B) distinguish between several momentous land acquisitions.
(C) comment on the price that was paid for the island.
(D) explain a cause of hostility between European settlers and Indians.
(E) commend Peter Minuit for outsmarting the Indians.

45. All of the following phrases are used to support the idea that the "sale lodged in the cultural memory" (line 13) EXCEPT

(A) "is known by everyone" (line 7).
(B) "durability to be riffed on" (line 8).
(C) "do service as a punchline" (line 10).
(D) "too delicious to let slip" (lines 18–19).
(E) "ruthless Europeans" (lines 19–20).

46. In line 19, the pronoun "our" refers to

(A) Native-Americans.
(B) specialists in early American history.
(C) everyone familiar with the details of the purchase of Manhattan Island.
(D) schoolchildren who have studied the history of New York.
(E) authors who write books about colonial America.

47. Which of the following inferences can be drawn from a reading of footnotes 3 and 4?

(A) That the information designated by footnote 3 (line 32) and footnote 4 (line 35) appeared in the works of both Sikes and King

(B) That *First People, First Contacts: Native Peoples of North America* is an eight-page pamphlet

(C) That the works of Sikes and King have been cited earlier in the book from which this passage has been taken

(D) That Sykes' work, *The Seven Daughters of Eve . . .*, is an article published in an unnamed periodical

(E) That the absence of a copyright dates in both footnotes suggests that the works of Sykes and King were published before the advent of copyright laws

48. The primary rhetorical purpose of the sentence "For this reason . . ." (lines 24–25) is to

(A) express a causal relationship between the sale of Manhattan and the island's future growth.

(B) link the idea expressed in the preceding sentence with the next paragraphs.

(C) restate the main idea of the passage.

(D) introduce important information that was deliberately left out of the second paragraph.

(E) suggest a symbolic interpretation of the events surrounding the sale of Manhattan.

49. In which of the following does the speaker exaggerate in order to create certain effects?

  I. "Everyone knows that" (line 1)
  II. "the most dramatic illustration . . . of their land" (lines 14–15)
  III. "linguistic richness unparalleled in human history" (line 33)

(A) I only
(B) III only
(C) I and II only
(D) II and III only
(E) I, II, and III

50. In describing the Indians who lived in areas that now are eastern states (lines 48–50), the speaker emphasizes their

(A) human qualities.
(B) cooperative nature.
(C) antagonism toward white settlers.
(D) courage in the face of danger.
(E) deceitfulness.

51. Which of the following best describes the footnoted material in the passage?

(A) It all contains ideas that originated in primary historical sources.
(B) Footnote 1 (line 1) refers to material that the author of the passage has paraphrased from his sources.
(C) Footnotes 1 (line 1) and 2 (line 12) refer to material containing general historical information.
(D) Footnotes 3 (line 32) and 4 (line 35) refer to material containing subjective interpretations of historical events.
(E) Footnote 2 (line 12) refers to material that contains a direct quotation.

52. In the sentence beginning "The Indians were . . ." (lines 48–50), all of the following words are parallel in function to "capable" (line 49) EXCEPT

(A) "skilled" (line 48).
(B) "duplicitous" (line 48).
(C) "technological" (line 49).
(D) "smart" (line 49).
(E) "cruel" (line 50).

53. The main rhetorical function of the last sentence of the passage (lines 54–56) is to

(A) offer a specific answer to the question that begins paragraph 4 (lines 26–27).
(B) put to rest a misconception that is discussed in the last paragraph of the passage.
(C) summarize the main idea of the passage.
(D) provide a series of generalizations that are drawn from evidence in the passage.
(E) introduce a new twist on the subject that readers would do well to think about.

SECTION II

Three Essay Questions

TIME: 2 HOURS AND 15 MINUTES

Write your essays on standard 8½" × 11" composition paper. At the exam you will be given a bound booklet containing 12 lined pages.

Essay Question 1

SUGGESTED TIME:
15 MINUTES FOR READING THE QUESTION AND SOURCES
40 MINUTES FOR WRITING AN ESSAY

Individuals and groups are invited into many high schools to inform students about colleges and job opportunities. By law, such schools must also allow representatives from the armed forces to talk with students about joining the military. Not everyone supports this policy. Peace groups as well as many parents, for instance, would like to change the law in order to keep military recruiters out of the schools.

Carefully read the following six sources, including the material that introduces each source. Then, in an essay that synthesizes at least three of the sources, take a position on the issue that a law denying military recruiters access to students on high school campuses should be passed.

Don't simply summarize the sources. Instead, weigh evidence from the sources to support and illustrate your position on the issue. You may paraphrase, review, and quote relevant material directly and indirectly from the sources. Be sure to indicate in your essay which sources you use. Refer to them as Source A, Source B, and so on, or by the key words in the parentheses below. In making your argument, you may, of course, also include any ideas of your own.

Source A (ACLU)
Source B (Inouye)
Source C (*Debate.org*)
Source D (Cartoon)
Source E (Hawk)
Source F (Hardcastle)

"Q & A About Military Recruitment at High Schools," ACLU of Washington, *www.aclu-wa.org,*
September 14, 2007.

*This passage is excerpted from an online article prepared by the American Civil Liberties Union,
a group devoted to protecting the constitutional rights of all Americans.*

Are schools required to allow military recruiters on campus?

. . . [L]aws require high schools to give military recruiters the same access to the campus
as they provide to other persons or groups who advise students about occupational or educational options. Therefore, if a school does not have any on-campus recruiting by employers or
colleges, it is not required to have on-campus military recruiting. For example, if a school has
a job fair with booths for many employers, it must offer a booth to military recruiters.

Can peace groups or military counseling groups get equal time as military recruiters?

Nothing would prevent a school from allowing peace groups to come on campus if it
wished. Whether peace groups could require the school to provide access against its wishes
depends on whether the school has created a public forum for that kind of expression. . . .

Can I prevent my school from giving contact information to military recruiters?

The law requires schools to release basic contact information about students (called "direc-
tory information") to military recruiters. However, schools are required to honor a family's
request that such information not be provided.

Arlene Inouye, "Should Military Recruiters Be Allowed on School Campuses?" *California Teachers Association Educator*, May 2013. *www.cta.org.*

Below is an excerpt from an article by a Los Angeles teacher who coordinates CAMS (Coalition for Alternatives to Militarism in Our Schools).

Public schools should not be the recruiting grounds for young people to be subjected to sophisticated, persuasive marketing techniques designed to sell them on joining the military. . . . Military recruitment is about the indoctrination of our young in a culture that glamorizes war and violence. Recruiters use deception and false promises to entice students who feel like they have few or no options. We call this the "poverty draft." The lure of the military particularly impacts youth of color, and more middle-class families as college becomes less affordable.

I witnessed Marine recruiters promising students from working-poor families a way to be "successful," go to college, buy a home for their parents and make their families proud. They promise male students a way to manhood, strength and independence. They promise females the best of all worlds: supervision and independence that will help them build strength of character. Recruiters know how to market the military in a way that speaks to the dreams and hopes of these young people.

. . . If we are a society that values our young, it is imperative we stop allowing the military to give them false and misleading information. It is wrong for the military to be afforded legitimacy and authority in our schools without also providing the truth about what it means to experience war.

"Should the Military Be Allowed to Recruit in Public Schools?", *Debate.org*, © 2013.

According to the keepers of Debate.org, their website is a place "where intelligent minds from around the world come to debate online and read the opinions of others."

I enlisted at the start of my senior year in high school—the best decision I ever made. I knew I wasn't going to college if I didn't join. (No money and lack of drive hurt my GPA.)

Now that I've left active duty, I'm a much better student. I'm focused, I'm driven, and I'm a lot more respectful of others. I'm a better person and I would not be this way if a recruiter had not visited my high school.

Military experience has opened doors for me and for those like me who have limited or even no options after high school. It turns boys and girls into men and women.

Every enlistee I ever met knew they were going to war, and 99% accepted it. Why? you may ask. Because they are the few who are willing to step up and fight, unlike those who hide behind those who fight.

So don't cry that high school students are easy targets for the propaganda spread by military recruiters. Think about it: Colleges do the exact same thing as military recruiters do.

—*Submitted by "Wild Bill," a U.S. Marine, 2006–2011*

"EP," "Military Recruitment Day," SouthWest Organizing Project, *swop.net*, Albuquerque, NM. Accessed from Google Images, July 2010.

This cartoon comes from the SouthWest Organizing Project, which works to empower communities to realize racial and gender equality as well as social and economic justice.

Ruby Hawk, "Military Recruitment in High Schools," *Socyberty.com.*, February 15, 2010.

This is excerpted from a position paper posted on the website of a group that publishes articles online on social issues from human psychology to politics and education.

The United States has long been against recruitment of child soldiers in other countries. So why do we have military recruiters going to high schools lecturing kids about all the advantages of joining the military? The pressure put on these students by aggressive recruiters has been unconscionable. Misconduct by recruiters includes deception, false promises, and hassling these kids at school and home. How can we call it volunteering when these youths are hounded and tricked into the service?

. . . [T]he U.S. continues its strategy to recruit youngsters under 17, and fails to protect 17 year olds from aggressive abusive recruitment. The ACLU [American Civil Liberties Union] also found that the U.S. military tactics targets kids from low income families. Last year a U.N. committee called on the U.S. to end military training in public schools and to stop targeting low income students and other venerable [*sic*] economic groups for military service.

In Georgia, violations are continuing. Federal law compels high schools to disclose student records of junior and seniors, including students under 17, to military recruiters. Parents can sign and submit a form asking that the data be withheld, but many schools do not make that information available to parents. . . .

Mike Hardcastle, "What Should You Do After High School?: A Look at Your Postgraduate Choices." *about.com*, accessed August 2010.

The passage consists of excerpts from an article posted online by a group that dispenses practical advice to teenagers.

Military life is for you if you thrive in a strict and structured environment, like helping people, have a sense of adventure and want to travel. ROTC [Reserve Officers Training Corps] is also a way to pay for university and ensure that you will have a job immediately after graduation.

Military life is not for everyone. Military service often puts you in high-risk situations and your life is often in danger even if you are not in a war zone. Depending on what type of service you choose even training can carry life-or-limb risks. Also, it is common for military service people to engage in peacekeeping missions that are anything but peaceful.

Whether you are deployed to a recognized war zone like the Middle East or are sent on a peacekeeping mission, a military career carries unusual risks. It also has incredible benefits. You get to see the world because military life involves travel. . . . You also get to learn crazy-fun skills that can't be learned anywhere else without having to pay for it like: skydiving, scuba diving, piloting aircraft, driving heavy-armored equipment, target shooting, to name a few. You don't just work in the military. It is a way of life. As the commercials state, it is really the toughest job you will ever love.

. . . While there is nothing wrong with jumping right in to the workforce after high school, be wary of accepting just any old job in order to bring home a paycheck. While you are still young you have so many opportunities to take advantage of that working in a dead end job or accepting a seemingly high paying position with no future is simply a waste. This is your life; make the best of it.

Essay Question 2

SUGGESTED TIME: 40 MINUTES

(This question counts as one third of the total score for Section II.)

> **Directions:** What follows is part of an essay, "Our March to Washington," written by Theodore Winthrop (1828–1861) about going off to fight in the Civil War. Carefully read the excerpt and then write an essay which analyzes the rhetorical strategies Winthrop used to convey his feelings about the experience.

At three o'clock in the afternoon of Friday, April 19, we took our peacemaker, a neat twelve-round brass howitzer, down from the Seventh Regiment Armory, and stationed it in the rear of the building. The twin peacemaker is somewhere near us, but entirely *Line* hidden by this enormous crowd.

(5)   An enormous crowd! of both sexes, of every age and condition. The men offer all kinds of truculent and patriotic hopes; the women shed tears, and say, "God bless you, boys."

This is a part of the town where baddish cigars prevail. But good or bad, I am ordered to keep all away from the gun. So the throng stands back, peers curiously over (10)   the heads of its junior members, and seems to be taking the measure of my coffin.

At a great house on the left, as we pass the Astor Library, I see a handkerchief waving for me. Yes! it is she who made the sandwiches in my knapsack. They were a trifle too thick, as I afterwards discovered, but otherwise perfection. Be these my thanks and the thanks of hungry comrades who had bites of them!

(15)   At the corner of Great Jones Street we halted for half an hour,—then, everything ready, we marched down Broadway.

It was worth a life, that march. Only one who passed, as we did, through that tempest of cheers, two miles long, can know the terrible enthusiasm of the occasion. I could hardly hear the rattle of our own gun-carriages, and only once or twice the (20)   music of our band came to me muffled and quelled by the uproar. We knew now, if we had not before divined it, that our great city was with us as one man, utterly united in the great cause we were marching to sustain.

This grand fact I learned by two senses. If hundreds of thousands roared it into my ears, thousands slapped it into my back. My fellow-citizens smote me on the (25)   knapsack, as I went by at the gun-rope, and encouraged me each in his own dialect. "Bully for you!" alternated with benedictions, in the proportion of two "bullies" for one blessing.

I was not so fortunate as to receive more substantial tokens of sympathy. But there were parting gifts showered on the regiment, enough to establish a variety-(30)   shop. Handkerchiefs, of course, came floating down upon us from the windows like a snow. Pretty little gloves pelted us with love-taps. The sterner sex forced upon us pocket-knives new and jagged, combs, soap, slippers, boxes of matches, cigars by the dozen and the hundred, pipes to smoke shag and pipes to smoke Latakia,[1] fruit, eggs, and sandwiches. One fellow got a new purse with ten bright quarter-eagles.

---

[1] *a type of tobacco*

Essay Question 3

SUGGESTED TIME: 40 MINUTES

(This question counts as one third of the total score for Section II.)

> **Directions:** The following passage was written by Sidney Smith (1771–1845), an English clergyman known as the wittiest man of his time. It has been adapted from Smith's review of *The Book of Fallacies* by Jeremy Bentham, published in London in 1824.
>
> Once you have read the passage, write an essay in which you support, refute, or qualify Smith's claim that to invoke our ancestors as a justification to act in a certain way is to rely on an "absurd and mischievous" fallacy. Use evidence from your reading, study, observation, or personal experience to develop your argument.

There are a vast number of absurd and mischievous fallacies, which pass readily in the world for sense and virtue, while in truth they tend only to fortify error and encourage crime. Mr. Bentham has enumerated the most conspicuous of these in

Line the book before us . . .

(5) OUR WISE ANCESTORS—*The Wisdom of Our Ancestors—The Wisdom of the Ages—Venerable Antiquity—Wisdom of Old Times*—This mischievous and absurd fallacy springs from the grossest perversion of the meaning of words. Experience is certainly the mother of wisdom, and the old have, of course, greater experience than the young; but the question is who are the old? and who are the young?

(10) Of *individuals* living at the same period, the oldest has, of course, the greatest experience; but among *generations* of men the reverse is true. Those who come first (our ancestors) are the young people, and have the least experience. We have added to their experience the experience of many centuries; and, therefore, as far as experience goes, are wiser and more capable of forming an opinion than they were.

(15) The real feeling should be, *not* can we be so presumptuous as to put our opinions in opposition to those of our ancestors? but can such young, ignorant, inexperienced persons as our ancestors necessarily were, be expected to have understood a subject as well as those who have seen so much more, lived so much longer, and enjoyed the experience of so many centuries?

END OF PRACTICE TEST C

ANSWER KEY
Practice Test C

Answers to Multiple-Choice Questions

1.	**B**	16.	**C**	31.	**B**	46.	**C**
2.	**A**	17.	**B**	32.	**E**	47.	**C**
3.	**B**	18.	**C**	33.	**C**	48.	**B**
4.	**B**	19.	**A**	34.	**E**	49.	**E**
5.	**B**	20.	**A**	35.	**E**	50.	**A**
6.	**E**	21.	**E**	36.	**C**	51.	**E**
7.	**A**	22.	**A**	37.	**E**	52.	**C**
8.	**E**	23.	**C**	38.	**C**	53.	**B**
9.	**C**	24.	**B**	39.	**D**		
10.	**D**	25.	**C**	40.	**C**		
11.	**B**	26.	**A**	41.	**C**		
12.	**D**	27.	**B**	42.	**C**		
13.	**E**	28.	**A**	43.	**D**		
14.	**A**	29.	**A**	44.	**A**		
15.	**A**	30.	**A**	45.	**E**		

Summary of Answers in Section I (Multiple-Choice)

Number of correct answers _____

Use this information when you calculate your score for this exam. See page 343.

ANSWER EXPLANATIONS

Passage 1—An excerpt from William Dean Howells' "I Talk of Dreams"

1. **(B)** The speaker's focus is on the delightfulness of his own dreams compared to the pointlessness of others' dreams.

2. **(A)** In the first sentence of the paragraph the speaker generalizes about the incredible "egotism of some people." In the next sentence he explains exactly what he means.

3. **(B)** The speaker finds fault with people who fail to realize how dull their dreams can be to others. (D) seems like a reasonable choice, too, but the phrase "mull over" suggests weighing the pros and cons of an issue. The people described by the speaker are so out of touch they don't realize that an issue exists.

4. **(B)** Throughout the passage the speaker inadvertently reveals shortcomings in his own personality and character. Primarily, he criticizes others' flaws while remaining unaware that he is flawed in the very same ways.

5. **(B)** The pronoun "they" refers to the dreams that can interest only the person who dreamt them. The people who tell their dreams may be just as "tedious and impertinent" as the dreams themselves, but grammatically speaking, "they" refers to dreams, not to people.

6. **(E)** The verb, "should be taught," is a clue that the speaker is proposing a course of action. In the second clause, the speaker adds a gratuitous slur.

7. **(A)** After criticizing people for imposing their dreams on others, it is ironic that the speaker is about to do just what he insists should not be done—tell the story of a dream. If you chose (B) as the answer, you may have overlooked the irony evident in the speaker's words or possibly, you may not have read far enough to observe the speaker's hypocrisy.

8. **(E)** By telling about his dream, the speaker supports his claim, made in the first paragraph, that unlike the dreams of others, his own dreams are worth hearing about. Although (B) may seem like a reasonable choice, it is a flawed answer because it refers specifically to the dreams of other people.

9. **(C)** The speaker finds fault with everyone but himself. Only the Duke of Wellington is beyond reproach, and that's because the Duke is, after all, a duke, not to mention the nobleman who defeated Napolean, and therefore is too high-class to be criticized.

10. **(D)** Out of respect for the Duke's status, the speaker does what "his Grace" requests, fetching a couple of towels. When the Duke treats him like a servant, however, the speaker seems slightly put off—although the passage ends before the speaker can go into detail.

11. **(B)** The adjective "Turkish" describes the two bath-gowns given to the speaker.

12. **(D)** The speaker devotes almost the entire passage to passing judgments on several matters, particularly people's propensity to relate their dreams to others. (A) cannot be the answer because the speaker in a dramatic monologue addresses a particular person or audience and responds to their cues. (B) and (E) apply only to minor segments of the passage. (C) is not a good answer because, in a soliloquy, the speaker customarily talks aloud to himself.

Passage 2—An excerpt from T. S. Eliot, "On Teaching the Appreciation of Poetry"

13. **(E)** Because the speaker has never "taught poetry," he cannot advise his audience on how to teach it. Rather, he can talk with authority about what he has observed from a distance of how poetry is taught in schools. In effect, he is defining the limits of what he will talk about.

14. **(A)** The speaker is alluding to the plight of many renowned poets and authors—namely being swamped by unsolicited requests by struggling writers for advice and critiques of their work.

15. **(A)** In contrast to the unique Egyptian boy, who boldly stated his purpose (he wants books), many youngsters did not make clear why they had written to him.

16. **(C)** The child's innocent question amuses the speaker. That he is able to laugh about it suggests that rumors of his elitism are unfounded, or at least overstated.

17. **(B)** A gentle, ironic humor pervades the speaker's account of his correspondence with students. You may have discerned a touch of nostalgia (D) throughout the passage, but this paragraph is shaped by the speaker's dry humor.

18. **(C)** Even if you don't know that Xanadu refers to an ideal, magical, other-worldly place or a remote, inaccessible realm, the context suggests that the "road to Xanadu" is a metaphorical expression. Check the Glossary on page 389 for definitions of the rhetorical terms you may not know.

19. **(A)** The sentence marks a slight change in the direction of the passage, but by using the phrase "this sort of thing" the speaker ties paragraph 3 to what he intends to say in paragraph 4.

20. **(A)** To some degree, all the choices except (A) are implied by the speaker's brief interjection.

21. **(E)** (A) refers to the names of past poets; (B) is found in "No," the first word of the paragraph. (C) is exemplified by "horse's mouth" (line 43), and (D) is used in lines 44–46. Only a rhetorical question is missing from the paragraph.

22. **(A)** The speaker surmises that some letters are motivated not by students' desire to learn, but by one-upmanship—a desire to find fault in their teachers' interpretations of poetry. Choice (C) deserves consideration, too, because it's hardly a secret that students sometimes get a kick out of annoying their teachers, but that's not what Eliot has in mind.

23. **(C)** The speaker mentions these poets of the past to stress the point that receiving letters from students is a development that only contemporary poets like himself have experienced. Choices (A) and (D) accurately describe these immortal poets, but Eliot put them on his list for a different reason.

24. **(B)** Although the speaker expresses misgivings over the way poetry is being taught, his criticism is tempered with gentle humor and understanding. At least one adjective in each of the other pairs (*e.g., agitated, sentimental, rigorous,* and *demanding*) disqualifies that choice as the best answer.

Passage 3—An excerpt from Robert Louis Stevenson, "Aes Triplex"

25. **(C)** The intent of both phrases—"death is not parallel" and "outdoes all other accidents"—is to emphasize the uniqueness of death. In other words, among life's experiences, there is nothing else quite like death.

26. **(A)** The "empty chairs" and "solitary walks," etc., are examples of the "sore havoc" (line 6) that follows the death of a friend or loved one.

27. **(B)** The phrase "like a Thug" is a simile. Personification occurs in "it leaps suddenly upon its victims" and "it lays regular siege." The repetition of "sometimes" serves to unify the first of the two sentences. The "pin," a device for holding things together, is an example of a metaphor. Only dramatic irony, a circumstance in which the reader knows more about a situation than a character in a story, is missing.

28. **(A)** The paragraph deals first with the seriousness of death for both the deceased and the survivors, and then with various consequences associated with dying. At the end of the paragraph, the speaker bemoans the fact that daily life leaves little time to reflect on the meaning of death. If you chose (B) as your answer, that's understandable because near the end of the paragraph a few social customs pertaining to funerals are listed. But the speaker's intent, in spite of calling the ceremonies "grimly ludicrous" (line 15), is not to mock them but to express reservations about their necessity.

29. **(A)** "It" refers to death, or as it is called in line 2, "the thing."

30. **(A)** The speaker cites the pyramids of Egypt, gallows, and hanging trees as "residue" that reminds us of death. Also "empty chairs, solitary walks, and single beds at night" (line 8)—all sights and customs that help keep us constantly aware of death.

31. **(B)** Because the sentence is constructed of a subordinate clause and a main clause, it is a complex sentence. It describes a paradox of human behavior: We fear death terribly but act as though it did not exist. The sentence also contains parallel phrases: "few things are spoken of" and "few have less influence." Only an analogy is missing from the sentence.

32. **(E)** The speaker compares having "serenades and supper. . . etc." with "delving gardens in England." Both are examples of routine, everyday endeavors.

33. **(C)** The repetition of initial consonant sounds—particularly the *s* and *m* sounds—is noteworthy. Turn to the Glossary on page 389 for definitions of the terms you don't know.

34. **(E)** The sentences develop the idea that residents of cities built on the side of fiery mountains appear to be indifferent to the mortal dangers of volcanic eruption.

35. **(E)** The opening sentence of the paragraph states a basic paradox: death frightens people, but it has no influence on their behavior. Much of the paragraph continues to discuss details about the inhabitants of cities built on the "side of fiery mountains." Paradoxically, the people are "not a jot more impressed by the solemnity of mortal conditions than if they were delving gardens . . . ." In other words, they lead ordinary lives, taking part in "serenades and suppers . . . etc.," in spite of the dangers lurking underfoot.

36. **(C)** The speaker alludes to umbrellas to suggest that these married couples take pains to protect themselves from the rain but mindlessly put themselves in harm's way by having "a bit of supper" on the side of a fiery mountain.

37. **(E)** Hermits pray for their own souls, are solitary figures, and suffer through their present lives in exchange for a heavenly life after death. The "born-devils" as described in the passage mindlessly drown their cares and sorrows in drink, unmindful of the consequences or long-term effects.

38. **(C)** The speaker is saying that much of what we do in life jeopardizes the health of our organs, hence our very lives.

39. **(D)** The repetition of "travelling blindly and swiftly" (lines 36–37) conjures the chaotic movement of a million worlds. The comparison of the human body and a ship is an analogy. Among the rhetorical questions are, "What woman would ever be lured into marriage . . . etc.?" (lines 45–46). In the last sentence "ice" is a metaphor for life. Only an anecdote is missing; nowhere does the speaker tell a story.

40. **(C)** The first and third paragraphs discuss the omnipresence of death. In the rest of the passage the speaker observes that, although death is a constant threat, people conduct their lives as though death were a phenomenon that has nothing to do with them. In effect, they ignore it because they can't control or understand it.

Passage 4—An excerpt from Russell Shorto,
The Island at the Center of the World

41. **(C)** While explaining the circumstances surrounding the purchase of Manhattan Island from the Indians, the speaker interprets the famous event and expresses opinions about it.

42. **(C)** The pair of terse back-to-back sentences convey the impression that the speaker has no doubt about the validity of his claim that Peter Minuit bought Manhattan Island.

43. **(D)** The footnote explains that historians differ on who actually purchased Manhattan Island. The speaker, after reading various accounts of the transaction, sides with those who believe it was Peter Minuit, but evidently no one knows for sure.

44. **(A)** In context, the reference to the song is meant to show that the story of Peter Minuit's purchase of Manhattan Island is unusually famous and well-remembered.

45. **(E)** All the phrases except "ruthless Europeans" to some degree develop the speaker's assertion that the story of Manhattan Island's purchase has become a well-known piece of America's cultural history.

46. **(C)** The speaker, explaining the legendary quality of the story, says that the "sale lodged in the cultural memory" (line 13). The pronoun "our" refers to those who make up the "cultural memory," namely anyone who knows the terms of sale agreed to by the Dutch and the Indians. Choices (B), (D), and (E) are not incorrect, but none of them is as valid as (C).

47. **(C)** The omission of information such as the publisher and date of publication indicates that a complete citation appeared earlier in the book.

48. **(B)** The speaker uses this brief sentence as a transition between the first and second halves of the passage. He has told the story of the purchase of Manhattan in general terms and is preparing to dig deeper into certain aspects of the event.

49. **(E)** Each statement is an exaggerated generalization that cannot be proven or disproven. Each is powerful and dramatic, leaving readers with a sense that this passage consists of unquestionably accurate, well-researched material.

50. **(A)** The speaker notes characteristics that are typically human: possession of technical and thinking skills, a capacity for cruelty and deception, curiosity about the world.

51. **(E)** Note 2 refers specifically to a quotation by comedian Dave Barry.

52. **(C)** All the words except (C) are predicate adjectives that describe "Indians," the subject of the sentence. "Technological" is also an adjective, but it modifies, or describes, "cunning," an object of the preposition *of*.

53. **(B)** The speaker uses the last sentence to clear up various stereotyped impressions of American Indians. In all respects, says the speaker, the Indians had many of the same characteristics—both favorable and unfavorable—as European settlers.

Answers to Essay Questions

Although answers to the essay questions will vary greatly, the following descriptions suggest a possible approach to each question and contain ideas that could be used in response to the question. Perhaps your essay contains many of the same ideas. If not, don't be alarmed. Your ideas may be at least as insightful, or even more so, as those below.

ESSAY QUESTION 1

Some Arguments <u>In Favor</u> of Changing the Law That Gives Military Recruiters Access to Students In High Schools:

- The quality of enlistees is high [Implying that recruiting in high schools is unnecessary]. (Source A)
- Recruiters use questionable methods to sway young and impressionable students into joining the military. (Source D)
- Military recruitment is about the indoctrination of young people in a culture that glamorizes war and violence. (Source B)
- The United States has a tradition of deploring the recruitment of very young soldiers in other countries. (Source E)
- Military recruiters use highly persuasive and often deceptive sales pitches that target low-income and noncollegebound students. (Source E)

Some Arguments <u>Against</u> Changing the Law That Gives Military Recruiters Access to Students in High Schools:

- The law is fair because it provides equal access to high school students by employers, colleges, and to the military. (Source A)

- Families of students can exercise the right to withhold student contact information from military recruiters. (Source A)
- Military experience opens doors for young men and women who face limited options after high school. (Source C)
- Military recruiters should be welcome in schools because their techniques are no different from those used by college recruiters. (Source C)
- Noncollegebound students can be given useful information about the vast educational and other opportunities available to service men and women. (Source F)

QUESTION 2, BASED ON AN EXCERPT FROM THEODORE WINTHROP'S "OUR MARCH TO WASHINGTON," 1861

The first-person narrator of this episode is a young man on his way to war. He and his regiment are parading through a city where people have gathered to send them off.

First he is assigned to keep onlookers away from a large cannon, a howitzer, named a "peacemaker." Whether he is aware of the irony of applying that label to a machine of war remains unclear, but in all likelihood he isn't, because he seems too caught up in the spirit of the moment.

Indeed, he is impressed by the size of the cheering crowd. Twice he uses the phrase "enormous crowd" (lines 4 and 5), once with an exclamation point for additional emphasis. He notes the men's expressions of "truculent and patriotic hopes" (line 6). He also notices that the "women shed tears and say, 'God bless you, boys'" (lines 6 7), but he seems unmindful of the feelings that evoke such responses. In other words, this is not a time for subtle observation or reflection. Yet, he reads in the faces of onlookers that they seem "to be taking the measure of my coffin" (line 10). In other words, before continuing his description of the parade, the speaker senses briefly the dark implications behind the noisy celebration.

"It was worth a life, that march" (line 17), he says, an opinion that can be interpreted in two ways. It could mean simply that the march was an experience of a lifetime. On the other hand, it suggests that the speaker knows that he, as well as many of his comrades, will soon be giving up their lives—a thought reinforced by the phrase "terrible enthusiasm" (line 18), in which "terrible" seems to be used in the sense of "terrifying" or "horrible," although at that time the word also carried a connotation of "awe-inspiring."

What is more, the speaker uses the term "tokens of sympathy" (line 28) for the small gifts—handkerchiefs, gloves, combs, soaps, etc.—that the crowd bestows on the troops. In a sense, this could also be the speaker's way of drawing attention to the discrepancy between the sacrifice he and his comrades may be about to make in battle and the trivial price paid by the people left behind. Or the seemingly insignificant gifts may also be interpreted as more personal expressions of support.

On one level, then, the passage is a rather superficial depiction of a typical farewell march of troops going to fight. On a deeper level, though, readers are privy to the apprehension felt by one young soldier. His fears and anxieties are presented not as blatant statements but by hints and indirections. Like most of the crowd—more inclined to shout "bullies'" than "benedictions" (line 26)—he puts up a brave front at a time of great peril and uncertainty.

QUESTION 3, BASED ON SIDNEY SMITH'S REVIEW OF *THE BOOK OF FALLACIES*

If you were to agree with Smith, your essay might begin with a rationale such as this: Young people need to make decisions on their own. Self-reliance is a sign of maturity. Therefore, on the verge of adulthood, the young will disregard the wisdom of the past. Beyond that, you could probably name several situations and endeavors in which young people are likely to be better informed than their elders. When it comes to modern electronic and digital technology, for instance, it's a truism that the young folks are far more savvy than the geezers. The same principle applies to such everyday activities as going to bed and getting up in the morning. Traditional wisdom says, "Early to bed and early to rise . . .," but modern youth knows better. They have the advantage of research into enzymes and body chemistry showing that most teenagers, biologically, tend to function more efficiently later in the day than early in the morning. No doubt you can think of additional ways in which to support Smith's surprising assertion that our ancestors are "the young people, and have the least experience."

If, on the other hand, you choose to poke holes in Smith's argument, you might cite several examples of how old-time wisdom and experience are valid today. You might argue, for instance, that governmental decisions and policies must be based on historical evidence. From World War II, the world learned, if nothing else, to be far more alert to the threats of genocide. From Iran and Afghanistan, America has presumably learned to be wary of political and military quagmires. In crisis after crisis, the wisdom of America's founders has proved to be a solid foundation for decision-making. In addition, ancient religious texts thousands of years old still serve as moral compasses for individuals as well as groups. Back in the 17th century, Rouchefoucauld said, "Nothing is given so profusely as advice," and, "The true way to be deceived is to think oneself more clever than others"—just two pieces of wisdom among countless others that are as apt today as they were generations ago.

Or let your essay take the middle ground between these two extremes. A strong case could be made that the past can serve as a beacon in some areas of life, but is hopelessly irrelevant in others. Certainly our ancestors can teach us little about treating cancer or AIDS. Their knowledge of diseases, health, nutrition, and genetics now seems quaint. Their understanding of the physical world was relatively primitive. But, when it comes to common sense about character and human relations, getting and spending money, morals and values, and so on, the wisdom of "old times" may still be instructive and useful.

SCORING SECTION II ESSAYS

Before scoring your essays, carefully review "How Essays Are Scored" (pages 36–37), a guide meant to help you judge as objectively as possible the quality of your writing.

Use the criteria listed below to evaluate each of your essays. Because it's tough to be totally impartial about your own writing, you may get a more accurate score by asking a well-informed friend, teacher, or counselor to rate your essays for you.

On the following Rating Chart, enter a number (from 1 to 6) that you think represents your level of performance in each category (A–F).

CATEGORY A: OVERALL PURPOSE/MAIN IDEA
6   extremely well-defined and insightful
5   clearly defined and generally insightful
4   mostly clear
3   somewhat clear but occasionally confusing
2   generally unclear and confusing
1   mostly incomprehensible or simplistic

CATEGORY B: HANDLING OF THE PROMPT
6   self-evident or extremely clear throughout
5   mostly clear
4   somewhat clear
3   somewhat unclear
2   generally unclear or ambiguous
1   confusing or nonexistent

CATEGORY C: ORGANIZATION AND DEVELOPMENT
6   insightfully organized; fully developed with excellent supporting evidence
5   reasonably well organized; developed with appropriate supporting material
4   appropriately organized; developed with some relevant material
3   inconsistent organization; weak development
2   poorly organized; little or no development
1   no discernible organization or development

CATEGORY D: SENTENCE STRUCTURE
6   varied and engaging
5   sufficiently varied to create interest
4   some variety
3   little variety; minor sentence errors
2   frequent sentence errors that interfere with meaning
1   serious sentence errors that obscure meaning

CATEGORY E: USE OF LANGUAGE
6   precise and effective word choice
5   competent word choice
4   conventional word choice; mostly correct
3   some errors in diction or idiom
2   frequent lapses in diction or idiom
1   meaning obscured by word choice

CATEGORY F: GRAMMAR AND USAGE
6   error-free or virtually error-free
5   occasional minor errors
4   basically correct but with several minor errors
3   meaning somewhat obscured by errors
2   meaning frequently obscured by errors
1   meaning blocked by several major errors

RATING CHART

Rate your essay	Essay 1	Essay 2	Essay 3
Overall Purpose/Main Idea			
Handling of the Prompt			
Organization and Development			
Sentence Structure			
Use of Language			
Grammar and Usage			
Composite Scores (sum of each column)			

By using the following scale, in which composite scores are converted to the nine-point AP rating scale, you may determine the final score for each essay:

Composite Score	AP Essay Score
33–36	9
29–32	8
25–28	7
21–24	6
18–20	5
15–17	4
10–14	3
7–9	2
6 or below	1

AP Essay Scores Essay 1 _____ Essay 2 _____ Essay 3 _____

TEST SCORE WORKSHEET

The scores you have earned on the multiple-choice and essay sections of the exam may now be converted to the AP five-point scale by performing the following calculations:

I. Determine Your Score for Section I (Multiple-Choice)

(STEP A) Number of correct answers _____

(STEP B) Multiply the figure in Step A by 1.2272 to find your Multiple-Choice Score _____. (Do not round.)

II. Determine Your Score for Section II (Essays)

(STEP A) Enter your score for Essay 1 (out of 9) _____

(STEP B) Enter your score for Essay 2 (out of 9) _____

(STEP C) Enter your score for Essay 3 (out of 9) _____

(STEP D) Add the figures in Steps A, B, and C _____

(STEP E) Multiply the figure in Step D by 3.0556 _____ (Do not round.) This is your Essay Score.

III. Determine Your Total Score

Add the scores for I and II to find your composite score _____. (Round to nearest whole number.)

To convert your composite score to the AP five-point scale, use the chart below. The range of scores only approximates what you would earn on the actual test because the exact figures may vary from test to test. Be aware, therefore, that your score on this test, as well as on other tests in this book, may differ slightly from your score on an actual AP exam.

Composite Score	AP Grade
111–150	5
97–110	4
80–96	3
53–79	2
0–52	1

AP essays are ordinarily judged in relation to other essays written on the same topic at the same time. Therefore, the scores you assign yourself for these essays may not be the same as the scores you would earn on an actual exam.

ANSWER SHEET
Practice Test D

Multiple-Choice Questions

Time—1 hour

1. Ⓐ Ⓑ Ⓒ Ⓓ Ⓔ 16. Ⓐ Ⓑ Ⓒ Ⓓ Ⓔ 31. Ⓐ Ⓑ Ⓒ Ⓓ Ⓔ 46. Ⓐ Ⓑ Ⓒ Ⓓ Ⓔ
2. Ⓐ Ⓑ Ⓒ Ⓓ Ⓔ 17. Ⓐ Ⓑ Ⓒ Ⓓ Ⓔ 32. Ⓐ Ⓑ Ⓒ Ⓓ Ⓔ 47. Ⓐ Ⓑ Ⓒ Ⓓ Ⓔ
3. Ⓐ Ⓑ Ⓒ Ⓓ Ⓔ 18. Ⓐ Ⓑ Ⓒ Ⓓ Ⓔ 33. Ⓐ Ⓑ Ⓒ Ⓓ Ⓔ 48. Ⓐ Ⓑ Ⓒ Ⓓ Ⓔ
4. Ⓐ Ⓑ Ⓒ Ⓓ Ⓔ 19. Ⓐ Ⓑ Ⓒ Ⓓ Ⓔ 34. Ⓐ Ⓑ Ⓒ Ⓓ Ⓔ 49. Ⓐ Ⓑ Ⓒ Ⓓ Ⓔ
5. Ⓐ Ⓑ Ⓒ Ⓓ Ⓔ 20. Ⓐ Ⓑ Ⓒ Ⓓ Ⓔ 35. Ⓐ Ⓑ Ⓒ Ⓓ Ⓔ 50. Ⓐ Ⓑ Ⓒ Ⓓ Ⓔ
6. Ⓐ Ⓑ Ⓒ Ⓓ Ⓔ 21. Ⓐ Ⓑ Ⓒ Ⓓ Ⓔ 36. Ⓐ Ⓑ Ⓒ Ⓓ Ⓔ 51. Ⓐ Ⓑ Ⓒ Ⓓ Ⓔ
7. Ⓐ Ⓑ Ⓒ Ⓓ Ⓔ 22. Ⓐ Ⓑ Ⓒ Ⓓ Ⓔ 37. Ⓐ Ⓑ Ⓒ Ⓓ Ⓔ 52. Ⓐ Ⓑ Ⓒ Ⓓ Ⓔ
8. Ⓐ Ⓑ Ⓒ Ⓓ Ⓔ 23. Ⓐ Ⓑ Ⓒ Ⓓ Ⓔ 38. Ⓐ Ⓑ Ⓒ Ⓓ Ⓔ
9. Ⓐ Ⓑ Ⓒ Ⓓ Ⓔ 24. Ⓐ Ⓑ Ⓒ Ⓓ Ⓔ 39. Ⓐ Ⓑ Ⓒ Ⓓ Ⓔ
10. Ⓐ Ⓑ Ⓒ Ⓓ Ⓔ 25. Ⓐ Ⓑ Ⓒ Ⓓ Ⓔ 40. Ⓐ Ⓑ Ⓒ Ⓓ Ⓔ
11. Ⓐ Ⓑ Ⓒ Ⓓ Ⓔ 26. Ⓐ Ⓑ Ⓒ Ⓓ Ⓔ 41. Ⓐ Ⓑ Ⓒ Ⓓ Ⓔ
12. Ⓐ Ⓑ Ⓒ Ⓓ Ⓔ 27. Ⓐ Ⓑ Ⓒ Ⓓ Ⓔ 42. Ⓐ Ⓑ Ⓒ Ⓓ Ⓔ
13. Ⓐ Ⓑ Ⓒ Ⓓ Ⓔ 28. Ⓐ Ⓑ Ⓒ Ⓓ Ⓔ 43. Ⓐ Ⓑ Ⓒ Ⓓ Ⓔ
14. Ⓐ Ⓑ Ⓒ Ⓓ Ⓔ 29. Ⓐ Ⓑ Ⓒ Ⓓ Ⓔ 44. Ⓐ Ⓑ Ⓒ Ⓓ Ⓔ
15. Ⓐ Ⓑ Ⓒ Ⓓ Ⓔ 30. Ⓐ Ⓑ Ⓒ Ⓓ Ⓔ 45. Ⓐ Ⓑ Ⓒ Ⓓ Ⓔ

Practice Test D

SECTION I

TIME: 1 HOUR

Directions: *Questions 1–14.* Carefully read the following passage and answer the accompanying questions.

The passage below is an excerpt from the autobiography of a 19th-century American literary figure.

PASSAGE 1

One day in June, 1854, young Adams walked for the last time down the steps of Mr. Dixwell's school in Boylston Place, and felt no sensation but one of unqualified joy that this experience was ended. Never before or afterwards in his life did he close
Line a period so long as four years without some sensation of loss—some sentiment of
(5) habit—but school was what in after life he commonly heard his friends denounce as an intolerable bore. He was born too old for it. The same thing could be said of most New England boys. Mentally they were never boys. Their education as men should have begun at ten years old. They were fully five years more mature than the English or European boy for whom schools were made. For the purposes of future advance-
(10) ment, as afterwards appeared, these first six years of a possible education were wasted in doing imperfectly what might have been done perfectly in one, and in any case would have had small value. The next regular step was Harvard College. He was more than glad to go. For generation after generation, Adamses and Brookses and Boylstons and Gorhams had gone to Harvard College, and although none of them,
(15) as far as known, had ever done any good there, or thought himself the better for it, custom, social ties, convenience, and above all, economy, kept each generation in the track. Any other education would have required a serious effort, but no one took Harvard College seriously. All went there because their friends went there, and the College was their ideal of social self-respect.
(20) Harvard College, as far as it educated at all, was a mild and liberal school, which sent young men into the world with all they needed to make respectable citizens, and something of what they wanted to make useful ones. Leaders of men it never tried to make. Its ideas were altogether different. The Unitarian clergy had given to the College a character of moderation, balance, judgment, restraint, what the French
(25) called *mesure*; excellent traits, which the College attained with singular success, so

that its graduates could commonly be recognized by the stamp, but such a type of character rarely lent itself to autobiography. In effect, the school created a type but not a will. Four years of Harvard College, if successful, resulted in an autobiographical blank, a mind on which only a water-mark had been stamped.

(30)   The stamp, as such things went, was a good one. The chief wonder of education is that it does not ruin everybody concerned with it, teachers and taught. Sometimes in after life, Adams debated whether in fact it had not ruined him and most of his companions, but, disappointment apart, Harvard College was probably less hurtful than any other University then in existence. It taught little, and that little ill, but it
(35)   left the mind open, free from bias, ignorant of facts, but docile. The graduate had few strong prejudices. He knew little, but his mind remained supple, ready to receive knowledge.

What caused the boy most disappointment was the little he got from his mates. Speaking exactly, he got less than nothing, a result common enough in education.
(40)   Yet the College Catalogue for the years 1854–1861 shows a list of names rather distinguished in their time. Alexander Agassiz and Phillips Brooks led it. H. H. Richardson and O. W. Holmes helped to close it. As a rule the most promising of all die early, and never get their names into a Dictionary of Contemporaries which seems to be the only popular standard of success. Many died in the war. Adams knew them all, more
(45)   or less; he felt as much regard, and quite as much respect for them then, as he did after they won great names and were objects of a vastly wider respect; but, as help toward education, he got nothing whatever from them or they from him until long after they had left College. Possibly the fault was his, but one would like to know how many others shared it. Accident counts for as much in companionship as in mar-
(50)   riage. Life offers perhaps only a score of possible companions, and it is mere chance whether they meet as early as school or college, but it is more than a chance that boys brought up together under like conditions have nothing to give each other.

1. Taken as a whole, the passage is best described as

    (A) a series of anecdotes about college life in the past.
    (B) a summary of academic customs during a particular era.
    (C) an assessment of a young man's educational experiences.
    (D) an indictment of an obsolete educational system.
    (E) a description of a historical period.

2. In line 3, the phrase "this experience" refers to Adams'

    (A) lack of sensation.
    (B) attendance at Mr. Dixwell's school.
    (C) walk down the steps.
    (D) graduation after four years.
    (E) boredom.

3. Which of the following best describes the rhetorical effect of the sentence in line 6 ("He was born too old for it")?

   (A) It succinctly summarizes all the ideas contained in the passage thus far.
   (B) It contrasts starkly to the structure and diction of the preceding sentence.
   (C) It suggests the simpleminded mentality of most New England boys.
   (D) It completely reverses the the tone of the passage.
   (E) It serves as a dramatic climax to the story of Adams' education.

4. The idea expressed in "He was born too old for it" (line 6) is reinforced by all of the following phrases EXCEPT

   (A) "some sentiment of habit" (lines 4–5).
   (B) "an intolerable bore" (line 6).
   (C) "never boys" (line 7).
   (D) "education as men should have begun at ten" (lines 7–8).
   (E) "fully five years more mature" (line 8).

5. The speaker mentions the "Adamses and Brookses and Boylstons and Gorhams" (lines 13–14) as examples of which of the following?

   I. Families that helped Harvard maintain its reputation as an exclusive finishing school for young men
   II. New England families that had traditionally sent their sons to Harvard
   III. Students whose names assured them of preferential treatment in Harvard's admission process

   (A) I only
   (B) I and II only
   (C) II and III only
   (D) III only
   (E) I, II, and III

6. The two sentences beginning with "Harvard College" and ending with "tried to make" (lines 20–23), employ all of the following EXCEPT

   (A) a compound subject.
   (B) predicate adjectives.
   (C) subordinate clause.
   (D) parallel syntax.
   (E) inverted sentence structure.

7. The effects of a Harvard education discussed in lines 20–22 are described elsewhere in the passage as which of the following?

   (A) "above all, economy" (line 16)
   (B) "serious effort" (line 17)
   (C) "less hurtful" (line 33)
   (D) "ready to receive knowledge" (lines 36–37)
   (E) "less than nothing" (line 39)

8. In context, the word "stamp" (line 26) is best interpreted to mean

    (A) a seal of approval.

    (B) a credential.

    (C) habit.

    (D) harmony.

    (E) a uniform image.

9. "[A] mind on which only a water-mark had been stamped" (line 29) is best understood as a metaphor for

    (A) an inhibited imagination.

    (B) an imperceptible amount of learning.

    (C) a lack of basic common sense.

    (D) a set of attitudes and values.

    (E) misinformation and confusion.

10. Which of the following best describes the tone of the sentence in lines 30–31 ("The chief . . . and taught")?

    (A) Cynical

    (B) Combative

    (C) Ironic

    (D) Resigned and contemplative

    (E) Agitated and moralistic

11. The rhetorical feature most in evidence in lines 34–36 is best described as

    (A) oxymoron.

    (B) pun.

    (C) antithesis.

    (D) hyperbole.

    (E) allusion.

12. The function of the sentences "Yet the College Catalogue . . . close it" (lines 40–42) is primarily to

    (A) qualify a statement made in the previous paragraph.

    (B) spell out the paragraph's main idea.

    (C) offer an explanation for the idea expressed in the previous sentence.

    (D) deny the truth of the first two sentences in the paragraph.

    (E) provide evidence that contrasts with ideas stated in the previous sentences.

13. The speaker employs an analogy between companionship and marriage (lines 49–50) mainly to

    (A) foreshadow Adams' marital difficulties.

    (B) analyze Adams' problems with friends.

    (C) argue in favor of co-education.

    (D) reflect on the unpredictability of life.

    (E) discuss life's losses and gains.

14. The speaker in the passage can best be described as a person inclined to believe all of the following EXCEPT that

(A) a Harvard education in the mid-19th century left much to be desired.
(B) the maturity of boys from abroad tended to lag behind the maturity of boys from New England.
(C) to be a Harvard student was socially desirable and advantageous.
(D) Harvard graduates were virtually indistinguishable from one another.
(E) Harvard's administration and faculty ought to have been held accountable for the College's deficiencies.

Directions: *Questions 15–25.* Carefully read the following passage and answer the accompanying questions.

The passage below is from an essay written by an early 20th-century British poet.

PASSAGE 2

Play is not for every hour of the day, or for any hour taken at random. There is a tide in the affairs of children. Civilization is cruel in sending them to bed at the most stimulating time of dusk. Summer dusk, especially, is the frolic moment for children,
Line baffle them how you may. They may have been in a pottering mood all day, intent
(5) upon all kinds of close industries, breathing hard over choppings and poundings. But when late twilight comes, there comes also the punctual wildness. The children will run and pursue, and laugh for the mere movement—it does so jolt their spirits.

What remembrances does this imply of the hunt, what of the predatory dark? The kitten grows alert at the same hour, and hunts for moths and crickets in the grass. It
(10) comes like an imp, leaping on all fours. The children lie in ambush and fall upon one another in the mimicry of hunting. The sudden outbreak of action is complained of as a defiance and a rebellion. Their entertainers are tired, and the children are to go home. But, with more or less of life and fire, the children strike some blow for liberty. It may be the impotent revolt of the ineffectual child, or the stroke of the conqueror;
(15) but something, something is done for freedom under the early stars.

This is not the only time when the energy of children is in conflict with the weariness of men. But it is less tolerable that the energy of men should be at odds with the weariness of children, which happens at some time of their jaunts together, especially, alas! in the jaunts of the poor.

(20) Of games for the summer dusk when it rains, cards are most beloved by children. Three tiny girls were to be taught "Old Maid" to beguile the time. One of them, a nut-brown child of five, was persuading another to play. "Oh, come," she said, "and play with me at 'New Maid.'"

The time of falling asleep is a child's immemorial and incalculable hour. It is full
(25) of traditions, and beset by antique habits. The habit of prehistoric races has been cited as the only explanation of the fixity of some customs in mankind. But if the inquirers who appeal to that beginning remembered better their own infancy, they

would seek no further. See the habits in falling to sleep which have children in their thralldom. Try to overcome them in any child, and his own conviction of their high (30) antiquity weakens your hand.

Childhood is antiquity, and with the sense of time and the sense of mystery is connected for ever to the hearing of a lullaby. The French sleep-song is the most romantic. There is in it such a sound of history as must inspire any imaginative child, falling to sleep, with a sense of the incalculable; and the songs themselves are old. "Le Bon (35) Roi Dagobert" has been sung over French cradles since the legend was fresh. The nurse knows nothing more sleepy than the tune and the verse that she herself slept to when a child. The gaiety of the thirteenth century, in "Le Pont d'Avignon," is put mysteriously to sleep, away in the *tête à tête* of child and nurse, in a thousand little sequestered rooms at night. "Malbrook" would be comparatively modern, were not (40) all things that are sung to a drowsing child as distant as the day of Abraham.

If English children are not rocked to many such aged lullabies, some of them are put to sleep to strange cradle-songs. The affectionate races that are brought into subjection sing the primitive lullaby to the white child. Asiatic voices and African persuade him to sleep in the tropical night. His closing eyes are filled with alien (45) images.

15. The sentence "There is a tide in the affairs of children" (lines 1–2) functions chiefly as

   (A) the topic sentence of the first paragraph.
   (B) an expression of the main idea of the passage.
   (C) a fact discussed in more detail later in the passage.
   (D) an analogy used to make an abstraction concrete.
   (E) an introduction to a paradox to be discussed later.

16. By using the word "tide" (line 2), the speaker emphasizes that

   (A) children are more changeable than adults.
   (B) consistency is difficult for children to learn.
   (C) some children follow parental rules; others don't.
   (D) children can be taught that there is a time and place for everything.
   (E) children's energy regularly comes and goes.

17. As used in line 4 "baffle" most nearly means

   (A) constrain.
   (B) confuse.
   (C) puzzle.
   (D) instruct.
   (E) schedule.

18. In lines 8–12, the speaker associates the wildness she observes in children at summer dusk with

(A) ancient survival techniques.
(B) a primitive impulse to kill.
(C) the instinctual behavior of predators.
(D) aggressive intimidation.
(E) extinct mammals.

19. The speaker's observation in the sentences, "But, with more or less . . . early stars" (lines 13–15) can best be described as an example of an

(A) expert's advice to parents.
(B) objective analysis of disobedient children.
(C) interpretation of children's behavior.
(D) appeal to authority.
(E) objection to excessively strict parental discipline.

20. Which of the following best describes a rhetorical shift that occurs in lines 24–30?

(A) The speaker's diction becomes less argumentative and contentious.
(B) The focus of the passage turns from children in general to a single child.
(C) The tone shifts from assertive to conjectural.
(D) The speaker adopts a highly poetic style of writing.
(E) The language is more concrete than in previous paragraphs.

21. In line 27, the pronoun "their" refers to

(A) "prehistoric races" (line 25).
(B) "customs" (line 26).
(C) "inquirers" (line 27).
(D) "habits" (line 28).
(E) "children" (line 28).

22. "Childhood is antiquity" (line 29) is an assertion supported by all of the following phrases from the passage EXCEPT

(A) "remembrances . . . of the hunt" (line 8).
(B) "the weariness of men" (16–17).
(C) "habit of prehistoric races" (line 25).
(D) "customs in mankind" (line 26).
(E) "the sense of time and . . . mystery" (line 31).

23. The speaker's central rhetorical strategy in the seventh paragraph (lines 31–40) can best be described as

(A) introducing a series of generalizations that will be supported later.
(B) citing specific examples to illustrate an abstract concept.
(C) comparing and contrasting a pair of suppositions.
(D) challenging a controversial thesis proposed earlier.
(E) anticipating objections raised by ideas presented in lines 32–34.

24. Which of the following phrases does the speaker use to illustrate the "mystery" (line 31) associated with lullabies?

(A) "The French sleep-song" (line 32)
(B) "the most romantic" (lines 32–33)
(C) "a sound of history" (line 33)
(D) "a sense of the incalculable" (line 34)
(E) "the tune and the verse" (line 36)

25. The author's tone in the passage as a whole is best described as

(A) contemplative and tender.
(B) casual and meandering.
(C) strict and dogmatic.
(D) scientific and aggressive.
(E) enthusiastic and extravagant.

Directions: *Questions 26–38.* Carefully read the following passage and answer the accompanying questions.

The passage below is from a essay written by a well-known novelist of the late 19th and early 20th centuries.

PASSAGE 3

There is a certain evening that I count as virtually a first impression— the end of a wet, black Sunday, twenty years ago, about the first of March. There had been an earlier vision, but it had turned gray, like faded ink, and the occasion I speak of was
Line a fresh beginning. No doubt I had a mystic prescience of how fond of the murky
(5) Babylon I was one day to become; certain it is that as I look back I find every small circumstance of those hours of approach and arrival still as vivid as if the solemnity of an opening era had breathed upon it. The sense of approach was already almost intolerably strong at Liverpool, where, I remember, the perception of the English character of everything was as acute as a surprise, though it could only be a
(10) surprise without a shock. It was expectation exquisitely gratified, superabundantly confirmed. There was a kind of wonder indeed that England should be as English as, for my entertainment, she took the trouble to be; but the wonder would have been greater, and all the pleasure absent, if the sensation had not been violent. It seems to sit there again like a visiting presence, as it sat opposite me at breakfast at a small
(15) table in a window of the old coffee-room of the Adelphi Hotel—the unextended (as it then was), the unimproved, the unblushingly local Adelphi. Liverpool is not a romantic city, but that smoky Saturday returns to me as a supreme success, measured by its association with the kind of emotion in the hope of which, for the most part, we betake ourselves to far countries.
(20) It assumed this character at an early hour—or rather indeed twenty-four hours before—with the sight, as one looked across the wintry ocean, of the strange, dark, lonely freshness of the coast of Ireland. Better still, before we could come up to the

city, were the black steamers knocking about in the yellow Mersey, under a sky so low that they seemed to touch it with their funnels, and in the thickest, windiest

(25) light. Spring was already in the air, in the town; there was no rain, but there was still less sun—one wondered what had become, on this side of the world, of the big white splotch in the heavens; and the gray mildness, shading away into black at every pretext, appeared in itself a promise. This was how it hung about me, between the window and the fire, in the coffee-room of the hotel—late in the morning for breakfast,

(30) as we had been long in disembarking. The other passengers had dispersed, knowingly catching trains for London (we had only been a handful); I had the place to myself, and I felt as if I had an exclusive property in the impression. I prolonged it, I sacrificed to it, and it is perfectly recoverable now, with the very taste of the national muffin, the creak of the waiter's shoes as he came and went (could anything be so

(35) English as his intensely professional back? it revealed a country of tradition), and the rustle of the newspaper I was too excited to read.

I continued to sacrifice for the rest of the day; it didn't seem to me a sentient[1] thing, as yet, to inquire into the means of getting away. My curiosity must indeed have languished, for I found myself on the morrow in the slowest of Sunday trains,

(40) pottering up to London with an interruptedness which might have been tedious without the conversation of an old gentleman who shared the carriage with me and to whom my alien as well as comparatively youthful character had betrayed itself. He instructed me as to the sights of London, and impressed upon me that nothing was more worthy of my attention than the great cathedral of St. Paul. "Have you

(45) seen St. Peter's in Rome? St. Peter's is more highly embellished, you know; but you may depend upon it that St. Paul's is the better building of the two." The impression I began with speaking of was, strictly, that of the drive from Euston, after dark, to Morely's Hotel in Trafalgar Square. It was not lovely—it was in fact rather horrible; but as I move again through dusky tortuous miles, in the greasy four-wheeler to

(50) which my luggage had compelled me to commit myself, I recognize the first step in an initiation of which the subsequent stages were to abound in pleasant things.

----

[1]sentient: aware; conscious; capable of making fine distinctions

26. The speaker in the passage focuses primarily on

(A) changes that have occurred since he arrived in London.
(B) a recollection of his state of mind upon arriving in England.
(C) memorable qualities that characterize England and the English people.
(D) his affection for all things English.
(E) the significance of his return to his ancestral homeland.

27. In lines 4–5, the phrase "murky Babylon" can best be described as

(A) an analogical comparison.
(B) an example of verbal irony.
(C) an elliptical construction.
(D) a metaphorical allusion.
(E) anecdotal development.

28. In paragraphs 1 and 2 (lines 1–36), the speaker's depiction of the setting emphasizes its

    (A) dark gloominess.
    (B) visual surprises.
    (C) distant views.
    (D) variety of color.
    (E) bustling activity.

29. In the first paragraph, all of the following contribute to the speaker's anticipation of a "fresh beginning" (line 4) EXCEPT

    (A) "the end of a wet, black Sunday" (lines 1–2).
    (B) "a mystic prescience" (line 4).
    (C) "the sense of approach" (line 7).
    (D) that "everything was as acute as a surprise" (line 9).
    (E) "a visiting presence" (line 14).

30. The sentence "It was expectation . . . confirmed" (lines 10–11) functions in all the following ways EXCEPT

    (A) it characterizes one of the speaker's reactions to setting foot on English soil.
    (B) it suggests that the speaker was well informed about England.
    (C) it helps to clarify the precise meaning of "surprise without a shock" in the preceding sentence.
    (D) it reveals still another dimension of the speaker's intense feelings.
    (E) it confirms that the speaker had lost control of his emotions.

31. To the speaker, the "Adelphi Hotel" (line 15) is associated with

    (A) the dreariness of traveling alone.
    (B) a fondly remembered feeling.
    (C) a shattered expectation.
    (D) a welcome relief.
    (E) a temporary bout with depression.

32. The "kind of emotion" mentioned in line 18 refers to

    (A) nostalgia.
    (B) "surprise without a shock" (line 10).
    (C) self-satisfaction.
    (D) gratification over having successfully achieved a long-sought goal.
    (E) a sense of wonder.

33. In line 20, the pronoun "It" refers to

    (A) "a first impression" (line 1).
    (B) "an earlier vision" (lines 2–3).
    (C) "the English character" (lines 8–9).
    (D) "a kind of wonder" (line 11).
    (E) "the coast of Ireland" (line 22).

34. The second paragraph (lines 20–36) derives its unity primarily through

    (A) an abundant use of sensual imagery.
    (B) using details to support a generalization.
    (C) a comparison of the land and the sea.
    (D) its emphasis on the weather.
    (E) contrasting the speaker's impressions of the night and the day.

35. In context, the phrase "sacrificed to it" (line 33) is best understood to mean that the speaker

    (A) abandoned his fellow passengers.
    (B) gave up his customary reading of the daily paper.
    (C) found himself being shunned by other passengers.
    (D) had given up a great deal in order to travel to England.
    (E) decided to linger in Liverpool before continuing his journey.

36. Which of the following best describes the speaker's tone in the parenthetical remark "could anything . . . of tradition" (lines 34–35)?

    (A) Curious and questioning
    (B) Slightly smug and worldly-wise
    (C) Uncertain and troubled
    (D) Puzzled and wary
    (E) Uncomfortable and insulting

37. The rhetorical function of the last sentence of the passage (lines 48–51) is to

    (A) bring the passage to an unexpected climax.
    (B) present a realistic picture of the speakers's emotional state.
    (C) unify the passage by reiterating its main theme.
    (D) reveal an inconsistency in the character of the speaker.
    (E) strengthen the coherence of the passage by alluding to the "earlier vision" (line 3).

38. The speaker in the passage can best be described as a person who

    (A) habitually boasts of his past successes.
    (B) nostalgically recalls earlier days.
    (C) tends to test the validity of his conjectures.
    (D) writes in order to recreate the pathos of a misspent youth.
    (E) promotes the advantages of traveling alone.

The passage below is an excerpt from a book written during the 20th century.

PASSAGE 4

In Massillon, Brown's rules had served as a sort of social welfare, teaching high-school boys to develop self-control and discipline. In Cleveland, his dress codes, his curfews, and his strict study regimen with playbooks, constant lectures, and testing, served a different postwar ethic: it enhanced an image, the image of a well-run organization. His model turned out to be less a throwback to wartime army discipline than a look forward to a new style of corporate control.

"We want you to reflect a special image in pro football," Brown told his players in a speech at the opening of each season.[1] They were not to smoke or drink *in public*; they were to wear jackets and ties, slacks and polished shoes *in public*; they were to display a proper "decorum" and not curse *in public*; if they so much as lounged on the ground during a game, they were fined; above all, they were never to behave in a manner that would make the team look "low class"—in other words, that would remind anybody of the league's origins in the mills and mines.

Brown demonstrated the seriousness of all this at the first opportunity: two days before the new league's first title game, he fired the team's captain, Jim Daniell, after the tackle had a few drinks and got into a minor spat with some local policemen. "I'll take my players high class, cold, deadly," Brown repeated in his seasonal speech. "We don't want any butchers on this team. No T-shirts in the dining hall. Don't eat with your elbows on the table and eat quietly." He told *Time* magazine in 1947, "There's no place on my team for Big Butch who talks hard and drinks hard. I like a lean and hungry look." When a young college lineman whom Brown was planning to recruit arrived at the team's training camp unshaven and "dressed like a laborer," Brown took one look, told him that he had been summoned mistakenly, and dismissed him at once.[2]

"Class always shows," Brown maintained, and what he wanted his men to show was the face of the new, white-collar bourgeoisie. "I didn't want them to look like the stereotype of the old-time pros," Brown said. "College players had a good reputation, but the public perception of the professional football player back then was of a big, dumb guy with a potbelly and a cheap cigar. That kind of person disgusted me, and I never wanted anyone associating our players with that image."[3] What Brown wanted was a managerial look: polished and uniform, college-educated but not effetely so, aspiring but conformist. What he wanted was a team represented by organization men. It was the sort of look he himself exemplified. With his contained demeanor, trim frame, and bland corporate suits, he looked like the archetypal sub-

---

[1] *Brown*, PB, p. 148.
[2] *Ibid.*, *pp.16, 148*; *Clary*, Cleveland Browns, *p. 18*; "Football: Brown Ohio," Newsweek, *Dec. 30, 1946*, *p. 66*; *Byrne, et al.*, The Cleveland Browns, *p. 17*; *Maule*, "A Man for This Season," *p. 32*; "Praying Professionals," Time, *Oct. 27, 1947, pp. 55–56.*
[3] *Clary*, The Gamesmakers, *p. 32*; *Clary*, Cleveland Browns, *p. 19*; *Brown*, PB, *p. 15.*

(35) urban husband about to board the commuter train to his desk job in the city. While Brown was insistent on his men flying first class and staying in fine hotels, it turned out this was not so much for their sakes as for the public profile of the team. He was intent on turning pro football into a sort of respectable middle class occupation that fit with the new white-collar bureaucracies and the rising corporate management
(40) ethic of postwar America.

39. Which of the following best states the subject of this passage?

    (A) Professional football at the crossroads
    (B) The role of a football coach
    (C) A football coach's vision of his team
    (D) The transformation of professional football teams
    (E) Turning college players into professionals

40. Which of the following rhetorical strategies does the author use in paragraph 1 of the passage?

    I. Parallel syntax
    II. Repetition of sentence structure
    III. Antithesis

    (A) I only
    (B) II only
    (C) I and II only
    (D) II and III only
    (E) I, II, and III

41. Which of the following best describes the rhetorical function of the second sentence (lines 2–5) of the passage?

    (A) It amends the tone of the first sentence.
    (B) It puts an idea expressed at the start of the passage into different words.
    (C) It presents a specific example in support of the preceding generalization.
    (D) It states the main idea of the passage.
    (E) It analyzes the author's purpose.

42. Which of the following phrases does the author use to reiterate the notion of a "different postwar ethic" (line 4)?

    (A) "social welfare" (line 1)
    (B) "self-control" (line 2)
    (C) "discipline" (line 2)
    (D) "playbooks" (line 3)
    (E) "image of a well-run organization" (lines 4–5)

43. In lines 8–10 of the passage, the author repeatedly uses "in public" in order to emphasize Brown's

(A) concerns about good manners.
(B) worries about the fans' impression of his players.
(C) uncontrollable paranoia.
(D) all-encompassing love of the game.
(E) concern for the physical and mental well-being of his team.

44. In line 12, "low class" implies all of the following EXCEPT

(A) a family living in poverty.
(B) a lack of breeding.
(C) a blue-collar background.
(D) coarse manners.
(E) the absence of self-respect.

45. In context, the expression "a lean and hungry look" (line 21) is best interpreted as having which of the following meanings?

(A) Unobtrusive and civilized
(B) Determined to succeed
(C) Starved for affection
(D) Versatile and adaptable
(E) Physically and emotionally well-balanced

46. Footnote 2 (line 24) gives readers all of the following information EXCEPT

(A) the incident of the young college lineman was widely reported.
(B) the words "dressed like a laborer" were quoted by Clary and Byrne.
(C) Brown discusses the dismissal of the young college lineman early in his book and then again later in the book.
(D) *The Cleveland Browns* was written by more than one author.
(E) the authors of articles published in *Newsweek* and *Time* received no bylines.

47. The author's observation that Brown wanted his players to show "the face of the new, white-collar bourgeoisie" (line 26) is best described as an example of

(A) poetic license.
(B) the author's explanation of Brown's values.
(C) the use of sarcasm.
(D) Brown's inflated way of speaking.
(E) the author's dismissal of a false claim.

48. Which of the following is being referred to by the abstract term "bourgeoisie" (line 26)?

(A) "dressed like a laborer" (lines 22–23)
(B) "stereotypes of the old-time pros" (line 27)
(C) "good reputation" (lines 27–28)
(D) "big, dumb guy" (line 29)
(E) "organization men" (line 33)

49. Which of the following pieces of information can be inferred from footnote 3?

(A) All of the works listed in the footnote have been cited in earlier footnotes.
(B) Clary writes articles for sports publications.
(C) *The Gamesmakers* was published prior to both *Cleveland Browns* and *PB*.
(D) Brown, the author of *PB*, interviewed Brown, the coach, while doing research.
(E) Clary collaborated with other authors in writing *The Gamesmakers* and *The Cleveland Browns*.

50. The sentence structure and diction of lines 30–35 ("What Brown wanted . . . in the city") suggest that the author views herself primarily as

(A) an impartial observer of human behavior.
(B) an interpreter of words and actions.
(C) a suspicious commentator.
(D) a well-meaning but selfish friend.
(E) a flattering admirer of celebrities.

51. Taken all together, the footnotes suggest that

(A) sports historians depend more on books than on news magazines as sources of information.
(B) Ohio is the center for publishing books about football and other sports.
(C) most of the material in the passage is anecdotal.
(D) Brown's work was a fertile source for the author of the passage.
(E) the passage was written roughly in the middle of the 20th century.

52. The development of the last paragraph (lines 25–40) can best be described as

(A) a selection of details leading to a generalized summary.
(B) a series of examples arranged chronologically.
(C) a statement of opinion followed by supporting evidence.
(D) an accumulation of generalizations.
(E) the movement from theory to a factual conclusion.

SECTION II

Three Essay Questions

TIME: 2 HOURS AND 15 MINUTES

Write your essays on standard 8½" × 11" composition paper. At the exam you will be given a bound booklet containing 12 lined pages.

Essay Question 1

SUGGESTED TIME:
15 MINUTES FOR READING THE QUESTION AND SOURCES
40 MINUTES FOR WRITING AN ESSAY

Open the newspaper almost any day and you'll find stories about sports accidents: skiers killed in avalanches, skydivers whose parachutes didn't open, football players knocked unconscious, even high school cheerleaders breaking their limbs.

Health and safety experts often deplore the lack of effective rules governing equipment and participation in sports. They say that some sports are too dangerous and should either be banned or strictly regulated. Safe sports, many claim, will attract more participants and in the long run improve the overall health and well-being of the population. Opponents of stricter regulation argue that regulations will take the fun out of sports. They say that participation in sports is voluntary, and in a free society no authority has the right to limit the choices that people make.

Carefully read the following six sources, including the material that introduces each source. Then, in an essay that synthesizes at least three of the sources, take a position on the claim that sports should be more strictly regulated in order to make them safer.

Don't simply summarize the sources. Instead, weigh evidence from the sources to support and illustrate your position on the issue. You may paraphrase, review, and quote relevant material directly and indirectly from the sources. Be sure to indicate in your essay which sources you use. Refer to them as Source A, Source B, and so on, or by the key words in the parentheses below. In making your argument, you may, of course, also include any ideas of your own.

Source A (Tuomey)
Source B (The Associated Press)
Source C (Jones)
Source D (Pie graphs)
Source E (BBC Online)
Source F (*Irish Independent*)

Enda Tuomey, "Should Dangerous Sports Be Banned? Yes!" *Writefix.com.*

What follows is part of an essay written by an English teacher currently at a college in Abu Dhabi in the United Arab Emirates.

Some sports are nothing but an excuse for violence. Boxing is a perfect example. The last thing an increasingly violent world needs is more violence on our television. The sight of two men (or even women) bleeding, with faces ripped open, trying to obliterate each other is barbaric. Other sports, such as American football or rugby, are also barely concealed violence.

Some people argue that the players can choose to participate. However, this is not always the case. Many boxers, for example, come from disadvantaged backgrounds. They are lured by money or by social or peer pressure and then cannot escape. Even in richer social groups, schools force unwilling students to play aggressive team sports, claiming that playing will improve the students' character (or the school's reputation), but in fact increasing the risk of injury.

Even when people can choose, they sometimes need to be protected against themselves. Most people approve of governments' efforts to reduce smoking. In the same way, governments need to act if there are unacceptably high levels of injuries in sports such as football, diving, mountaineering, or motor-racing.

I accept that all sports involve challenge and risk. However, violence and aggression should not be permitted in the name of sport. Governments and individuals must act to limit brutality and violence so that children and adults can enjoy and benefit from sports.

The Associated Press, "Big Hits, Macho Players and Dangers of NFL," *Abilene Reporter-News* online.

The following is an excerpt from a feature story published in the e-edition of an online newspaper, TODAY, *in January 2009.*

In football, where big hits bring big celebrations, every player must deal silently with the thought that he is always just one play away from being strapped on a gurney and carted off the field.

"This is just football," said Arizona receiver Larry Fitzgerald. "This is a man's game, and I know that every time I go up for a pass there is a possibility that I could be knocked out, and I'm willing to take that risk because I love what I do, and you play for the love of the game."

The machismo is shared by fellow players and celebrated by their many fans. It's why Ben Roethlisberger can come back from a concussion in the last game of the regular season to start in the playoffs, and why Anquan Boldin needed only two weeks off after a vicious hit that required seven plates and over 40 screws to fix multiple fractures of his face. . . . Got to show you're tough. Got to earn that paycheck.

. . . Repeated hits to the head aren't just causing damage on the field. They may be killing former players. Researchers say they have found evidence of a condition called chronic traumatic encephalopathy in the brains of six former players who died at relatively young ages. The condition, which can bring on dementia in people in their 40s and 50s, is more commonly found in boxers who have taken too many blows to the head.

Lola Jones, "Banging on about High Diving and Extreme Sports Rules and Regulations," *www.extremesport4u.com*, April 24, 2009.

What follows is an excerpt from an online article published by a group that promotes so-called "extreme sports." The writer is also a skier, snow boarder, and kite surfer.

Lawmakers . . . have been pushing for laws regulating fate-tempting sports, which often involve inexperienced participants, but passing such laws, whether involving caving, canyoning, paragliding, ice climbing or bungee jumping, has proved difficult. . . .

The problem is people take up an extreme sport because it gives them a feeling of freedom—an escape from the nanny state we all live in. If everything became too regimented these people would be pushed toward activities that are even less controlled.

Anyway, what has happened to freedom of choice? I am not advocating that you go out there and do something so ludicrously stupid that the result is death. But, if you do an extreme sport, you are obviously aware of the risks. And having evaluated them and deciding to continue, that, *surely*, is your choice. And having made that decision, you are not likely to be the type of person to squeal if something goes wrong.

. . . For this very reason a chunk of society, in a last ditch attempt to have some control over their own lives, takes to extreme sports, where they learn the art and then make their own decisions. . . .

R. Dawn Comstock, et al. "Time Loss by Type of Exposure, High School Sports-Related Injury Surveillance Study, United States, 2012–2013 School Year.

The graphs below come from the Summary Report *based on a study of high school sports by the Center for Injury Research and Policy, Columbus, Ohio, 2014.*

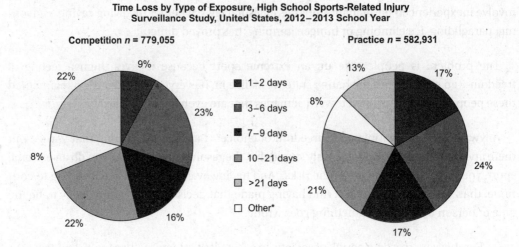

Time Loss by Type of Exposure, High School Sports-Related Injury Surveillance Study, United States, 2012–2013 School Year

Competition *n* = 779,055

Practice *n* = 582,931

- 1–2 days
- 3–6 days
- 7–9 days
- 10–21 days
- >21 days
- Other*

*Other category is made up of medical disqualification for season, medical disqualification for career, athlete chooses not to continue, and season ended before athlete returned to play.

British Broadcasting Co., "Are Sports Becoming Too Dangerous?" "Talking Points."

The text below consists of responses to the question "Are sports becoming too dangerous?" posed to readers of the BBC Online Network in 1999.

"The very fact that this question is being asked is symptomatic of a neurosis which has reached epidemic proportions. There is no such thing as a 'risk-free' life, and misguided (and often self-serving) attempts to create one will soon reach a point where demands for further regulation of our lives make any sort of life not worth living. The truth is that we are living in an age when there isn't much to worry about and, as a consequence, we seem to worry about everything."

David, United Kingdom

"The choice is individual. I think people are highly aware of the dangers that extreme sports have. What needs to be regulated is the preparation of the group leaders. The marketing of extreme sports is not properly regulated. Even elementary precautions are not taken."

Alessandro, Italy

"Certainly sports are becoming too dangerous. We see it when boxers like Mike Tyson bite the ears off opponents and then get back into the ring again. We see it when daredevils do stupid things. We see it when men and women do nutty things to prove themselves. We see it in our ignorance of the common sense of life."

Adam, USA

"I have no problem dying doing a sport I love. You have to get a kick from somewhere, and it's not going to be at your 9 to 5."

Dave, United Kingdom

"Smoking is regulated, airline travel is regulated, food and drugs are regulated. Then why not sports? Society suffers when people do idiotic things to hurt themselves. Pointless injuries often result in lifelong disabilities and divert medical resources from where they are truly needed. It may seem oppressive to place restrictions on sports, but foolhardy people need to be protected from themselves."

Kate, Scotland

"Is Boxing the Most Dangerous Sport?" posted on *www.independent.ie*, the website of the *Irish Independent*, December 7, 2007.

The following is an excerpt from a column published in the sports pages of an Irish newspaper.

Is boxing the most dangerous sport?

Not in terms of deaths. On that measure, horse racing, skydiving, mountaineering, and scuba diving are more dangerous. An assessment of their relative fatality rates conducted more than 20 years ago concluded that boxing caused 1.3 deaths per 100,000 participants compared with 11 for scuba diving, 51 for mountaineering, and more than 120 for skydiving and horse racing. But the British Medical Association (BMA) says it is not death but the chronic brain damage that is most worrying about boxing.

Why is the BMA not calling for other sports to be banned?

. . . The majority view is that if people want to take part in dangerous activities that is a matter for them in which the state should not interfere. The BMA argues that boxing is different because it is the only sport in which the purpose is to cause harm. In other sports, harm is an accidental side effect.

Why not introduce head guards or ban blows to the head?

. . . Boxing fans are drawn to major bouts for their naked display of aggression and by the prospect of a knockout—something that is very difficult to deliver with a blow to the body. Stricter rules or protective gear might save boxers' lives, but they would kill the sport.

Essay Question 2

SUGGESTED TIME: 40 MINUTES

(This question counts as one third of the total score for Section II.)

> **Directions:** The following sketch, "A Fair and Happy Milkmaid," written in 1615 and credited to two possible authors—Thomas Overbury and John Webster—pays tribute to a lovely young lass.
>
> Read the passage carefully. Then write an essay in which you analyze how the speaker uses rhetorical strategies and stylistic devices to convey his affection for the milkmaid.

A fair and happy milkmaid is a country wench, that is so far from making herself beautiful by art, that one look of hers is able to put all outsides face-physic out of countenance. She knows a fair look is but a dumb orator to commend virtue, there-
Line fore minds it not. All her excellencies stand in her so silently, as if they had stolen
(5) upon her without her knowledge. The lining of her apparel . . . is far better than the outsides of tissue: for though she be not arrayed in the spoil of the silk-worm, she is decked in innocency, a far better wearing. She doth not, with lying long abed, spoil both her complexion and conditions; nature hath taught her, too immoderate sleep is rust to the soul: she rises therefore with chanticleer, her dame's cock, and at night
(10) makes the lamb her curfew. In milking a cow, and straining the teats through her fingers, it seems that so sweet a milk-press makes the milk the whiter or sweeter; for never came almond glove or aromatic ointment on her palm to taint it. The golden ears of corn fall and kiss her feet when she reaps them, as if they wished to be bound and led prisoners by the same hand that felled them. Her breath is her own, which
(15) scents all the year long of June, like a new made haycock. She makes her hand hard with labour, and her heart soft with pity: and when winter evenings fall early (sitting at her merry wheel), she sings a defiance to the giddy wheel of fortune. She doth all things with so sweet a grace, it seems ignorance will not suffer her to do ill, being her mind is to do well. She bestows her year's wages at next fair; and in choosing her
(20) garments, counts no bravery in the world, like decency. The garden and the bee-hive are all her physic[1] and chirurgery,[2] and she lives the longer for it. She dares go alone, and unfold sheep in the night, and fears no manner of ill, because she means none: yet to say truth, she is never alone, for she is still accompanied with old songs, honest thoughts, and prayers, but short ones; yet they have their efficacy, in that they are not
(25) palled with ensuing idle cogitations. Lastly, her dreams are so chaste, that she dare tell them; only a Friday's dream[3] is all her superstition: that she conceals for fear of anger. Thus lives she, and all her care is that she may die in the spring time, to have store of flowers stuck upon her winding sheet.

---

[1] *physic: medicine, cures*
[2] *chirurgery: surgery*
[3] *Friday's dream: Christ's passion took place on a Friday; hence, Friday's dreams are ominous*

Essay Question 3

SUGGESTED TIME: 40 MINUTES

(This question counts as one third of the total score for Section II.)

> **Directions:** The following lines from Edwin Arlington Robinson's poem, "Richard Cory," written in 1897, describe what people often feel when they see others who apparently lead happier, richer, more satisfying lives than they do.

> *We thought that he was everything*
> *To make us wish that we were in his place.*

The kind of envy to which Robinson refers may serve as a strong motivating force for some people to improve their condition and place in life. On the other hand, envy may be frustrating, crippling and destructive because it compels people to strive in vain for unattainable goals.

After considering the meaning and implications of the quotation, plan and write an essay which supports, refutes, or qualifies the claim that envy is generally an unfavorable force in people's lives. Use evidence from your reading, studies, observations, or personal experience to develop your argument.

END OF PRACTICE TEST D

Answers to Multiple-Choice Questions

1.	C	16.	E	31.	B	46.	B
2.	B	17.	A	32.	E	47.	B
3.	B	18.	C	33.	D	48.	E
4.	A	19.	C	34.	A	49.	A
5.	B	20.	E	35.	E	50.	B
6.	A	21.	C	36.	B	51.	D
7.	D	22.	B	37.	C	52.	A
8.	E	23.	B	38.	B		
9.	D	24.	D	39.	C		
10.	A	25.	A	40.	E		
11.	C	26.	B	41.	D		
12.	E	27.	D	42.	E		
13.	D	28.	A	43.	B		
14.	E	29.	A	44.	A		
15.	B	30.	E	45.	A		

Summary of Answers in Section I (Multiple-Choice)

Number of correct answers _____

Use this information when you calculate your score for this exam. See page 381.

ANSWER EXPLANATIONS

Passage 1—An excerpt from Henry Adams, *The Education of Henry Adams*

1. **(C)** Through most of the passage, the speaker appraises the evolution of Adams' education from his last day at Mr. Dixwell's school through his graduation from Harvard and beyond. If you chose (D) as the answer, you may have overlooked the word "obsolete." Young Adams complained about the school because it was "an intolerable bore" (line 6), not because it was old-fashioned or out of date.

2. **(B)** The experience is young Adams' career at Mr. Dixwell's school. The boy is overjoyed that it has come to an end. Adams is pleased to be walking down the steps for the last time (C), but his joy springs from awareness that he's leaving Mr. Dixwell's school forever.

3. **(B)** Coming on the heels of two lengthy introductory sentences, this stark seven-word, seven-syllable sentence stands out startlingly and tersely.

4. **(A)** All the phrases except (A) in one way or other develop the idea that Adams was too mentally and emotionally advanced for Mr. Dixwell's school.

5. **(B)** The names are those of old and influential New England families that enjoyed long affiliations with Harvard and helped to build the stature of the college. It would be reasonable to assume that applicants bearing those names would be given preferential treatment, but the passage does not discuss the admissions process.

6. **(A)** Neither sentence contains a compound subject. The words "mild" and "liberal" are predicate adjectives; "which" (line 20) begins a subordinate clause; that portion of the sentence beginning with "with" (line 21) contains parallel syntax; and in the second sentence the predicate precedes the subject, indicating inverted word order. For an explanation of the grammatical terms, see pages 91–92 and 155–195.

7. **(D)** The phrase "something of what they wanted to make useful [citizens]" (line 22) suggests that a Harvard degree was not the end of a young man's education. Rather, it marked just the start. Once the graduate left Harvard, he was "ready to receive knowledge"—that is, he could now begin to acquire the knowledge needed to make something of himself.

8. **(E)** The speaker maintains that Harvard graduates project a certain uniform and easily identifiable image.

9. **(D)** Graduates of Harvard became recognizable types, inevitably endowed with a certain set of qualities, among them supple, but docile, minds and few strong prejudices (lines 34–36). Although the passage claims that Harvard's students suffered a shortage of learning, the college left an indelible mark on the character of each of them.

10. **(A)** The sentence, which is a broad statement about the deleterious effects of education, reveals a cynical state of mind. It reflects both the speaker's and Adams' attitude.

11. **(C)** The speaker uses a succession of antitheses: "taught little . . . but left the mind open," "free from bias . . . but docile," and "knew little . . . but . . . remained supple." For definitions of rhetorical features, see the Glossary, page 389.

12. **(E)** The conjunction "Yet" at the beginning of the sentence is a clue that the speaker is about to offer a contradiction or contrast to a preceding idea. Indeed, the sentence offers evidence meant to show that Adams' experience at Harvard could not have been caused by the absence of distinguished fellow students.

13. **(D)** The speaker uses the analogy to emphasize the effect of "accident" or "chance" in human life. In other words, no one can predict when one will meet one's lifelong friends or one's future spouse. It is a matter completely out of our hands.

14. **(E)** The speaker holds many opinions, but in the passage he makes no judgments about Harvard's administrators or teachers.

Passage 2—An excerpt from Alice Meynell, "Under the Early Stars"

15. **(B)** The passage consists largely of impressions of children's behavior at various times during the day. Like the tides, children's energies and interests come and go. Choice (A) is too narrow an answer. If you chose (C), note that the passage consists not of facts *per se*, but rather of the speaker's observations and interpretations of children's moods and actions.

16. **(E)** In its context, the word "tide" is used as a metaphor to suggest the ebb and flow of children's moods, energy, and inclinations to play. In the remainder of the paragraph the speaker discusses a problem caused by such changes.

17. **(A)** According to the speaker, children will frolic at dusk in the summertime regardless of what may be tried to constrain or control them.

18. **(C)** The wildness of children conjures thoughts of predatory creatures, including prehistoric man, although a kitten on the prowl more vividly manifests the primitive hunting instinct and is a more appropriate example in a passage about children's behavior.

19. **(C)** The speaker sees in children's activities at twilight a struggle for freedom. Others, of course, may interpret the children's wild behavior as something else.

20. **(E)** Of all the paragraphs in the passage, this one contains the least amount of interpretation and analysis of children and their lives. In addition, no other paragraph contains the sort of anecdote found here. Moreover, readers are urged indirectly to recall their own experiences as children rather than intellectualize about instincts inherited from prehistoric races.

21. **(C)** Grammatically, the pronoun refers directly to "inquirers."

22. **(B)** The statement "Childhood is antiquity" conveys the idea that children's impulses and behaviors have their roots in mankind's early ancestry. All answers but (B) allude to characteristics of our ancient forebears.

23. **(B)** The paragraph's main idea is that lullabies have their origins in antiquity and are imbued with mystery and a sense of timelessness. To support that assertion, the speaker comments on three popular lullabies.

24. **(D)** The phrase implies something unknowable, something mysterious and puzzling.

25. **(A)** The speaker observes children affectionately, almost sentimentally. Her interpretations of children's behavior appear to have been thoughtfully developed over a long period observing small children.

Passage 3—An excerpt from Henry James, *From London*

26. **(B)** Most of the passage discusses the speaker's emotions as he arrives in England and makes his way to London. As the speaker approaches London, his feelings certainly include those described by choices (C) and (D), but those are secondary to the speaker's main concern.

27. **(D)** The phrase alludes to Babylon, an ancient city that has become a metaphor for a large, luxurious metropolis given to gratifying the senses of its inhabitants and visitors. For definitions of rhetorical terms, turn to the Glossary, page 389.

28. **(A)** Beginning with the phrase "wet, black Sunday" (line 2) until the description of "the gray mildness, shading away into black" (line 27), the speaker stresses the bleakness of the land and sky.

29. **(A)** All the phrases except "the end of a wet, black Sunday" suggest the speaker's high level of emotional anticipation as he approached London. In contrast, a "wet, black Sunday, . . . about the first of March" is primarily a piece of incidental information.

30. **(E)** Although arriving in England evoked strong feelings, there is no evidence that the speaker's emotions leapt beyond his control.

31. **(B)** At breakfast in the hotel soon after his arrival in England, the speaker rediscovered with a sense of wonder how "English" it was in England (lines 11–16). Choice (D) may be partly true, but the word "relief" incorrectly suggests that the speaker, upon returning to England, had been concerned that the country might not live up to his recollections.

32. **(E)** As the speaker says, it's the kind of emotion (line 18) that often makes us yearn for strange and faraway places—in other words a sense of wonder. Nostalgia (choice A) helps to show the speaker's emotions, but his sense of wonder is generated mainly from the anticipation of reliving a previous experience as though it never happened before.

33. **(D)** Through much of the first paragraph the speaker describes his sense of wonder. The pronoun "It" carries the discussion into the next paragraph.

34. **(A)** Pervasive throughout the paragraph are sensual images evoking sights, sounds, smells, tastes, and physical sensations; for example: "strange, dark, lonely freshness of the coast" (lines 21–22), "the gray mildness, shading away into black" (line 27), and "the creak of the waiter's shoes" (line 34). These images have moved the speaker deeply—so deeply that he prolongs his stay in the coffee-room to reflect on them.

35. **(E)** In order to remain on an emotional high a while longer, the speaker stays put for a day, thereby sacrificing, as it were, the pleasure and anticipation of a timely arrival in London, his final destination.

36. **(B)** The remark is somewhat boastful. It sends a message to the reader that says: Look how clever I am to make this witty and perceptive observation about the waiter's back.

37. **(C)** The last sentence contains another reference to the speaker's fondness for London. Even the "rather horrible" ride on the "greasy fourwheeler" could not keep him from recognizing that his friendship with the city is about to be renewed.

38. **(B)** Not only is the speaker similar to a memoirist, he actually *is* one, fondly recalling his arrival in England about twenty years before (line 2) when he was still "comparatively youthful" (line 42).

Passage 4—An excerpt from Susan Faludi, *Stiffed*

39. **(C)** Like every "main-idea" question, this one can't be answered until you have read most, or all, of the passage. By the end, you'll see that the author focuses on Brown's efforts to reshape the image of players on his team. Choice (B) has some merit, but it is too broad, because a coach does far more than manage his players' appearance and behavior.

40. **(E)** Parallel syntax is exemplified by the series phrases in lines 3 and 4. The structure of the first two sentences of the passage is virtually identical: Both begin with prepositional phrases, and both contain the same verb, *served*. The last sentence of the paragraph employs antithesis (not a "throwback" but a "look forward").

41. **(D)** Lines 2–5 introduce tactics that Brown first used as a high school football coach. The rest of the passage consists almost completely of how he adapted and developed these measures to improve the public image of players on his professional football team.

42. **(E)** Choices (A), (B), and (C) refer to Brown's days as a high-school football coach. In Cleveland, Brown's plan for a "well-run organization" more fully refers to the new ethic he had in mind for his players.

43. **(B)** The author's repeated use of the italicized phrase "in public" is meant to show that Brown's paramount interest was the team's public image.

44. **(A)** What mattered most to Brown was that his players reflected conventional middle-class values, or as the author puts it in line 26, "the face of the new, white-collar bourgeoisie." The economic condition of their families didn't matter.

45. **(A)** In context, the expression describes someone just the opposite of a "Big Butch who talks hard and drinks hard" (line 20)—in other words, someone whose behavior is discreet and restrained.

46. **(B)** Based on the footnote, the source of the quotation "dressed like a laborer" remains unclear.

47. **(B)** Throughout the passage, the author illuminates and widens the meaning and implications of Brown's ideas. The author may be exercising poetic license (A) with the phrase "white collar bourgeoisie," which in the context may be a conspicuous example of grandiose diction. Because the paragraph discusses class structure in America, however, the author's choice of words is neither inappropriate nor overblown.

48. **(E)** The author explains the term in lines 30–39. What Brown evidently wanted was a team full of bland, corporate types—in other words, men who looked and acted in a particular way, who gave up some of their individuality on behalf of the team, i.e., for the organization.

49. **(A)** Because the works cited contain only the author, title, and page number, it's reasonable to infer that each of the works has been listed before. The previous citations probably contained full information about each work. (It's also possible that the author of the book used another documentation method in which all footnotes refer to works listed in a separate bibliography.)

50. **(B)** The author analyzes Brown's words and spells out what she thinks Brown is really saying. In other words, she examines the implications of Brown's down-to-earth ideas and articulates them in the more sophisticated language of, say, a sociologist or historian.

51. **(D)** Because all the footnotes accompanying the passage refer to Brown, the author evidently found Brown's work a fruitful source.

52. **(A)** The paragraph contains a number of quotations amplified by the author's commentary. The last sentence summarizes Brown's intentions and generalizes the overall point of the passage.

Answers to Essay Questions

Although answers to the essay questions will vary greatly, the following descriptions suggest a possible approach to each question and contain ideas that could be used in response to the question. Perhaps your essay contains many of the same ideas. If not, don't be alarmed. Your ideas may be at least as insightful, or even more so, as those below.

ESSAY QUESTION 1

Some Arguments <u>In Favor</u> of Stricter Regulation of Sports:

- Some sports are little more than organized violence. (Source A)
- Athletes are often unwilling participants in violent sports, having been drawn in by circumstances such as the lure of money or peer pressure. (Source A)
- Placing limits on brutality and violence will permit more people to enjoy and derive benefits from sports. (Source A)
- Because people often behave recklessly and ignore common sense, they need to be protected from themselves. (Source E)

Some Arguments <u>Against</u> Stricter Regulation of Sports:

- Some athletes' love for sports is greater than their fear of injury or death. (Source B)
- In a free society, individuals should have the right to choose whether to risk injury and death by participating in dangerous sports. (Source C)
- Because more than half of the injuries suffered in high school sports are relatively minor, stricter regulations are unnecessary. (Source D)
- Restrictions will drain the excitement out of sports. (Sources E and F)

ESSAY QUESTION 2, BASED ON "A FAIR AND HAPPY MILKMAID" BY EITHER THOMAS OVERBURY OR JOHN WEBSTER

The equivalent of a prose poem, this sketch idealizes the subject's appearance, behavior, and state of mind. Using the language and sentence structure of his day—the 17th century—the speaker compiles a list of the young maid's virtues, endowing her with the qualities of a saint.

The girl embodies excellence. She is innocent, beautiful, natural, and good in every way. And best of all she is unaware of these extraordinary assets: Her "excellencies stand in her so silently, as if they had stolen upon her without her knowledge" (lines 4-5). To create this portrait of near-perfection the speaker relies mainly on images taken from nature and rural life: the girl rises "with chanticleer" (rooster) and retires with the lambs. Her breath smells fresh like a "new made haycock" (line 15); the "garden and the beehive" assure her good health. What's more, she is devout. Spinning at her wheel on winter evenings, she sings a "defiance to the giddy wheel of fortune," (line 17) implying her belief that God is watching over her.

Using hyperbole, the speaker gives the maid her own godlike qualities: Ears of corn, for example, "fall and kiss her feet when she reaps them" (line 13); milk that passes through her fingers becomes whiter and sweeter. Because she "fears no manner of ill" (line 22), she is immune to worry and apprehension. In spite of such qualities, however, she is still subject to human anxieties. She fears being overcome with anger (lines 26-27) toward those who crucified Jesus, and she has concerns about death. The maid even displays a touch of vanity, for she hopes to die in the springtime in order have flowers available to decorate her "winding sheet," (line 31) the garment in which corpses are wrapped.

ESSAY QUESTION 3, BASED ON A QUOTATION FROM "RICHARD CORY" BY EDWIN ARLINGTON ROBINSON

Envy usually ranks up there with anger, vengefulness, and hate as an undesirable—even a sinful—emotion. Beginning with that assessment, you might argue that envy is always insidious and destructive, breeds despair, erodes self-confidence, incites hatred, and worse. The title character of Shakespeare's Othello, is an example. A brave and respected warrior, he is brought to a catastrophic end by rage sprung from uncontrollable jealousy. Or consider a hypothetical high school senior—let's call her Jessie—who is over-the-top envious of her friend Astrid's success in school and in life. Jessie feels that she can't match Astrid's intellect, physical prowess, social graces, or any other of her enviable gifts. So, instead of rejoicing in Astrid's good fortune, Jessie sulks and scowls and suffers in silence.

Like a toxic weed, envy can grow almost anywhere. The owners of a small business, envying a competitor's reputation or success in controlling a certain market, can try to undermine, or even sabotage, their rival. Or how about a workplace where an employee envies the performance of certain colleagues? Over time, he may begin to perceive imaginary slights or insults, and then take action—sometimes deadly action—against them. History is rife with instances of nations coveting land, resources, seaports, or the riches of other countries and sending armies to seize them. Germany's actions in the 1930s provoked the world into war for that very reason.

In spite of its bad reputation, envy now and then has the potential to do good. Your essay, therefore, could take the position that envy has salutary effects—at least on occasion. Should you adopt this as your main idea, you could argue that in some circumstances envy can motivate people to improve themselves. Say, for instance, that an acquaintance Nicky, is blessed with a generous and compassionate nature. She never fails to help needy people in any way she can. Others admire Nicky, or perhaps even envy her natural affability and altruism. Seeing the good that she does could spur them to emulate Nicky and begin their own efforts to help those in need.

A similar dynamic might occur among the world's downtrodden multitudes—say, the poor, the dispossessed—perhaps refugees from war ravaged lands who crave what others enjoy: peace, opportunity, and a degree of stability in their lives. Envy may inspire them to break from their plight and strive to achieve goals that initially may have seemed way out of reach. Or consider what took place not long ago when American car manufacturers looked enviously at the safety and reliability of vehicles made by Japanese companies. After years of plummeting sales, General Motors and Chrysler struggled to restore their reputation for quality and gradually regained consumers' trust.

Countless other scenarios of envy as a force for good or ill could be incorporated into your essay. But once you have determined your main idea, build an argument using only a small number of specific situations in which envy plays a part. Aim to show AP essay readers the depth rather than the breadth of your thinking.

SCORING SECTION II ESSAYS

Before scoring your essays, carefully review "How Essays Are Scored" (pages 36–37), a guide meant to help you judge as objectively as possible the quality of your writing.

Use the criteria listed below to evaluate each of your essays. Because it's tough to be totally impartial about your own writing, you may get a more accurate score by asking a well-informed friend, teacher, or counselor to rate your essays for you.

On the following Rating Chart, enter a number (from 1 to 6) that you think represents your level of performance in each category (A–F).

CATEGORY A: OVERALL PURPOSE/MAIN IDEA

6   extremely well-defined and insightful
5   clearly defined and generally insightful
4   mostly clear
3   somewhat clear but occasionally confusing
2   generally unclear and confusing
1   mostly incomprehensible or simplistic

CATEGORY B: HANDLING OF THE PROMPT

6   self-evident or extremely clear throughout
5   mostly clear
4   somewhat clear
3   somewhat unclear
2   generally unclear or ambiguous
1   confusing or nonexistent

CATEGORY C: ORGANIZATION AND DEVELOPMENT

6   insightfully organized; fully developed with excellent supporting evidence
5   reasonably well organized; developed with appropriate supporting material
4   appropriately organized; developed with some relevant material
3   inconsistent organization; weak development
2   poorly organized; little or no development
1   no discernible organization or development

CATEGORY D: SENTENCE STRUCTURE

6   varied and engaging
5   sufficiently varied to create interest
4   some variety
3   little variety; minor sentence errors
2   frequent sentence errors that interfere with meaning
1   serious sentence errors that obscure meaning

CATEGORY E: USE OF LANGUAGE

6   precise and effective word choice
5   competent word choice
4   conventional word choice; mostly correct
3   some errors in diction or idiom
2   frequent lapses in diction or idiom
1   meaning obscured by word choice

CATEGORY F: GRAMMAR AND USAGE

6   error-free or virtually error-free
5   occasional minor errors
4   basically correct but with several minor errors
3   meaning somewhat obscured by errors
2   meaning frequently obscured by errors
1   meaning blocked by several major errors

RATING CHART

Rate your essay	Essay 1	Essay 2	Essay 3
Overall Purpose/Main Idea			
Handling of the Prompt			
Organization and Development			
Sentence Structure			
Use of Language			
Grammar and Usage			
Composite Scores (sum of each column)			

By using the following scale, in which composite scores are converted to the nine-point AP rating scale, you may determine the final score for each essay:

Composite Score	AP Essay Score
33–36	9
29–32	8
25–28	7
21–24	6
18–20	5
15–17	4
10–14	3
7–9	2
6 or below	1

AP Essay Scores Essay 1 _____ Essay 2 _____ Essay 3 _____

TEST SCORE WORKSHEET

The scores you have earned on the multiple-choice and essay sections of the exam may now be converted to the AP five-point scale by performing the following calculations:

I. Determine Your Score for Section I (Multiple-Choice)

(STEP A) Number of correct answers _____

(STEP B) Multiply the figure in Step A by 1.2272 to find your
Multiple-Choice Score _____. (Do not round.)

II. Determine Your Score for Section II (Essays)

(STEP A) Enter your score for Essay 1 (out of 9) _____

(STEP B) Enter your score for Essay 2 (out of 9) _____

(STEP C) Enter your score for Essay 3 (out of 9) _____

(STEP D) Add the figures in Steps A, B, and C _____

(STEP E) Multiply the figure in Step D by 3.0556 _____ (Do not round.)
This is your Essay Score.

III. Determine Your Total Score

Add the scores for I and II to find your composite score _____.
(Round to nearest whole number.)

To convert your composite score to the AP five-point scale, use the chart below. The range of scores only approximates what you would earn on the actual test because the exact figures may vary from test to test. Be aware, therefore, that your score on this test, as well as on other tests in this book, may differ slightly from your score on an actual AP exam.

Composite Score	AP Grade
112–150	5
97–111	4
80–96	3
55–79	2
0–54	1

AP essays are ordinarily judged in relation to other essays written on the same topic at the same time. Therefore, the scores you assign yourself for these essays may not be the same as the scores you would earn on an actual exam.

Appendix

PASSAGE FOR ANNOTATION

At one point several hundred thousand years ago, snow began falling over the center of the earth's largest island. The snow did not melt, and in the years that fol-
Line lowed, storms brought even more. All around Greenland,
(5) the arctic temperatures remained low enough for snow to last past spring and summer. It piled up, year after year, century after century, millenium after millenium. Eventually, the snow became the Greenland ice sheet, a blanket of ice so huge that it covered 650,000 square
(10) miles and reached the thickness of 10,000 feet in places. Meanwhile, in Antarctica, a similar process was well underway. There, as snow fell upon snow for years without end, the ice sheet spread out over a much vaster area: 5.4 million square miles, an expanse far larger than
(15) the lower 48 states. By the start of the modern era, when power plants and electric lights began illuminating the streets of Manhattan, about 75 percent of the world's fresh water had been frozen into the ice sheets that lay over these lands at the opposite ends of the earth.

(20) The ice sheets covering Greenland and large areas of Antarctica are now losing more ice every year than they gain from snowfall. The loss is evident in the rushing meltwater rivers, blue gashes that crisscross the ice surface in warmer months and drain the sheets' mass
(25) by billions of tons annually. Another sign of imbalance is the number of immense icebergs that, with increasing regularity, cleave from the sheets and drop into the seas. In late August, for instance, a highly active glacier in Greenland named Jakobshavn calved one of the largest
(30) icebergs in history, a chunk of ice about 4,600 feet thick and about five square miles in area.

If the ice sheets on Greenland and Antarctica were to collapse and melt entirely, the result would be a sea-level rise of 200 feet or so. This number, though fearsome, is
(35) not especially helpful to anyone but Hollywood screen-

writers: No scientist believes that all that ice will slide into the oceans soon. During the last year, however, a small contingent of researchers has begun to consider whether sea-level-rise projections, increased by the (40) recent activity of collapsing glaciers on the periphery of the ice sheets, point toward a potential catastrophe. It would not take 200 feet to drown New Orleans. Or New York. A mere five or ten feet worth of sea-level rise due to icebergs, and a few powerful storm surges, would (45) probably suffice.

How soon could that happen? When it comes to understanding the implications of ice-sheet collapse, the speed of that breakdown is everything. It could mean sea levels that rise slowly and steadily, perhaps a (50) foot or two per century, which might allow coastal communities to adapt and adjust. Or it could mean levels that rise at an accelerating pace, perhaps five feet or more per century—forcing the evacuation of millions of refugees and almost unimaginable financial costs. (55) The difference between slowly and rapidly is a crucial distinction that one scientist described as "the trillion-dollar question."

—Excerpt from Jon Gertner, "Ice,"
New York Times Magazine,
November 15, 2015, pp. 48–57, 80–81.

Here is the same passage annotated by the author:

[1] At one point several hundred thousand years ago, snow began falling over the center of the earth's largest island. The snow did not melt, and in the years that
Line followed, storms brought even more. [2] All around
(5) Greenland, the arctic temperatures remained low enough for snow to last past spring and summer. It piled up, year after year, century after century, millenium after millenium. Eventually, the snow became the Greenland ice sheet, a blanket of ice so huge that it covered [3] 650,000
(10) square miles and reached the thickness of 10,000 feet in places. Meanwhile, in Antarctica, a similar process was

[1] The writer refers to a "point" in prehistory, a rhetorical tactic meant to draw curious readers into the passage. After all, who can know what happened on the earth "several hundred thousand years ago? That much of our planet got buried in snow that didn't melt for thousands of years is a startling fact.

[2] By alluding to the familiar concepts of spring and summer (line 6), the writer keeps the reader interested. Then, using a series of repetitive phrases ("year after year, century after century, millenium after millenium") the writer not only emphasizes the vastness of the earth's accumulated snowfall but offers readers still another amazing bit of information.

[3] Statistics tell the reader about amount of the world's ice. Knowing that figures such as "650,000 square miles" and "10,000 feet" are not easy to grasp, the writer declares that the size of the Antarctic ice sheet is "far larger than the lower 48 states" (lines 14-15), thereby adding a straightforward and comprehensible fact to the discussion.

well underway. **[4]** There, as snow fell upon snow for years without end, the ice sheet spread out over a much vaster area: 5.4 million square miles, an expanse far (15) larger than the lower 48 states. By the start of the modern era, when power plants and electric lights began illuminating the streets of Manhattan, about 75 percent of the world's fresh water had been frozen into **[5]** the ice sheets that lay over these lands at the opposite ends (20) of the earth.

[6] The ice sheets covering Greenland and large areas of Antarctica are now losing more ice every year than they gain from snowfall. The loss is evident in the rushing meltwater rivers, blue gashes that crisscross (25) the ice surface in warmer months and drain the sheets' mass by billions of tons annually. Another sign of imbalance is the number of immense icebergs that, with increasing regularity, cleave from the sheets and drop into the seas. In late August, for instance, a highly active (30) glacier in Greenland named Jakobshavn calved one of the largest icebergs in history, a chunk of ice about 4,600 feet thick and about five square miles in area.

[4] In line 13, hyperbole ("years without end") emphasizes once more how long it took for earth's ice sheets to form, in contrast—as readers will soon see—to the rapid melting to be described in the next paragraph. Indicated by the writer's diction: "rushing meltwater," "gashes that crisscross the ice," "icebergs . . . cleave from the sheets and drop into the seas." In lines 29-32, the writer cites a specific example of an immense loss.

[5] The first paragraph has explained that ice formed in both the northern (Greenland) and in the southern (Antarctica) hemispheres. This leads to the observation that the earth's frozen fresh water covers lands "at the opposite ends of the earth" (lines 19-20) and implies that the ice sheets have worldwide implications—a topic discussed in the next paragraph.

[6] The writer now uses the present tense to discuss the status of the world's ice: It is vanishing rapidly and uncontrollably, as indicated by the writer's diction: "rushing meltwater," "gashes across the ice," "icebergs . . . cleave from the sheets and drop into the seas." In lines 29-32, the writer cites a specific example of an immense loss.

[7] If the ice sheets on Greenland and Antarctica were to collapse and melt entirely, the result would (35) be a sea-level rise of 200 feet or so. This number, though fearsome, is not especially helpful to anyone but Hollywood screenwriters: No scientist believes that all that ice will slide into the oceans soon. During the last year, however, a small contingent of researchers has (40) begun to consider whether sea-level-rise projections, increased by the recent activity of collapsing glaciers on the periphery of the ice sheets, point toward a potential catastrophe. [8] It would not take 200 feet to drown New Orleans. Or New York. A mere five or ten feet worth of (45) sea-level rise due to icebergs, and a few powerful storm surges, would probably suffice.

How soon could that happen? When it comes to understanding the implications of ice-sheet collapse, the speed of that breakdown is everything. It could (50) mean sea levels that rise slowly and steadily, perhaps a foot or two per century, which might allow coastal communities to adapt and adjust. Or it could mean levels that rise at an accelerating pace, perhaps five feet or more per century—forcing the evacuation of millions (55) of refugees and almost unimaginable financial costs. [9] The difference between slowly and rapidly is a crucial distinction that one scientist described as "the trillion-dollar question."

[7] In this paragraph the writer begins to speculate on the future—on the consequences of a vast disappearance of ice.

(Clearly, the passage has been organized into three sections—a narrative form that deals with the past, the present, and the future. Use of this structure helps attract a more interested audience. Storytelling, as a rhetorical device, tends to hold readers more firmly than textbook versions of the same material.)

Because the future is always uncertain, the tone in the passage is speculative: "If the ice sheets. . .," "would probably suffice," "It could mean . . .," etc.

[8] The phrase "potential catastrophe" (lines 42-43) sets the tone for the remainder of the passage, for the writer focuses on the possible consequences—none of them favorable—of sea-level rise. Using allusions to such things as forced "evacuations," "millions of refugees," and "unimaginable financial costs," the writer has created a frightening doomsday scenario. References to specific places (New Orleans, New York) vividly suggest the immediacy of the threat.

[9] The conclusion serves as a kind of disclaimer for the writer. Whether sea-level rise will cause havoc throughout the world remains to be seen. At present it is still a "trillion-dollar question."

Annotation Summary

    The purpose of the passage is to inform the reader about the earth's ice fields and glaciers and to sound an alert about the potential consequences of their disappearance, brought about by global warming. To achieve this goal, the writer describes first the origin, location, and dimensions the earth's frozen water. He then focuses on the current meltdown of ice in both the northern and southern hemispheres and speculates on the effects of worldwide sea-level rise caused by steadily increasing temperatures. The writer uses factual material, especially statistics, to highlight both the dimensions of the world's ice and its rapid decline. His language choices describing mankind's potentially catastrophic future are meant to both educate and unsettle the reader, but at the very end, the writer implies that scientists, uncertain about what lies in store, have adopted a wait-and-see attitude.

Glossary

The list that follows is made up of words and phrases used by scholars, critics, writers—in fact, all literate people—to exchange ideas and information about language. Most of the words and phrases have appeared in recent years in the multiple-choice or essay sections of AP Language and Composition exams.

abstract (*n.*) An abbreviated synopsis of a longer work of scholarship or research. (*adj.*) Dealing with or tending to deal with a subject apart from a particular or specific instance.

ad hominem Directed to or appealing to feelings or prejudices instead of to intellect or reason.

adage A saying or proverb containing a truth based on experience and often couched in metaphorical language. Example: "There is more than one way to skin a cat."

allegory A story in which a second meaning is to be read beneath the surface.

alliteration The repetition of one or more initial consonants in a group of words or lines in a poem.

allusion A reference to a person, place, or event meant to create an effect or enhance the meaning of an idea.

ambiguity A vagueness of meaning; a conscious lack of clarity meant to evoke multiple meanings or interpretations.

anachronism A person, scene, event, or other element that fails to correspond with the appropriate time or era. Example: Columbus sailing to the United States.

analogy A comparison that points out similarities between two dissimilar things; a passage that points out several similarities between two unlike things is called an *extended analogy*.

anecdote A brief narrative often used to illustrate an idea or make a point.

annotation A brief explanation, summary, or evaluation of a text or work of literature.

antagonist A character or force in a work of literature that, by opposing the *protagonist*, produces tension or conflict.

antecedent A word to which a pronoun refers.

antithesis A rhetorical opposition or contrast of ideas by means of a grammatical arrangement of words, clauses, or sentences, as in the following: "They promised freedom but provided slavery." "Ask not what your country can do for you, but what you can do for your country."

aphorism A short, pithy statement of a generally accepted truth or sentiment. Also see *adage* and *maxim*.

Apollonian In contrast to *Dionysian*, it refers to the most noble, godlike qualities of human nature and behavior.

apostrophe A locution that addresses a person or personified thing not present. Example: "Oh, you cruel streets of Manhattan, how I detest you!"

arch (*adj.*) Characterized by clever or sly humor, often saucy, playful, and somewhat irreverent.

archetype An abstract or ideal conception of a type; a perfectly typical example; an original model or form.

assonance The repetition of two or more vowel sounds in a group of words in prose or poetry.

bard A poet; in olden times, a performer who told heroic stories to musical accompaniment.

bathos Insincere or overdone sentimentality.

belle-lettres A French term for the world of books, criticism, and literature in general.

bibliography A list of works cited or otherwise relevant to a particular subject.

bombast Inflated, pretentious language.

burlesque A work of literature meant to ridicule a subject; a grotesque imitation.

cacophony Grating, inharmonious sounds.

canon The works considered most important in a national literature or period; works widely read and studied.

caricature A grotesque or exaggerated likeness of striking qualities in persons and things.

carpe diem Literally, "seize the day"; "enjoy life while you can," a common theme in life and literature.

circumlocution Literally, "talking around" a subject; i.e., discourse that avoids direct reference to a subject.

classic A highly regarded work of literature or other art form that has withstood the test of time.

classical, classicism Deriving from the orderly qualities of ancient Greek and Roman culture; implies formality, objectivity, simplicity, and restraint.

clause A structural element of a sentence, consisting of a grammatical subject and a predicate. *Independent clauses,* sometimes called *main clauses,* may stand on their own as complete sentences; *dependent clauses,* which are used as nouns or modifiers, are incomplete sentences and cannot stand alone grammatically. Dependent clauses are sometimes called *subordinate clauses.* Dependent clauses that function as adjectives, nouns, or adverbs are known, respectively, as *adjective, noun,* and *adverbial clauses.*

climax The high point, or turning point, of a story or play.

comparison and contrast A mode of discourse in which two or more things are compared and contrasted. Comparison often refers to similarities, contrast to differences.

conceit A witty or ingenious thought; a diverting or highly fanciful idea, often stated in figurative language.

concrete detail A highly specific, particular, often real, actual, or tangible detail; the opposite of abstract.

connotation The suggested or implied meaning of a word or phrase. Contrast with *denotation.*

consonance The repetition of two or more consonant sounds in a group of words or a unit of speech or writing.

critique An analysis or assessment of a thing or situation for the purpose of determining its nature, limitations, and conformity to a set of standards.

cynic One who expects and observes nothing but the worst of human conduct.

deductive reasoning A method of reasoning by which specific definitions, conclusions, and theorems are drawn from general principles. Its opposite is *inductive reasoning*.

denotation The dictionary definition of a word. Contrast with *connotation*.

dénouement The resolution that occurs at the end of a narrative or drama, real or imagined.

descriptive detail Graphic, exact, and accurate presentation of the characteristics of a person, place, or thing.

deus ex machina In literature, the use of an artificial device or gimmick to solve a problem.

diction The choice of words in oral and written discourse.

didactic Having an instructive purpose; intending to convey information or teach a lesson, usually in a dry, pompous manner.

digression That portion of discourse that wanders or departs from the main subject or topic.

Dionysian As distinguished from *Apollonian*, the word refers to sensual, pleasure-seeking impulses.

dramatic irony A circumstance in which the audience or reader knows more about a situation than a character.

elegy A poem or prose selection that laments or meditates on the passing or death of someone or something of value. The adjective describing an elegy is *elegiac*.

ellipsis Three periods (. . .) indicating the omission of words in a thought or quotation.

elliptical construction A sentence containing a deliberate omission of words. In the sentence "May was hot and June the same," the verb *was* is omitted from the second clause.

empathy A feeling of association or identification with an object or person.

epic A narrative poem that tells of the adventures and exploits of a hero.

epigram A concise but ingenious, witty, and thoughtful statement.

epithet An adjective or phrase that expresses a striking quality of a person or thing; *sun-bright topaz*, *sun-lit lake*, and *sun-bright lake* are examples. Can also be used to apply to vulgar or profane exclamations.

eponymous A term for the title character of a work of literature.

ethos A speaker's or author's authority to express opinions on a subject. The ethos of a professional wrestler, for instance, to speak credibly about, say, philosophy or metaphysics, is questionable.

euphemism A mild or less negative usage for a harsh or blunt term. Example: *pass away* is a euphemism for *die*.

euphony Pleasing, harmonious sounds.

exegesis A detailed analysis or interpretation of a work of prose or poetry.

explication The interpretation or analysis of a text.

exposé A factual piece of writing that reveals weaknesses, faults, frailties, or other short-comings.

exposition The background and events that lead to the presentation of the main idea or purpose of an essay or other work; setting forth the meaning or purpose of a piece of writing or discourse.

extended metaphor A series of comparisons between two unlike objects.

fable A short tale, often with nonhuman characters, from which a useful lesson or moral may be drawn.

fallacy, fallacious reasoning An incorrect belief or supposition based on faulty data, defective evidence, false information, or flawed logic.

fantasy A story containing unreal, imaginary features.

farce A comedy that contains an extravagant and nonsensical disregard of seriousness, although it may have a serious, scornful purpose.

figure of speech, figurative language In contrast to literal language, figurative language implies meanings. Figures of speech include, among many others, *metaphor*, *simile*, and *personification*.

frame A structure that provides a premise or setting for a narrative or other discourse. Example: a group of pilgrims exchanging stories while on the road is the frame for Chaucer's *Canterbury Tales*.

genre A term used to describe literary forms, such as novel, play, and essay.

harangue A forceful sermon, lecture, or tirade.

homily A lecture or sermon on a religious or moral theme meant to guide human behavior.

hubris Excessive pride that often affects tone.

humanism A belief that emphasizes faith and optimism in human potential and creativity.

hyperbole Overstatement; gross exaggeration for rhetorical effect.

idyll A lyric poem or passage that describes a kind of ideal life or place.

image A word or phrase representing that which can be seen, touched, tasted, smelled, or felt; *imagery* is the use of images in speech and writing.

indirect quotation A rendering of a quotation in which actual words are not stated but only approximated or paraphrased.

inductive reasoning A method of reasoning in which a number of specific facts or examples are used to make a generalization. Its opposite is *deductive reasoning*.

inference A conclusion or proposition arrived at by considering facts, observations, or some other specific data.

invective A direct verbal assault; a denunciation; casting blame on someone or something.

irony A mode of expression in which the intended meaning is the opposite of what is stated, often implying ridicule or light sarcasm; a state of affairs or events that is the reverse of what might have been expected.

kenning A device employed in Anglo-Saxon poetry in which the name of a thing is replaced by one of its functions or qualities, as in "ring-giver" for king and "whale-road" for ocean.

lampoon A mocking, satirical assault on a person or situation.

litotes A form of understatement in which the negative of the contrary is used to achieve emphasis or intensity. Example: *He is not a bad dancer.*

logos The logic used by a speaker or writer to support a claim or point of view. In an argument in favor of more healthful food in the school cafeteria, for example, statistics about teenage obesity can be persuasive.

loose sentence A sentence that follows the customary word order of English sentences, i.e., subject-verb-object. The main idea of the sentence is presented first and is then followed by one or more subordinate clauses. See also *periodic sentence*.

lyrical prose Personal, reflective prose that reveals the speaker's thoughts and feelings about the subject.

malapropism A confused use of words in which the appropriate word is replaced by one with a similar sound but inappropriate meaning.

maxim A saying or proverb expressing common wisdom or truth. See also *adage* and *aphorism*.

melodrama A literary form in which events are exaggerated in order to create an extreme emotional response.

metaphor A figure of speech that compares unlike objects. When several characteristics of the same objects are compared, the device is called an *extended metaphor*. A metaphor referring to a particular person, place, or thing is called a *metaphorical allusion*; for example, referring to someone as "a Hercules."

metaphysical A term describing poetry that uses elaborate conceits, expresses the complexities of love and life, and is highly intellectual. More generally, *metaphysical* refers to ideas that are neither analytical nor subject to empirical verification; that is, ideas that express an attitude about which rational argument is impossible.

metonymy A figure of speech that uses the name of one thing to represent something else with which it is associated. Example: *"The White House says . . ."*

Middle English The language spoken in England roughly between 1150 and 1500 A.D.

mock epic A parody of traditional epic form.

mock serious Characterized by feigned or deliberately artificial seriousness, often for satirical purposes.

mode The general form, pattern, and manner of expression of a piece of discourse.

montage A quick succession of images or impressions used to express an idea.

mood The emotional tone or prevailing atmosphere in a work of literature or other discourse. In grammar, mood refers to the intent of a particular sentence. The *indicative mood* is used for statements of fact; *subjunctive mood* is used to express doubt or a conditional attitude; sentences in the *imperative mood* give commands.

moral A brief and often simplistic lesson that a reader may infer from a work of literature.

motif A phrase, idea, or event that through repetition serves to unify or convey a theme in an essay or other discourse.

muse (*n.*) One of the ancient Greek goddesses presiding over the arts; the imaginary source of inspiration for an artist or writer. (*v.*) To reflect deeply; to ponder.

myth An imaginary story that has become an accepted part of the cultural or religious tradition of a group or society.

narrative A form of verse or prose (both fiction *and* nonfiction) that tells a story. A storyteller may use any number of *narrative devices*, such as skipping back and forth in time, ordering events chronologically, and ordering events to lead up to a suspenseful climax. Also see *frame*.

naturalism A term often used as a synonym for *realism*; also a view of experience that is generally characterized as bleak and pessimistic.

non sequitur A statement or idea that fails to follow logically from the one before.

objective (*adj.*) Of or relating to facts and reality, as opposed to private and personal feelings and attitudes. Its opposite is *subjective*.

ode A lyric poem usually marked by serious, respectful, and exalted feelings toward the subject.

Old English The Anglo-Saxon language spoken from approximately 450 to 1150 A.D. in what is now Great Britain.

omniscient narrator A narrator with unlimited awareness, understanding, and insight of characters, setting, background, and all other elements of the story.

onomatopoeia The use of words whose sounds suggest their meaning. Example: *bubbling, murmuring brooks.*

oxymoron A term consisting of contradictory elements juxtaposed to create a paradoxical effect. Examples: *loud silence, jumbo shrimp.*

parable A story consisting of events from which a moral or spiritual truth may be derived.

paradox A statement that seems self-contradictory but is nevertheless true.

parallel structure The structure required for expressing two or more grammatical elements of equal rank. Coordinate ideas, compared and contrasted ideas, and correlative constructions call for parallel construction. For example: Colleges favor applicants with *good academic records, varied interests,* and they should earn a high score on the AP exam. The underlined section of the sentence lacks the same grammatical form as the italicized phrases. To be correct, it should read *high scores.*

paraphrase A version of a text put into simpler, everyday words or summarized for brevity.

parody An imitation of a work meant to ridicule its style and subject.

pastoral A work of literature dealing with rural life.

pathetic fallacy Faulty reasoning that inappropriately ascribes human feelings to nature or nonhuman objects.

pathos That element in literature that stimulates pity or sorrow. Also, the emotional appeal used to persuade an audience to accept a certain point of view or opinion.

pedantic Narrowly academic instead of broad and humane; excessively petty and meticulous.

periodic sentence A sentence that departs from the usual word order of English sentences by expressing its main thought only at the end. In other words, the particulars in the sentence are presented before the idea they support. See also *loose sentence.*

persona The role or facade that a character assumes or depicts to a reader or other audience.

personification A figure of speech in which objects and animals are given human characteristics.

plot The interrelationship among the events in a story; the *plot line* is the pattern of events, including exposition, rising action, climax, falling action, and resolution.

point of view The relation in which a narrator or speaker stands to a subject of discourse. A matter discussed in the first person has an *internal* point of view; an observer uses an *external* point of view.

predicate The part of a sentence that is not the grammatical subject. It often says something about the subject. A noun that provides another name for the subject is called a *predicate nominative*, as in:

Lynn (subject) is the *president* (predicate nominative) of the company.

An adjective that describes the subject is called *a predicate adjective*, as in:

Harold (subject) is *courageous* (predicate adjective).

prose Any discourse that is not poetry. A *prose poem* is a selection of prose that, because of its language or content, is poetic in nature.

proverb A short pithy statement of a general truth that condenses common experience into memorable form. See also *adage* and *maxim*.

pseudonym A false name or alias used by writers.

pulp fiction Novels written for mass consumption, often emphasizing exciting and titillating plots.

pun A humorous play on words, using similar-sounding or identical words to suggest different meanings.

realism The depiction of people, things, and events as they really are without idealization or exaggeration for effect. See also *naturalism*.

rebuttal or **refutation** The part of discourse wherein opposing arguments are anticipated and answered.

reiteration Repetition of an idea using different words, often for emphasis or other effect.

repetition Reuse of the same words, phrases, or ideas for rhetorical effect, usually to emphasize a point.

retraction The withdrawal of a previously stated idea or opinion.

rhetoric The language of a work and its style; words, often highly emotional, used to convince or sway an audience.

rhetorical mode A general term that identifies discourse according to its chief purpose. Modes include *exposition* (to explain, analyze, or discuss an idea), *argumentation* (to prove a point or to persuade), *description* (to recreate or present with details), and *narration* (to relate an anecdote or story).

rhetorical question A question to which the audience already knows the answer; a question asked merely for effect with no answer expected.

rhetorical stance Language that conveys a speaker's attitude or opinion with regard to a particular subject.

rhyme The repetition of similar sounds at regular intervals, used mostly in poetry but not unheard of in prose.

rhythm The pattern of stressed and unstressed syllables that make up speech and writing.

romance An extended narrative about improbable events and extraordinary people in exotic places.

saga A long, historical, episodic narrative often focusing on a single hero, family, or group. A popular modern-day saga is *Lord of the Rings*.

sarcasm A sharp, caustic attitude conveyed in words through jibes, taunts, or other remarks; sarcasm differs from *irony*, which is more subtle.

satire A literary style used to poke fun at, attack, or ridicule an idea, vice, or foible, often for the purpose of inducing change.

sentence structure The arrangement of the parts of a sentence. A sentence may be *simple* (one subject and one verb), *compound* (two or more independent clauses joined by a conjunction), or *complex* (an independent clause plus one or more dependent clauses). Sentences may also contain any of these structures in combination with each other. Each variation leaves a different impression on the reader, and along with other rhetorical devices, may create a countless array of effects.

sentiment A synonym for *view* or *feeling*; also a refined and tender emotion in literature.

sentimental A term that describes characters' excessive emotional response to experience; also nauseatingly nostalgic and mawkish.

setting An environment that consists of time, place, historical milieu, and social, political, and even spiritual circumstances.

simile A figurative comparison using the words *like* or *as*. Example: She sings *like a canary*.

stream of consciousness A style of writing in which the author tries to reproduce the random flow of thoughts in the human mind.

style The manner in which an author uses and arranges words, shapes ideas, forms sentences, and creates a structure to convey ideas.

stylistic devices A general term referring to diction, syntax, tone, figurative language, and all other elements that contribute to the "style" or manner of a given piece of discourse.

subject complement The name of a grammatical unit that is comprised of *predicate nominatives* and *predicate adjectives*.

subjective (*adj.*) Of or relating to private and personal feelings and attitudes as opposed to facts and reality. Its opposite is *objective*.

subtext The implied meaning that underlies the main meaning of an essay or other work.

syllogism A form of deductive reasoning in which given certain ideas or facts, other ideas or facts must follow, as in *All men are mortal; Mike is a man; therefore, Mike is mortal.*

symbolism The use of one object to evoke ideas and associations not literally part of the original object. Example: The American flag may symbolize freedom, the fifty states, and the American way of life, among many other things.

synecdoche A figure of speech in which a part signifies the whole (*fifty masts* for *fifty ships*) or the whole signifies the part (*days* for *life*, as in *He lived his days under African skies*). When the name of a material stands for the thing itself, as in *pigskin* for *football*, that, too, is synecdoche.

syntax The organization of language into meaningful structure; every sentence has a particular syntax, or pattern of words.

theme The main idea or meaning, often an abstract idea upon which an essay or other form of discourse is built.

thesis The main idea of a piece of discourse; the statement or proposition that a speaker or writer wishes to advance, illustrate, prove, or defend.

tone The author's attitude toward the subject being written about. The tone is the characteristic emotion that pervades a work or part of a work—the spirit or quality that is the work's emotional essence.

tragedy A form of literature in which the hero is destroyed by some character flaw or by a set of forces that cause the hero considerable anguish.

transition A stylistic device used to create a link between ideas. Transitions often endow discourse with continuity and coherence.

trope The generic name for a figure of speech such as image, symbol, simile, and metaphor.

understatement A restrained statement that departs from what could be said; a studied avoidance of emphasis or exaggeration, often to create a particular effect.

verbal irony A discrepancy between the true meaning of a situation and the literal meaning of the written or spoken words.

verisimilitude Similar to the truth; the quality of realism in a work that persuades readers that they are getting a vision of life as it is or could have been.

verse A synonym for poetry; also a group of lines in a song or poem; also a single line of poetry.

voice The real or assumed personality used by a writer or speaker. In grammar, *active voice* and *passive voice* refer to the use of verbs. A verb is in the active voice when it expresses an action performed by its subject. A verb is in the passive voice when it expresses an action performed upon its subject or when the subject is the result of the action.

> ACTIVE: The crew raked the leaves.
> PASSIVE: The leaves were raked by the crew.

Stylistically, the active voice leads to more economical and vigorous writing.

whimsy An object, device, or creation that is fanciful or rooted in unreality.

wit The quickness of intellect and the power and talent for saying brilliant things that surprise and delight by their unexpectedness; the power to comment subtly and pointedly on the foibles of the passing scene.

Index

How to Use the CD-ROM

The software is not installed on your computer; it runs directly from the CD-ROM. Barron's CD-ROM includes an "autorun" feature that automatically launches the application when the CD is inserted into the CD-ROM drive. In the unlikely event that the autorun feature is disabled, follow the manual launching instructions below.

Windows®

1. Click on the Start button and choose "My Computer."
2. Double-click on the CD-ROM drive, which is named **AP_English_Language_and_Composition.exe.**
3. Double-click **AP_English_Language_and_Composition.exe** to launch the program.

MAC®

1. Double-click the CD-ROM icon.
2. Double-click the **AP_English_Language_and_Composition** icon to start the program.

SYSTEM REQUIREMENTS

(Flash Player 10.2 is recommended)

Microsoft® Windows®	**MAC® OS X**
Processor: Intel Pentium 4 2.33GHz, Athlon 64 2800+ or faster processor (or equivalent).	Processor: Intel Core™ Duo 1.33GHz or faster processor.
Memory: 128MB of RAM.	Memory: 256MB of RAM.
Graphics Memory: 128MB.	Graphics Memory: 128MB.
Platforms:	Platforms:
Windows 7, Windows Vista®, Windows XP, Windows Server® 2008, Windows Server 2003.	Mac OS X 10.6, Mac OS X 10.5, Mac OS X 10.4 (Intel) and higher.